The Write Start
Paragraphs to Essays

WITH PROFESSIONAL
AND STUDENT READINGS

The Write Start
Paragraphs to Essays

WITH PROFESSIONAL AND STUDENT READINGS

Fifth Edition

Gayle Feng-Checkett
St. Charles Community College

Lawrence Checkett
St. Charles Community College

WADSWORTH
CENGAGE Learning

Australia • Brazil • Japan • Korea • Mexico • Singapore • Spain • United Kingdom • United States

**The Write Start: Paragraphs to Essays
with Professional and Student Readings,
Fifth Edition**
Gayle Feng-Checkett and Lawrence Checkett

Director of Developmental Studies: Annie Todd

Assistant Editor: Beth Rice

Editorial Assistant: Luria Rittenberg

Media Editor: Christian Biagetti

Market Development Manager: Linda Yip

Content Project Manager: Dan Saabye

Art Director: Faith Brosnan

Manufacturing Planner: Betsy Donaghey

Rights Acquisition Specialist: Ann Hoffman

Production Service: S4Carlisle Publishing
Services

Text Designer: Icons by Jay Purcell

Cover Designer: RHDG/Riezebos Holzbaur

Cover Image: Chad Baker/Digital Vision/Getty
Images

Compositor: S4Carlisle Publishing Services

For product information and technology assistance, contact us at
Cengage Learning Customer & Sales Support, 1-800-354-9706

For permission to use material from this text or product,
submit all requests online at **cengage.com/permissions**
Further permissions questions can be e-mailed to
permissionrequest@cengage.com

Library of Congress Control Number: 2012950392

ISBN-13: 978-1-285-17514-0
ISBN-10: 1-285-17514-X

Wadsworth
20 Channel Center
Boston, MA 02210
USA

Cengage Learning is a leading provider of customized learning solutions with
office locations around the globe, including Singapore, the United Kingdom,
Australia, Mexico, Brazil, and Japan. Locate your local office at:
international.cengage.com/region

Cengage Learning products are represented in Canada by Nelson
Education, Ltd.

For your course and learning solutions, visit **academic.cengage.com**

Purchase any of our products at your local college store or at our preferred
online store **www.ichapters.com**

Printed in the United States of America
1 2 3 4 5 6 7 16 15 14 13

BRIEF CONTENTS

Lan Shaw/Alamy

Chapter 6

The Concluding Paragraph   70

PART TWO

Moving Forward: Strategies for Developing Essays   83

Chapter 7

The Descriptive Essay   85

Songquan Deng/Shutterstock.com

cesar liana/Alamy

Chapter 14

The Cause or Effect Essay   208

Andrey Armyagov/Fotolia LLC

Chapter 15

The Persuasive Essay   226

AP Photo

Design Pics/Ron Nickel/Jupiter Images

Image Source/Jupiter Images

PREFACE

A Message from the Authors

It is particularly gratifying when textbook authors see their long hours of diligent work over many years come to fruition with publication. However, they soon discover that an even greater reward is uncovered—the bond that begins to develop when writing instructors throughout the country employ the textbooks in their classrooms. As writing teachers ourselves, this is an act of trust that we do not take lightly. We wish to thank all of you for the confidence you have placed in us by entrusting the writing instruction of your students to the first four editions of *The Write Start: Paragraphs to Essays* and its companion volume, *The Write Start with Readings: Sentences to Paragraphs*—already in its fifth edition.

The feedback has been overwhelmingly positive, supporting the approach we have taken with both texts. In this new fifth edition of *The Write Start: Paragraphs to Essays*, we hope that the trust and confidence you have already placed in our texts will not diminish. The fifth edition keeps its focus on the end goal of writing quality essays using the various modes of development.

An increase in developmental writing instruction is being demanded of community colleges in particular because of burgeoning student bodies and a corresponding growth in their multicultural makeup. The new fifth edition of *The Write Start: Paragraphs to Essays* meets this challenge in several ways. In the modes chapters, we have organized the essays into discrete chapters with the chapters expanded to include more exercises with a renewed emphasis on addressing ESL/EFL concerns in developmental writing classrooms. You have told us you like this new restructuring, and we agree.

As always, we continue to listen closely to pertinent criticisms as well as praise, and in this fifth edition we have made some significant changes that will make the series even more relevant to the writing demands and needs of your students.

Thank you again for allowing us into your classrooms and giving us the opportunity and privilege of assisting you in the vitally important work of teaching your students to communicate more effectively.

Gayle Feng-Checkett and Lawrence Checkett

What's New in the Fifth Edition

The changes in the fifth edition are based on the excellent criticisms and suggestions made by instructors and reviewers familiar with the fourth edition. With each new edition, our foremost desire is to expand and improve our treatment of the writing process: the interrelationship of reading, critical thinking, and writing.

In Chapter 5, a new technique, the summary paragraph, has been introduced.

B U I L D I N G

"Building block" icons have been added to all exercises to show students how their skills are building with each chapter.

> **I = Identifying.** The student is asked to identify various parts of speech and sentence constructions devices.
>
> **B = Building.** The student is asked to add a word or part of a sentence to a partially constructed sentence in order to complete it.
>
> **W = Writing.** The student is asked to create an entire sentence or paragraph.
>
> **E = Editing.** The student is asked to alter and add to an existing sentence or paragraph to enhance its clarity and meaning.
>
> **A = Analyzing.** The student is asked to read and comment on the meaning of a paragraph or essay.

A "**Common Error**" **icon** has been added to appropriate exercises in the "Writer's Resources" section. A common error icon draws the student's attention to those errors that most frequently occur in student writing.

The number of chapters in the Writer's Resources section has been condensed from 35 chapters to 30 chapters to better organize and connect parts of speech and their particular usages and usage problems.

In the Undergraduate Research Paper section, the topic of evaluating online sources has been expanded. With the ubiquitous use of online Web sites for sourcing paper material, evaluating Web sites for reliability and relevance is a growing necessity.

In the Additional Readings section, we have removed essays, at our readers' suggestions, that no longer appeal to today's students. We have replaced some of them with essays, such as Jane Goodall's "In the Shadow of Man." In one case, we have shifted an essay from one mode to another, such as "Two Ways to be in America" from Comparison and Contrast to Process because the comments from our readers have suggested it. We hope these changes will provide students with an interesting and thought-provoking experience.

Flesch-Kincaid Grade Reading Levels have been added to the three new essays in the Additional Readings section. We realize the challenge instructors and departments face in their classrooms with the variance in reading abilities with students. The Flesch-Kincaid readability test is designed to point out students' difficulties in comprehending the types of material they are expected to read in their academic experience. Hopefully, the Flesch-Kincaid Grade Reading Level scores will assist students in achieving success in their reading and writing experience. The Flesch-Kincaid Grade Reading Levels can be used with other reading and writing assessments to help instructors individually and in concert with other members of the English/reading departments to coordinate instruction within their disciplines to help students achieve success. The scoring is simple: A 7.0 score indicates a grade-school level of seventh grade, meaning a seventh grader could read and comprehend the material. An 11.1 score indicates the material could be read and comprehended by an eleventh grader, a junior in high school. All essays in the Additional Readings section have a Flesch-Kincaid Grade Reading Level score in brackets following the title of the essay, marked with an "Accessible" for easy reading and comprehension, "Medium" for intermediate reading and comprehension, and "Challenging" for more advanced reading and comprehension.

The Write Start Series

The Write Start is a two-book series designed to meet the needs of students taking developmental writing courses. The first text, *The Write Start: Sentences to Paragraphs*, addresses the most basic writing skills: grammar, sentence and paragraph structure, the integration of reading and writing, the special concerns of students with English as a second language, the various modes of developing topics, and an introduction to the essay.

This text, *The Write Start: Paragraphs to Essays*, is the second book of the series. It continues the developmental writing sequence, focusing first on writing paragraphs that express thoughts about a topic by using the various modes of development. It then focuses on expanding the topic by applying the techniques of the mode to the longer essay format. Some grammar, sentence structure, and ESL concerns are embedded in the mode chapters, but the bulk of this material is expanded on in Part Four of the text, the comprehensive Writer's Resources section. We believe that presenting the material in this manner keeps the writing process instruction more fluid and dynamic.

Organization of the Text

We have organized the text in an effort to introduce the developing writer to the basic elements and skills necessary for writing effective essays in the academic environment. While these skills also will help students communicate more effectively in their personal and work correspondence, the primary focus is to ready developing writers for the rigors of their first college-level composition course (for credit) at the next level. Many developing writers are taking courses requiring college-level writing skills while concurrently enrolled in developmental writing courses, and as a result they face problems doing the written work that is expected of them. Thus we have attempted to illustrate the processes and skills necessary for effective writing in as simple and straightforward a manner as possible, so students can begin applying their new writing skills immediately to their work in other courses.

Introduction: Chapters 1 and 2

Chapter 1 reinforces the idea that writing is important. The developing writer might at first resist this idea, but it is our belief, through years of experience, that the developing writer knows this to be true. This chapter stresses the idea that writing is difficult, but like other skills, it can be developed with the proper attitude, information, and work ethic. The chapter also emphasizes the important link between reading and writing, the need for writing presentable papers without significant grammar, punctuation, and sentence structure errors. Students are encouraged to develop the mature writing and thinking that comes from writing about topics in a variety of mode, and the techniques for making the transition from paragraphs to essays.

Chapter 2 introduces the developing writer to the elements of reasoning that underpin the critical thinking processes for analyzing and evaluating reading and writing. At the end of each essay in Chapters 7 through 15 and in the Additional Readings section, the developing writer is given a set of questions to answer based on the critical reading questions discussed in Chapter 2.

The Fundamentals: Chapters 3 through 6

Chapters 3 through 6 focus on the total writing process, from prewriting to the final draft. Part One begins with an overview of the major elements of the essay: the sentence, the paragraph, the thesis sentence, topic sentences, support sentences, audience, unity, and coherence. Chapter 3 discusses the entire writing process: prewriting, drafting, revising, and proofreading. The chapter includes a sustained example of a paragraph in various stages of development as well as practice exercises.

Chapter 4 introduces the developing writer to the introductory paragraph, including lead-in techniques and the thesis sentence. Chapter 5 describes the body paragraphs, including the topic sentence and support sentences. Part One closes with Chapter 6 and an examination of the concluding paragraph, focusing on several techniques to bring an essay to a successful end. Throughout Chapters 4 through 6, the developing writer will see a single essay as it is developed from the prewriting stage, through revisions of the rough draft, to the final proofread and corrected draft. This instruction will reinforce the rules and processes that have been introduced, and it will actually show how the processes help to create the essay.

Strategies for Developing Essays: Chapters 7 through 15

These nine chapters introduce the developing writer to the modes of development for examining topics. Each chapter begins with a photo warm-up exercise to get students writing and to get them to think about writing. Each mode chapter uses the paragraph to explain the basic concepts and techniques of the mode. Then, the chapter shows students how to make the transition to the full essay. A list of transitional expressions is provided in each chapter to aid the developing writer in creating rhythm, connecting related ideas, and combining sentences. Student essays are used to model the concepts, techniques, and processes of each mode, as well as the thesis sentence with essay map approach. In addition, professional essays are provided in each chapter to give students exposure to writing that has a less structured format. Each chapter ends with additional writing prompts, a writing checklist for the mode, and a review of the major points discussed in the chapter.

Special Writing Situations: Chapters 16 and 17

Because this text focuses on preparing the developing writer for the rigors of academic writing—specifically the first college composition course—these chapters focus on writing the research paper and the in-class essay examination.

Chapter 16 introduces the developing writer to the steps involved in writing a paper that requires research in primary and secondary sources and in documenting that research using the Modern Language Association format. The chapter uses one student-written and one professionally written research paper to model the techniques and process for research writing.

Chapter 17 focuses on the key terms that developing writers should look for in the prompts they are given on examinations to help them organize an essay in just a few minutes. The thesis statement with essay map is offered as a technique to quickly identify and organize subtopics into a clearly defined approach in response to the overall topic parameters. A number of prompts from various disciplines are illustrated with accompanying thesis statements.

The Writer's Resources: Chapters 18 through 30

The Writer's Resources section is a veritable warehouse of chapters with specific information on sentence skills, grammar, punctuation, word choice, spelling, and sentence combining. Examples and exercises accompany the material for illustration, clarification, and additional practice. Material that is especially helpful to English as a Second Language (ESL) students is tagged by an ESL icon.

Additional Readings

To give developing writers more exposure to good writing, the Additional Readings section contain one or more professional essays to accompany each of the modes covered in Chapters 7 through 15. Each essay has its own apparatus, including Flesch-Kincaid Grade Reading Level score, vocabulary, writing technique questions, critical reading and thinking questions, and writing opportunities.

Limited Answer Key

An answer key provides half the answers to the in-chapter objective practices. Students can check their own work to see how their skills are developing. (A complete answer key is included in the Annotated Instructor's Edition.)

Glossary

At the end of *The Write Start*, a glossary of terms provides a convenient resource for students to look up the meanings of key terms used in the text.

Special Features of *The Write Start*

The features of *The Write Start: Paragraphs to Essays* have been carefully developed with the needs of developmental English students and instructors in mind.

- **Clarity and Simplicity.** Concepts and techniques are simply described and illustrated, with key terms boldfaced and defined in each chapter as well as in the end-of-book glossary. The writing style is friendly, clear, and easy for students to understand. The topical presentation is logically sequenced and flows easily from chapter to chapter, yet all chapters are entirely modular, allowing instructors to determine their own order of presentation and to structure their classes however they choose. To support the clarity of the presentation, a simple, uncluttered, attractive design has been used.

- **Smooth Flow of Concepts within Each Chapter.** In each chapter, concepts flow logically from the simple to the more complex. Students are presented with concepts in a fashion that allows them to understand a little at a time and build on what they have just learned.

- **Examples.** One of the best ways for developmental students to learn is through example, and examples are used liberally to illustrate all the concepts presented. Examples are presented with a background color to make them pop out for clear emphasis and easier reference.

- **Practices.** Numerous practices reinforce learning and help students apply what they have just read. The practices are narrowly focused on the content just covered, and they range from making lists, to writing sentences, to writing and rewriting paragraphs.

- **Highly Structured Presentation of the Essay as a Form.** Writing a good essay is a complex undertaking. To help students develop their essay writing skills, *The Write Start* first presents a five-paragraph essay structure (introductory paragraph with thesis sentence and essay map, three body paragraphs, concluding paragraph) and then presents instruction on each essay mode (description, narration, etc.) using the five-paragraph essay as a structural model. Thus students can improve their organizational and writing skills within a highly structured form defined by the thesis sentence with essay map. All the model student essays use the essay map and are written in this five-paragraph form to reinforce the instruction.

- **A Word about the Thesis Sentence.** As you will find in Chapter 4, this textbook uses the thesis sentence with essay map as the tool for organizing the essay. However, we understand that each instructor needs to be adaptive with each class. So, feel free to use the thesis construction mechanism (single sentence or multi-sentence statement) with which you are most comfortable.

- ■ **The need for structure and rhythm.** Some writing teachers complain that the essay map forces the writer into a mechanical style. We believe this to be untrue. In writing this text, we have made two assumptions, one about the developing writer and one about writing.

- ■ **Structure.** First, we believe that the developing writer, to be successful in academic work, needs structure. The essay map in the thesis sentence allows the developing writer to create a mini outline of the essay, helping the writer to stay focused on the subtopic at hand and on the order in which the subtopics should be discussed. In fact, the feedback we have received from our students indicates that they rely on the thesis sentence in many of their other classes, particularly during in-class essay exams.

- ■ **Rhythm.** Second, we believe that mechanical writing results from the failure to make good use of techniques that promote a fluid, rhythmical style. In each of the mode chapters, we illustrate the transitional devices that help connect related ideas, foster rhythm in the paragraphs, and combine sentences to reduce choppiness and introduce variety, a hallmark of good writing. In fact, many professionals use the essay map as the organizing tool in their writing, yet one would hardly call the writing styles of professional writers such as Barbara Ehrenreich—who has used the essay map—stodgy, stolid, or mechanical.

- ■ **Focus on ESL.** The developmental writing market overlaps with the ESL market. Many ESL instructors need to use developmental texts, and many developmental instructors have ESL students enrolled in their courses. Gayle Feng-Checkett is a certified ESL instructor, so much of the text was written with ESL students in mind. This book uses ESL research and pedagogy to the benefit of all developmental English students.

- ■ **Critical Thinking Skills: The Connection between Reading and Writing.** Good writers are also good readers, and many of the skills used in reading are also used in writing. Chapter 2, on critical thinking, explains why critical thinking skills are important in today's information-overloaded society, provides students with an explanation of key critical thinking skills, and models the use of the skills on a reading. The skills covered in this introductory chapter are picked up in later essay mode chapters. In each of these chapters, a critical reading activity requires students to analyze the chapter's model essays using particular critical thinking skills.

- ■ **Model Essays.** Each of the essay mode chapters has two model essays. The first is a student essay written in the five-paragraph essay structure on which instruction is built. The second is a professionally written essay that departs from the five-paragraph structure and gives students exposure to less-structured but excellent writing. All essays have been chosen not only for their technical merit, but also because they are about high-interest topics.

- ■ **Writing Technique Questions and Critical Reading and Thinking Questions.** Each model essay in the mode chapters as well as in the Additional Readings is followed by a series of questions that help students analyze the techniques as well as the content of the essay.

- ■ **More Topics for Writing.** At the end of each essay mode chapter are more suggested topics for essay writing. Students may choose a topic, or instructors may assign topics. At least one of the topics is related to a photo on which an essay can be based.

■ **The Writer's Resources.** In the Writer's Resources section, the treatment of sentence problems has been expanded and many additional exercises have been added. These provide additional practice for students who need help with grammar, punctuation, style, and word choice. These exercises encourage students to compose and create their own correct sentences, and the "Read All about It" features encourage students to work with and study the specific style of the professional writers who have contributed essays to this text.

■ **Writing Checklists.** Writing checklists appear at the end of each of the essay mode chapters. These help students identify strategies and tasks needed to write an essay using the mode.

■ **Read All about It.** Many exercises in the Writer's Resources section are based on the essays in the Additional Readings section. An icon indicates the reading from which the exercise is excerpted so that students can refer to the complete essay for additional context.

The Teaching and Learning Package

Each component of the teaching and learning package has been crafted to ensure that the course is rewarding for instructors and students. In addition to the book-specific supplements discussed previously, a series of other skills-based supplements is available for both instructors and students. All of these supplements are available either free or at greatly reduced prices.

For Instructors
Annotated Instructor's Edition
This book is a replica of the student text, but it includes answers printed directly on the fill-in lines provided in the text. 978-1-285-17765-6.

Instructor's Manual and Test Bank provides additional teaching support for each chapter, including tips and suggestions for classroom activities, establishing a learning environment, collaborative writing assignments, and additional support for teaching classes that include ESL students. The test bank provides a wealth of quizzes for each chapter in the text, and is formatted in a way that simplifies copying and distribution. 978-1-285-17777-9

ExamView® allows instructors to create, deliver, and customize test bank content for both print and online exams.

Acknowledgments

We would like to thank everyone who has helped us write and publish *The Write Start*. Special thanks goes to the team at Cengage Learning including Cate Richard Dodson, Development Editor; Annie Todd, Director of Developmental English; Melanie Opacki, Editorial Assistant; Aimee Chevrette Bear, Content Project Manager; and Melena Fenn, Senior Project Manager at Pre-Press PMG. Our students contributed paragraphs and essays to the text and demonstrated through their own writing that our techniques work, while challenging us to keep improving them. Finally, many thanks to the devoted English instructors around the country who reviewed our text and made valuable suggestions for improvement, Patricia A. Mosele, Central Carolina Technical College; Larry Silverman, Seattle Central Community College; Diana Nystedt, Palo Alto College; Andrew Nessett, Century College; Melissa McCoy, Clarendon College; Michael Bodek, Bergen College; Richard Turner, Ozarks Tech Community College; and Joseph Fly, South Plains College.

Gayle Feng-Checkett
Lawrence Checkett

The Write Start
Paragraphs to Essays

WITH PROFESSIONAL AND STUDENT READINGS

1

To the Student

As a college student, you face multiple demands each day, and writing is an integral part of most of these challenges. This book has been written to help you, the developing college writer, to reach your immediate and long-term goals. You have made the decision to go to college to learn the skills that will help you succeed in your learning, as well as help you secure a rewarding career. Whether or not you already know your career path, you will find that writing will play a large part in your successfully completing college work and in reaching your future work-related goals.

How This Book Can Help You Reach Your Goals

Good writing is hard, but good writing is achievable. People are not born good writers. With hard work, the right techniques, and helpful advice, you can master the skills of writing. This book will give you the tools, the strategies, and the advice that have been used successfully for years with students like you in classes just like yours.

This book will help you achieve your writing goals in the following ways.

- ■ **By emphasizing the important link between reading and writing.** The student and professional essays in this book are used to model the writing techniques demonstrated in the instructional chapters. By understanding how these techniques are used in the readings, you will improve your own writing skills.
- ■ **By helping you read and write with more depth and understanding through the use of critical thinking skills.** In Chapter 2, you will be introduced to the key critical thinking questions that will help you analyze and evaluate the information coming to you. Learning how to analyze what you read will help you improve your ability to communicate your ideas to others. At the end of Chapters 7 through 15, you will find a number of writing opportunities based on critical thinking skill elements.
- ■ **By introducing you to a variety of methods you can use to develop your ideas about specific topics.** Not every topic can best be developed using the same approach. One piece of information might be best presented by using definition, while another might be clarified using example, and another might be best explained by comparing or contrasting

1

it to something else. In this book, you will be introduced to the traditional methods used for developing topics.

■ **By teaching you a few techniques to develop a topic and write about it.** In Chapter 3, you will be introduced to the writing process: prewriting, drafting, revising, and proofreading. (1) Prewriting activities, such as brainstorming, clustering, and cubing, can help you develop subtopics to support your ideas concerning the main topic. For instance, you may want to write about investing (the main topic), but investing covers a lot of possible areas (the subtopics): investing for immediate income as opposed to investing for retirement, investing in stocks versus investing in bonds, or whether to do your own investing or let a brokerage firm do it for you. Prewriting activities will help you map out a variety of subtopics so that you can focus on those that you think will best develop the main topic. (2) Drafting is the stage at which you write the first, rough version of your paragraph or essay. You write the draft to get your ideas down, however roughly. (3) Revising techniques can help you sharpen what you want to say, better organize and develop your thoughts, and express your ideas more clearly. You can revise at any time during the writing process. (4) Proofreading takes place after you have written the final draft. When proofreading, you correct errors in spelling, punctuation, word choice, and grammar. These distract from clear content and presentation.

■ **By demonstrating how the different parts of an essay are written.** In Chapters 4 through 6, we will model the writing process using the introductory, body, and concluding paragraphs of an essay. This will help you get an overview of how an essay is written.

■ **By showing you how to make the transition from writing the paragraph to writing the longer essay.** In Chapters 7 through 15, you will be introduced to different methods of developing a topic. At the start of each chapter, the method will be explained using the paragraph as the instructional model. The paragraph is used because it is short but still

Lan Shaw/Alamy

© 2014 Wadsworth, Cengage Learning

enables us to illustrate the key concepts of the method under discussion. Once the basic elements and techniques are demonstrated, the transition to a longer unit of writing, the essay, follows.

■ **By helping you present your thoughts more professionally, using good grammar, punctuation, and sentence structure.** Constructing logical and reasonable content is only half of the writing process. The other half has to do with proper presentation. For instance, you might have the most talented mind in the world, but if you show up at a job interview wearing torn jeans and a shirt with food stains all over it, having unwashed and uncombed hair, and with a cigarette hanging out of the side of your mouth, you are not likely to get the job. You may have the right content, but your presentation is wrong. So it is with writing. If you have too many errors in punctuation or mechanics, your writing will not be successful, no matter how good the content is. Part 4 of this text, The Writer's Resources, is a complete guide to correct grammar, punctuation, and usage. It also contains information and helpful techniques for students whose first language is not English.

Writing Can Be Learned

Writing skills are essential not only in academia, but also in the business world as well, and many in the business community have a growing concern about the writing abilities of the graduates they hire and work with. Executives need their employees to have excellent communication skills—to foster increased productivity and enhanced performance. Whether it is a term paper or a business report you are asked to complete, good writing skills are a necessity. This book will help you establish and maintain the skills necessary for good writing. Once again, writing is a skill that can be learned with practice and dedication. In this way, good writing is no different from any other skill you want to learn and improve upon. There is an old joke that captures the essence of this undertaking.

> A person carrying a violin case and walking along a street in New York City stops another person walking by and asks, "Excuse me, but how do I get to Carnegie Hall?" The second person answers sternly, "Practice, practice, practice."

 ## Visit *The Write Start* Online!

For additional practice with the materials found in this chapter, visit our Student Companion Web site by going to cengagebrain.com and searching for this text. The Web site also features additional readings, quizzes, writing activities, and Internet links.

Critical Thinking: The Connection between Reading and Writing

You often will be asked to write about a topic you have studied. In the academic world, this is the most common form of communication you will have with your instructors. However, before you can write about what you have learned and the conclusions you have come to, you first must think critically about what you have heard, read, observed, or discussed. An effective way to start the **critical thinking** process is to ask yourself some questions about the material you are reading.

The point of asking questions about the material you are exploring is so you do not blindly accept the opinions and conclusions of others. Every person and organization has an agenda with which you may or may not agree. It is necessary to understand the points of view of others in order to evaluate their arguments and conclusions. Once you have analyzed the points of view of others, you are in a better position to reach your own conclusions.

Questions for Thinking Critically

To assess a piece of information critically, ask the following four critical thinking questions. By doing so, you will come to a better understanding of why you are convinced or unconvinced by the material's point of view or conclusions. The critical thinking questions also will help you identify the major strengths and weaknesses of the material.

1. **What is the main idea?** The **main idea** is the writer's basic approach to the subject matter. The main idea is the most important aspect of the essay; it is the problem to be solved or the issue being raised for consideration. In an essay about the topic of national ID cards, for example, the main idea might be that the United States should consider issuing ID cards to residents. You can usually find the topic and main idea in the first paragraph of an essay.

2. **What conclusions are reached regarding the main idea?** The writer's conclusions might include steps to solve the problem or possibilities that might lead to a solution. In the national ID card essay, the writer might conclude that national ID cards would be useful because they would help combat crime and terrorism.

3. **What reasons or evidence does the writer give to support the conclusions?** *Reasons* is another word for *evidence*. Evidence can be

personal experience; the experiences of others; the ideas of experts regarding the topic; statistics; or information from articles, magazines, journals, books, lectures, videos, or other sources.

4. **Are the reasons or evidence fact or opinion?** Generally, *fact* is distinguished from *opinion* in the following way. Facts are accepted as *true*. Water freezes at 0° Celsius or 32° Fahrenheit—this is a fact. It cannot be disputed. That the United States is a member of the United Nations (UN) is also a fact in the same way. However, *opinions* are interpretations of the facts. While it is a fact that the United States is a member of the UN, is its membership positive or negative for you personally, for the nation as a whole, or for the international community? Do you think the United States' membership costs too much for the results produced? Should other countries bear more of the UN's operating costs? Do small nations have too much voice in UN decisions? While we all agree that it is a fact that the United States is a member of the UN, we will have a variety of opinions about whether that fact is good or bad.

Applying the Critical Thinking Questions

To help you see how asking the critical thinking questions works, we have provided an example. First, read the following excerpt from a student essay. Then, read through the brief model analysis that uses the four critical thinking questions.

Sample Student Essay: ARE TWO MILLION AMERICAN INMATES TOO MANY?

Tom Weidemann

> The following is an excerpt from an essay by student writer Tom Weidemann. In the essay, Tom is concerned with how the U.S. criminal justice system deals with people found guilty of committing minor drug-related crimes.

Are Two Million American Inmates Too Many?

Crime has always been one of society's major concerns, as have the ways to deal with it. According to a report from the Government Accounting Office (GAO), as of February 15, 2000, an estimated two million Americans were doing jail time in the American penal system. And the number is increasing each year. The cost of housing, feeding, guarding, and providing medical care for inmates is spiraling upward. Columnist Neal Janny, in an article appearing in the editorial section of the *Denver Post*, states, "America has the largest prison population in the world, and an inordinate number of the prison population is comprised of black males serving time for minor drug-related crimes." Janny concludes that there is something dreadfully wrong when a wealthy, well-educated society handles a problem in such a ham-fisted and shortsighted way. Michael Cartine, in his book *Mindless Revenge*, explains, "While black males represent only 5–6 percent of the American

population, they represent 50 percent of the prison population." This kind of disproportionate outcome should be a flashing danger signal to all Americans and to the leaders of our judicial and penal systems. It is time to recognize that our society is wasting money and potentially productive lives by the way it handles criminals convicted of minor drug-related crimes. Imprisoning petty crooks is too costly and does little to change the adverse effects caused by both the crime and the incarceration.

Some people believe that placing small-time drug dealers in prison is a way to ensure the safety of the general public. They believe that it is necessary to separate criminals from society for the common good. In Sheila Adkins' article "The Wrong Sentence," appearing in the journal *American Prison Quarterly*, she explains that both Japan and China have effectively reduced the drug problems in their countries by arresting and re-educating, not arresting and imprisoning, drug users and, thereby, ending the vicious supply and demand circle. Our prisons have not done a good job in rehabilitating inmates. Most inmates, after being paroled, return to prison within a short time. Adkins' solution is, then, one that should merit society's attention. America can help solve some of its drug problems by decriminalizing minor drug-related crimes and focusing on rehabilitating rather than imprisoning those found guilty of minor drug-related offenses. Decriminalization and rehabilitation would lower the cost of operating our penal system. It also would lead to a lower crime rate. Re-educating petty criminals also would deliver productive and law-abiding citizens rather than recycling yet another batch of criminals whose actions are to society's detriment.

Model Critical Thinking Analysis of "Are Two Million American Inmates Too Many?"

1. What is the main idea?

The topic of the essay is the treatment of people who commit minor drug-related crimes. In this case, there are several ideas in the opening paragraph.

The main idea is the one that specifies the essay's purpose. For instance, in the preceding excerpt, the paragraph begins with a broad concept, *crime*, in the first sentence; moves to a more specific idea in the fourth sentence, *The cost of housing, feeding, guarding, and providing medical care for inmates is spiraling upward*; and finishes in the second to last sentence with the most specific and focused statement, one that announces a purpose and, therefore, is the main idea: *It is time to recognize the fact that our society is wasting money and potentially productive lives by the way it handles criminals convicted of minor drug-related crimes.* The rest of the essay, then, will give the reader information on how society can save money and generate more productive lives by changing how it treats petty criminals convicted of minor drug-related crimes.

2. What conclusions are reached regarding the main idea?

One conclusion is stated in the second to last sentence of the first paragraph, that *society is wasting money and potentially productive lives by the way it handles criminals convicted of minor drug-related offenses*. Other conclusions are found in paragraph 2, sentence 4, *Our prisons have not done a good job in rehabilitating inmates*; sentence 7, *America can help solve some of its drug problems by decriminalizing minor drug-related crimes and focusing on rehabilitating rather than imprisoning those found guilty of minor drug-related offenses*; sentence 8, *Decriminalization and rehabilitation would lower the cost of operating our penal system*; sentence 9, *It also would lead to a lower crime rate*; and sentence 10, *Re-educating petty criminals also would deliver productive and law-abiding citizens rather than recycling yet another batch of criminals whose actions are to society's detriment.*

3. What reasons or evidence does the writer give to support the conclusions?

The evidence in paragraph 1 includes sentence 2, *an estimated two million Americans were doing jail time*; sentence 3, *the number [of inmates] is increasing each year*; sentence 4, *The cost of housing, feeding, guarding, and providing medical care for inmates is spiraling upward*; sentence 5, *the prison population is comprised of black males serving time for minor drug-related crimes*; and sentence 7, *While black males represent only 5–6 percent of the American population, they represent 50 percent of the prison population.*

The evidence in paragraph 2 includes sentence 3, *both Japan and China have effectively reduced the drug problems in their countries by arresting and re-educating, not arresting and imprisoning, drug users and, thereby, ending the vicious supply and demand circle*; and sentence 5, *Most inmates, after being paroled, return to prison within a short time.*

4. Are the reasons or evidence fact or opinion?

All of the evidence is factual. In paragraph 1, sentences 2, 3, and 4, the source of the evidence is the Government Accounting Office (GAO), not the author's opinion; in sentence 5, the source is a newspaper columnist, a professional expected to gather such evidence from reliable sources, not from personal opinion; in sentence 7, the evidence comes from a book and is statistical and, therefore, most probably taken from a study or survey done by a reputable organization; in paragraph 2, sentence 3, the information comes from a journal article and indicates an objective source other than the author's opinion. Finally, in sentence 7, the evidence is statistical in nature and most likely was taken from a source other than the author's opinion.

Note that even if the source of factual evidence is not stated in the essay or references, it is still presumed that the author can produce the source if necessary. To make up information as if it came from a reliable source or to be unable to document factual evidence is considered a serious error in writing.

Finally, ask yourself how convincing are the evidence and conclusions in supporting the main idea. The answer to this question will vary from reader to reader, but you should examine all the information with this purpose in mind.

Using the four critical thinking questions will enable you to analyze critically information with depth and clarity, and it will allow you to communicate your thoughts about an essay clearly and confidently.

Questions for Thinking Critically

What Is the Main Idea?	What Are the Conclusions?	What Evidence Is Presented?	Is the Evidence Fact or Opinion?
The writer's approach to the subject. The problem to be solved or the issue being raised for consideration.	The writer's analysis of a problem, proposed steps to solve it, or possibilities leading to solution.	Reasons and support for the writer's conclusions. Evidence may be experience, expert opinions, statistics, or information from books, articles, lectures, and other sources.	Facts can be proved true. Opinions are interpretations of the facts.

Sample Professional Essay: DESIGNER BABIES

Sharon Begley

In the following essay, *Newsweek* writer Sharon Begley looks at one of the potential consequences stemming from the Human Genome Project (the effort to map the genetic makeup of humans). What she finds is a disturbing possibility that may affect the very nature of evolution.

Vocabulary

Before you begin reading, look up the definitions of the following terms that appear in the essay. The number in parentheses after each term indicates the paragraph in which the term appears.

anecdotal (6)	eradicate (7)	presto (5)
bequeathed (2)	gene (1)	protocol (6)
chromosome (1)	insinuate (6)	quirk (4)
disposition (3)	in vitro fertilization (1)	Rubicon (2)
embryo (1)	momentous (2)	

Designer Babies

It is only a matter of time. One day—a day probably no more distant than the first wedding anniversary of a couple who are now teenage sweethearts—a man and a woman will walk into an in vitro fertilization clinic and make scientific history. Their problem won't be infertility, the reason couples now choose IVF. Rather, they will be desperate for a very special child, a child who will elude a family curse. To create their dream child, doctors will fertilize a few of the woman's eggs with her husband's sperm, as IVF clinics do today. But then they will inject an artificial human chromosome, carrying made-to-order genes like pearls on a string, into the fertilized egg. One of the genes will carry instructions ordering cells to commit suicide. Then the doctors will place the embryo into the woman's uterus. If her baby is a boy, when he becomes an old man he, like his father and grandfather before him, will develop prostate cancer. But the cell-suicide gene will make his prostate cells self-destruct. The man, unlike his ancestors, will not die of the cancer. And since the gene that the doctors gave him copied itself into every cell of his body, including his sperm, his sons will beat prostate cancer, too.

Genetic engineers are preparing to cross what has long been an ethical Rubicon. Since 1990, gene therapy has meant slipping a healthy gene into the cells of one organ of a patient suffering from a genetic disease. Soon, it may mean something much more momentous: altering a fertilized egg so that genes in all of a person's cells, including eggs or sperm, also carry a gene that scientists, not parents, bequeathed them. When the pioneers of gene therapy first requested government approval for their experiments in 1987, they vowed they would *never* alter patients' eggs or sperm. That was then. This is now. One of those pioneers, Dr. W. French Anderson of the University of Southern California, recently put the National Institutes of Health on notice. Within two or three years, he said, he would ask approval to use gene therapy on a fetus that has been diagnosed with a deadly inherited disease. The therapy would cure the fetus before it is born. But the introduced genes, though targeted at only blood or immune-system cells, might inadvertently slip into the child's egg (or sperm) cells, too. If that happens, the genetic change would affect that child's children unto the nth generation. "Life would enter a new phase," says biophysicist Gregory Stock of UCLA, "one in which we seize control of our own evolution."

Judging by the 70 pages of public comments NIH has received since Anderson submitted his proposal in September, the overwhelming majority of scientists and ethicists weighing in oppose gene therapy that changes the "germline" (eggs and sperm). But the position could be a boulevard wide and paper thin. "There is a great divide in the bioethics community over whether we should be opening up this Pandora's box," says science-policy scholar Sheldon Krimsky of Tufts University. Many bioethicists are sympathetic to using germline therapy to shield a child from a family disposition to cancer, or atherosclerosis or other illness with a strong genetic component. As James Watson, president of the Cold Spring Harbor Laboratory and codiscoverer of the double-helical structure of DNA, said at a recent UCLA conference, "We might as well do what we finally can to take the threat of Alzheimer's or breast cancer away from a family." But something else is suddenly making it OK to discuss the once forbidden possibility of germline engineering: molecular biologists now think they have clever ways to circumvent ethical concerns that engulf this sci-fi idea.

There may be ways, for instance, to design a baby's genes without violating the principle of informed consent. This is the belief that no one's genes—not even an embryo's—should be altered without his or her permission. Presumably few people would object to being spared a fatal disease. But what about genes for personality traits, like risk-taking or being neurotic? If you like today's blame game—it's *Mom's fault* that you inherited her temper—you'll love tomorrow's: she intentionally stuck you with that personality quirk. But the child of tomorrow might have the final word about his genes, says UCLA geneticist John Campbell. The designer gene for, say, patience could be paired with an on-off switch, he says. The child would have to take a drug to activate the patience gene. Free to accept or reject the drug, he retains informed consent over his genetic endowment.

There may also be ways to make an end run around the worry that [it] is wrong to monkey with human evolution. Researchers are experimenting with tricks to make the introduced gene self-destruct in cells that become eggs or sperm. That would confine the tinkering to one generation. Then, if it became clear that eliminating genes for, say[,] mental illness also erased genes for creativity, that loss would not become a permanent part of man's genetic blueprint. (Of course, preventing the new gene's transmission to future generations would also defeat the hope of permanently lopping off a diseased branch from a family tree.) In experiments with animals, geneticist Mario Capecchi of the University of Utah has designed a string of genes flanked by the molecular version of scissors. The scissors are activated by an enzyme that would be made only in the cells that become eggs or sperm. Once activated, the genetic scissors snip out the introduced gene and, presto, it is not passed along to future generations. "What I worry about," says Capecchi, "is that if we start messing around with [eggs and sperm], at some point—since this is a human enterprise—we're going to make a mistake. You want a way to undo that mistake. And since what may seem terrific now may seem naive in 20 years, you want a way to make the genetic change reversible."

There is no easy technological fix for another ethical worry, however; with germline engineering only society's "haves" will control their genetic traits. It isn't hard to foresee a day like that painted in last year's film "Gattaca," where only the wealthy can afford to genetically engineer their children with such "killer applications" as intelligence, beauty, long life or health. "If you are going to disadvantage even further those who are already disadvantaged," says bioethicist Ruth Macklin of Albert Einstein College of Medicine, "then that does raise serious concerns." But perhaps not enough to keep designer babies solely in Hollywood's imagination. For one thing, genetic therapy as done today (treating one organ of one child or adult) has been a bitter disappointment. "With the exception of a few anecdotal cases," says USC's Anderson, "there is no evidence of a gene-therapy protocol that helps." But germline therapy might actually be easier. Doctors would not have to insinuate the new gene into millions of lung cells in, say, a cystic fibrosis patient. They could manipulate only a single cell—the fertilized egg—and still have the gene reach every cell of the person who develops from that egg.

How soon might we design our children? The necessary pieces are quickly falling into place. The first artificial human chromosome was created last year. The Human Genome Project decoded all 3 billion chemical letters that spell out our 70,000 or so genes. Animal experiments designed to show that the process will not create horrible mutants are underway. No law prohibits germline engineering. Although NIH now refuses to even consider funding proposals for it, the rules are being updated. And where there is a way, there will almost surely be a will: none of us, says USC's Anderson, "wants to pass on to our children lethal genes if we can prevent it—that's what's going to drive this." At the UCLA symposium on germline engineering, two-thirds of the audience supported it. Few would argue against using the technique to eradicate a disease that has plagued a family for generations. As Tuft's Krimsky says, "We know where to start." The harder question is this: do we know where to stop?

PRACTICE 1   **Using the Critical Thinking Questions to Evaluate "Designer Babies"**

I B W E A

A N A L Y Z I N G

1. What is the main idea?

_____

_____

_____

2. What conclusions are reached regarding the main idea?

_____

_____

_____

_____

_____

_____

_____

_____

3. What are the reasons or evidence given to support the conclusions?

_____

_____

_____

_____

_____

_____

4. Are the reasons or evidence fact or opinion?

_____

_____

_____

_____

_____

Critical Reading Questions

At the end of each essay in Chapters 7 through 15 and the Additional Readings, you will find a set of Critical Reading Questions based on the critical thinking questions you have studied in this chapter: main idea, conclusions, reasons or evidence, and the nature of the reasons or evidence (fact or opinion). By answering the critical reading questions, you will improve your reading comprehension and thinking abilities, and your writing will become clearer and more meaningful.

CHAPTER REVIEW

- It is important to think critically about what you are reading so you can evaluate the point of view and conclusions of the writer.
- There are four main questions to ask when reading critically: (1) What is the main idea? (2) What conclusions are reached regarding the main idea? (3) What reasons or evidence does the writer give to support the conclusions? (4) Are the reasons or evidence fact or opinion?
- The topic is the subject matter of the essay. The main idea is the writer's basic point about the subject matter. Both are often found in the first paragraph of an essay.
- Conclusions about the main idea need to be supported by sound evidence and reasons.
- Evidence and reasons can be fact-based (accepted as true) or opinions (interpretations that may or may not be sound).
- Your evaluation of an essay's conclusions is based on your answers to the four critical thinking questions.

 ## Visit *The Write Start* Online!

For additional practice with the materials found in this chapter, visit our Student Companion Web site by going to cengagebrain.com and searching for this text. The Web site also features additional readings, quizzes, writing activities, and Internet links.

Getting Started: The Fundamentals

While sentences are good for expressing short pieces of information, a longer format is necessary for longer, more developed ideas. The following four chapters will enable you to understand and write the basic paragraphs that make up an even longer format called the essay. Writing paragraphs is good practice because paragraphs contain many of the elements you will find in longer pieces of writing, such as letters, reports, essays, and research papers.

Prewriting, Drafting, Revising, and Proofreading

When you begin writing a paragraph or essay, you should consider what needs to be done prior to drafting the paragraph or essay you hand in. In Chapter 3, with a few short examples, we will explain the **prewriting** strategies for getting started, the **drafting** stages, the need for **revising** to take your rough drafts to a final draft, and **proofreading** techniques that remove any technical errors in the finished draft.

After you have studied the short prewriting, drafting, revising, and proofreading examples in Chapter 3, you can follow an entire essay being written using these techniques in Chapters 4 through 6 as you study the introductory, body, and concluding paragraphs.

The Paragraph

A paragraph consists of a number of sentences that develop a single idea called a **topic**. In fact, you are reading a paragraph right now, and its topic is "the paragraph." Four to eight sentences is the length of most paragraphs, although they can be as short or as long as the topic or assignment demands. A good paragraph is long enough to develop the topic adequately, but no longer.

On the page, a paragraph is formatted like this:

- The first line of a paragraph should be indented five spaces from the left margin, or one tab stop.
- Each additional line of the paragraph should begin at the left margin, but each line does not have to end exactly at the right margin. Your computer will automatically adjust the line endings for you.

■ If the last word of a line comes before the right margin, leave the remainder of the line blank.

Types of Sentences in Paragraphs

There are two basic types of sentences in a paragraph: the **topic sentence** and **support sentences**. The topic sentence tells the reader what the main idea, or topic, of the paragraph is. Although there is no set place in the paragraph for the topic sentence, making the topic sentence the first sentence in the paragraph will help you organize and develop the topic. The topic sentence is followed by support sentences that explain, clarify, and define the topic by using specific detail. Support sentences should demonstrate a variety of styles to show the relationship between the various pieces of information and to create rhythm.

To summarize the characteristics and elements of a paragraph:

■ A topic sentence announces one main idea (the topic).
■ Support sentences use specific details to develop the topic.
■ Sentence variety connects related ideas and adds rhythm.

Let us look at an example paragraph that exhibits the characteristics and elements you have been reading about.

> **Example Paragraph**
>
> Edward Kennedy "Duke" Ellington was an American composer, pianist, and conductor greatly admired for bringing jazz from nightclubs into mainstream concert halls. "Sophisticated Lady" and "Mood Indigo" were two of his most famous shorter jazz pieces, but his longer compositions, such as *Paris Blues* and *Far East Suite*, were styled after the classical concerto form, modified for his jazz stylizations. This creativity led to appearances on radio and television, in theaters and nightclubs, and on worldwide tours. Even though Duke Ellington was so prolific, his music won critical acclaim worldwide.

■ The first sentence is the topic sentence, and it announces the main idea of the paragraph (Duke Ellington) and what specific information will be used in the support sentences to explore the main idea. The specific support information also can be called the **controlling idea** (Ellington was greatly admired for his ability to make jazz appreciated by the mainstream public).
■ The following three support sentences develop the topic and controlling idea by naming his most famous compositions (sentence 2), by explaining that critics and the public enjoyed his music (sentences 3 and 4), and by giving the vast numbers of venues in which he played his music (sentence 3).
■ The sentences also exhibit variety. The second sentence is coordinated with the conjunction **but**; it also contains extra information between two commas. The third sentence is a simple sentence. The fourth sentence is subordinated by using an introductory dependent clause preceding the independent clause.

The Essay

Effective paragraph writing is useful for short pieces of communication, such as memos, short-answer exams, and brief writing assignments, but many business reports and longer college writing assignments require multiple paragraphs to explain many ideas.

Just as sentences are joined together to make paragraphs, paragraphs are used to make longer pieces of writing, including the **essay**. An essay is a number of related paragraphs that develop a particular topic. Essays can be developed using many of the techniques for developing the paragraph.

Although an essay can have any number of paragraphs, this book will use the five-paragraph model to introduce the basic elements of the essay.

The Essay Title

Almost all essays should have a title, one that should pique the reader's interest. It should be a catchy or dramatic phrase, usually comprising two to six words. Longer titles can become wordy and cumbersome to read. If you cannot come up with something clever or dramatic, use the main idea as your title. It is a good idea to wait until your essay is finished before you create a title. In that way, you give yourself enough time to fully understand the point of your essay and create the most appropriate title for it.

When writing your title, do the following:

- Capitalize all words except articles (a, an, the) and prepositions (in, of, on, to) unless the article or preposition is the first or last word of the title. First words of titles are always capitalized.
- Center the title on the page and leave two line spaces between it and the introductory paragraph.

Essay Elements

Most essays begin with the **introductory paragraph**. Its purpose is to introduce the reader to the topic of the essay. The paragraph consists of **introductory sentences** and the **thesis statement**. The purpose of introductory sentences (sometimes called "lead-in sentences") is to create a context that makes the topic interesting or important. The thesis statement clarifies the specific subject matter to be explored, and it gives the writer's attitude about the topic. The thesis statement also may outline how the subject will be explored by including an optional organizational idea, often called an "essay map" (a series of subtopics that will be used in the body paragraphs to explore the main topic).

After the introductory paragraph come the **body paragraphs**. Their purpose is to develop, support, and explain the topic idea stated in the thesis statement. Body paragraphs consist of a **topic sentence** followed by **support sentences**.

The essay ends with the **concluding paragraph**. Its purpose is to bring the essay to a conclusion that gives the reader a sense of completeness.

These essay elements will be discussed in detail in Chapters 4 through 6. Chapter 4 discusses the introductory paragraph, Chapter 5 discusses body paragraphs, and Chapter 6 discusses the concluding paragraph.

Audience

Before writing an essay, you should think about your **audience**, for whom you are writing. In college, you will almost always be writing for your professor. However, you also may be writing for other members of the class if peer reading and assessment is part of the assignment. In some cases, you will be writing for your employer, for someone in a company with which you want to do business, for members of a club to which you belong, or for a select group having special interest in your topic. Depending on your intended audience, you should think about the type, depth, and presentation of the information you want to include in your work. Consider the following points:

1. How much specific knowledge does your audience have about the topic?

   For example, if you are writing about a new computer program, ask yourself how much your audience knows about computers. If you are writing for a group of novices—people who may not yet have a computer or have just recently purchased one—the information you provide will be very basic, and you will use simple wording and plenty of definitions for unfamiliar terms and, perhaps, many examples to illustrate what you mean. Conversely, if your audience is a group of computer programmers, who work every day with computer programs in a variety of applications, you will likely omit basic concepts that they are likely to know. Your word choices can be more sophisticated, and you will most likely use only a few examples to clarify information.

2. How much persuading do you need to do?

   For instance, does the audience you are writing for agree or disagree with your ideas? If you know they agree with your position, typically you will use information that will assure them that their beliefs are acceptable. Your task is easy as long as you keep your audience comfortable and feeling good about themselves. You are, in essence, "preaching to the choir." If, however, you know that your audience disagrees or is uncomfortable with your topic, then your job becomes much tougher. You will need to present information to reduce the level of negative emotion and bias. You might want to begin by offering an olive branch to your audience. Instead of being confrontational—telling them, in effect, that it is "your way or the highway"—you might concede that theirs is a legitimate point of view and that people of goodwill can disagree without being disagreeable. In this way, you diffuse some of the opposition to your ideas before you actually dig into the substance of your position. Most often, you will never turn an audience completely to your side of things. However, if you can at least convince them to listen, to give you a reasonable hearing, you have done as much as you can do with a short piece of communication.

Unity

Unity means that each paragraph's topic sentence supports an essay's thesis statement, and each support sentence within a paragraph supports the paragraph's topic sentence. Ideas other than those that help develop, support, or clarify the topic and subtopics in the writing may not be introduced.

> **Example of a Paragraph without Unity**
>
> (1) When a space shuttle catastrophe occurs, funding of NASA's space program is threatened. (2) Many Americans consider space travel too dangerous, and they do not want Congress to fund such programs. (3) Many members of Congress agree that the cost of manned space travel is too expensive, in terms of both money and loss of life. (4) Some astronauts come from the ranks of teachers.

(5) When a crew of astronauts is lost in a tragic accident, the intense, widespread media coverage causes many viewers to have a negative emotional response toward NASA. (6) Opponents of space exploration use the incident and the emotional response as evidence that funding should be stopped.

The first sentence, the topic sentence, states the main idea: *space shuttle accidents threaten NASA funding*. The remainder of the support sentences in the paragraph must support this idea. Other ideas may not be introduced. Sentence number 4, then, should be removed from the paragraph because it does not develop, support, or clarify the main idea in the topic sentence.

PRACTICE 1   **Paragraph Unity**

I D E N T I F Y I N G

Read the following paragraph. If the paragraph is not unified, identify on the line provided the number of the sentence or sentences in the paragraph that should be removed.

(1) Owning guns should be illegal because they cause too much death.

(2) Guns kill over 11,000 people each year in the United States. (3) There are more than 200 million guns held privately in America. (4) Men and women in the Armed Forces train regularly with firearms. (5) Polls suggest that almost everyone agrees the numbers of firearms should be reduced and stricter gun laws enforced. (6) Great Britain, for example, has very strict gun laws, and there are fewer than 100 gun-related deaths per year. (7) Some guns are specially made for buyers who keep them in expensive gun showcases. (8) Firearms should be treated as any other consumer product because most gun-related deaths occur between people who know each other. (9) As the saying goes, "Guns don't kill people. People kill people."

Coherence

Coherence means that the ideas expressed in your writing are presented so that the content is clear and convincing. Coherence keeps readers moving from idea to idea, keeps them focused on relevant information, and presents ideas with clarity and precision. Your thoughts should not be presented chaotically, in a random and confusing manner. Generally, you can order ideas by **time**, **space**, and **importance**.

Time Order

Time order means that ideas are arranged chronologically, either past to present or present to past. The time can be given in seconds, minutes, hours, days, weeks, months, years, decades, or centuries. Additionally, time can be divided into transitional expressions, such as "morning," "afternoon," and "evening," or with phrases such as "before breakfast," "after lunch," and "during dinner." "First," "second," "third," and "then," "next," and "finally" also are useful time-ordering transitional expressions. The important concept to remember is that presenting material in chronological order reduces the possibility of confusion.

In the following paragraph, instructions for diffusing a bomb are given.

Example of Poor Time Order

First, unscrew the nose cone. Second, remove the plastic housing covering the clock mechanism. Third, identify the black button with the red wire attached and the red button with the black wire attached. Fourth, press the black button. Fifth, before pressing the black button, make certain you first cut the black wire attached to the red button.

Ouch! You never got to instruction number 5! Instructions 4 and 5 should have been reversed. Using proper time order can be *extremely* important.

PRACTICE 2   Time Order

B U I L D I N G

To explain how to use an ATM for a cash withdrawal, arrange the following list in the proper sequence by numbering each item from 1 to 9.

_____ Remove cash

_____ Select Amount of Withdrawal

_____ Enter PIN Number

_____ Remove Card

_____ Select "Debit" or "Credit"

_____ Remove Receipt

_____ Insert Card

_____ Do You Want Another Transaction: Press "Yes" or "No"

_____ Select "Deposit" or "Withdrawal"

PRACTICE 3   Writing a Paragraph in Time Order

Using the steps in Practice 2 that you have placed in chronological order, write a paragraph using transitional expressions to connect the steps in the process.

Space Order

If you describe a person, place, or thing from inside to outside, from back to front, from top to bottom, from right to left, and so on, you are using **space order**. Describing details about a subject using space order is very much like the experience of an audience watching a movie as the camera explores various people or places. The following paragraph is written with space order. It describes a house from outside to inside.

> **Example of Space Order**
>
> Whenever I think of the house I grew up in, I always envision myself coming home after school. The wooden gate in the front yard always squeaked when I pushed it. As I walked toward the porch, I skipped over each crack in the sidewalk because stepping on a crack was always considered bad luck. The smell of freshly baked cookies beyond the expanse of green lawn guided me up the porch steps, across the freshly painted wooden boards, and through the screen door with six small holes caused by my misplaced bow and arrow practice. My mouth was already watering by the time I stepped into the hallway. As I dropped my books on the hall table, I could hear sounds of my mother cooking in the kitchen. After passing through the living room in the center of the house, I would watch cartoons for a half hour in the den at the rear of the house. This is how I passed many a weekday afternoon after school in the warm comfort of my house.

In this paragraph, the writer describes his house by moving through it from outside to inside, from front to back. The space order follows a path from the front gate to the back den. The space order transitional expressions "front," "beyond," "across," "center," and "rear" assist the reader in following the journey.

PRACTICE 4   Writing a Paragraph Using Space Order

Write a paragraph using space order. The paragraph can describe a person, a place, or a thing. Select a topic that interests you. Familiarity will help you select details and their arrangement. Use transitional expressions that enhance the details that you use.

Order of Importance

By beginning your writing with the most important point and finishing with the least important point, you are arranging your ideas by **order of importance**.

Example of Order of Importance

Many profound differences exist between upper management and middle management in terms of compensation. The most important difference is salary. While upper management salaries are generally six figures, middle managers usually do not break that barrier. The next factor is portfolio compensation. Most middle management must rely on company pension plans and IRAs for retirement, but upper management can increase retirement income with stock options, sick leave accrual buyouts, and postemployment "consulting" fees. Finally, middle management, after retirement, must find private health insurance, which is expensive and normally does not offer the same coverage as the plans they had with the company. In contrast, upper management is often given "paid for" policies for life, often including long-term and catastrophic coverage.

In this paragraph, the three ideas of importance are presented from most important to least important: salary, retirement compensation, and health insurance. The order of importance transitional expressions—"most important," "less likely," "next," and "finally"—help the reader connect ideas and move smoothly from one idea to the next.

You also can arrange ideas from least important to most important. The effect can be dramatic because the intensity builds to a climax.

PRACTICE 5 | **Rewriting a Paragraph Using Order of Importance**

Rewrite the paragraph about upper and middle management compensation by reversing the order of importance from least important to most important. You will have to replace or move some of the transitional expressions to fit the new arrangement. After you have finished, compare the two paragraphs. Which do you think is the more powerful or convincing order?

3

The Writing Process

Ask almost any writer what is the hardest part of the writing process and the typical response will be "Getting started!" You have probably had problems getting started with some of your own writing assignments. Coming up with a topic is usually easy enough, but deciding what to write and how to say it can be paralyzing.

Over the years, writers have developed numerous **prewriting** methods for getting started with a piece of writing. Some of the more popular prewriting methods include **listing**, **clustering**, **cubing**, **cross-examination**, and **brainstorming**.

In this chapter, you will be introduced to these strategies to help you choose your topic, develop your thesis, and expand your ideas. Your instructor can probably suggest several other prewriting techniques. You might find that using one method will work very well, or you might find it effective to use more than one strategy each time you write. The key is to experiment with as many prewriting methods as you need to get started writing.

In this chapter, you also will be introduced to three additional skills that will help you take the ideas you discovered in the prewriting processes through various stages of an essay's development to a finished product: **drafting**, **revising**, and **proofreading**.

By learning and practicing the techniques illustrated in this chapter, you can develop the skills that will allow you to approach any writing assignment with confidence. Nothing builds confidence like success, and nothing engenders success like confidence.

Prewriting

The prewriting techniques that follow will help you decide if there is enough to say about a particular topic to warrant writing about it. These techniques also will help you identify subtopics that will be developed in the body paragraphs of your essay.

Listing

Listing is exactly what it sounds like—making a list. Here is how it works. Take a blank piece of paper and write the topic at the top. If you are using a computer, write the topic at the beginning of the document. Next, as quickly as possible, write down any idea that pops into your head. Do not stop to think about how to develop each idea. This thinking technique is called *free association*. Let the words come quickly, and write them down as they come. Remember, do not revise, correct, or edit your thoughts—just let them flow. A list of ideas on the topic of writing might look like this:

Example

Writing

assignment	thesis	paragraphs	content
grammar	topic	punctuation	analysis
sentences	spelling	development	conclusion
subtopics	coordination	essay	research
facts	opinion	title	body paragraphs

Continue listing for at least ten minutes, because one idea often inspires another. The act of writing helps the thinking process for most writers. When you have finished listing, see which ideas are related, and rearrange the items into groups. Your new page might look something like this:

Example

Writing

Group 1	**Group 2**	**Group 3**
grammar	sentences	thesis
spelling	paragraphs	topic
punctuation	conclusion	subtopics
	body paragraphs	

After you have put the ideas into lists of related terms, try to find a logical order for them, perhaps by chronology (what you would do first, then second, third, etc.) or by priority or importance (most important to least important, or vice versa). This step can help you outline your topic.

PRACTICE 1　　Listing

List at least ten words that come to mind about each of the following topics.

1. Your favorite vacation spot.

_____

_____

_____

2. A sport or sporting event.

_____

_____

_____

3. Ending a relationship.

_____

_____

_____

4. A memorable person.

_____

_____

_____

5. A phobia or fear (snakes, heights, spiders, enclosed spaces).

_____

_____

_____

Clustering (Mapping)

A technique similar to listing but more visual is **clustering**, or **mapping**. Clustering can help you see relationships among possible ideas more clearly. First, draw a circle at the center of your paper and write the topic inside it. Then, think of related topics and write them in circles around it. Link these to the topic circle by connecting lines. Next, focus on the new circles, one by one. Think of topics related to these, and put them in another layer of circles. Note the diagram on page 24. The main topic is educational television.

After studying the individual clusters, select the group that best develops the topic. You can expand on your options by continuing to add to the groups you have chosen. For instance, you could add Polynesian and Tex-Mex circles to the Cooking cluster. You could add Northern and Southern to the Italian circle. Then, you could write a paper about Northern Italian cooking versus Southern Italian cooking. The possibilities are as endless as the number of circles you can add to the clusters.

PRACTICE 2	Clustering or Mapping

Place each of the following topics in the middle of a piece of paper. As related ideas come to you, make clusters with lines connecting them to one another if the ideas are also related.

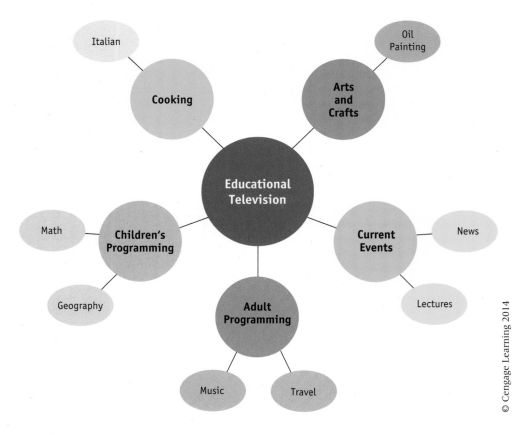

The Internet

Video games

Parenting

Cubing

Another method to generate new approaches to a topic is called **cubing**. To do this, imagine a cube with six sides with the following questions on each side:

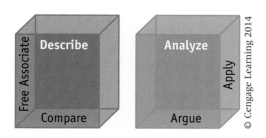

1. *Describe the topic:* What does the subject look like? What is the size, color, shape, texture, smell, and sound? Which details are unique?
2. *Compare or contrast the topic:* What is your subject like? How does it differ from other subjects? How is it similar? Give details.
3. *Free associate about the topic:* What does your subject remind you of? What further ideas can you think of?
4. *Analyze the topic:* What are the parts of the topic? How does each part function? How are the parts connected? What is the significance of the subject?

5. *Argue for or against the topic:* What are the arguments for and against your topic? What are its advantages and disadvantages?
6. *Apply the topic:* How can the topic be used?

Approach your topic from each of the six perspectives, freewriting your answers as with listing or clustering. Give yourself ten minutes to explore your ideas. Do not worry about topic development at this point; just get your ideas down. Finally, review your responses. See if any are appropriate to your assignment. Sometimes, doing this will generate ideas for your writing assignment.

PRACTICE 3	Cubing

I B W E A

B U I L D I N G

Choose one of the following topics. Answer the questions on each side of the cube to develop ideas for the topic.

Ways to relax	A favorite room
A theatrical play	A type of music
An exciting city	Advertising a new product

1. Describe

_____

_____

_____

_____

2. Compare or contrast

_____

_____

_____

_____

3. Free associate

_____

_____

_____

_____

4. Analyze

_____

_____

_____

_____

5. Argue for or against

_____

_____

_____

_____

6. Apply

_____

_____

_____

_____

Cross-Examination

You can use cross-examination on your own or with a partner. Depending on the type of essay assignment or the type of essay you would like to write, the questions can be grouped differently. You can interview yourself or your partner regarding the topic, using the following sets of questions:

Definition

How is the subject defined or explained by the dictionary or encyclopedia?

How do most people define the topic informally?

How do I define the subject?

What is the history, origin, or background of the topic?

What are some examples of the topic?

Relationship

What is the cause of the topic?

To what larger group or category does the subject belong?

What are the values or goals of the subject?

What are the effects of the subject?

Comparison and Contrast

What is the subject similar to?

What is the subject different from?

What is the subject better than?

What is the subject worse than?

What is the subject opposite to?

Testimony

What do people say about the topic?

What authorities exist on this topic?

Has anything been written on this topic?

What are the important statistics?

Is there any further research on the topic?

Have I had any personal experience with this topic?

Circumstance

Is this subject possible?

Is this subject impossible?

When has this subject happened before?

What might prevent it from happening?

Why might it happen again?

Who or what is associated with the topic?

Of course, not all of these questions will apply to every topic. Choose those that help you develop your topic most thoroughly and effectively.

PRACTICE 4   Cross-Examination

For one of the following topics, quickly write down answers for as many of the questions in each category as you can. Do not hesitate to write down answers for questions that come to you that are not listed in the categories provided here.

Mandatory handgun registration   Parental control lockouts for the Internet

A prison without guards   Commercial-free television

1. Definition

_____

_____

_____

_____

2. Relationship

_____

_____

_____

_____

3. Comparison and contrast

_____

_____

_____

_____

4. Testimony

_____

_____

_____

_____

5. Circumstance

_____

_____

_____

_____

Brainstorming

Brainstorming can be done in a variety of ways. First, it can be accomplished through discussion with others: friends, family, or students engaged in a similar process. By brainstorming, you can expand your ideas about a topic by listening to one or two different perspectives and taking notes. Second, brainstorming can be done in writing using the following techniques, such as listing or freewriting. Following is a sample of verbal brainstorming focusing on notes a student has taken when presenting the topic of violence in society to a partner.

> **Example**
>
> **_Topic: Violence in Today's Society_**
>
> | | |
> |---|---|
> | Is it caused by television? | Movies are violent also. |
> | Not everyone is affected by violence | Parent's role |
> | What about guns, murders? | Why so many in America? |
> | Is there more here than other places? | The cities more violent than the country? |
> | Gun control | Constitutional rights |
> | What can reduce crime? | What is the effect of war? |

Recent events	Columbine
Why do kids kill others?	Bullying?
What are we afraid of?	Racism

PRACTICE 5   Brainstorming

In a classroom setting, students should break into small groups of two or three. Each student should present the topic they wish to explore to the other members of the group, and for five or ten minutes, the students should discuss what they think about each topic while the original author takes notes and joins in the discussion. After the assigned time period, the next student presents a new topic for a brainstorming session.

Freewriting

Freewriting is a warm-up technique similar to **listing** (already discussed). However, in freewriting, the writer chooses a topic and writes freely for five or ten minutes about whatever comes to mind, without an assigned structure or format, in order to explore any possible ideas that could be associated with the topic. The writer continues to write even when there is writer's block, saying honestly, "I don't know what else to say on the topic," or words to that effect. Additionally, the writer does not worry about grammar, punctuation, or spelling. The following is an example of a student's five-minute freewrite on the topic of "the environment."

Example

I am not sure what to say on the topic of the environment. It seems to me that people have been discussing ideas about how to improve the situation with the environment for a long time but there is not too much being done about it. No one in this country wants to really pay for new forms of energy. We want to drive the cars we like and we want to use electricity. I don't think we have done very much with solar power or wind power even though I think there are some people who try these things. I hear that there is a lot of pollution in the water and in the air. The problem seems so big that it is hard for us to think about how to solve this. I wonder why the ideas are not made into laws. Why do some cities have buses or subways and others rely on cars? It is overwhelming to think of what should be done regarding the environment.

PRACTICE 6   Freewriting

To practice freewriting, take out several sheets of paper and choose one of the topics mentioned in the **listing** activity (pp. 22–23). Place the topic at the top of the first sheet of paper and write for five or ten minutes without stopping. If you have trouble thinking of what to write, write that down as well.

A Final Word about Prewriting

If you practice a variety of prewriting strategies, you are likely to find one or two with which you are most comfortable and that allow you to write with a sense of confidence. You will probably learn which strategies best apply to different topics. Getting started on a writing project can be the most difficult part of the assignment, but using prewriting strategies can make the entire process get off the ground with less frustration and more success. Never forget that the goal of prewriting is *discovery*, not completion. Progress through your writing assignment step by step, do not get ahead of yourself, and you will find the total experience much more enjoyable and worthwhile.

Drafting

When prewriting activities are completed, you are ready to begin writing your first **draft**. A *draft* is another word for *version*. In other words, you will write more than one version, or draft, of your ideas before handing in your work. You probably have heard the term *rough draft*. This is another name for an unfinished piece of writing—writing that must be revised and proofread before submission.

Focusing and Developing Ideas

In the clustering example on page 24, *educational television* is the overall topic being explored. If you write a paragraph about educational television, possible subtopics include *cooking, arts and crafts, current events, adult programming,* and *children's programming*. Let us say you have chosen *children's programming, adult programming,* and *current events* because all three have at least two items or subcategories within their grouping by which the topic can be developed. (Children's programming subdivides, for example, into "math" and " geography," and adult programming subdivides into "music" and "travel," and current events subdivides into "news" and "lectures.")

Writing the Paragraph's Topic Sentence

Now that you have chosen the topic and subtopics, you can write a topic sentence:

> *Educational television* [the main idea] *should be supported because children's programming, adult programming, and current events programming are valuable* [the focus the writer will use to explore the main idea].

Developing the Paragraph

The paragraph will be developed using the subcategories linked to the subtopics:

> *Children's programming—math* and *geography* to show how they support similar instruction children receive in school.
>
> *Adult programming—music* and *travel* to show how they can help make more enjoyable the lives of people who have a difficult time getting out because of physical limitations or illness.
>
> *Current events—news programming* and *lectures* to show how they help make the public better aware of happenings in the world.

Writing the Rough Draft Paragraph

To write the first draft of the paragraph, begin with the topic sentence, and follow it with the subtopic sentences.

Example 1: Rough Draft—The Basic Ideas

> Educational television should be supported because children's programming, adult programming, and current events programming are valuable. Children's programs help support instruction received at school. News programs and lectures by experts are essential. Adult shows make programming an enjoyable experience for a wider audience.

Of course, this is only the first draft. The next step on the road to the finished product is revising.

Revising the Rough Draft

Revising is not just another word for *rewriting*. **Revising** means to rewrite for both content and organization. As you reread and rewrite your assignment, you often will notice that one idea is not as good as another one that you have thought of. If so, you need to replace the initial idea with what you think will make the writing even better. The ideas in the paragraph should follow a plan—hopefully, the one stated in your topic sentence. Revising means to present your ideas in the best way possible to make them clear and interesting to the reader.

For example, in the first draft of the paragraph on educational television, there are several flaws.

1. The organization does not follow the order given in the topic sentence: children's programming, adult programming, and current events programming. The writer has switched "news programming" and "adult programming." In the next draft of the paragraph, the writer should switch them back to their original sequence as stated in the topic sentence. Following a stated plan helps the reader to remain focused and clear about the paragraph's purpose.
2. The paragraph is not well developed. The writer has not included information about the subcategories within each subtopic: "math and geography" in the *children's programming* subtopic, "music and travel" within the *adult programming* subtopic, and "news programming and lectures" within the *current events programming* subtopic.

Using the revising notes, we rewrote the first rough draft, this time reordering the information and developing the paragraph by including the subcategory information.

Example 2: Rough Draft Revision—Developing the Basic Ideas

> Educational television should be supported because children's programming, adult programming, and current events programming are valuable. Children's programs help support instruction

received at school. Programs about math can include counting, addition, subtraction, multiplication, and division. Geography programming might include state capitals and countries around the world. Adult shows, such as those involving big band music, can help the elderly think about happier, carefree days of their youth; travel programs can take shut-ins and sick people to places they might not otherwise be able to travel to. Current events programming, both news and lectures, helps make viewers aware of important things worldwide. Worldwide ideas also are given, so the viewer is made aware that every issue has many people for it and against it.

This second draft of the paragraph is better than the first draft because it is easier to follow (the paragraph's organization follows that in the topic sentence), and the topic is more fully developed (additional, specific information is given about the topic). However, many of the ideas could be expressed more clearly with better word choices and a bit of sentence polishing to make the presentation better.

You can use a thesaurus to locate more specific, descriptive nouns and verbs. Remember, one of your tasks as a writer is to choose language that makes your writing clearer and more interesting for the reader.

Example 3: Rough Draft Revision—Expanding the Content

Educational television should be supported because children's programming, adult programming, and current events programming are valuable. Children's programs help support instruction received in school. Programs about math can include counting, addition, subtraction, multiplication, and division. Geography programming might include state capitals and countries around the world. Adult shows, such as those involving ~~big band~~ "Big Band" music, can help the elderly ~~think about~~ remember [reminisce would even be a better choice] happier, ~~carefree days of their youth~~ times [not all your readers might have been young when they listened to Big Band music, and they may have been listening to it all through the years, not just when they were young]; travel programs can take transport shut-ins and ~~sick people~~ the infirmed to ~~places~~ exotic locales they may not ~~have been able to get to~~ otherwise have been able to visit ~~travel to~~. Current events programming, both news and lectures, helps make keep viewers aware of important things happenings worldwide. ~~Worldwide~~ [do not repeat the same word after having just used it] International ~~ideas~~ points of view also are ~~given~~ presented, so the viewer is made aware that every issue has many ~~people for it and many people against it~~ supporters and opponents.

With the corrections and additions completed, compare the second rough draft with the third. The third draft's content is much more detailed and complete than in the earlier drafts, which enables the reader to comprehend and develop a better understanding of the topic.

Now that the content is developed, we can add transitional expressions and create sentence variety. **Transitional expressions** accomplish three important things in good writing: They create rhythm within the writing, helping the communication flow from point to point in a smooth and enjoyable manner; they help to show relationships that exist between ideas, such as cause and effect and comparisons and contrasts; and they can help create sentence variety.

Sentence variety is important for communications to be clear and convincing. Simple sentences are fine for simple ideas, but complex ideas need to be presented in more sophisticated sentences. A paragraph consisting of nothing but simple sentences appears somewhat childlike in its presentation and rhythm, and it lacks the complexity to properly develop and show relationships between bits of information.

Example 4: Rough Draft—Adding Transitional Expressions and Creating Sentence Variety

In a depressed economy, educational television should be supported because children's programming, adult programming, and current events programming are valuable. Children's programs help support instruction received in school; **for example**, programs about math can include counting, addition, subtraction, multiplication, and division. Geography programming might include state capitals and countries around the world. Adult shows, such as those involving "Big Band" music, can help the elderly remember happier times; **additionally**, travel programs can transport shut-ins and the infirmed to exotic locales they may not otherwise have been able to visit. Current events programming, both news and lectures, helps keep viewers aware of important happenings worldwide. **For instance**, international points of view also are presented, so the viewer is made aware that every issue has many supporters and opponents.

Notice how much more effective the paragraph is because the transitional phrases move the reader from idea to idea quickly and smoothly. The four transitional expressions also help the reader understand the content. "In a depressed economy" helps the reader understand why educational television, which is largely publicly funded, needs more help. When the economy is bad, governments earmark less money for organizations such as public television, which they do not consider as critical as national defense and highway improvement. "For example," "additionally," and "For instance" cue the reader that they are about to receive additional examples that will help them understand the topic more clearly and with more depth.

Proofreading—Catching the "Little" Errors That Can Mean "Big" Trouble

The final step in the writing process is **proofreading**. After your paper is written, you should read it two or three times, looking for the following types of errors:

Note: The Writer's Resources section of this text in Chapters 18 through 30 covers the following topics with additional practice and exercises.

■ **Spelling**—Correct *misspelled words* (*liason* instead of *liaison*); *typos* (you hit the keys out of order, so *ball* looks like *blal*), and *sound-alike errors* (you meant to write *lean* meaning thin, but you wrote *lien* instead, a financial term). By the way, although most word-processing programs include a spellchecker, the program does not understand the context in which a word is used. The spellchecker, as its name implies, only checks to see if a word is spelled correctly. [Writer's Resources, "Commonly Misspelled Words" pages 375–376].

■ **Punctuation**—Check for *run-on or fused sentence errors* (two independent clauses without punctuation between them) and *comma splice errors* (two independent clauses separated only by a comma), in addition to other punctuation errors. [Writer's Resources, "Correcting Common Errors" (Fragments, Comma Splices, Run on Sentences); "Sentence Combining Practice" pages 355–358.]

■ **Sentence fragments**—Look for *incomplete sentences* with a subject or verb missing from the independent clause or sufficient meaning missing from the clause, as is the case when a dependent clause is mistakenly used as a complete sentence. [See preceding Writer's Resources reference.]

■ **Grammar**—Check for *grammatical errors* such as subjects and verbs that do not agree, pronouns with no antecedents, and other types of mistakes. [Writer's Resources, "Nouns and Pronouns" Pronoun–Antecedent Agreement pages 279–288; "Verbs and Verbals" (Subject–Verb Agreement pages 289–302).]

The "Final" Final Step

After you have proofread your paragraph or essay, print it in black ink on high-quality (20-pound white bond) paper. Make sure your name, class, and date appear on the printed paragraph or essay. Check to see if margins are consistent on each page. Make sure there are no ink smudges, wrinkles, or tears in the paper. The paper should look professional in every respect. After all, if it appears that you do not care for your work, why should the reader take it seriously?

From First Rough Draft to Finished Product

Look again at the first rough draft of the educational television paragraph, and compare it with the final version. By using just a few techniques in a few drafts, the paragraph has evolved from an underdeveloped, unfocused, amateurish effort into a coherent, developed, and polished piece of professional-quality writing. Here is the first rough draft.

> Educational television should be supported because children's programming, adult programming, and current events programming are valuable. Children's programs help support instruction received at school. News programs and lectures by experts are essential. Adult shows make programming an enjoyable experience for a wider audience.

Now look at the finished product.

> In a depressed economy, educational television should be supported because children's programming, adult programming, and current events programming are valuable. Children's programs help support instruction received in school; for example, programs about math can include counting, addition, subtraction, multiplication, and division. Geography programming might include state capitals and countries around the world. Adult shows, such as those involving "Big Band" music, can help the elderly remember happier times; additionally, travel programs can transport shut-ins and the infirm to exotic locales they may not otherwise have been able to visit. Current events programming, both news and lectures, helps keep viewers aware of important happenings worldwide. For instance, international points of view also are presented, so the viewer is made aware that every issue has many supporters and opponents.

Writing is a learned skill. By practicing a few techniques and employing them in a few drafts, you can improve your writing dramatically. Work the processes, and they will work for you.

© 2014 Wadsworth, Cengage Learning

PRACTICE 7   Drafting, Revising, and Proofreading a Paragraph

In the following exercise, use the techniques discussed in this chapter to develop a paragraph on a specific topic.

1. Choose a topic from the following list: The Power of Role Models; How Fear Affects Behavior; War as a Means of Solving International Disputes; Diplomacy as a Means of Solving International Disputes; The Value of a Positive Attitude; Stopping a Bad Habit; The Negative Effects of Eating Fast Food.

2. Apply one or more of the prewriting techniques to your topic to uncover subtopics; create a topic sentence; write a first draft; revise the first draft; develop the basic ideas; expand the content; add transitional expressions; proofread; and, finally, print your paragraph.

CHAPTER REVIEW

- Prewriting activities help you develop ideas for your writing. They include listing, clustering or mapping, cubing, cross-examination, freewriting, and brainstorming.
- Writing a rough draft of a paragraph or essay enables you to develop the content and organization of a piece based on your prewriting ideas. The rough draft may need several revisions.
- Revising a rough draft means evaluating its content and organization to ensure the ideas make sense and are presented in a way the reader will easily understand. Improvements to content and organization are made at this stage. Revising also includes improving the writing by using appropriate transitional expressions.
- Proofreading involves reading your paragraph or essay and correcting mistakes in spelling, punctuation, and grammar.
- The final step of your writing activity is to print the paragraph or essay, properly formatted, on good-quality paper. Use black ink.

Visit *The Write Start* Online!

For additional practice with the materials found in this chapter, visit our Student Companion Web site by going to cengagebrain.com and searching for this text. The Web site also features additional readings, quizzes, writing activities, and Internet links.

4

The Introductory Paragraph

In Chapter 3, you learned about the entire writing process. In this and the next two chapters, you will be introduced to the three major segments of the expository essay: the introductory paragraph in this chapter, the body paragraph in Chapter 5, and the concluding paragraph in Chapter 6. **To illustrate the parts of the essay, an essay about the city of San Francisco will be developed one segment at a time at the end of these three chapters.** The essay will go through the entire writing process, from prewriting activity, to rough draft revision, to proofreading, to final version.

The Five-Paragraph Essay: An Instructional Model

We realize that there are as many methods of writing essays as there are different assignments. In this book, for ease and clarity of instruction, we use the **five-paragraph model essay** to introduce writing students to the elements of the essay. That is why all the student essays shown in the text are five-paragraph essays.

Most likely, you will never be asked to write a five-paragraph essay in any class you will ever take, nor will you be asked to write a report or business letter or document of precisely five paragraphs. That also is why all the professional essays in this text vary in length. An essay's length is determined by the complexity of the assignment and the development necessary to explain, convince, and clarify the topic.

Each five-paragraph model essay in this text contains an **introductory paragraph**, **three body paragraphs**, and a **concluding paragraph**. The five-paragraph model is used because it is short enough to demonstrate and keep you, the developing writer, focused on the elements of good writing, and it is long enough to provide you with room to develop your ideas. Once you learn the elements of good writing using the five-paragraph model, you will be able to expand it to longer and more complex writing assignments.

The first part of an expository essay is the introductory paragraph, which introduces the reader to your essay's topic. It provides your first chance as a writer to engage your audience and set up the purpose of your essay. An introductory paragraph consists of a series of **introductory sentences** and a **thesis statement** (which can be announced in several sentences), or it can be called a **thesis sentence** if the main idea is announced in a single sentence.

The Thesis Statement with Three-Item Essay Map

The thesis statement is the most important element in any essay because it sets the tone for the entire essay. It also provides a roadmap for the entire essay. It states what you are going to clarify, explain, or argue for or against about the topic. Although there are no rules about where to place the thesis statement in the introductory paragraph, it usually will appear near the end, so it is the last idea the reader considers.

Because we are using the five-paragraph instructional model, we are confining our thesis statement to a single sentence called the **thesis sentence**. This will help you stay focused on the topic and the elements you need to clarify about the topic.

As we stated earlier, the five-paragraph essay has three body paragraphs. Therefore, the thesis sentence with a **three-item essay map** will be demonstrated. This type of sentence also is called the **forecasting thesis sentence** because it clarifies the items and organizational structure of the essay prior to the reader actually reading the essay. Each item in the essay map corresponds to the topic of each body paragraph. This is a highly organized structure; you can think of it as a *mini-outline* of your entire essay. The thesis sentence with three-item essay map will help both you and your audience stay focused on the topic and where it is headed.

The Attitude in the Thesis Sentence

A thesis sentence is the author's opinion about a particular subject. Opinion is not fact; it is a possible position that not everyone agrees with. An opinion opens the subject up for debate. Therefore, the thesis sentence must contain a word or phrase that clarifies the writer's **attitude** regarding the subject. This expressed attitude prevents the thesis sentence from being stated as a fact. The thesis sentence, then, states how the writer feels about the subject; it is what makes the subject important or worth writing about. Readers do not have to agree with the writer's position, but they do have to understand clearly what the writer's position is and how the writer feels about the topic.

A **verb** can be the basis of expressing your attitude about the topic. For example, the verbs *are/are not, is/is not, should/should not,* and *can/cannot* begin to tell the reader how you feel about a topic. **Adjectives** and **adverbs** also can express the attitude about the topic. *Important, better, more worthwhile, beautifully, adversely,* and *harshly* can suggest to the reader what the writer feels is important regarding the topic. Verbs, adjectives, and adverbs can work together to form the attitude in a thesis sentence.

For instance, you might believe that reading to young children every day will make them more informed on a variety of subjects, thus making them better students. The thesis sentence might read: *Parents should read to young children every day to make their children better students.* The verb *should read* begins to express your attitude about the topic. The adjective *better* also helps establish the writer's attitude about reading because doing so will make the children "better" students.

The Controlling Idea in the Thesis Sentence

Along with the topic and the attitude, the thesis sentence should clarify how the topic will be discussed. This is called the **controlling idea** because it clarifies how the topic will be developed in the body paragraphs. In the thesis sentence *Parents should read to young children every day to make their children better students,* "should read" and "better" are connected as the attitude toward the topic "parents reading to their children." The controlling idea is "make their children better students." Therefore, in the body paragraphs, the writer will discuss how parents reading to their young children should make the children better students.

As a writer, your attitude and controlling idea express not only why the subject is important to you, but also why it should be important to the reader.

> **Examples**
>
> In each of the following thesis sentences, the attitude and controlling idea are italicized, with the attitude circled.
>
> Lunch (is) an (important) *meal during the day.*
>
> Psycho (is) a (scary) *movie because of the shower scene.*
>
> Chevrolet (makes better) *trucks than Ford.*
>
> Tanning beds (do less) *damage to your skin than the sun.*
>
> Tanning beds (do as much) *damage to your skin as the sun.*
>
> Voting (should be important) *to all 18- to 20-year-old citizens.*
>
> Divorce (should not be) *the first thought when problems surface in a marriage.*

Providing readers with a thesis sentence containing a clearly defined attitude and controlling idea will help them understand your focus before they begin reading the body of the essay.

PRACTICE 1   Identifying the Topic and Controlling Idea

In each of the following sentences, underline the attitude word or phrase once and the controlling idea twice.

I D E N T I F Y I N G

> **Examples**
>
> The Rolls-Royce <u>is considered</u> <u>by many as the finest car in the world.</u>
>
> The Lemonaire <u>is not considered</u> <u>by anyone as the finest car in the world.</u>

1. Reading a newspaper each day is important because it keeps you informed about current events.

2. Regular tune-ups can keep a car running efficiently for years.

3. Working while going to school should teach young people responsibility.

4. Laptop computers can make the workplace anywhere a worker happens to be sitting.

5. The Beatles remain popular, even after their breakup decades ago, because of their versatile musical style.

The Essay Map in the Thesis Sentence

One easy way to make sure that your essay is well organized is to include an **essay map** in your thesis sentence. The essay map is a series that lists the subtopics supporting your thesis in the body paragraphs. Each of the essay map items will become the topic for one of the three body paragraphs. The thesis sentence with an essay map automatically organizes your essay and limits its scope. As we stated earlier, because this text uses the five-paragraph essay model, with three body paragraphs, the essay map in the thesis sentence will contain three subtopics. If there were four items mentioned in the essay map, there would be a corresponding four body paragraphs, and so forth.

In the following sentences, each element of the three-item essay map is identified by color. Notice that the essay map can be placed at the beginning, middle, or end of the thesis statement. There is no preferred placement. This is up to each writer and depends on how each one thinks the items are best presented.

Examples

1. To prevent fires in the home, people should *hide matches from children, never smoke in bed,* and *keep a fire extinguisher in the kitchen.*
2. *Practice, conditioning,* and a *proper diet* help athletes perform at a high level.
3. Communist countries worldwide, because of *insufficient international trade strategies, poor farming methods,* and *excessive military budgets,* were not very successful.

IDENTIFYING

PRACTICE 2   Identifying the Essay Map

Underline the three-item essay map in each of the following sentences.

1. Airlines, trucking companies, and railroads should be regulated by the federal government because they transport people and goods over state lines, they must ensure safe transportation, and the national economy depends on their remaining in business.

2. The aging process, talented newcomers, and constant travel make maintaining a sports career a difficult lifestyle.

3. Savings bonds, because of liquidity, safety, and interest, are a better investment vehicle than annuities.

4. A successful career often hinges on hard work, dedication, and intelligence.

5. New York is an exciting city to visit because of its many points of historical interest, excellent music and theater, and fine restaurants.

Parallelism in the Essay Map

For items in a list or series to work properly, they must be the same type of word, or they must be the same grammatical form. For instance, the items in the series all must be pronouns, or nouns, or single words, or the same type of phrase. This is known as **parallelism**.

Mixing different categories of words or phrases in the same list makes the sentence hard to read and understand. This is particularly damaging in a thesis sentence because it controls the entire essay; therefore, it must be very clear and well-organized.

> **Example**
> High-priced gasoline causes at-the-pump-anger, tax rates are high, and increasingly.

In this example, a prepositional phrase, an independent clause, and an adverb have been mixed inappropriately as the items in the list. See how confusing this sentence is. It also sounds choppy and rhythmically uneven. Additionally, the reader might be confused as to which item is increasing: the anger or the taxes. Parallel lists should be smooth, rhythmic, and clear.

> **Examples**
> Phil and Samantha enjoyed the concert because they heard a sonata, a concerto, and a symphony.
> (nouns)
> The frightened cat ran under the porch, over the flower bed, and around the garage.
> (prepositional phrases beginning with *under*, *over*, and *around*)

In each example, the items in the series are parallel because they are the same type of word or the same grammatical form. The sentences are easy to read, and the information in them is clear and easy to understand.

PRACTICE 3   Rewriting the Thesis Sentence Essay Map

In each of the following thesis sentences, rewrite the essay map so that each construction demonstrates parallelism. Answers will vary.

1. Exercise is important to Clarisse because of health, her complexion clears up, and work output.

_____

_____

_____

2. Energy costs, after taxes, and spiraling mortgage rates adversely affect most people's savings accounts.

_____

_____

_____

3. The morning greeting of birds chirping, deer, and a refreshing breeze made the campers feel the day would be wonderful.

_____

_____

_____

4. Politicians feel it is important to fundraise, visit with lobbyists, and put forward legislation that will benefit the voters back home.

_____

_____

_____

5. The ability to save information to a CD-ROM, software, and gray coloring are important components of any computer system.

_____

_____

_____

Important Points to Remember about the Thesis Sentence
The thesis sentence:
- announces the overall topic
- has only one topic and never more than one
- states the importance of the topic (the writer's attitude about the topic)
- limits the scope of the essay (the controlling idea)
- expresses the topic as an opinion that can be discussed
- can outline the organizational structure of the essay (the essay map)
- does *not* express the topic as a fact
- does *not* express the topic as a question

If the answer to any of these questions is "no," your thesis sentence does not match these guidelines, and you need to rewrite your thesis sentence.

Examples

Poor	Voting and military service are important activities for all citizens. (*two topics with a clear attitude and controlling idea, but no essay map*)
Better	Voting is an important responsibility for all citizens. (*one topic and clear attitude and controlling idea, but no essay map*)
Best	Voting is an important responsibility for all citizens because it gives people a voice in how the government is run, removes ineffective politicians from office, and influences political decision-making. (*one topic, clear attitude, clear controlling idea, and a three-item essay map that outlines the essay's structure*)
Poor	Many students work while going to school. (*statement of fact, no attitude, no essay map, no controlling idea*)
Better	Working while going to school can teach students valuable lessons. (*one topic, clear attitude, a controlling idea, but no essay map*)
Best	Working while going to school can teach students responsibility, organizational skills, and teamwork. (*one topic, clear attitude, good controlling idea, and a three-item essay map that outlines the essay's structure*)
Poor	Are regular automobile oil changes really necessary? (*the sentence is in the form of a question, not a clearly stated opinion*)
Better	Regular oil changes can keep a car running better. (*one topic, an attitude, a clearly stated controlling idea, but no essay map*)
Best	Regular oil changes can keep a car running more efficiently, improve gas mileage, and reduce long-term maintenance costs. (*one topic, clear attitude, good controlling idea, and a three-item essay map that outlines the essay's structure*)

PRACTICE 4   Identifying the Parts of a Thesis Sentence

In each of the following thesis sentences, underline the topic once, the attitude and controlling idea twice, and the essay map three times. On the line provided, indicate if any element is missing.

1. Fruits are a good source for vitamin C.

_____

2. Fast serves, pinpoint lobs, and slice volleys make tennis an exciting sport to watch.

_____

3. Many students make college a worthwhile experience by joining fraternities and sororities, playing intramural sports, and participating in student government.

_____

4. Lightweight sleeping bags are good for camping trips.

_____

5. Styling, construction, and value make the Breitling a popular wristwatch for collectors.

_____

6. Fuel cell cars should be an industry priority because of skyrocketing fuel costs, environmental pollution, and diminishing fuel reserves.

_____

7. Skydiving and bungee jumping are dangerous activities.

_____

8. The St. Louis Cardinals are a major league baseball team.

_____

9. *Star Trek* has been a long-running television series because of special effects, interesting characters, and fascinating stories.

_____

10. Cruises are a popular form of vacationing because of good food, entertainment, and stops in exotic places.

_____

PRACTICE 5   Rewriting Thesis Sentences

Rewrite the following thesis sentences if the essay map items do not clarify the organizational structure of the essay. If the essay map does clarify the organizational structure of the essay, write "Correct" in the space provided.

BUILDING

> **Example**
>
> The television program *Cops* is unfair to African and Mexican Americans because it shows their pets, kitchen appliances, and lawns.
>
> *Problem*: The three essay map items do not support why the program is "unfair" to minorities. *Cops* is a show about crime. What do "pets," "kitchen appliances," and "lawns" have to do with crime and "unfair" treatment?
>
> *Revision*: <u>The television program *Cops* is unfair to African and Mexican Americans</u> because it focuses on them as criminals, creates racial stereotypes, and distorts elements of their cultures.

In the revised sentence, the essay map items do clarify why the program is unfair to African American and Mexican American groups by organizing the structure of the essay's subtopics. Remember, readers do not have to agree with your position; however, they do have to understand where you stand on the issue.

1. A new car is superior to a used car because of better viewing, colors, and the neighbors.

_____

_____

_____

2. Reducing air pollution, expanding the economy, and supporting education are good reasons to vote for a political candidate.

_____

_____

_____

3. A successful small business, built on spectacular vistas, aromatic candles, and U.S. Grade A ground beef, is easy to franchise.

_____

_____

_____

4. Hiring a housecleaning crew can help cure dizzy spells, make pets happier, and cause cars to get better gas mileage.

_____

_____

_____

5. A professional wrestling career can be easier to attain by studying classical music, ballet, and the opera.

_____

_____

_____

_____

PRACTICE 6   Writing Thesis Sentences

Write a thesis sentence for the following topics. Use the criteria for writing an effective thesis sentence that you have learned.

1. A popular book.

_____

_____

2. A controversial movie.

_____

_____

3. Privacy on the Internet.

_____

_____

4. What makes a relationship work.

_____

_____

5. College drinking.

_____

_____

PRACTICE 7   **Writing Thesis Sentences**

Write a thesis sentence for each of the paragraph examples on page 48. Do not forget to create an essay map that clarifies the organizational structure of the essay.

1. _____

_____

_____

_____

2. _____

_____

_____

_____

_____

3. _____

_____

_____

_____

Introductory Sentences

In the introductory paragraph, the thesis sentence is introduced by **introductory sentences**, also called **lead-in sentences**. The purpose of introductory sentences is to catch the reader's attention and clarify your **tone** (for example, humorous, serious, or satiric). Some effective techniques for introducing the thesis sentence include using a shocking statistic or statement, posing a series of questions, or stating a common problem or misconception.

Examples

Shocking statistic or statement

One out of every three families is directly affected by alcoholism. Of the 50,000 people killed in automobile accidents each year, two-thirds have a direct link to drinking and driving. The numbers are increasing each year. *Place thesis sentence here.*

Series of questions

When is the last time you enjoyed the process of buying a car? Are you tired of worrying about whether you are going to end up with a lemon? Do you resent smooth-talking sales people who are more interested in their commission than concerned with your satisfaction? *Place thesis sentence here.*

Common problem or misconception

Most people define welfare as money going to the poor living in the inner city. However, many corporations receive tax abatements when they move to a new city or town. Military dependents receive free medical and dental coverage and discounted food and merchandise at base stores. Many college students receive money for tuition and living expenses that they do not have to repay. *Place thesis sentence here.*

PRACTICE 8 — Writing Introductory Sentences

Write introductory sentences for each of the following thesis sentences. Try to create at least three sentences using one of the introductory sentence techniques you have learned.

1. _____

_____

_____

_____

_____

_____

_____

Visiting foreign lands can make travelers appreciate their own country, understand other people's points of view, and learn more about current international issues.

2. _____

_____

_____

_____

_____

_____

_____

Canning fruits and vegetables, keeping the thermostat set at 68° in the winter, and making clothes can reduce monthly bills by half.

3. _____

_____

_____

_____

_____

_____

_____

Senior citizens who continue learning, have a hobby, and exercise regularly can live longer and happier lives.

Writing an Essay from Start to Finish

San Francisco or Bust!

Students in one writing class have been given an assignment to write about a city that they have a great deal of knowledge about. One student, having lived in San Francisco for many years, decides to make that city the topic. For the remainder of this chapter, and in the two following chapters, you will see how the student developed the essay from beginning to end. You can find the finished essay at the end of Chapter 6.

Drafting an Introductory Paragraph for the San Francisco Essay

Prewriting Activities: Creating Ideas to Write About

To create some ideas concerning San Francisco, the writer has chosen the clustering technique:

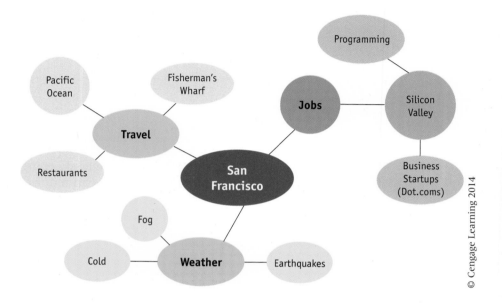

© Cengage Learning 2014

Possible topics to write about in regard to San Francisco are "Jobs," "Weather," "Expense," and "Travel." With "Jobs" as the organizational idea, the writer can perhaps explore "Silicon Valley," the center of computer-related jobs located nearby. If "Weather" is chosen, the writer can write about

David W. Hamilton/The Image Bank/Getty Images

© 2014 Wadsworth, Cengage Learning

the cold current in the ocean, the well-known San Francisco fog, and the potential for serious earthquakes. However, because San Francisco is such a beautiful city with a variety of activities and attractions, "Travel" is selected as the reason for writing the essay.

To create ideas concerning travel, the writer can construct another cluster or use a different prewriting technique to explore this concept. You will see the listing technique demonstrated in Chapter 5, "The Body Paragraphs."

Drafting the Introductory Sentences

From personal experience, the writer knows that many people vacation at the same places each year. A trip to San Francisco, however, would be a very different and exciting experience. The writer explores the problem of boring vacations in the introductory paragraph by asking the reader a series of questions:

Example

Are you tired of going to see the same trees and hills year after year? Have you been going to the same time-share for so long that you have names for all the squirrels and chipmunks? Tired of hiking from museum to museum, until you become lost in a faceless crowd moving from one room to another? Thinking of separate vacations just so you can be assured of "not seeing the same old thing"? Well, if you want a memorable vacation, one packed with new experiences and invigorating activities, run—don't walk—to San Francisco.

In the introductory sentences, the writer has posed the problem (one lead-in technique) by creating a series of questions (another lead-in technique). More than one lead-in technique can be used in the introductory sentences.

Drafting the Thesis Sentence

After posing the problem, *many vacations become boring because of familiarity*, the writer must state an opinion about how to solve the problem. This is the purpose of the thesis sentence. By looking at the clustering diagram, the writer chooses the subtopics for the body paragraphs: Fisherman's Wharf, the Pacific Ocean, and Restaurants. These items will be the elements in the essay map in the thesis sentence. Next, the writer must express an attitude and controlling idea about San Francisco that will be clarified organizationally by the essay map items. While considering the introductory sentences, the writer used the word *exciting*, and that seems like an appropriate attitude about visiting San Francisco. The controlling idea is *visiting the city*. Putting together the topic, attitude, controlling idea, and essay map, the writer creates the thesis sentence.

San Francisco is an exciting city to visit because of Fisherman's Wharf, the Pacific Ocean, and fine restaurants.

The introductory paragraph is now in rough draft form.

> Are you tired of going to see the same trees and hills year after year? Have you been going to the same time-share for so long that you have names for all the squirrels and chipmunks? Tired of hiking from museum to museum until you become lost in a faceless crowd moving from one room to another? Thinking of separate vacations just so you can be assured of "not seeing the same old thing"? Well, if you want a memorable vacation, one packed with new experiences and invigorating activities, run—don't walk—to San Francisco. San Francisco is an exciting city to visit because of Fisherman's Wharf, the Pacific Ocean, and fine restaurants.

This paragraph is in rough draft form. It still needs to be revised and proofread for errors in grammar, punctuation, spelling, word choice, organization, and content. This will be demonstrated at the end of Chapter 6 when the entire rough draft of the essay is revised and proofread. The introductory paragraph is good enough to leave, for now, so that the body paragraphs can be drafted in Chapter 5.

CHAPTER REVIEW

- The thesis sentence of an essay states the topic, the writer's controlling idea and attitude about the topic, and the essay map for the essay's structure.
- In the thesis sentence for a five-paragraph essay, the essay map has three subtopics. Each subtopic is developed by one of the body paragraphs.
- Introductory sentences usually precede the thesis sentence. They catch the reader's attention and clarify the tone of the essay. Techniques for introductory sentences include using a surprising statistic or statement, posing a series of questions, or stating a common problem or misconception.

 ## Visit *The Write Start* Online!

For additional practice with the materials found in this chapter, visit our Student Companion Web site by going to cengagebrain.com and searching for this text. The Web site also features additional readings, quizzes, writing activities, and Internet links.

5

The Body Paragraphs

The purpose of the **body paragraphs** of an essay is to develop, support, and explain the thesis sentence in the introductory paragraph. Each body paragraph's topic is based on one of the items in the essay map of the thesis sentence. Body paragraphs follow the general organizational model for a paragraph as presented in Part One: topic sentence and supporting sentences.

The Topic Sentence

The topic sentence of the body paragraph, like the thesis sentence of the essay, has three parts: the **topic** (also called the **subject**), the **attitude**, and the **controlling idea**. Because this text demonstrates the essay map in the thesis sentence, the subject of each topic sentence is taken from the items listed in the essay map. Sometimes, the subject or topic of a topic sentence also is called a **subtopic** when referring to the overall topic of the essay as stated in the thesis sentence. If this sounds a bit confusing, think of it this way.

Thesis Sentence Example

The controlling idea in the following thesis sentence is underlined for instructional purposes: *Mutual funds are beneficial because of <u>the need for college tuition, retirement income, and as a hedge against high taxation rates</u>*. In this sentence, the controlling idea and the essay map are merged. This often happens in thesis sentences with essay maps.

Overall Topic of Essay	Attitude	Controlling Idea/Essay Map
↓	↓	↓

Mutual funds are beneficial because of <u>the need for college tuition, retirement income, and as a hedge against high taxation rates</u>.

Subtopic 1: Tuition	Subtopic 2: Retirement	Subtopic 3: Taxes
↓	↓	↓
The topic of the topic sentence in Body Paragraph 1	The topic of the topic sentence in Body Paragraph 2	The topic of the topic sentence in Body Paragraph 3

In this thesis sentence, the controlling idea and the items in the essay map limit the scope of the information that can be used to develop, support, and explain the overall topic in the body paragraphs. New subjects or ideas cannot be introduced in the body paragraphs. They must follow the essay map items. For instance, in a paragraph about how novelists use description to create a violent atmosphere, the author cannot talk about other aspects of the novel, such as critical reviews, sales figures, or awards the novel may have won. The controlling idea and the essay map items force the writer to talk only about those descriptive features that develop the violent aspects of the novel. Otherwise, the reader can become confused as to the subject matter and focus of the essay.

Just as a thesis sentence without a controlling idea and essay map lacks focus and organizational structure, a body paragraph topic sentence without a clearly defined controlling idea lacks focus and specific direction. Without a controlling idea, the writer's thoughts or feelings about the subject may be unclear to the reader.

Examples

Poor topic sentences

Sammy Sosa is a baseball player.

(No controlling idea or attitude; this is simply a statement of fact)

Jogging is a popular form of exercise.

(No controlling idea)

Better topic sentences

Sammy Sosa's ability to hit home runs makes him an exciting baseball player.

(Controlling idea: *hit home runs*—Attitude: *exciting*)

Jogging is a popular form of exercise because it promotes cardiovascular fitness.

(Controlling idea: *cardiovascular fitness*—Attitude: *popular*)

Again, the controlling idea in a thesis sentence or a topic sentence does not have to be series of items (an essay map). However, because we are using the five-paragraph model with three body paragraphs, we are consistently demonstrating and referring to the three-item series (essay map) because it illustrates for the reader in advance the topics for the body paragraphs. Also, in a short thesis sentence, the controlling idea and the essay map often are expressed together. However, depending on the class you are in and the complexity of the assignment, the essay map is an optional tool to be used at your or your instructor's discretion.

PRACTICE 1   Improving Topic Sentences

The following sentences are inadequate as topic sentences because they lack a controlling idea and attitude. Turn them into topic sentences by adding a controlling idea and an attitude.

1. Commuters drive cars every day.

_____

_____

2. Marathoners wear running shoes.

_____

_____

3. Many young people attend rock concerts.

_____

_____

4. Jonathan attends pre-calculus classes.

_____

_____

5. The World Series is played during October.

_____

_____

6. Most businesses use computers.

_____

_____

7. Millions diet each day.

_____

_____

8. Voting in presidential elections takes place every four years.

_____

_____

9. A relationship exists between farming and the rainforest.

_____

_____

10. The police respond to emergency situations.

_____

_____

PRACTICE 2   Writing Topic Sentences

B U I L D I N G

Write topic sentences for the following subjects. Do not forget to add a controlling idea and an attitude.

1. Clothes

_____

_____

2. Hurricanes

_____

_____

3. Political races

_____

_____

4. Summer jobs

_____

_____

5. Exercising

_____

_____

6. Soap operas

_____

_____

7. Television reruns

_____

_____

8. Rollerblading

_____

_____

9. Music

_____

_____

10. Astrology

_____

_____

Support Sentences

Support sentences follow the topic sentence in a body paragraph and help develop, support, and explain the subject by using specific facts, details, and examples. The supporting ideas must be consistent with the controlling idea and the attitude. The controlling idea and attitude help determine the kind of support ideas you can use in the support sentences.

> **Example**
> Teachers are most effective when helping students learn _how_ to learn.

In this example, the topic is underlined once, and the controlling idea and attitude are underlined twice.

Support sentences for this topic would focus on _what_ teachers do to help students and might include teaching students the following activities:

- what information to take down as notes during a lecture
- what to identify as important information in reading assignments
- what techniques help make for effective studying

PRACTICE 3   Writing Topic Sentences for Support Sentences

Write a topic sentence with a controlling idea and an attitude for the support sentences in the following paragraphs.

1. _____

_____

First, the rafting trip down the river provided a thrill a minute as we hit the rapids. Next, the horseback ride along a winding trail took us through a dense forest filled with the sounds of many birds and other wildlife. After all the day's activities were complete, we sat around a roaring campfire and sang songs beneath a canopy of twinkling stars.

2. _____

_____

Monet's impressionistic paintings, with their muted colors and wispy, fog-like quality, seemed to be part of a dream. On the other hand, the shiny, brightly colored glass sculptures of Dale Chihuly appeared like fantastic clouds plunging from the sky, and the rigid, metallic armor suits of the knights seemed to stand guard over the earthly domain.

3. _____

_____

Uncle Morgan seemed about ten pounds heavier than the last time the family got together. Twins Marleena and Marlaana, first cousins from Mom's side of the genealogy chart, were wearing their hair in long curls instead of their usual Peter Pan cut. The twinkle in Aunt Bessy's eyes had been replaced with a sad, almost mournful gaze.

4. _____

_____

China's population is already over one billion, and India's population will be over one billion in the near future. The total population for the United States, which has many well-advertised family planning organizations, has increased by thirty million in only a few decades. The amount of world resources being consumed is increasing at a staggering speed.

Parallelism in Paragraphs

Parallelism is very important in your body paragraphs. Similar words and phrases throughout the paragraph create balanced rhythm and clearly expressed ideas just as it did for the thesis sentence that you studied in Chapter 4. Parallelism helps the reader make connections and emphasize points you are trying to make.

In the paragraphs that follow, the parallel constructions have been underlined.

Read All About It . . . To read the full essay from which this paragraph is excerpted, see page 395.

Example

I met Mary's mother once, years later. I worked as a real estate developer and wanted to buy some land in the area. More as an excuse than out of necessity, I called up to schedule a tour of her listings. She never placed me, and after an hour in her car, I began to accept that Mary was right. Her mother was not a racist—at least not in the sense that I had imagined in high school. She was comfortable with me. Nothing in her manner betrayed nervousness or artificial cordiality.

In the paragraph, the parallel constructions help to emphasize the process that the narrator is going through and that the narrator is reflecting on what happened to her.

Read All About It …

To read the full essay from which this paragraph is excerpted, see page 405.

Example

    I think a little learning is in order on both sides. <u>Korean immigrants, like other newcomers</u>, need orientation before they leave their country as well as when they <u>arrive in the United States</u>. It's also important for <u>Korean immigrants, like other Asians</u> who <u>live in the United States</u>, <u>to realize</u> that they are indebted to blacks for the social gains won by their civil rights struggle. They face less discrimination today because blacks have paved the way. Instead of looking down on their culture, it would be constructive <u>to learn</u> their history, literature, music, and values and see our African American brothers and sisters in their full humanity.

In the paragraph, the parallel constructions clarify who the focus of the paragraph is about (*Korean immigrants*), and they emphasize the comparison between Korean immigrants and other immigrants to the United States and what they need to understand.

PRACTICE 4   Rewriting for Parallelism

Rewrite the following paragraphs. Create parallel form by adding similar phrases and clauses in the sentences you revise. You can add new ideas if necessary.

1. Many people watch television programs starring celebrities such as Dr. Phil, Oprah, Montel Williams, and Maury Povich. Viewers often gain insight into their problems by seeing people with similar concerns to their own. This lends authenticity to any solutions that might come from the show. Those watching the stars of the shows sometimes miss the answers because they are too engrossed in the famous personalities.

_____

_____

_____

_____

_____

_____

_____

_____

2. More people in America voted for performers on *American Idol* than went to the polls during the last presidential election. Americans seem to think choosing an elected official is less important than selecting the future stars they want to watch on television. Viewers should change their attitudes when opting for the important things in their lives. Certainly, new actors and singers are important for our entertainment, but they should never overshadow who we want as the most important politician in the land.

_____

_____

_____

_____

_____

_____

_____

_____

_____

Drafting a Working Outline for a Body Paragraph

Before you begin writing your paragraph, you may want to sketch out the major ideas that will appear in your paragraph. This can help you discover whether or not you have a topic, a controlling idea, an attitude, and supporting ideas that work in unison for proper development. To create a working outline, you can write your topic, controlling idea, attitude, and support ideas in a ladder-like list. (For other prewriting techniques, see Chapter 3.)

Example

Topic:	Smoking
Attitude:	can cause
Controlling idea:	harmful effects
Supporting ideas:	lung cancer
	emphysema
	gum disease

The paragraph outlined in the example will discuss the harmful effects of smoking. This topic will be developed and supported by using lung cancer, emphysema, and gum disease as the negative outcomes that smoking can produce. The finished paragraph might look like this.

> **Example 5**
>
> Smoking can cause many harmful effects. It can lead to lung cancer, a potentially deadly condition for which cures are almost nonexistent. Emphysema, a chronic problem that worsens with time, is a disease wherein the air spaces in the lung increase, causing labored breathing and a susceptibility to infection. Additionally, smoking can cause excessive gum bleeding and gum cancer. Consult with a doctor for the best method to quit smoking.

Outlining helps you and your reader keep focused on the topic under discussion and the supporting ideas that explain, clarify, and support your ideas.

PRACTICE 5   Outlining a Paragraph

I B W E A
BUILDING

To practice creating working outlines, create a controlling idea and an attitude for each of the following topics. List three specific support details that develop the controlling idea and attitude. After you have finished, you will have a list of all the basic ideas that will go into a paragraph on the topic. This is called a *working outline* because the paragraph is still unfinished.

1. Topic: The Mission Impossible movies

Controlling idea: _____

Attitude: _____

Supporting ideas:

a. _____

b. _____

c. _____

2. Topic: Dating

Controlling idea: _____

Attitude: _____

Supporting ideas:

a. _____

b. _____

c. _____

3. Topic: School violence

Controlling idea: _____

Attitude: _____

Supporting ideas:

a. _____

b. _____

c. _____

4. Topic: Welfare

Controlling idea: _____

Attitude: _____

Supporting ideas:

a. _____

b. _____

c. _____

5. Topic: Recycling

Controlling idea: _____

Attitude: _____

Supporting ideas:

a. _____

b. _____

c. _____

PRACTICE 6   **Writing Paragraphs**

Write a paragraph for each of the working outlines you created in Practice 5.

Writing the Body Paragraphs for the San Francisco Essay

In Chapter 4, we illustrated, step by step, the creation of an *introductory paragraph* with a *thesis sentence* for an essay about reasons to visit San Francisco.

Justin Sullivan/Getty Images

Using the essay map items in the thesis sentence, this section will develop the body paragraphs using the techniques you have studied.

Prewriting Activities: Creating Ideas to Write About

In Chapter 4, we demonstrated the clustering prewriting activity to uncover that "travel" was the focus of our attention in regard to the topic and that the specific topics for our body paragraphs were Fisherman's Wharf, the Pacific Ocean, and restaurants. The *listing* or *free association* prewriting technique is demonstrated following to uncover the specific items that will develop the topic in each body paragraph.

Listing or Free Association

Fisherman's Wharf	Pacific Ocean	Restaurants
Museums	Golden Gate Bridge	North Beach
Jefferson Street	Marinas	Chinatown
Pier 45	Fog	Italian food
Fishing fleets	Ships	Mission District
Ghirardelli Square	Museums	Russian delis
Specialty shops	Alcatraz	South American food
Sourdough bread	*Balclutha*	Richmond District
Medieval dungeon		
Submarine		
Wax museum		

Now that a significant number of ideas have been uncovered, the task of grouping the ideas into appropriate categories needs to be done. After the groups have been classified, other ideas can be added if they come to mind.

Fisherman's Wharf	Pacific Ocean	Restaurants
Museums	*Golden Gate Bridge*	*North Beach*
Wax museum	Fog	Italian food
Ripley's Museum	*Marinas*	California food
Medieval dungeon	Boat rental	*Richmond District*
Pier 45	Alcatraz	Russian delis
Submarine	*Museums*	*Chinatown*
Jefferson Street	Maritime museum	Mandarin
Fishing fleets	*Ships*	Szechuan
Specialty shops	*Balclutha*	Hunan
Ghirardelli Square	*Eureka*	*Mission District*
Specialty shops		Central American food
Sourdough bread		South American Food

Drafting the Body Paragraphs' Topic Sentences

The body paragraph topics are the essay map items we have already uncovered using the clustering prewriting activity: Fisherman's Wharf, Pacific Ocean, and restaurants. An attitude should be included in each topic sentence to support the overall attitude expressed in the thesis sentence: "exciting." The controlling idea in the topic sentence is usually a word or phrase that can describe the elements that will clarify or explain the topic of the paragraph. These are the elements uncovered using the preceding listing or free association prewriting activity.

Body Paragraph 1

Topic: Fisherman's Wharf

Attitude: fascinating (supports "exciting")

Controlling idea: attractions

Topic sentence: Fisherman's Wharf offers the visitor a wide array of fascinating attractions.

Body Paragraph 2

Topic: Pacific Ocean

Attitude: unbelievable (supports "exciting")

Controlling idea: boating

Topic sentence: The Pacific Ocean, like an unbelievable expanse of blue glass, is a boater's paradise.

Body Paragraph 3

Topic: Restaurants

Attitude: delectable variety (supports "exciting")

Controlling idea: international cuisines

Topic sentence: The city's restaurants serve a delectable variety of international cuisines.

Checking the Outline

At this point in the drafting process, it is a good idea to check to make sure that your topic sentences actually support the thesis sentence.

> Thesis sentence: San Francisco is an exciting city to visit because of the fantastic Fisherman's Wharf, the incredible Pacific Ocean, and the extraordinary restaurants.
>
> Topic sentence 1: Fisherman's Wharf offers the visitor a wide array of fascinating attractions.
>
> Topic sentence 2: The Pacific Ocean, like an unbelievable expanse of blue glass, is a boater's paradise.
>
> Topic sentence 3: The city's restaurants serve a delectable variety of international cuisines.

As illustrated in the preceding outline, the essay's body paragraphs are organized according to elements of the essay map in the thesis sentence, and the "exciting" attitude regarding San Francisco will be supported in the body paragraphs as well. The next step is to write the body paragraph rough drafts using the items discovered in the listing or free association prewriting activity. If other items come to mind as the rough drafts are being written, feel free to include them.

Drafting the Body Paragraphs

Using the groups of items discovered in the prewriting activities, you can complete the rough draft of each body paragraph. Remember, if new ideas come to you during the rough-drafting process, feel free to use them.

Example of Body Paragraph 1

   Fisherman's Wharf offers the visitor a wide array of fascinating attractions. The fishing fleets docks along the Jefferson Street promenade. An early morning stroll along "Fish Alley" **[new idea]** will allow you to see fishermen at work. Jefferson Street has a host of specialty shops and entertainment for the entire family. The Wharf has its share of museums, but they are a bit out of the ordinary. There's a wax museum, the Ripley's *Believe It or Not!* Museum, and a museum in the guise of a medieval dungeon. If you're not to claustrophobic, you can visit Pier 45 and tour the USS *Pampanito*, a retired WWII submarine. Also, you might want to visit Ghirardelli Square and pick a souvenir or two from the many specialty shops located there. Finally, before you leave the Wharf, make certain you take with you a loaf or too of San Francisco's famous sourdough bread. You'll probably want to visit Fisherman's Wharf several times before your vacation is over.

Example of Body Paragraph 2

The Pacific Ocean, like an unbelievable expanse of blue glass, is a boater's paradise. In San Francisco, boating enthusiasts can participate in activities in and out of the water. The San Francisco Maritime National Historical Park contains four national landmark ships, including the famous square-rigger *Balclutha* and the ferry boat *Eureka*, which houses a collection of classic cars **[new idea]**. The park's Maritime Museum houses a fascinating array of model ships, figureheads, paintings, photographs, and artifacts in an art deco building shaped to resemble a cruise ship **[new ideas]**. But, if it's the high seas you want, you can head for several marinas and rent a boat or take an excursion tour boat **[new idea]** out into the bay. Or, you can take a ferry to the infamous "Rock," Alcatraz Island. The former maximum-security prison now offers guided tours, a self-guided hiking trail, and a slide show illustrating the penitentiary's notorious history. Or sail or motor out into the bay to view the enormous expanse of the Pacific Ocean and the incredible Golden Gate Bridge. Even when the fog is clouding and shrouding the enormous structure, the sight of fog rolling over the 1.2–mile-long bridge is both spectacular and haunting.

Example of Body Paragraph 3

The city's restaurants serve a delectable variety of international cuisines. The real difficulty is making a choice between so many delicious options. The Richmond district is well known for Russian delis. Chinatown offers traditional Mandarin, Szechuan, and Hunan food and an array of Asian restaurants, such Cambodian, Laotian, Burmese, and Indian **[new ideas]**. The North Beach area is famous for Italian and California cuisines, while Central and South American food is the specialty in the Mission District. To borrow from the Swedish—what a *smorgasbord*! If you like dining out, San Francisco is the place.

Note that the body paragraphs are not finished. They remain in a rough draft state, and they must be revised, proofread, and rewritten before the final draft is complete. This process will be illustrated at the end of Chapter 6. For now, however, the body paragraphs can be put aside, so the concluding paragraph can be drafted, as will be demonstrated in Chapter 6, "The Concluding Paragraph."

The Summary Paragraph

The outline and paragraph techniques described previously can also be used for a very important type of paragraph used in essay, research, and literary analysis: the summary paragraph. When students are reading long, complex documents, it is necessary to summarize the information to emphasize the most important ideas. The following steps, used also in outlining, should be followed. The focus is making a distinction between main ideas and those that are less important, and this skill is surprisingly difficult!

1. Read the chosen selection and underline the topic sentence of the paragraph. (Usually, these target paragraphs are not introductory paragraphs).
2. Underline the key subtopics that illustrate, define, or develop the topic of the paragraph.
3. Make an outline of these elements in your own words.
4. Giving credit to the author of the original source, create a topic sentence that restates the main idea of the paragraph,
5. In your own words, briefly state each subtopic and define it in a concise way, using one to two sentences for each subtopic and using transitional words to tie the sentences together.
6. You may end the paragraph, by emphasizing the main idea, or transition to the next paragraph.

This process will be illustrated by using body paragraph 2 from the model essay "San Francisco or Bust."

1. and **2.** (Read and underline *topic* and *subtopics*).
   The Pacific Ocean, like an unbelievable expanse of blue glass, is a boater's paradise. (**underline topic sentence**) In San Francisco, boating enthusiasts can participate in activities in and out of the water. The San Francisco Maritime National Historical Park contains four national landmark ships, including the famous square-rigger *Balclutha* and the ferry boat *Eureka*, which houses a collection of classic cars. (**subtopic 1**) The park's Maritime Museum houses a fascinating array of model ships, figureheads, paintings, photographs, and artifacts (**examples**) in an art deco building shaped to resemble a cruise ship. But, if it is the high seas you want, you can head for several marinas and rent a boat or take an excursion tour boat out into the bay. (**subtopic 2**) Or, you can take a ferry to the infamous Alcatraz Island. (**example**) The former maximum-security prison now offers guided tours, a self-guided hiking trail, and a slide show illustrating the penitentiary's notorious history. Or sail or motor out into the bay to view the enormous expanse of the Pacific Ocean (**example**) and the incredible Golden Gate Bridge. (**example**) Even when the fog is clouding and shrouding the enormous structure, the sight of fog rolling over the 1.2–mile-long bridge is both spectacular and haunting.
3. Make an outline of these elements in your own words, or if you use any quoted phrases, put them in quotation marks.
   Topic: The Pacific Ocean is "a boater's paradise"

   Supporting Ideas:
   a. The San Francisco Maritime National Historical Park displays four landmark ships, including the *Eureka* and the *Balclutha*.
   b. Tourists can also rent a boat, take a tour or ferry ride, and see the attractions of the San Francisco bay, such as Alcatraz Island, the Pacific Ocean, and the San Francisco Bay Bridge.
4. Create summary topic sentence.
   According to the author, the Pacific Ocean is "a boater's Paradise."
5. Add the subtopics and key examples, using transitions.
   According to the author, the Pacific Ocean is "a boater's Paradise." First (**transition**), the San Francisco Maritime National Historical Park displays four historical ships, including the *Eureka* and the *Balclutha*. Tourists

can also (**transition)** rent a boat, take a tour or ferry ride, and see the attractions of the San Francisco bay, such as Alcatraz Island, the Pacific Ocean, and the San Francisco Bay Bridge.

6. End the paragraph by emphasizing the main idea or creating a transition to the next paragraph. The goal is to create a summary that is approximately one-quarter the length of the original paragraph.

According to the author, the Pacific Ocean is "a boater's Paradise." First **(transition)**, the San Francisco Maritime National Historical Park displays four historical ships, including the *Eureka* and the *Balclutha*. Tourists can also **(transition)** rent a boat, take a tour or ferry ride, and see the attractions of the San Francisco bay, such as Alcatraz Island, the Pacific Ocean, and the San Francisco Bay Bridge. The San Francisco Bay is truly a "spectacular and haunting" experience for visitors who enjoy boating! (Conclusion emphasizing the topic).

The Summary process also can be expanded to condense multiparagraph works. In the summary essay, the topic sentence becomes a thesis at the end of an introductory paragraph that gives information about the background of the author or topic, each subtopic becomes a topic sentence and a concise paragraph, and the conclusion is added at the end. This process is a very important skill for all college writers!

Additional Writing Assignments

The following paragraph writing assignments will help you practice the techniques you have learned. Create a working outline before you write each paragraph.

1. Write about an event: a public event such as an Olympic competition, a religious ceremony, a birthday or graduation party, an operation, an athletic event, or a historical event. The topic sentence should name the event and exhibit an organizational idea and attitude to be developed in the support sentences.

2. Write about a person: a parent, sibling, relative, friend, teacher, coworker, or a historical figure. The topic sentence should identify the individual and clarify the organizational idea and attitude to be developed in the support sentences.

3. Write about a location: a room, house, school, workplace, or a historical location. The topic sentence should name the location, the organizational idea, and attitude to be developed in the support sentences.

4. Write about an important time: childhood, the teenage years, or a well-known time in history. In the topic sentence, clarify the timeframe, and include an organizational idea and attitude to be developed in the support sentences.

5. Write about why something happened: a recent event in the United States or in another country or the reason something happened in history. In the topic sentence, name the reason for the occurrence, and write an organizational idea and attitude to be developed in the support sentences.

6. Write about how something happens or is done: a significant accomplishment by an individual or group, something that occurred in nature, or how something happened historically. In your topic sentence, name the process, and write an organizational idea and attitude to be developed in the support sentences.

CHAPTER REVIEW

- The body paragraphs of an essay develop and support the essay's topic as set forth in the essay map of the thesis sentence.
- Each essay map item corresponds to a body paragraph topic.
- The topic sentence of a body paragraph states the topic, the controlling idea, and the attitude toward the topic of the paragraph.
- Support sentences follow the topic sentence and help develop the topic by using specific facts, details, and examples.
- A working outline that states the topic, organizational and controlling idea and attitude, and support ideas can help you organize your paragraph.

 Visit *The Write Start* Online!

For additional practice with the materials found in this chapter, visit our Student Companion Web site by going to cengagebrain.com and searching for this text. The Web site also features additional readings, quizzes, writing activities, and Internet links.

6

The Concluding Paragraph

Essays should not stop abruptly after the final body paragraph. Instead, you should leave your reader with a sense that your essay is complete. Use a **concluding paragraph** to bring a sense of completion to your essay and to reemphasize the central thesis. A concluding paragraph can simply be a summation of the points you have made, but it can also urge your readers to action, predict an outcome, or provide a warning based on the information in your essay. There are some things, however, that a concluding paragraph should *not* do.

- The concluding paragraph is not used to introduce new points; developing new points is the function of the body paragraphs.
- A concluding paragraph in a short essay should not simply restate your thesis sentence. Your reader is not likely to have forgotten the points you have developed in your body paragraphs. In a longer, more complex essay, restating the thesis in the concluding paragraph can be helpful because doing so reminds the reader of the major points that were used to support your ideas about the essay's topic.

There are several techniques you can use in the concluding paragraph to place emphasis on the points you have made throughout the essay. These techniques include the following:

- call to action
- warning
- prediction
- evaluation

© 2014 Wadsworth, Cengage Learning

Call to Action

In a concluding paragraph that uses a call to action, the reader is asked to take some action—to do something based on the essay's content.

Example of a Concluding Paragraph

New procedures are necessary to handle the burgeoning number of yearly visitors to national parks, but simply increasing entrance fees to generate more revenues is not an acceptable answer. <u>Write to senators and representatives and suggest that they need to hold hearings to determine what can be done to save these treasures.</u> If the destruction of national parks can be stemmed, future generations will be able to enjoy the natural beauty of America's great outdoors.

Call to Action ⟶

In this concluding paragraph, the reader is asked to contact a senator or representative. A prediction also is given: if destruction halts, future generations will be able to enjoy the parks.

Warning

In some concluding paragraphs, the reader is warned that negative events might occur.

Example

Buying insurance on the Internet is becoming a commonplace practice. The amount of money spent online for insurance is doubling every year. The main reason for the popularity of buying insurance on the Internet is convenience. However, consumers should be careful when purchasing insurance online. <u>Make certain the company has an A1 Superior rating by a reputable rating service.</u> There have been cases where consumers paid for policies that didn't exist because the companies that sold the policies weren't actual insurance companies.

Warning ⟶

In this concluding paragraph, the reader is given a warning about past fraudulent Internet companies. The paragraph also includes an evaluation: convenience is the reason more and more people shop for insurance on the Internet.

Prediction

A concluding paragraph may predict potential outcomes stemming from the discussion of the essay's topic. The writer looks into the future, so to speak.

Example

The new SUVs are becoming larger every year. They look like military Humvee rejects. Families love the extra room, great for all kinds of shopping around town and vacationing with the children (pets included). However, handling the bigger vehicles can become a problem. Also, because their bumper height causes more damage to smaller cars, insurance companies are charging

Prediction →
> their owners higher premiums. <u>With the increasing popularity of SUVs, insurance rates will rise for all vehicles over the next few years.</u> It is incumbent upon the manufacturers of SUVs to plan for ways to reduce the spiraling insurance costs associated with these vehicles.

In this concluding paragraph, the writer predicts higher insurance rates for all vehicles. The paragraph also includes a warning about how handling bigger vehicles is a problem and a call-to-action: manufacturers need to plan for ways to alter big vehicles to help reduce insurance costs.

Evaluation

The importance of the overall topic may be summarized and judged in a concluding paragraph.

> **Example**
>
> Many bacteria that cause diseases are becoming resistant to antibiotics used to treat them. The rainforest provides many of the plants from which these antibiotics are made. But with so much of the rainforest being destroyed each year, a different method of producing antibiotics is necessary. <u>New synthetic drugs can be effective in combating diseases currently resistant to natural drugs. Additionally, new synthetic derivatives can be created by studying both natural and existing synthetics.</u> With assistance from the government, pharmaceutical companies should find new synthetic drug research a lucrative endeavor.

Evaluation →
Evaluation →

In this paragraph, the writer evaluates the topic by focusing on the importance of synthetic drugs. The writer also includes a warning about the deforestation of the rainforests and, thus, the difficulty in discovering new, natural drugs; additionally, the author includes a call to action: the government should work with industry to discover new synthetic drugs.

Drafting the Concluding Paragraph for the San Francisco Essay

While visiting San Francisco is certainly an exciting activity, big cities present some problems that visitors need to be aware of. With this in mind, a *warning* and a *call to action* seem appropriate techniques to use in drafting the concluding paragraph for the San Francisco essay. A paragraph using these techniques might look like this.

> As enjoyable as your vacation in San Francisco is likely to be, remember a few things. It's a big city, and it comes with the usual cautions. When you're in crowded places, keep your wallet in your front pocket, and hold onto your purse tightly. There

are pickpockets in all large cities, and San Francisco is no different. Lock care doors, and don't leaving anything in plane sight. Discourage thieves from taking advantage of you. On a lighter but important topic, San Francisco, while blessed with a moderate climate, can get downright chilly at times. Remember, the city is quite far north, so always carry a windbreaker, and wearing shorts is only encouraged if you have listen carefully to the local weather before you go out. With just a bit of planning and precaution, your vacation to San Francisco, the "City by the Bay," will be an experience that you and your family will remember for years to come.

In this paragraph, the *warnings* are twofold: Beware of pickpockets and consider the possibility of chilly weather. The *calls to action* advise the vacationer to keep valuables in secure places, lock care doors, and listen to local weather reports. Notice that the advice is presented in a matter-of-fact manner so as not to scare potential visitors. The writer is not attempting to alarm readers, just inform them about reasonable precautions to take while traveling. With the rough draft of the concluding paragraph finished, the first revision draft of the entire essay can begin. Remember, this is a rough draft of the concluding paragraph, and it still needs to be revised and proofread prior to producing the final draft.

Revising the First Rough Draft of the San Francisco Essay

As written, the first rough draft of the entire essay looks like this.

Are you tired of going to see the same trees and hills year after year? Have you been going to the same time-share for so long that you have names for all the squirrels and chipmunks? Tired of hiking from museum to museum until you become lost in a faceless crowd moving from one room to another? Thinking of separate vacations just so you can be assured of "not seeing the same old thing"? Well, if you want a memorable vacation, one packed with new experiences and invigorating activities, run— don't walk—to San Francisco. San Francisco is an exciting city to visit because of the Fisherman's Wharf, the Pacific Ocean, and the fine restaurants.

Fisherman's Wharf offers the visitor a wide array of fascinating attractions. The fishing fleets docks along the Jefferson Street promenade. An early morning stroll along "Fish Alley" will allow you to see fishermen at work. Jefferson Street has a host of specialty shops and entertainment for the entire family. The Wharf has its share of museums, but they are a bit out of the ordinary. There's a wax museum, the Ripley's *Believe It or Not!* Museum, and a museum in the guise of a medieval dungeon. If you're not to claustrophobic, you can visit Pier 45 and tour the USS *Pampanito*, a retired WWII submarine. Also, you might want to visit Ghirardelli Square and pick a souvenir or two from the many specialty shops located there. Finally, before you leave the Wharf, make certain you take with you a loaf or too of San Francisco's famous sourdough bread. You'll probably want to visit Fisherman's Wharf several times before your vacation is over.

The Pacific Ocean, like an unbelievable expanse of blue glass, is a boater's paradise. In San Francisco, boating enthusiasts can participate in activities in and out of the water. The San Francisco Maritime National Historical Park contains four national landmark ships, including the famous square-rigger *Balclutha* and the ferryboat *Eureka*, which houses a collection of classic cars. The park's Maritime Museum house a fascinating array of model ships, figureheads, painting, photographs, and artifacts in an art deco building shaped to resemble a cruise ship. But, if it's the high seas you want, you can head for several marinas and rent a boat or take an excursion tour boat out into the bay. Or, you can take a ferry to the infamous "Rock," Alcatraz Island. The former maximum-security prison now offers guided tours, a self-guided hiking trail, and a slide show illustrating the penitentiary's notorious history. Or sail or motor out into the bay to view the enormous expanse of the Pacific Ocean and the incredible Golden Gate Bridge. Even when the fog is clouding and shrouding the enormous structure, the sight of fog rolling over the 1.2-mile-long bridge is both spectacular and haunting.

The city's restaurants serve a delectable variety of international cuisines. The real difficulty is making a choice between so many savory and delicious options. The Richmond District is well known for Russian delis. Chinatown offers traditional Mandarin, Szechuan, and Hunan fare and an array of Asian restaurants, such Cambodian, Laotian, Burmese, and Indian. The North Beach area is famous for Italian and California cuisines, while Central and South American food is the specially in the Mission District. To borrow from the Swedish—what a *smorgasbord!* If you like dining out, San Francisco is the place.

As enjoyable as your vacation in San Francisco is likely to be, remember a few things. It's a big city, and it comes with the usual cautions. When you're in crowded places, keep your wallet in your front pocket, and hold onto your purse tightly. There are pickpockets in all large cities, and San Francisco is no different. Lock care doors, and don't leaving anything in plane sight. Discourage thieves from taking ad advantage of you. On a lighter but important topic, San Francisco, while blessed with a moderate climate, can get downright chilly at times. Remember, the city is quite far north, so always carry a windbreaker, and wearing shorts is only encouraged if you have listen carefully to the local weather before you go out. With just a bit of planning and precaution, your vacation to San Francisco, the "City by the Bay," will be an experience that you and your family will remember for years to come.

In revising the first draft, eliminate poor noun and verb choices and unnecessary pronoun usage, and replace them with more specific nouns and verbs. Additionally, adding descriptive adjectives and adverbs helps to develop and clarify the content. Also, unless specifically assigned to do so, do not write in the first or second person; in other words, do not use "I," "me," "myself," "you," and "your." Substituting "person," "people," or "one" for these nouns and pronouns is not good writing, either. Use specific words to achieve developed, specific ideas that present clear content to your audience. As you focus on removing and replacing words, look for misspelled words and correct them.

A revision of the first draft might look like this.

~~Are you~~ Many vacationers are tired of ~~going~~ looking ~~to see~~ **at** the same trees and hills year after year. ~~Have you been going to~~ Visiting the same time-share each summer can become so commonplace that the visitors give all the squirrels and chipmunks pet names! Tired of hiking from museum to museum? ~~until you~~ Upset at becom**ing** lost in a faceless crowd ~~moving~~ **shuffling** from one **overcrowded, stuffy** room to another? Thinking of separate vacations ~~just so you can~~ to be assured of "not seeing the same old thing"? Well, ~~if you want~~ for a memorable vacation, one packed with new experiences and invigorating activities, run—don't walk—to San Francisco. San Francisco is an exciting city to visit because of the **fantastic** Fisherman's Wharf, the **incredible** Pacific Ocean, and the ~~fine~~ **extraordinary** restaurants.

Fisherman's Wharf offers the visitor a wide array of fascinating attractions. The fishing fleets docks along the Jefferson Street promenade. An early morning stroll along "Fish Alley" ~~will allow you to see~~ **uncovers** fishermen at work. Jefferson Street has a host of specialty shops and entertainment for the entire family. The Wharf has its share of museums, but they are a bit out of the ordinary. There's a wax museum, the Ripley's *Believe It or Not!* Museum, and a museum in the guise of a medieval dungeon. If ~~you're not to~~ claustrophobi**a** ~~you can~~ **is not a problem,** visit Pier 45 and tour the USS *Pampanito*, a retired WWII submarine. Also, ~~you might want to~~ visit Ghirardelli Square and pick a souvenir or two from the many specialty shops ~~located there~~. Finally, before you leav**ing** the Wharf, ~~make certain you take with you~~ **buy** a loaf or ~~too~~ **two** of San Francisco's famous sourdough bread. ~~You'll probably want to~~ **V**isit Fisherman's Wharf several times before ~~your~~ vacation **time** is ~~over~~ **runs out**.

The Pacific Ocean, like an unbelievable expanse of blue glass, is a boater's paradise. In San Francisco, boating enthusiasts can participate in activities in and out of the water. The San Francisco Maritime National Par**k** contains four national landmark ships, including the famous square-rigger *Balclutha* and the ferryboat *Eureka*, which houses a collection of classic cars. The park's Maritime Museum houses a fascinating arr**a**y of model ships, figurehead**s**, painting**s**, photograph**s**, and artifacts in an art deco building shaped to resemble a cruise ship. But, if ~~it's~~ the high seas ~~you want~~ **is a must-see**, ~~you can~~ head for several marinas ~~and~~ **to** rent a boat or ~~take~~ **board** an excursion tour boat **motoring** out into the bay. Or, ~~you can take~~ **ride** a ferry to the infamous "Rock," Alcatraz **I**sland. The former maximum-security prison now offers guided tours, a self-guided hiking trail, and a slide show illustrating the penitentiary's notorious history. ~~Or~~ **S**ail or motor out into the bay to view the enormous expanse of the Pacific Ocean and the incredible Golden Gate Bridge. Even when the fog is clouding and shrouding the enormous structure, the sight of fog rolling over the 1.2-mile-long bridge is both spectacular and haunting.

The city's restaurants serve a delectable variety of international cuisines. The real difficulty is ~~making a choice~~ **choosing** between so many savory and delicious options. The Richmond District is well known for Russian delis. Chinatown offers traditional Mandarin, Szechuan, and Hunan fare and an array of Asian restaurants, such **as** Cambodian, Laotian, Burmese, and Ind~~aii~~an. The North Beach area is famous for Italian and California cuisines, while Central and South American food is the special**ty** in the Mission District. To borrow from the Swedish—what a *smorgasbord!* ~~If you like dining out~~, San Francisco is "the place" for dining out!

As enjoyable as ~~your vacation in~~ **a** San Francisco **vacation** is likely to be, remember a few ~~things~~ **important points**. It's a big city, and it comes with the usual cautions. ~~When you're~~ **In** crowded places, keep ~~your~~ wallet**s secured** in ~~your~~ front pockets, and hold ~~onto your~~ purse**s** tightly. ~~There are~~ **P**ickpockets ~~in~~ **infest** all large cities, and San Francisco is no different. Lock care doors, and don't ~~leaveing anything~~ **packages or video equipment** in plaine sight. Discourage thieves ~~from taking advantage of you~~ **by being prepared in advance**. On a lighter but important topic, San Francisco, while blessed with a moderate climate, can ~~get~~ **become** downright chilly at times. Remember, the city is quite far north, so always carry a wi~~nddn~~breaker, and wearing shorts is only encouraged if ~~you have listen carefully~~ to the local weather **channel has predicted a warm forecast** ~~before you go out~~. With just a bit of planning and precaution, ~~your~~ **a** vacation to San Francisco, the "City by the Bay," will be an experience ~~that you and your~~ **any** family will remember for years to come.

In the first draft revision, the second person pronoun "you" has been removed, and bland verbs, such as *going, moving, make,* and *take* have been replaced. Descriptive adjectives, such as *fantastic, incredible, extraordinary, overcrowded, stuffy,* and *important* have been added. Misspelled words, such as *too* [two], *Indain* [Indian], and *Pard* [Park] have been corrected.

Revising the Second Rough Draft of the San Francisco Essay

In revising the second rough draft, correct punctuation errors. Additionally, create sentence variety by adding introductory phrases and clauses, and connect related ideas by using coordinating conjunctions, adverbial conjunctives, and transitional expressions. Finally, where applicable, help order information by using the "time," "space," and "ideas of importance" techniques you studied in Part One, "Getting Started: The Fundamentals."

The revised second rough draft might look like this.

Many vacationers are tired of looking at the same trees and hills year after year. Visiting the same time-share each summer can become so commonplace that the visitors give all the squirrels and chipmunks pet names! Tired of hiking from museum to museum? Upset at becoming lost in a faceless crowd**,** shuffling from one overcrowded, stuffy room to another? Thinking of separate vacations to be assured of "not seeing the same old thing"? **Well**, **for a memorable vacation**, one packed with new experiences and invigorating activities, run—don't walk—to San Francisco. San Francisco is an exciting city to visit because of the fantastic Fisherman's Wharf, the incredible Pacific Ocean, and the extraordinary restaurants.

Fisherman's Wharf offers the visitor a wide array of fascinating attractions. The fishing fleets dock along the Jefferson Street promenade. **First,** an early morning stroll along "Fish Alley" uncovers fishermen at work. Jefferson Street has a host of specialty shops and entertainment for the entire family. **Second,** the Wharf has its share of museums, **but** they are a bit out of the ordinary. There's a wax museum, the Ripley's *Believe It or Not!* Museum, and a museum in the guise of a medieval dungeon. **Third, if claustrophobia is not a problem**, visit Pier 45 and tour the USS *Pampanito*, a retired WWII submarine. **Also**, visit Ghirardelli Square, and pick a souvenir or two from the many specialty shops. **Finally**, **before leaving the Wharf**, buy a loaf or two of San Francisco's famous sourdough bread. Visit Fisherman's Wharf several times before vacation time runs out.

The Pacific Ocean, like an unbelievable expanse of blue glass, is a boater's paradise; **consequently, in San Francisco**, boating enthusiasts can participate in activities in and out of the water. The San Francisco Maritime National Historical Park contains four national landmark ships, including the famous square-rigger *Balclutha* and the ferryboat *Eureka*, which houses a collection of classic cars. The park's Maritime Museum houses a fascinating array of model ships, figureheads, paintings, photographs, and artifacts in an art deco building shaped to resemble a cruise ship. **But, if the high seas are a must-see**, head for several marinas to rent a boat or board an excursion tour boat motoring out into the bay, **or** ride a ferry to the infamous "Rock," Alcatraz Island. The former maximum-security prison now offers guided tours, a self-guided hiking trail, and a slide show illustrating the penitentiary's notorious history. **S**ail or motor out into the bay to view the enormous expanse of the Pacific Ocean and the incredible Golden Gate Bridge. **Even when the fog is clouding and shrouding the enormous structure**, the sight of fog rolling over the 1.2-mile-long bridge is both spectacular and haunting.

The city's restaurants serve a delectable variety of international cuisines. **Initially,** the real difficulty is choosing between so many savory and delicious options. The Richmond District is well-known for Russian delis. **Next,** Chinatown offers traditional Mandarin, Szechuan, and Hunan fare and an array of Asian restaurants, such as Cambodian, Laotian, Burmese, and Indian. **Then,** the North Beach area is famous for Italian and California cuisines, **while** Central and South American food is the specialty in the Mission District. **To borrow from the Swedish**—what a *smorgasbord!* San Francisco is "the place" for dining out!

As enjoyable as a San Francisco vacation is likely to be, remember a few important points. It's a big city, **and** it comes with the usual cautions. **In crowded places**, keep wallets secured in front pockets, **and** hold purses tightly. Pickpockets infest all large cities**, and** San Francisco is no different. Lock car doors**, and** don't leave packages or video equipment in plain sight. Discourage thieves by being prepared in advance. **However, on a lighter but important topic**, San Francisco, while blessed with a moderate climate, can become downright chilly at times. **Remember**, the city is quite far north**, so** always carry a windbreaker**, and** wearing shorts is only encouraged if the local weather channel has predicted a warm forecast. **Lastly, with just a bit of planning and precaution**, a vacation to San Francisco, the "City by the Bay," will be an experience any family will remember for years to come.

In the second rough draft, sentence variety and rhythm have been achieved through the use of introductory phrases and clauses, coordinating conjunctions, adverbial conjunctives, and transitional expressions. Punctuation errors have been corrected, and the ideas have been given a logical order through the addition of key words and phrases. Additionally, misspelled words have been corrected.

Now it is time to take one last look at the essay. The essay should flow rhythmically from sentence to sentence. The ideas should be organized logically and orderly. In other words, the essay should be professional in both content and presentation. The final draft would look like this:

Sample Essay: SAN FRANCISCO OR BUST!

1   Many vacationers are tired of looking at the same trees and hills year after year. Visiting the same time-share each summer can become so commonplace that the visitors give all the squirrels and chipmunks pet names. Tired of hiking from museum to museum? Upset at becoming lost in a faceless crowd, shuffling from one overcrowded, stuffy room to another? Thinking of separate vacations to be assured of "not seeing the same old thing"? Well, for a memorable vacation, one packed with new experiences and invigorating activities, run—don't walk—to San Francisco. San Francisco is an exciting city to visit because of the fantastic Fisherman's Wharf, the incredible Pacific Ocean, and the extraordinary restaurants.

2   Fisherman's Wharf offers the visitor a wide array of fascinating attractions. The fishing fleets dock along the Jefferson Street promenade. First, an early morning stroll along "Fish Alley" uncovers fishermen at work. Jefferson Street has a host of specialty shops and entertainment for the entire family. Second, the Wharf has its share of museums, but they are a bit out of the ordinary. There's a wax museum, the Ripley's *Believe It or Not!* Museum, and a museum in the guise of a medieval dungeon. Third, if claustrophobia is not a problem, visit Pier 45 and tour the USS *Pampanito*, a retired WWII submarine. Also, visit Ghirardelli Square, and pick a souvenir or two from the many specialty shops. Finally, before leaving the Wharf, buy a loaf or two of San Francisco's famous sourdough bread. Visit Fisherman's Wharf several times before vacation time runs out.

3   The Pacific Ocean, like an unbelievable expanse of blue glass, is a boater's paradise; consequently, in San Francisco, boating enthusiasts can participate in activities in and out of the water. The San Francisco Maritime National

Morton Beebe/CORBIS

Historical Park contains four national landmark ships, including the famous square-rigger *Balclutha* and the ferryboat *Eureka*, which houses a collection of classic cars. The park's Maritime Museum houses a fascinating array of model ships, figureheads, paintings, photographs, and artifacts in an art deco building shaped to resemble a cruise ship. But, if the high seas are a must-see, head for several marinas to rent a boat or board an excursion tour boat motoring out into the bay, or ride a ferry to the infamous "Rock," Alcatraz Island. The former maximum-security prison now offers guided tours, a self-guided hiking trail, and a slide show illustrating the penitentiary's notorious history. Sail or motor out into the bay to view the enormous expanse of the Pacific Ocean and the incredible Golden Gate Bridge. Even when the fog is clouding and shrouding the enormous structure, the sight of fog rolling over the 1.2-mile-long bridge is both spectacular and haunting.

4   The city's restaurants serve a delectable variety of international cuisines. Initially, the real difficulty is choosing between so many savory and delicious options. The Richmond District is well-known for Russian delis. Next, Chinatown offers traditional Mandarin, Szechuan, and Hunan fare and an array of Asian restaurants, such as Cambodian, Laotian, Burmese, and Indian. Then, the North Beach area is famous for Italian and California cuisines, while Central and South American food is the specialty in the Mission District. To borrow from the Swedish—what a *smorgasbord*! San Francisco is "the place" for dining out!

5   As enjoyable as a San Francisco vacation is likely to be, remember a few important points. It's a big city, and it comes with the usual cautions. In crowded places, keep wallets secured in front pockets, and hold purses tightly. Pickpockets infest all large cities, and San Francisco is no different. Lock car doors, and don't leave packages or video equipment in plain sight. Discourage thieves by being prepared in advance. However, on a lighter but important topic, San Francisco, while blessed with a moderate climate, can become downright chilly at times. Remember, the city is quite far north, so always carry a windbreaker, and wearing shorts is only encouraged if the local weather channel has predicted a warm forecast. Lastly, with just a bit of

planning and precaution, a vacation to San Francisco, the "City by the Bay," will be an experience any family will remember for years to come.

When you are satisfied that the essay is well organized and presents its ideas clearly, you can print it and hand it in. Then, and only then, can you consider your essay finished.

Essay Writing Technique Questions

1. What technique is used in the introductory sentences to introduce the thesis sentence?

   _____

2. Identify the thesis sentence, and write it on the following lines. Circle the subject. Underline each of the essay map items twice.

   _____

   _____

   _____

3. Identify the topic sentence in each of the three body paragraphs, and write the sentences on the following lines. Circle the subject of each topic sentence. Are the subjects the same as the essay map items that you underlined twice in Question 2?

   _____

   _____

   _____

   _____

4. Identify the techniques used in the concluding paragraph, and write your answer on the following lines. Then, answer this question: If you were thinking about traveling to San Francisco for a vacation, would the concluding paragraph affect your decision?

   _____

   _____

   _____

   _____

CHAPTER REVIEW

■ The concluding paragraph of an essay brings a sense of completion to the essay and reemphasizes its general thesis.
■ Techniques for writing a concluding paragraph include call to action, warning, prediction, and evaluation.

 Visit *The Write Start* Online!

For additional practice with the materials found in this chapter, visit our Student Companion Web site by going to cengagebrain.com and searching for this text. The Web site also features additional readings, quizzes, writing activities, and Internet links.

© 2014 Wadsworth, Cengage Learning

Moving Forward: Strategies for Developing Essays

Now that you have learned the steps in the writing process and how to write introductory, body, and concluding paragraphs, it is time to put these skills together and construct a longer unit of writing called an essay, theme, paper, or composition. Essays are an important part of the college learning process because the essay helps you in three important respects: (1) writing an essay helps you to learn, (2) writing an essay helps you to learn about a topic from a variety of viewpoints, and (3) your essay tells your instructor what you have learned.

The Modes of Development

The different viewpoints from which you can write about a topic are called **modes of development**. *Mode* simply means method or process. You can develop a topic in more than one way, thereby learning something different about it each time, depending upon the mode of development you use.

In Part Two of the text, you will be exploring, in order, the following modes of development:

Description: developing a topic through the use of vivid detail.

Narration: developing a topic through a recounting of events.

Example: developing a topic by using illustrations as clarification.

Classification: developing a topic by categorizing its characteristics.

Process: developing a topic by explaining how to do something or how something operates.

Comparison or contrast: developing a topic by focusing on similarities and differences.

Definition: developing a topic by explaining what it is and, at times, is not.

Cause or/and effect: developing a topic by focusing on why it occurs or the consequences or results of it occurring.

Persuasion: developing a topic by convincing the audience to agree with a particular point of view.

For instance, in an engineering course, your instructor might ask you to write an essay about a piece of machinery. The modes of development can guide you in making choices about your approach to the assignment. You can use *description* to tell about the physical dimensions and visual characteristics of the machine, or you can use *description* to give your reader an emotional sense of the machine: what it sounds like and feels like when you use it. You can use *process* to explain how the machine works. You can *compare* or *contrast* the machine to other machines with similar or different characteristics. A *cause and effect* essay might explore what effects the machine has had on product development, company profitability, or later developments in technology or commerce.

Of course, you can increase your essay's depth and vision by combining one or more of the modes of development. In fact, you will do this to some degree whether you plan to do it or not. That is, you cannot *describe*, *compare*, or show *cause and effect* about a person, place, or thing without *defining* it; likewise, it is difficult to *compare*, *contrast*, *define*, *describe*, or show *cause and effect* without using *examples*.

The modes of development are tools to assist you in writing your paper by helping you to choose your approach to the topic. As you learn to use these techniques, your writing will become more developed in content and more varied in style—both signs of a mature, intelligent thinker and communicator.

Beyond the College Essay

In the chapters that follow, student essays, as we have explained earlier, are used to model the five-paragraph essay. While this essay format is useful in teaching developing writers the elements of effective essay writing for an academic setting, other formats are used by more advanced student writers and professional writers.

Form Follows Function: The Form of Professional Essays

There's an old saying that "form follows function." This means that the format the writing takes is usually created to best suit the ideas the author is trying to get across to the reader. In other words, the form of your essay will fit the assignment you have been given. For instance, while paragraphs in college essays usually are at least four or five sentences long, paragraphs in professional essays sometimes consist of a single sentence. Perhaps the writer wishes to emphasize a particular idea or image by presenting it in a stand-alone sentence. This focuses the reader's attention on the idea or image without the distraction of other ideas and images in other sentences in a longer paragraph. So, as you read the professional essays in Chapters 7 through 15 and in the Additional Readings section, *be aware that their formats are designed specifically to present the author's ideas in the best manner.*

As You Become a Better Writer: Good Things to Come

As you become more proficient in your writing, you also will be able to build on the basic elements learned by writing in the five-paragraph format. You will be able to create essays of a varying number of paragraphs exhibiting a varied number of sentences that will best illustrate and express your ideas to fit the assignment you have been given. As your college writing assignments become longer and more complex, you will be able to build on the basic elements you have learned in this text. Soon, you will be writing with the same proficiency and style as other professional writers. Learning to write is like learning to ride a bicycle: once you learn how, you will never forget. So, a little hard work and dedication now will last you a lifetime and provide a lifetime of good writing experiences.

The Descriptive Essay

All essays develop a topic. One method to build on a topic is by describing it in detail. Effective **description** creates images in the reader's mind by using specific details. Like a painter using color on a canvas, the writer uses words (the color) to create pictures in the reader's mind (the canvas).

Instead of merely writing

> The bowl contained three scoops of ice cream.

a writer using effective description might write

> The glistening white bowl, decorated with bright blue spirals, overflowed with three gigantic mounds of vanilla, chocolate, and strawberry ice cream covered by a thick layer of whipped cream and garnished with a bright red cherry.

Bon Appetit/Alamy

Write a paragraph describing the party food in the above picture. Focus on the following characteristics as you write your description: types of food, tastes, colors, and shapes.

The specific details help develop the word-painting that describes persons, places, things, and emotions.

Identifying Your Purpose

The purpose of writing a descriptive essay is to clarify, explain, or create a particular mood about a person, place, or thing. Sometimes you want to be objective (factual) in your description. For instance, **objective description** can be useful in describing a medical procedure, a legal concept, or a new piece of technological hardware.

Most of the time, you will use **subjective description** to create a more emotionally charged impression. For instance, a subjective (or impressionistic) description may relate how a medical advance will affect the lives of patients and their families, how a legal concept can affect an entire population, or how a technological advance can change the economic outlook of an entire industry.

At times, you will want to convey a feeling of sadness. At other times, you might want to evoke a feeling of happiness, or frustration, or hope, or sarcasm. Effective description evokes emotion and adds clarity and depth to your writing.

Objective versus Subjective Description

Objective description relies on factual detail without much embellishment. You write down what you see, hear, taste, smell, or touch without any emotional response or interpretation.

> The old mansion sat in the middle of the unkempt property.

From this objective description, it is difficult to recognize what emotion or impression the writer wants the reader to understand.

In contrast, subjective description creates an easily identifiable emotion or impression.

> The hulking, old mansion, its windows covered with broken spider webs and darkened by a thick covering of dust, sat like a lurking beast hiding in a yard overgrown with weeds and creeping vines.

From this subjective description, it is clear that the writer wants the site of the mansion to evoke a mysterious or dreadful emotion. Objective description describes what the writer actually perceives. Subjective description conveys the writer's emotional response to what he or she encounters.

PRACTICE 1   Writing an Objective Description

On a separate piece of paper, write a paragraph about the room you are now sitting in. Describe the room objectively by simply writing down, in four or five sentences, what you see, hear, smell, or touch.

Dominant Impression

Your descriptive writing will be clearer and more enjoyable if you focus on just one **dominant impression** (sometimes identified as the **DI**). The dominant impression is the overall feeling or emotional response you want the reader to take away from the description. When you write a descriptive paragraph, each support sentence should build on the dominant impression you create in the topic sentence. Be careful to add only those details that support the dominant impression. Do not add details that suggest a different impression, as in the first example that follows.

Examples

Poor dominant impression
On a bright, sunny day, Meiling played joyously with her frisky, new puppy until it fell into a drainage ditch full of sewage.

Better dominant impression
On a bright, sunny day, Meiling romped joyously with her frisky, new puppy, and she could not contain herself from laughing out loud at the cute little dog's frolicking antics.

In the first example, the reader will not know what dominant impression the writer is attempting to convey. Is the writer trying to convey a positive impression (Meiling playing joyously with her puppy) or a negative impression (the puppy falling into a ditch full of sewage)? The second example is more convincing and focused on the writer's intentions. The descriptions of the dog, its actions, and Meiling's responses are consistent with the same happy mood. The positive dominant impression is clear, supported by such word choices as "bright," "sunny," "romped," "joyously," "frisky," "laughing," and "frolicking."

Use Effective Dominant Impression Words

The word you choose for your dominant impression should be as emotionally specific as possible, so the reader can understand what feeling you are trying to convey. Dominant impression choices, such as "good," "nice," "fine," and "great," are not emotionally specific. For instance, "good" can mean *tasty, well, honorable,* or *healthy;* "nice" can mean *pleasant, attractive,* or *friendly;* "fine" can mean *delicate, pure,* or *acceptable;* and "great" can mean *big, wide, heroic,* or *important.*

The following list illustrates dominant impression words that are emotionally specific.

aggressive	angry	bitter	boisterous	bumbling
cheerful	clumsy	cluttered	comfortable	cozy
crowded	dazzling	depressing	drab	dreadful
eerie	fierce	friendly	gaudy	generous
gigantic	inviting	peaceful	pessimistic	placid
restful	restless	romantic	rustic	shy
silent	snobbish	spacious	stuffy	sullen
tasteless	tense	ugly	uncomfortable	unfriendly

EDITING

PRACTICE 2   Rewriting an Objective Description as Subjective Description

In Practice 1, you wrote an objective description of a room. On a separate piece of paper, rewrite your paragraph subjectively. Focus on the dominant impression the room suggests to you, perhaps because of the room's color scheme, some object in the room, or the type of activity that happens in the room. You can choose one of the dominant impression words from the preceding list if you cannot think of one. After you have finished, compare the two paragraphs. Which one do you think paints a sharper, clearer image in the reader's mind?

Writing the Descriptive Paragraph

A descriptive paragraph has a topic sentence that conveys the dominant impression. It also can include emotionally specific details described by the use of sensory images and figurative language.

The Topic Sentence in a Subjective Description Paragraph

The topic sentence in a subjective description paragraph states the topic to be discussed and clearly states the dominant impression that will be developed in the supporting sentences that follow. Topic sentences without a dominant impression are usually statements of fact; in other words, they are too objective for a subjective description paragraph.

Examples

Topic sentences without a dominant impression:

The parade passed down the street.

Sareena wore a dress to the prom.

The hockey game was played Saturday night.

Yoshi had an interesting personality.

Topic sentences with a dominant impression:

The parade passing down the street was **dazzling**.

The dress Sareena wore to the prom was **tasteless**.

The hockey game played Saturday night was **exciting**.

Yoshi's personality was **bitter**.

Resource Note: A useful type of book to help you select better dominant impression words is a *thesaurus*. This type of reference book contains lists of synonyms, homonyms, and antonyms for almost any word you can think of. You can buy an inexpensive paperback thesaurus at any bookstore or from an online book source, and some computer programs have a thesaurus built in. You can also access a thesaurus on the Internet.

PRACTICE 3   Adding a Dominant Impression to Topic Sentences

Rewrite the following topic sentences by adding a dominant impression to each one.

1. William Jefferson Clinton was president of the United States.

_____

_____

2. Students use the Internet to find information.

_____

_____

3. Ecstasy is a drug used mostly by young people.

_____

_____

4. Security police help keep order on campuses.

_____

_____

5. Date rape is a new crime.

_____

_____

Supporting Details: Sensory Images

Once you have decided on the dominant impression you wish to create, you need to choose language and details to develop that impression. Writers can choose from a rich array of language to create and support description, including **sensory images**. These sensory images are based on the five senses with which we are all familiar: sight, touch, smell, sound, and taste. Because description creates images, it can tell the reader what a person, place, or thing

- looks like
- feels like
- smells like
- sounds like
- tastes like

By using sensory images, writers can draw a more fully developed picture of what they are describing. Good description actually causes readers to remember similar persons, places, or things from their own experiences. This personal interaction between the reader and the writing is a wonderful and powerful process.

> **Examples**
>
> *Sight*
> **Nondescriptive:** The sky was blue.
> **Descriptive:** The sky was a **deep, azure blue, dotted** by **fluffy, white clouds.**
>
> *Touch*
> **Nondescriptive:** The hospital bed sheets were uncomfortable.
> **Descriptive:** The hospital sheets were **stiff and scratchy**, like **sandpaper scraping** against my skin.
>
> *Smell*
> **Nondescriptive:** The cab of Miguel's truck smelled awful.
> **Descriptive:** The cab of Miguel's truck smelled like a **gym locker stuffed** with a year's worth of **dirty socks.**
>
> *Sound*
> **Nondescriptive:** The jetliner was loud as it took off.
> **Descriptive:** As it took off, the jetliner was so loud that it **made your teeth vibrate, as if a dozen motorcycles were passing by.**
>
> *Taste*
> **Nondescriptive:** The bagels tasted old.
> **Descriptive:** The bagels **tasted musty, like moldy cheese** I remember eating at my brother-in-law's house last New Year's Eve.

PRACTICE 4   **Adding Sensory Details to a Paragraph**

B U I L D I N G

Using the subjective paragraph you completed in Practice 2, add sensory description to some of the sentences. Try to use at least two different sensory techniques. After you are finished, compare this new paragraph with your previous version. Are the images more vivid in your mind?

Supporting Details: Comparisons Using Figurative Language

Another device that writers can use to describe something is **comparison**. Comparisons to well-known or everyday objects or images provide descriptions that readers can immediately recognize. Many writers find comparison the easiest descriptive tool because comparisons allow writers to provide clear ideas to the reader by tapping into images and emotions that the reader has already experienced.

    Figurative language is one tool writers use to make comparisons. Figurative language describes a person or thing in terms usually associated with something very different. The three most effective figurative language devices are **similes**, **metaphors**, and **personification**.

A *simile* is a comparison using either *like* or *as* to show a similarity between two dissimilar things. Notice how similar the words *simile* and *similarity* are.

> **Examples**
> The huge football lineman is **like** a mountain.
> The clouds covered the city **like** a thick, wool blanket.
> The workman is **as** strong **as** a bull.
> The gymnast is **as** agile **as** a monkey.

A *metaphor* is a stronger comparison between two things without using *like* or *as*. The implication is that one thing "is" the same as the other.

> **Examples**
> The huge football lineman **is** a mountain.
> The cloud cover **is** a thick blanket smothering the city.
> The workman **is** a bull.
> The gymnast **is** an agile monkey.

Personification gives human emotions or characteristics to animals, objects, or ideas.

> **Examples**
> The wind **howled** past my ears.
> Love **danced** in their eyes.
> The fox **cheated** the farmer by **stealing** eggs from the henhouse.
> The candle in the window **winked** at the passing cars.
> The sun **slept** as the moon **kept watch** over the campers.

PRACTICE 5   Using Figurative Language

Using the completed paragraph from Practice 4, add several figurative language techniques to several ideas. After you are finished, compare the paragraph with the previous ones. There is quite a difference. Your paragraph illustrates the creative power of effectively written description.

Moving from Paragraph to Essay

Now that you have studied and practiced the techniques to create effective subjective description paragraphs, it is time to expand your ideas to a larger writing unit: the **descriptive essay**. The descriptive essay is a union of the paragraph techniques you learned in Part One regarding developing the essay and the subjective description techniques you have just learned.

Creating the Introductory Paragraph

Description often can seem free-flowing and without purpose. But a descriptive essay is a piece of writing—and all good writing has a purpose and a clearly defined organization. The thesis sentence of the introductory paragraph should clearly indicate the purpose of the essay and how the essay will develop.

The thesis in a descriptive essay should blend naturally into the rest of the introductory paragraph. In the following example, notice how the thesis announces the topic (*storms*), the writer's controlling attitude—the dominant impression—toward the topic (*devastation*), and the essay map containing the body paragraph subtopics (*lightning, winds, and flooding*). The thesis statement is underlined for instructional purposes.

Example

The sky darkened like a ceiling scorched by fire. Raindrops as big as marbles began to pelt the ground, hurling bits of mud and grass into the air as the creek's banks began to overflow. The wind swirled and muscled trees into spaghetti-like shapes. Brilliant flashes of light split the air like a hot knife through butter. Lightning, raging winds, and flooding all added to the storm's devastation. Such was the storm's vengeance; all in its path was destroyed.

Notice how the specific detail and the figurative language all support the dominant impression of devastation. There are specific sensory details: *darkened, scorched, hurling, swirled, muscled, flashes, split, raging, vengeance, destroyed*. There are similes: *sky darkened like a ceiling scorched by fire; raindrops as big as marbles; flashes of light split the air like a hot knife through butter*. There is also personification: *the wind… muscled; such was the storm's vengeance*.

Creating the Body Paragraphs

For a paper describing *a storm's devastation*, the focus of the body paragraphs will be the paragraph topics listed in the thesis statement's essay map.

- The first body paragraph's topic will be about *lightning*.
- The second body paragraph's topic will be about *raging winds*.
- The third body paragraph's topic will be about *flooding*.
- Your focus should be that these elements *added to the storm's devastation*.
- Your focus should not be *how the National Weather Service tracks storms*, or *how local authorities marshal their forces to help victims*, or *how people take precautions when preparing for severe weather*.

Keep your focus on the controlling idea and attitude as stated in your thesis sentence.

Burton McNeely/Stone/Getty Images

Creating the Concluding Paragraph

The approach of the concluding paragraph should flow naturally from the essay's main topic. Because the essay's focus is on how various elements can make a storm devastating, *evaluating* each element that might be part of a devastating storm would seem an appropriate choice. You might describe how each different element (lightning, wind, and flooding) can affect people's lives and property. Whereas the body paragraphs were used to describe the effects of the elements, you can use the concluding paragraph to present the more personal effects of the storm on its victims.

Sample Student Essay: MR. ROGERS DON'T LIVE HERE

Blanche Wade

> The following essay, "Mr. Rogers Don't Live Here," by student writer Blanche Wade, is an emotionally intensive look at her inner-city neighborhood. The essay relies on sharply honed images that capture the sense of danger and broken dreams the neighborhood symbolizes. The numerous descriptive images paint a picture recognizable to anyone who has lived in or near a big city.

Vocabulary

Before you start reading, use a dictionary to look up the definitions of the following words that appear in the essay. (The paragraph number is shown in parentheses.)

fatalistic (3)	foreboding (4)	formidable (2)
imps (2)	neurotic (3)	shroud (1)
obscure (1)	paraphernalia (2)	wily (4)
spawn (3)	waning (1)	

Mr. Rogers Don't Live Here

1   On a night when the inky sky is wearing a shroud, and the moon eyes weary travelers, the wind is whistling through vacant spaces like a broken phonograph playing ghostly melodies. Sluggish souls tremble as supernatural organs play tunes of terror in the waning light. While thoughts swarm of "things that go bump in the night" and devilish demons dance, the green and yellow eyes of obscure creatures watch from the shadows. The neighborhood has become a dangerous jungle of broken bodies, vacant eyes, and wild creatures waiting to pounce on unsuspecting souls.

2   Broken buildings are like bodies that have been used and tossed aside. These hulking, crumbling structures fling concrete boulders from their rooftops; consequently, the fused stones, as if tossed by evil imps, become murderous missiles of destruction. The unsuspecting traveler, unaware of their formidable firing power, now wears a bandage on his head, a reminder of the neighborhood's ability to strike swiftly and painfully. Windows, framed but without glass, squint as they watch passersby stumble on rippled sidewalks. Snake-like cracks wait to ambush unsuspecting victims. The menacing walkways connect the vacant spaces of deserted lots and the streets that are as mean as lions chasing lambs. The neighborhood is littered with a variety of paraphernalia: the unfulfilled visions lost in bottles of drowned dreams and needles of forgotten promises, the obstacles to the art of survival.

3   Vacant eyes are connected to lost souls. Dealers of every type of drug are lurking in deepening shadows; buyers rushing in to purchase the ability to forget. Dreams are forever lost after these transactions, like Satan's spawn. Pushers are cackling witches during a late October's eve as they collect all debts due from hopeless junkies. The wasted eyes are only capable of searching for someone to rob. Fatalistic criminals are prepared to relieve hardworking citizens of their pay, and ladies of the evening are sometimes the forgotten players in this hellish nightmare. Young and not so young women, neurotic and high-strung, slither through the damp and filthy ruins seeking profits in exchange for pleasure but not enjoying the trade; these ladies, driven by desperation, work doggedly for their needs. The malignant obsession of their addictions compels them to continually abuse their temples. The patchwork existence within the neighborhood resembles a puzzle with missing pieces.

4   Meanwhile, once tame animals, mirroring the fate of their former masters, hasten to sanctuaries filled with unrecognizable rubble. Rats like cats, large and fearless, move swiftly through the outer limits of decay; wily and foreboding, they strike terror as they sprint past. Dogs, fierce and beyond approach, snarl at any movement, real or imagined; thin, starving, unwanted and on the prowl for mayhem and deadly dealing, they are killers in a dangerous nightmare come to life. Little tabbies have mutated into ferocious, menacing beasts. These clawing, scratching, and sneaky assassins wait silently and patiently for their next meal. Shrewd and able hunters, these night-stalkers patrol their concrete forest with survival skills matching that of any well-trained mercenary: stalk and kill!

5   Even closed eyes can see the possibilities of hopelessness. The lost community, the depressing statistics, and the war on drugs are all too real, not a horrible fantasy. Demons are within all of us; be aware that one neighborhood lost is one too many. Small children, if neglected, have the potential to become large and powerful monsters. There are no quick fixes to the many causes of despair. Only caring for our children and pets and tearing down houses so they cannot be used as hideouts for delinquents from responsibility can possibly slow the neighborhood decay.

Descriptive Technique Questions

1. Identify the thesis statement by listing the topic, the attitude, and the three-item essay map.

Topic:

_____

Attitude:

_____

Essay Map Items:

_____

_____

_____

2. The author uses personification to enhance the menacing tone of the essay. Point out instances of personification, and explain how they help create the essay's tone.

_____

_____

_____

3. Underline as many similes and metaphors as you can find. How do they help support the writer's attitude concerning the neighborhood?

_____

_____

_____

4. Point out as many sensory images as you can. How do they help develop the essay's tone?

_____

_____

_____

5. Sentence variety helps to create rhythm and to connect related ideas. Identify different types of coordinated and subordinated sentences.

_____

_____

_____

Critical Reading and Thinking Questions

ANALYZING

1. How does the title affect your understanding of the author's feeling about her neighborhood? Do you know what the reference to "Mr. Rogers" means? How did the title affect you before you read the story? Did it have more significance once you had finished the story?

_____

_____

_____

_____

2. What dominant impression do you think the author is trying to achieve?

_____

3. Beside people, the author uses buildings and animals to describe her neighborhood. How does her using these "nonhuman" elements help create the dominant impression?

_____

Descriptive Writing Exercises

WRITING

1. Write a descriptive paragraph about your neighborhood. First, what is the dominant impression you have about your neighborhood? Pick out one person, place, or thing, and use it as the focus of your paragraph. How does the person, place, or thing represent your feeling about your neighborhood? Use descriptive adjectives, sensory images, and figurative language to describe the element you have chosen. Even though you are writing about your neighborhood, do not use the first- or second-person point of view: in other words, no "I" or "you" writing. Both Blanche Wade and Mario Suarez (the author of the next essay) are writing about their neighborhoods, but neither uses the first- or second-person point of view to tell their story.

2. Now, write a descriptive essay about your neighborhood. Expand your vision by including descriptions of the two elements you did not use in Exercise 1 as other paragraph topics to support the dominant impression you want to convey. Create images using the descriptive techniques as you did in Exercise 1. Remember, do not use first- or second-person point of view.

Sample Professional Essay: EL HOYO

Mario Suarez

Although written in his first year of college at the University of Arizona, this essay by Mario Suarez is as professional as any you will ever read. It was published in the *Arizona Quarterly*. Suarez's audience was probably not very familiar with the Latino culture and some of the words he uses. Also, some of the words, such as *barrio*, probably had negative connotations for the reader. To create a more positive image of the Latino culture, Suarez builds one positive event upon another with unrelenting descriptive imagery until the dignity of the Chicano shines through the rubble and the squalor.

Vocabulary

Before you start to read, use a dictionary to look up the definitions for the following words appearing in the essay.

benevolent (2)	bicker (1)	conquistador (3)	famine (1)
imply (1)	inundated (1)	solace (2)	solicited (2)

See the Glossary at the end of the story for an explanation of words marked with an asterisk (*).

El Hoyo

1   From the center of downtown Tucson the ground slopes gently away to Main Street, drops a few feet, and then rolls to the banks of the Santa Cruz River. Here lies the section of the city known as El Hoyo. Why it is called El Hoyo is not very clear. In no sense is it a hole as its name would imply; it is simply the river's immediate valley. Its inhabitants are chicanos who raise hell on Saturday night and listen to Padre Estanislao on Sunday morning. While the term chicano is the short way of saying Mexican, it is not restricted to the paisanos who came from old Mexico with the territory or the last famine to work for the railroad, labor, sing, and go on relief. Chicano is the easy way of referring to everybody. Pablo Gutierrez married the Chinese grocer's daughter and now runs a meat department; his sons are chicanos. So are the sons of Killer Jones who threw a fight in Harlem and fled to El Hoyo to marry Cristina Mendez. And so are all of them. However, it is doubtful that all these spiritual sons of Mexico live in El Hoyo because they love each other—many fight and bicker constantly. It is doubtful they live in El Hoyo because of its scenic beauty—it is everything but beautiful. Its houses are simple affairs of unplastered adobe, wood, and abandoned car parts. Its narrow streets are mostly clearings which have, in time, acquired names. Except for some tall trees which nobody has ever cared to identify, nurse, or destroy, the main things known to grow in the general area are weeds, garbage piles, dark-eyed chavalos,* and dogs. And it is doubtful that the chicanos live in El Hoyo because it is safe—many times the Santa Cruz has risen and inundated the area.

2   In other respects living in El Hoyo has its advantages. If one is born with weakness for acquiring bills, El Hoyo is where the collectors are less likely to find you. If one has acquired the habit of listening to Octavio Perea's Mexican Hour in the wee hours of the morning with the radio on at full blast, El Hoyo

is where you are less likely to be reported to the authorities. Besides, Perea is very popular and sooner or later to everyone "Smoke in the Eyes" is dedicated between the pinto beans and white flour commercials. If one, for any reason whatever, comes on an extended period of hard times, where, if not in El Hoyo, are the neighbors more willing to offer solace? When Teofila Malacara's house burned to the ground with all her belongings and two children, a benevolent gentleman carried through the gesture that made tolerable her burden. He made a list of 500 names and solicited from each a dollar. At the end of a month he turned over to the tearful but grateful señora* $100 in cold cash and then accompanied her on a short vacation. When the new manager of a local store decided that no more chicanos were to work behind the counters, it was the chicanos of El Hoyo who, on taking their individually small but collectively great buying power elsewhere, drove the manager out and the girls returned to their jobs. When the Mexican Army was en route to Baja California and the chicanos found out that the enlisted men ate only at infrequent intervals, it was El Hoyo's chicanos who crusaded across town with pots of beans and trays of tortillas to meet the train. When someone gets married, celebrating is not restricted to the immediate friends of the couple. Everybody is invited. Anything calls for a celebration and a celebration calls for anything. On Memorial Day there are no less than half a dozen good fights at the Riverside Dance Hall. On Mexican Independence Day more than one flag is sworn allegiance to amid cheers for the queen.

3   And El Hoyo is something more. It is this something more which brought Felipe Suarez back from the wars after having killed a score of Vietnamese with his body resembling a patchwork quilt to marry Julia Armijo. It brought Joe Zepeda, a gunner, . . . back to compose boleros.* He has a metal plate for a skull. Perhaps El Hoyo is proof that those people exist, and perhaps exist best, who have as yet failed to observe the more popular modes of human conduct. Perhaps the humble appearance of El Hoyo justifies the indifferent shrug of those made aware of its existence. Perhaps El Hoyo's simplicity motivates an occasional chicano to move away from its narrow streets, babbling comrades, and shrieking children to deny the bloodwell from which he springs and to claim the blood of a conquistador while his hair is straight and his face beardless. Yet El Hoyo is not an outpost of a few families against the world. It fights for no causes except those which soothe its immediate angers. It laughs and cries with the same amount of passion in times of plenty and of want.

4   Perhaps El Hoyo, its inhabitants, and its essence can best be explained by telling a bit about a dish called capirotada. Its origin is uncertain. But, according to the time and the circumstance, it is made of old, new or hard bread. It is softened with water and then cooked with peanuts, raisins, onions, cheese, and panocha.* It is fired with sherry wine. Then it is served hot, cold, or just "on the weather" as they say in El Hoyo. The Sermenos like it one way, the Garcias another, and the Ortegas still another. While it might differ greatly from one home to another, nevertheless it is still capirotada. And so it is with El Hoyo's chicanos. While being divided from within and from without, like the capirotada, they remain chicanos.

Glossary of Terms

chavalo = young man; lad   bolero = a type of dance

señora = Mrs.; woman   panocha = corn

Descriptive Technique Questions

1. Suarez describes El Hoyo by examining many aspects of the community. Point out examples of where El Hoyo is located, who lives there, how the inhabitants live, and why.

   _____

   _____

   _____

   _____

   _____

   _____

   _____

2. In the last paragraph, Suarez describes chicanos by comparing them to something else. Describe the details of the comparison. In what other parts of the essay do you find details to support your answer?

   _____

   _____

   _____

   _____

   _____

3. Considering all the description about El Hoyo, what dominant impression do you think Suarez is trying to create in the reader's mind?

   _____

Critical Reading and Thinking Questions

1. What do you think Suarez's purpose is for writing the essay? Is his thesis implied, or can you find a sentence that states his thesis?

   _____

   _____

   _____

2. How do you think Suarez feels about El Hoyo? Is the image he creates positive or negative? Support your answer with specific details from the essay.

_____

_____

_____

3. How does Blanche Wade's description of her neighborhood differ from Suarez's? What does Wade focus on that Suarez does not, and vice versa? Does Suarez's essay feel more like a story? Does it appear more "realistic"? If so, why?

_____

_____

_____

Descriptive Writing Exercises

1. Create a thesis sentence with a three-item essay map for "El Hoyo." Use the dominant impression you chose for your answer in the preceding Question 3 as the attitude in the thesis statement.
2. One of the important elements in thinking critically is to have a *purpose* to your writing. Suarez's essay is not simply a description of a neighborhood with which he is familiar. For instance, he may be attempting to familiarize his readers with an environment with which they might not be familiar or about which they may have a misunderstanding. He might be describing the neighborhood with an eye toward convincing his readers that this environment is not one we need to fear but one that could use our financial help or some other kind of understanding.

   Write an essay describing a neighborhood or area with which you are familiar. This can be a place where you once lived or the one in which you currently reside. You will most likely want to include descriptions of the houses or apartment buildings, the businesses, the surrounding neighborhood and environs, and the people living there. After you have completed your prewriting techniques, create a thesis statement that expresses the underlying purpose for writing your descriptive essay.

More Topics for a Descriptive Essay

Here are some possible topics for descriptive writing assignments. Remember, descriptive writing has purpose, so do not forget to create a thesis sentence with an appropriate attitude. Use an essay map to organize the topics for your body paragraphs. Be certain that all specific information supports your topic sentences.

Songquan Deng/Shutterstock.com

1. A spectacular event, such as a fireworks display or a lightning storm, or a famous event in history (the attack on Pearl Harbor or the marriage of Britain's Prince Charles and Diana).
2. A messy desk.
3. A piece of art, such as a painting or sculpture.
4. A holiday event, such as Christmas or Thanksgiving.
5. A bustling office.
6. An ethnic restaurant.
7. A busy street or intersection (this can be a famous location, such as London's Piccadilly Circus or New York's Times Square).
8. A nature setting.
9. A famous building or monument.
10. An interesting or unusual person (this can be a famous historical person).
11. A description of what you have seen under a microscope in a biology class (for example, blood cells, amoebae or paramecia, a strand of hair, or an insect's wing).
12. A magazine or newspaper photograph of a dramatic event.
13. An interesting professor at your school.
14. A homeless person.
15. A run-down building or structure.

☑ Writing Checklist for a Descriptive Essay

❏   Choose a topic.

❏   Explore the topic using one or more of the prewriting techniques you studied in Chapter 3.

❏   Choose two to five (or whatever number the assignment calls for) of the characteristics you have uncovered during the prewriting phase as the topics for the body paragraphs (or as your essay map items).

❏   Create a dominant impression about the topic that can be supported by the body paragraph topics.

❏   Create the thesis sentence.

❏   Use descriptive adjectives, sensory images, and figurative language to develop your topic and the dominant impression.

❏   Write a first draft of the introductory, body, and concluding paragraphs.

❏   Revise the first draft.

❏   Proofread the final draft.

❏   Print or type the essay and submit it.

CHAPTER REVIEW

■ Description is a technique that creates images in the reader's mind by using specific details. Description can be objective or factual, or it can be subjective, evoking an emotion or mood. Good descriptive writing makes a dominant impression, creating a single mood or emotion.

■ The topic sentence of a subjective description paragraph states the dominant impression, and all the details support the dominant impression. Supporting details in descriptive writing include sensory images and figurative language—similes, metaphors, and personification.

■ In the introductory paragraph of a descriptive essay, the dominant impression is the controlling idea or attitude to the topic as a whole, and the body paragraphs focus on the items in the essay map. Evaluation is often used as the approach to the concluding paragraph.

 Visit *The Write Start* Online!

For additional practice with the materials found in this chapter, visit our Student Companion Web site by going to cengagebrain.com and searching for this text. The Web site also features additional readings, quizzes, writing activities, and Internet links, as well as a bulletin board and interactive chat.

Pages 97–98: Mario Suarez, "El Hoyo." Reprinted from *Arizona Quarterly*, 47.2 (1947), by permission of the Regents of the University of Arizona.

8

The Narrative Essay

To use **narration** is to tell a story, either to entertain or to inform. Narration can be made up, such as a short story or novel, or it can be nonfiction, the retelling of an incident that actually happened. When you listen to a news program, the anchor narrates the day's events to you, perhaps reporting how an airplane disaster was averted or explaining the background of the Supreme Court's latest legal decision. Also, if you read a novel, you are reading a narrative.

Identifying Your Purpose

In college, you will be asked to write narrative essays quite frequently. In English classes, your instructor might ask you to retell an incident from your life, such as the always fascinating "What I Did Last Summer" essay. In a science class, you might be asked to recount how a famous experiment led to an important discovery, such as Marie and Pierre Curie's discovery

Write a narrative paragraph about the people and the disaster in the preceding pictures. Focus on the events that may have preceded the current dilemma.

PHOTO 24/Brand X Pictures/Getty Images

David McNew/Getty Images

of radium. In a history course, you might be asked to write about a famous event, such as Germany's invasion of Poland in 1939 that started World War II. Whatever the writing assignment, the narrative, like all writing, must have a purpose.

Writing the Narrative Paragraph

In addition to recounting events, the narrative paragraph must indicate **why the events are important**. Techniques for writing an effective narrative paragraph can include using the six reporters' questions to focus the narrative and using transitional expressions to sequence the events being recounted.

The Topic Sentence and the Point of the Story

There must be a point to every narrative paragraph; otherwise, the reader will lose interest in it. Narrative writing, then, must have a clear point or purpose. This might seem obvious, but too many writers lose sight of it. The topic sentence of a narrative paragraph should announce the subject and clarify what is interesting about the subject. That interest is the **point of the story** as shown in Exhibit 8.1.

**Exhibit 8.1
The Point of
the Story**

Subject: abuse

Point of the story: abuse can change the victim's life

The Paragraph:

Topic Sentence ⟶ From the first moment I felt his large, cold hand strike my face, my life changed forever. For the first six months of our marriage, I truly believed he was my dream partner for a lifetime. I had done nothing wrong—I thought I was the perfect wife. I worked a 40-hour-a-week job, did the food shopping, house cleaning, cooking, and even made snacks for his weekly poker parties. He was tall, dark, blonde with blue eyes, and at first he seemed as perfect as a person could be but, at the end of six months, he was the devil in disguise. I have never been able wholly to trust another person since.

PRACTICE 1   **Writing Narrative Topic Sentences**

WRITING

Write a narrative topic sentence for each of the following subjects. Be certain that the sentence expresses the point of the story, the idea that will keep the reader's interest. You will have to make up the point of each story.

1. Visiting a new place

_____

_____

_____

2. An important event

_____

_____

_____

3. An important person

_____

_____

_____

Supporting Details: The Six Reporters' Questions

Once you have chosen the subject and the point of the story, you must decide how to develop the subject. What details, facts, and examples will develop the ideas and get the point of the story across? The simplest method to develop the subject and maintain focus is to use the six reporters' questions: who, what, where, when, why, and how.

For the topic sentence example in Exhibit 8.1, the developing focus could be any of the following.

Examples	
Who:	Who was affected by the abuse?
	As the topic sentence states, the writer was.
What:	What was the abuse?
	The abuse was physical, but the paragraph might also detail emotional abuse.
Where:	Where did the abuse take place?
	Although the inference is "in the home," abuse at other locations might be explored.

When:	When did the abuse take place?
	In this paragraph, the abuse took place early in the marriage.
Why:	Why did the abuse take place?
	The writer states that she did not do anything to cause the violence. Something in the husband's experience may have to be examined.
How:	How did the abuse happen?
	The abuse may have happened spontaneously, or a pattern of behavior may have preceded it.

From the list of examples, the answers to *who*, *where*, and *when* may be fairly obvious, or they may be the least important of the factors. Thus, they probably do not need to be developed. The most important factors to develop would be *what* (the emotional abuse might be even more damaging over the long run than the physical abuse), *why* (why did the abuse occur), and *how* (what were the patterns of behavior that led up to the abuse). Other ideas might come to your mind as you ask these questions, and you can pick and choose depending on your own experience.

Model Paragraphs

The three model paragraphs that follow were developed for the topic sentence in Exhibit 8.1 using the three focus questions *what*, *why*, and *how*.

Focus on What: developing the emotional effects stemming from the physical abuse.

Topic Sentence →

The daily physical beatings took their toll. Their effects were short-lived compared to the devastating emotional effects that remain with me till this day. I used to be a very trusting individual. I would lend my car or give money to almost anyone if they were in need. My first thoughts about people were that they were as kind and generous as I was. If I showed kindness to someone, I expected the same in return. Now I am suspicious of everyone. It doesn't matter how good or nice they are to me. In the back of my mind there is a fear of what monster might crouch hidden behind the friendly mask looking at me. People have become like the famous creature of literature—Dr. Jekyll and Mr. Hyde.

In this paragraph, the topic is developed by those details that support the "what" focus question: the narrator used to be trusting; she would lend her car or money; she thought people were as kind and generous as she was; but now she is suspicious; she sees everyone as having a hidden personality.

Focus on Why: developing the reasons for the abuse.

Topic Sentence →

> From the beginning, I couldn't figure out why he was abusing me. I had done everything possible to please him and to keep a good home. It wasn't until after the divorce that his sister confided in me. My husband had been physically abused when he was a child. It turns out that his father was an alcoholic who had trouble keeping a job. He took his troubles out on Dennis. I have since learned that almost all abusers were abused as children—a terrible cycle of pain for everyone involved.

In this paragraph, the topic is developed by those details that support the "why" focus question: at first, the narrator could not figure out why the abuse was occurring; later she learned that her husband had been abused by an alcoholic father and that abused children grow up to be adults who abuse.

Focus on How: developing the patterns of behavior that led to the abuse.

Topic Sentence →

> Thinking back about how each of the horrible attacks occurred, I have come to the conclusion that each encounter was preceded by my husband being angry about something else, not me. He struck me when we had been discussing what bills to pay immediately and what bills could wait. He was angry that we couldn't pay them all at once. An attack came immediately after he had returned home from work. His boss had chewed him out because he had shipped some materials to the wrong buyer. Each time something made him angry, he took his anger out on me. It could be something as big as his boss threatening to fire him or something as small as bird droppings on his car. It didn't matter. I became the object of his anger.

In this paragraph, the topic is developed by those details that support the "how" focus question: the attacks were preceded by the husband being angry at things other than his wife, such as not being able to pay all the bills, his boss getting angry at him, and bird droppings on his car.

The important thing to remember is that each paragraph develops the same general topic—abuse—yet the topic is developed using information that places emphasis on a different aspect of the abuse.

PRACTICE 2   Writing Narrative Paragraphs

Using the narrative topic sentences you created in Practice 1, write a narrative paragraph for each. Choose one of the six reporters' questions (who, what, where, when, why, and how) to develop the topic for each paragraph.

Using Transitional Expressions to Order Events

Narrative writing tells a story. Therefore, it is important to present the events of the story in proper order so that the reader can remain focused without being confused about the sequence of how things happened. To help keep track of the chronological order of events, you need to use **transitional expressions**. Transitional expressions connect related ideas appropriately, and they also add rhythm to your writing.

Transitional Expressions for Narration		
after	first, second, . . .	soon
afterward	last(ly)	then
as	later	thus
as soon as	meanwhile	upon
before	next	when

Transitional expressions are simply words and phrases that indicate when one event happens in relation to another. When transitional expressions are added to the *Focus on How* paragraph, they help keep the events in chronological order, add rhythm, and connect related ideas.

Example

Thinking back about how each of the horrible attacks occurred, I have come to the conclusion that each encounter was preceded by my husband being angry about something else, not me. The **first** time he struck me was **when** we had been discussing what bills to pay immediately and what bills could wait. He was angry that we couldn't pay them all at once. The **next** attack came immediately **after** he had returned home from work. **Upon** arriving at work, his boss had chewed him out because he had shipped some materials to the wrong buyer. **Afterward**, each time something made him angry, he took his anger out on me. It could be something as big as his boss threatening to fire him, or something as small as bird droppings on his car. It didn't matter. I became the object of his anger.

PRACTICE 3   Using Transitional Expressions

Add at least three transitional expressions to each of the paragraphs you wrote in Practice 2. Choose the expressions that help order the events chronologically and connect related ideas appropriately.

Moving from Paragraph to Essay

Now that you have studied and practiced the techniques to create effective narration, it is time to expand your ideas by writing a narrative essay. The narrative essay is a union of the techniques you learned in Part One regarding developing the essay paragraphs and the narration techniques you have just learned. Return to Part One if you need to review the instruction concerning writing the essay.

Creating the Introductory Paragraph

Even though narration is the retelling of an event, do not let the reader become lost in a myriad of details, facts, and examples. Be certain that the purpose of the story remains the focus of the story. Your story should have a thesis around which the events unfold.

The thesis in the narration essay should blend naturally into the rest of the introductory paragraph. In the following introductory paragraph for a narrative essay, the thesis identifies the topic (drinking and driving), the writer's attitude about the topic (negative consequences arise from this activity), and the essay map containing the subtopics that will be developed in the body paragraphs (risking your life, risking the lives of others, and the possibility of a lifelong injury). The thesis sentence in the example is underlined for instructional purposes.

Example

It started out as a night full of anticipation. My four best friends and I were driving to a high school graduation party. We knew there would be some drinking at the party, but we never suspected how it would impact our lives. Why would we? We were young and fearless—invincible! We had all of our lives ahead of us. At least that's what we thought as we began the evening looking forward to another rite of passage. But risking your life, risking the lives of others, and the possibility of a lifelong injury are negative consequences of drinking and driving.

Notice that while the story will be about the night of revelry by the group of graduating high school seniors, the point of the story (the story's purpose) will be the negative consequences of drinking and driving.

Creating the Body Paragraphs

For an essay on *drinking and driving*, the focus of the body paragraphs will be the paragraph topics listed in the thesis sentence's essay map.

- The first body paragraph's topic will be *risking your life*.
- The second body paragraph's topic will be *risking the lives of others*.
- The third body paragraph's topic will be *the possibility of a lifelong injury*.
- Your focus should be that these are the *negative consequences of drinking and driving*.
- Your focus should not be on *medical expenses or the need for tougher national drunk driving laws*.

Keep your focus on the point of the story: the negative *physical* possibilities stemming from driving drunk.

Creating the Concluding Paragraph

The approach of the concluding paragraph should flow naturally from the essay's main topic. Because this essay's focus is the negative consequences stemming from drinking and driving, a *warning* would seem an appropriate choice for the concluding paragraph. You might identify other negative consequences that might come from driving under the influence. Unlike the body paragraphs, the concluding paragraph is the proper place to mention medical expenses, the effects on family and friends should you be killed, or the potential legal problems that can occur if you are convicted of a related crime in a court of law. Other, more positive narrative essay topics might lend themselves to *prediction* rather than warning in the concluding paragraph. (Refer to Chapter 6 for other approaches for concluding paragraphs.)

Sample Narrative Student Essay: SHORT—YET NOT SWEET

Kate Smith

> Tennessee Williams, the great American playwright, wrote in his play *The Glass Menagerie* that time, not distance, is the shortest path between two points. In the following essay, "Short—Yet Not Sweet," student writer Kate Smith recounts the terrible amount of pain and suffering her mother's mental illness caused in a relatively short period of time. Notice the many specific word choices the author uses in order to develop the feelings she is describing in her story. They create an emotional immediacy to her story that is both compelling and intense.

Vocabulary

Before you start reading, use a dictionary to look up the definitions of the following words appearing in the essay.

bipolar disorder (1)	chaotic (3)	distraught (3)
endure (2)	inspired (5)	manic depression (2)
multitask (3)	pillaged (3)	ransacked (3)
vibrant (4)	vital (2)	

Short—Yet Not Sweet

1   My mother, Rita Ann, suffered from a mental illness called *manic-depressive bipolar disorder*. This illness had damaging effects on her life throughout the years. The differences in her from 1987 to 2001 showed the horrific conclusion to a life hardly lived. This disease took her life from her and took her away from her family. Manic depression adversely affected my mother's appearance, comprehension, and her family.

2   My mother had been a beautiful woman. She was fashion-model-thin with black, shiny hair that fell like a waterfall of smooth, shiny oil. She was tall and athletic. Perhaps this was due to her love of exercise. I can remember her waking every morning, jogging and stretching, rain or shine or snow, then taking a shower and putting on her makeup. Not that she had anywhere to go, but it was very important for her to look attractive. She didn't do anything out of the ordinary; in fact, she did what any ordinary housewife and mother would do each day. She appeared to be a vital woman. It wasn't until 1995 that manic depression made her endure several changes. She was

no longer full of life as she once proved herself to be. She stopped waking at a reasonably early hour each day. She stopped exercising and, when she did awaken, she did not comb her hair, nor did she even bother to dress which, at one time, had been a very important and popular activity for her. She no longer had a routine. Because exercise became a chore for her, she became unhealthy and overweight. My mother was no longer the vital woman we had known and loved.

3   Before this devastating illness pillaged her senses, she was very smart and could talk with anyone about anything. She read the newspaper from beginning to end each day, and she listened to "talk radio" shows while doing her daily routine. Yet, as the disease began to invade her mind, she never let it be known that she hated her world and wanted out. Someone looking in from the outside would have never thought twice about her inner chaotic life. She was careful not to let that show. My family and I were hopeful that throughout her battle she would continue to keep her head above water; however, as her ability to function each day grew weaker, so did her willingness. If anyone would try to talk to her, they would end up repeating themselves several times. When she finally did comprehend what was being said, she would merely shake her head. She spoke in jumbled sentences, mirroring her jumbled thoughts. We were distraught at the fact that her condition had taken her away and left us with a stranger. Furthermore, before the disease, her high level of energy allowed her to paint and draw for hours. Besides being many other things, such as a cook, a nurse, a teacher, a friend, a washer and ironer of clothes, she was a role model of efficiency and organization. Her ability to multitask is something I have yet to achieve as a mother myself. She could cook dinner on a regular basis, walk the dogs, and then go running. She was able to do for herself as well as for others before the depression ransacked her mind. As each month went by, her energy level became almost nonexistent.

4   By this point, our family was being greatly affected: cold dinner, if any at all; emotional stress that was never, ever talked about; and constant bickering between me <and> my siblings. Suddenly, she could not give us direction, to guide us, to say "How was your day?" At first, no one ever talked about my mother's depression. We simply carried on as normal as we could pretend. My dad was certainly not to blame—poor man. He worked two jobs to support us, days at Southwestern Bell and several nights at a college teaching computer classes. The bills were becoming rather intense, but as a family, we had to stick together. My mother had been a beautiful, vibrant woman who I had looked up to; as the disease progressed, and before I fully understood it, she became someone I thought to be selfish and embarrassing. Over the years, as I learned more about her disease, I could see that she was doing the best she could, even trying to make an effort to be something within the limitations of her possibilities. But, due to the years of mental and physical hardship her mind and body had endured, it was, ultimately, impossible for her to accomplish much.

5   The tragedy of her life was finally erased by the blessing of her passing. She had put up the best fight she could against a powerful, unrelenting enemy, and although I miss her, I feel good that she no longer has to suffer. I feel much sorrow and regret in my heart at the thought of never seeing her again. People who have not seen the effects of manic depression cannot imagine the result it has on the person who lives with it daily. My mother was dead to the world long before she died. Her illness had damaging consequences on her and the life of her family. However, it has inspired me to become a nurse, so that I may help others in her situation. And, in that way, she'll always be with me.

Narrative Technique Questions

ANALYZING

1. Identify the thesis statement. What is the author's attitude about the topic?

   _____

   _____

   _____

   _____

2. Identify the essay map subtopics in the thesis sentence. Do they appear in the topic sentence of each of the body paragraphs?

   _____

   _____

   _____

   _____

   _____

3. Sentence variety helps to create rhythm, connect related ideas, and show relationships between ideas. Identify different types of coordinated and subordinated sentences, and comment on how the sentences accomplish the functions described previously.

   _____

   _____

   _____

   _____

   _____

   _____

   _____

   _____

   _____

   _____

Critical Reading Thinking Questions

A N A L Y Z I N G

1. What do you think is the point of the story?

_____

_____

_____

_____

_____

2. How did the author's feelings about her mother change over the life of the illness?

_____

_____

_____

_____

_____

_____

Narrative Writing Exercises

W R I T I N G

1. Write a narrative paragraph about someone you know who has struggled with a disease. Point out how the disease affected the person.

2. Now, write an essay and expand on the topic you wrote about in Exercise 1. Include how the disease also affected the family and friends and even coworkers of the person.

Sample Professional Essay: TIME TO LOOK AND LISTEN

Magdoline Asfahani

> Magdoline Asfahani is of Lebanese and Syrian ethnicity. When she was a student at the University of Texas at El Paso, she wrote this essay with a dual purpose in mind: to honor her parents' cultural backgrounds and to reflect and honor her American heritage. As you read, think about how your ethnicity and American heritage influence your own values.

Vocabulary
Meaning comes primarily from words. Before you start reading, use a dictionary to look up the meanings of the following words that appear in the essay.

Chanukah (5)	diverted (3)	ethnicity (4)
incompatible (2)	Judaism (5)	Koran (8)
monotheistic (5)	nuances (8)	taunted (3)

Time to Look and Listen

1   I love my country as many who have been here for generations cannot. Perhaps that's because I'm the child of immigrants, raised with a conscious respect for America that many people take for granted. My parents chose this country because it offered them a new life, freedom and possibilities. But I learned at a young age that the country we loved so much did not feel the same way about us.

2   Discrimination is not unique to America. It occurs in any country that allows immigration. Anyone who is unlike the majority is looked at a little suspiciously, dealt with a little differently. I knew that I was an Arab and a Muslim. This meant nothing to me. At school I stood up to say the Pledge of Allegiance every day. These things did not seem incompatible at all. Then everything changed for me, suddenly and permanently, in 1985. I was only in seventh grade, but that was the beginning of my political education.

3   That year a TWA plane originating in Athens was diverted to Beirut. Two years earlier the U.S. Marine barracks in Beirut had been bombed. That seemed to start a chain of events that would forever link Arabs with terrorism. After the hijacking, I faced classmates who taunted me with cruel names, attacking my heritage and my religion. I became an outcast and had to apologize for myself constantly.

4   After a while, I tried to forget my heritage. No matter what race, religion or ethnicity, a child who is attacked often retreats. I was the only Arab I knew of in my class, so I had no one in my peer group as an ally. No matter what my parents tried to tell me about my proud cultural history, I would ignore it. My classmates told me I came from an uncivilized, brutal place, that Arabs were by nature anti-American, and I believed them. They did not know the hours my parents spent studying, working, trying to preserve part of their old lives while embracing, willingly, the new.

5   I tried to forget the Arabic I knew, because if I didn't I'd be forever linked to murderers. I stopped inviting friends over for dinner, because I thought the food we ate was "weird." I lied about where my parents had come from. Their accents (although they spoke English perfectly) humiliated me. Though Islam is a major monotheistic religion with many similarities to Judaism and Christianity, there were no holidays near Chanukah or Christmas, nothing to tie me to the "Judeo-Christian" tradition. I felt more excluded. I slowly began to turn into someone without a past.

6   Civil war was raging in Lebanon, and all that Americans saw of that country was destruction and violence. Every other movie seemed to feature Arab terrorists. The most common questions I was asked were if I had ever ridden a camel or if my family lived in tents. I felt burdened with responsibility. Why should an adolescent be asked questions like "Is it true you hate Jews and you want Israel destroyed?" I didn't hate anybody. My parents had never said anything even alluding to such sentiments. I was confused and hurt.

7   As I grew older and began to form my own opinions, my embarrassment lessened and my anger grew. The turning point came in high school. My grandmother had become very ill, and it was necessary for me to leave school a few days before Christmas vacation. My chemistry teacher was very sympathetic until I said I was going to the Middle East. "Don't come back in a body bag," he said cheerfully. The class laughed. Suddenly, those years of watching movies that mocked me and listening to others who knew nothing about Arabs and Muslims except what they saw on television seemed like a bad dream. I knew then that I would never be silent again.

8   I've tried to reclaim those lost years. I realize now that I come from a culture that has a rich history. The Arab world is a medley of people of different religions; not every Arab is a Muslim, and vice versa. The Arabs brought tremendous advances in the sciences and mathematics, as well as creating a literary tradition that has never been surpassed. The language itself is flexible and beautiful, with nuances and shades of meaning unparalleled in any language. Though many find it hard to believe, Islam has made progress in women's rights. There is a specific provision in the Koran that permits women to own property and ensures that their inheritance is protected—although recent events have shown that interpretation of these laws can vary.

9   My youngest brother, who is 12, is now at the crossroads I faced. When initial reports of the Oklahoma City bombing pointed to "Arab-looking individuals" as the culprits, he came home from school crying. "Mom, why do Muslims kill people? Why are the Arabs so bad?" She was angry and brokenhearted, but tried to handle the situation in the best way possible through education. She went to his class, armed with Arabic music, pictures, traditional dress and cookies. She brought a chapter of the social-studies book to life and the children asked intelligent, thoughtful questions, even after the class was over. Some even asked if she was coming back. When my brother came home, he was excited and proud instead of ashamed.

10   I only recently told my mother about my past experience. Maybe if I had told her then, I would have been better equipped to deal with the thoughtless teasing. But, unfortunately, the world is changing. Although discrimination and stereotyping still exist, many people are trying to lessen and end it. Teachers, schools and the media are showing greater sensitivity to cultural issues. However, there is still much that needs to be done, not for the sake of any particular ethnic or cultural groups but for the sake of our country.

11   The America that I love is one that values freedom and the differences of its people. Education is the key to understanding. As Americans we need to take a little time to look and listen carefully to what is around us and not rush to judgment without knowing the facts. And we must never be ashamed of our pasts. It is our collective differences that unite and make us unique as a nation. It's what determines our present and our future.

Narrative Technique Questions

1. Which sentence sums up the point of the story?

_____

_____

_____

_____

_____

_____

2. What introductory paragraph lead-in technique does the writer use?

_____

_____

_____

_____

_____

3. Identify at least five transitional expressions that help establish coherence, rhythm, and relationships between ideas.

_____

_____

_____

Critical Reading and Thinking Questions

1. What do you think is the purpose behind Asfahani writing this essay?

_____

_____

_____

2. Narration allows the author to write a personal story. Identify the world events the author mentions, and then identify the more personal events. How did the two types of events affect her and her family? Give specific examples.

_____

_____

_____

_____

_____

_____

_____

_____

3. What do you think the author learned about herself and her feeling about her ethnicity and American heritage?

_____

_____

_____

_____

_____

Narration Writing Exercises

1. Write a paragraph about how your ethnic heritage or another person's ethnic heritage has caused problems for you.
2. Using the topic of your paragraph in Exercise 1, write an essay. Expand your ideas by including how world events and personal events affected you and your thoughts about ethnicity, both personally and in general.

More Topics for a Narrative Essay

Here are some possible topics for narration writing assignments. Remember, your narrative essay should have a clearly defined point or purpose.

1. Being different from others (at work, school, or in a specific neighborhood).
2. Being insensitive to another's needs.
3. An incident that challenged opinions.
4. A trip or place that triggers a change in self-awareness.
5. A pet's meaningfulness.
6. A happy or lonely time.
7. Heroism during an event.
8. The positive and/or negative effects of an accident, treatment, and recovery.
9. How stories, movies, and plays affect people.
10. How an acquaintance's lifestyle can affect family, loved ones, and friends.
11. A story that's been told in your family for generations.
12. Make up an Urban Legend (such as people swallowing spiders in their sleep or the deranged psychopathic killer in your backseat).

NASA Photography/Alamy

13. A story about yourself as a superhero.
14. A day in a space shuttle or the International Space Station.
15. What it would be like to be buried alive in a coffin.

☑ Writing Checklist for a Narrative Essay

❏ Choose a topic.

❏ Explore the topic using one or more of the prewriting techniques you have studied, or use the six reporters' questions to uncover topics for the body paragraphs (or as your essay map items).

❏ Create the thesis statement.

❏ Write your narrative essay, remembering to use transitional expressions to create rhythm, to connect related ideas, and to order the events.

❏ Revise the first draft.

❏ Proofread the final draft.

❏ Print or type the essay and submit it.

CHAPTER REVIEW

■ A narrative essay tells a story, fictional or true. An effective narrative has a point, a reason that the story is important.

■ Techniques for writing narrative paragraphs include stating the point of the narrative in the topic sentence, using the six reporters' questions to focus the narrative, and using transitional expressions to order events.

■ In a narrative essay, the thesis sentence should state the point of the story as well as lay out the essay map. The body paragraphs pick up the topics of the essay map. The last paragraph can use any of the techniques for concluding paragraphs, but warning and prediction are often suitable for concluding a narrative essay.

 Visit *The Write Start* Online!

For additional practice with the materials found in this chapter, visit our Student Companion Web site by going to cengagebrain.com and searching for this text. The Web site also features additional readings, quizzes, writing activities, and Internet links, as well as a bulletin board and interactive chat.

The Example Essay

Using **example** is one of the most popular and effective methods for developing an essay topic. Good examples can help focus the reader's attention and illustrate a topic quickly and clearly. Maybe you have heard a friend say, "School isn't any fun!" Your first thought might be to ask why

Noel Hendrickson/Digital Vision/Jupiter Images

cesar liana/Alamy

Tom Grill/Corbis

© 2014 Wadsworth, Cengage Learning

Write an example paragraph focusing on the variety of courses you have taken at your school. Give at least three examples of skills you learned in each class that will help you prepare for success in your future academic and business environments.

your friend feels this way. You might ask her what specifically makes her feel the way she does. Your friend will probably respond by giving you examples: the teachers are uncaring, there is too much homework, the tests are too difficult, and the teachers assign too many papers. By giving you specific examples, your friend supports and clarifies her general critical view about her school experience.

Identifying Your Purpose

Detailed examples are used to illustrate, clarify, convince, or make concrete a general idea about a subject. Most people find specific, concrete examples easier to understand than general concepts. For instance, the topics in Exhibit 9.1 are accompanied by a list of examples that can be used to develop the subject.

Exhibit 9.1
Creating Detail through Examples

Topic	Examples
clothing	formal, casual, athletic
food	ethnic, holiday, diet
airplanes	acrobatic, commercial, military
politicians	mayors, presidents, senators
glasses	reading, bifocals, sun

PRACTICE 1   Writing an Example Paragraph

Using one of the other topics in Exhibit 9.1, make a list of three examples that you could use to develop the subject you have chosen. Use one or more of the prewriting techniques you have studied to discover subtopics to use in the body paragraphs to develop your thesis about the topic. Next, write a paragraph using your chosen examples to develop the topic.

Writing the Example Paragraph

An example paragraph should include a topic sentence identifying the topic of the paragraph and how it will be developed. The paragraph should use transitional expressions to connect the examples and maintain coherence.

The Topic Sentence in an Example Paragraph

The topic sentence in an example paragraph states the general topic to be discussed and the controlling idea and attitude that will guide the development of the paragraph.

The controlling idea is a statement that tells the reader what your focus will be as you develop the topic and how you feel about it (your attitude). In Exhibit 9.2, the topic is *airplanes*, and the controlling idea is *they have many uses besides transporting travelers*.

**Exhibit 9.2
The Adaptable
Airplane**

Topic Sentence ⟶

Exhibit 9.2 is an example paragraph using one of the topics and specific examples taken from Exhibit 9.1.

Airplanes have many uses besides transporting travelers. At county fairs and Fourth of July celebrations, the festivities often include a demonstration of aerial acrobatics. Usually, either a single biplane or a team of biplanes will dive and tumble their way through a series of flight patterns designed to bring "oohs" and "aahs" from the crowd below. Airplanes, since early in the 20th century, have been used to deliver mail. Big companies, such as FedEx and UPS, owe much of their success to the airplane because it allows them to deliver mail overnight, instead of the normal three to five days. Of course, no one uses the airplane more extensively than the military. Fighters, bombers, refueling tankers, cargo transports, and communication jets are only a few of the planes the armed services use to complete their varied missions.

PRACTICE 2   Identifying the Topic and Controlling Idea

I D E N T I F Y I N G

Underline the topic once and the controlling idea or attitude twice in the topic sentences that follow.

1. Cybersex is becoming a popular activity.

2. Religion is an important aspect of most people's lives.

3. Binge drinking at parties is increasing.

4. Date rape is hard to prove in court.

5. A positive attitude can help fight illness.

6. Plagiarism defeats the purpose of writing assignments.

PRACTICE 3   Writing an Example Paragraph

Using one of the topic sentences in Practice 2, select one of the prewriting techniques from Chapter 3, and use it to discover subtopics you will use to develop the controlling idea. Second, make a list of three examples that explain the focus you have chosen for developing the controlling idea. Third, write one or more sentences for each of the examples you have chosen. Finally, rewrite your sentences into standard paragraph form.

Using Transitional Expressions to Connect Examples to the Topic

While each example helps to clarify, explain, and develop the topic, **transitional expressions** help to connect the examples to the topic, and they add rhythm to the paragraph. Use transitional expressions so that the examples do not appear merely as a list. Examples should act in unison to develop the subject expressed in the topic sentence.

> **Transitional Expressions for Example**
>
> | | |
> |---|---|
> | a case in point is | for example |
> | another example of | for instance |
> | another instance of | to illustrate |
> | another illustration of | specifically |

Look how using transitional expressions can help identify examples, connect related ideas, and add rhythm to the paragraph from Exhibit 9.2.

> Airplanes have many uses besides transporting travelers. **For instance**, at county fairs and Fourth of July celebrations, the festivities often include a demonstration of aerial acrobatics. Usually, either a single biplane or a team of biplanes will dive and tumble their way through a series of flight patterns designed to bring "oohs" and "aahs" from the crowd below. Airplanes, since early in the 20th century, have been used to deliver mail. **To illustrate**, big companies, such as FedEx and UPS, owe much of their success to the airplane because it allows them to deliver mail overnight, instead of the normal three to five days. Of course, no one uses the airplane more extensively than the military. **For example**, fighters, bombers, refueling tankers, cargo transports, and communication jets are only a few of the planes the armed services use to complete their varied missions.

In the preceding example paragraph, the transitional expressions "for instance," "to illustrate," and "for example" are used to announce to the reader that an example is forthcoming. This technique helps keep the reader focused on the specific example you are using to explain, clarify, and develop the topic.

PRACTICE 4   **Using Transitional Expressions**

Using the paragraph you wrote for Practice 3, add at least three transitional expressions to connect related ideas, add rhythm, and announce upcoming examples. After you have finished, compare the two paragraphs. The paragraph with the transitional expressions should be easier to read and understand.

Moving from Paragraph to Essay

Now that you have studied and practiced the techniques to create effective example paragraphs, it is time to expand your ideas to a larger writing unit: the example essay. You will use the techniques you learned in Part One regarding developing the essay paragraphs and the example techniques you have just learned to create the example essay. This might be a good time to return to Part One and review the techniques for developing the full essay.

Creating the Introductory Paragraph

Because examples are such good devices to clarify ideas, it is easy for a writer to think that there need not be any special concern regarding the organization and focus of an example essay. However, an example essay is writing, and all writing has a specific purpose. Therefore, an example essay needs a clearly defined purpose and organization. The thesis sentence in an example essay should state the essay's purpose and organization.

The thesis in an example essay should blend naturally into the rest of the introductory paragraph. In the following introductory paragraph, notice how the thesis sentence announces the topic (*required courses*), the writer's controlling idea about the topic (*are essential to a student's education*), and the essay map containing the body paragraph topics (*refining communication skills, developing a wide range of interests*, and *building practical skills*). The thesis sentence in the example is underlined for instructional purposes.

> Freshman students attending college each fall soon discover that they have few choices in putting together their class schedule. Regardless if they have declared a major field of study, all students find out that they are required to take a minimum number of hours in general course work (introductory courses in history, civics, sociology, and writing, for example) before they can receive a degree. Many students think taking these courses is a waste of time because they have already taken these courses in high school. However, the amount of material covered and the specialized knowledge of college professors make these courses valuable assets to college students as they prepare themselves for life in college and beyond. <u>Required courses are essential to a student's education because they help refine communication skills, develop a wide range of interests, and build practical skills.</u>

While this essay's topic is *required courses*, the focus of the essay is the idea that the required courses are essential to a student's education.

Creating the Body Paragraphs

For a paper on the *required courses* topic, the focus of the body paragraphs will be the topics listed in the thesis sentence's essay map.

- The first body paragraph's topic will be they *help refine communication skills*.
- The second body paragraph's topic will be they *help develop a wide range of interests*.
- The third body paragraph's topic will be they *help build practical skills*.

Keep your focus on the fact that required courses *are essential to a student's education*.

Creating the Concluding Paragraph

The concluding paragraph should flow naturally from the essay's main topic. Because the essay's focus is that required courses are essential for a student's education, a *prediction* would seem an appropriate choice. You might point out that students should not resent taking required courses; rather, if they apply themselves to their required course work, their educational development will be substantially rewarded. The concluding paragraph is the proper place to mention rewards other than those mentioned in the body paragraphs, such as nomination to honor societies, reference letters from teachers, and teaching assistantships during graduate studies.

Sample Student Essay: OPPORTUNITIES IN THE ARMED FORCES

Jennifer Staggs

In today's world of corporate downsizing and job insecurity, many young people are not prepared for the competitive world of job hunting and retention. Even college graduates can find it difficult to find employment because they lack specific skills. In this essay, student writer Jennifer Staggs, who spent four years in the U.S. Navy immediately following high school, suggests that many young people would benefit from a tour in the armed forces. While this particular essay uses many examples to support the thesis, it also uses many descriptive adjectives to help bring the examples to life.

Vocabulary

Before you start reading, use a dictionary to look up the definitions of the following words that appear in the essay.

acquiring (1)	apprehension (1)	burden (1)
distinct (4)	encounter (2)	impeccable (4)
initial (3)	invigorating (2)	propel (5)
rigorous (2)	sculpting (2)	sufficient (4)

Note: Icarus, in Greek mythology, was the son of Daedalus. Trapped in a labyrinth, Icarus attempted to escape by flying out of the labyrinth with wax wings. Although he thought he was properly prepared to be successful, he flew too close to the sun, the wax wings melted, and he fell into the ocean and was drowned.

Opportunities in the Armed Forces

1   Since the days of Icarus, young people have awaited the day to spread their wings and gain freedom and independence; however, although the future may seem sunny and bright, dark clouds can quickly appear on the horizon. An uncertain unemployment environment and the economic burden of college can also create apprehension in both student and parent. Even college graduates have difficulty acquiring employment because they may lack specific skills. Many of these young people do not have the proper advice and guidance from more experienced adults, and they also are unaware of an exciting world awaiting discovery. Because of discipline, travel, and work experience, young people should consider enlisting in the military.

Thesis Statement with Essay Map →

Topic Sentence →

2   In the armed forces, a new recruit will encounter many forms of discipline. During basic training, lasting eight to 13 weeks, trainees learn rigorous, invigorating exercises for achieving fitness and sculpting the body's shape. Maintaining a nutritious diet helps to fuel the vigorous routine that the

PATRICK BAZ/AFP/Getty Images

trainee meets with each new day. The recruit will eat three balanced meals each day, including plenty of fruit and fresh vegetables—no more junk food! Most important, the trainee will learn to respect authority and to understand the life-saving elements of teamwork. There is no "I" in "team."

Topic Sentence →
3   After initial training, overseas assignments or other travel opportunities often become available. Imagine experiencing the mysteries of the Far East, the breathtaking landscapes of Ireland, or the magnificent Rhineland castles of Germany! Gourmet foods, exotic dress, and colorful arts and crafts are just some of the many aspects that make other cultures so fascinating. All the branches of the armed forces have duty stations worldwide that broaden the horizons of military personnel.

Topic Sentence →
4   The armed forces have an impeccable record of sending veterans out into the civilian world with superior work experience and skills. Because of sufficient funding, the military has some of the best equipment and training in the world. Many veterans return to civilian businesses with the knowledge and experience to operate or repair some of the most up-to-date and sophisticated machinery and electronic equipment in existence. Veterans of the military, because of their operating within a distinct chain of command, bring excellent communication abilities, organization strengths, and teamwork readiness to be successful in whatever work environment they enter. Employers find these "ready-to-work" veterans an invaluable resource for their companies.

5   Following a successful enlistment period, men and women are better prepared for the future. In addition to receiving the best education, honor is bestowed upon those serving the people of the United States. In the past, many young people have used their military experience to propel themselves into careers in business, industry, and politics. Most of our past and present congresspersons, senators, and presidents have served honorably and proudly in the military. All in all, from any employer's perspective, a veteran is a well-rounded person, an outstanding worker, and a trustworthy citizen.

Example Technique Questions

A N A L Y Z I N G

1. What lead-in technique(s) does the author use to introduce the thesis sentence?

   _____

2. The writer's attitude toward military service is that young people "should consider" it. What are some of the examples the writer uses in the body paragraphs to develop and support this attitude?

   _____

   _____

   _____

   _____

   _____

   _____

_____

_____

_____

_____

_____

_____

_____

_____

_____

_____

3. List some occupations that young people not going to college might consider exploring. What examples does the writer point out that could help young people have a better chance at success in these occupations?

_____

_____

Critical Reading and Thinking Questions

ANALYZING

1. How does the reference to Icarus help the writer establish the seriousness of the topic?

_____

_____

2. Underline the adjectives in the essay. How do they enhance and support the writer's attitude that serving in the military can be a rewarding experience for young people?

_____

_____

_____

Example Writing Exercises

1. In her essay "Opportunities in the Armed Forces," student writer Jennifer Staggs points out a *problem* that she notices about many young people (a lack of proper advice and guidance from adults and a lack of awareness of an exciting world around them). Her attempt to answer the problem is to introduce young people to the opportunities in the armed forces that help solve the problem. Write an example paragraph that explains how to solve a problem you see affecting young people or those in your age group. Some problems might be voting apathy, distrust in working for a large corporation, or a feeling that a high school or college degree is not important.

2. Expand the ideas in the paragraph you wrote in Exercise 1, and write an example essay. Do not forget to formulate a clearly expressed thesis statement. Discover subtopics by using one or more of the prewriting techniques you have studied.

Sample Professional Essay: DARKNESS AT NOON

Harold Krents

> The following article originally appeared in the *New York Times* in 1976. Author Harold Krents, blind from birth, was a lawyer and writer who never allowed his "handicap" to stand in the way of his accomplishments. In the article, Krents points out many examples of discrimination that he had to endure as a result of his being blind.

Vocabulary

Meaning comes primarily from words. Before you start reading, use a dictionary to look up the meanings of the following words that appear in the essay.

converse (2)	cum laude (15)	dependent (1)
disposition (13)	enunciating (2)	graphically (5)
intoned (12)	invariably (3)	narcissistic (1)

Darkness at Noon

1 Blind from birth, I have never had the opportunity to see myself and have been completely dependent on the image I create in the eye of the observer. To date it has not been narcissistic.

2 There are those who assume that since I can't see, I obviously cannot hear. Very often people will converse with me at the top of their lungs, enunciating

each word very carefully. Conversely, people will also often whisper, assuming that since my eyes don't work, my ears don't either.

3   For example, when I go the airport and ask the ticket agent for assistance to the plane, he or she will invariably pick up the phone, call a ground hostess and whisper: "Hi, Jane, we've got a 76 here." I have concluded that the word "blind" is not used for one of two reasons: either they fear that if the dread word is spoken, the ticket agent's retina will immediately detach, or they are reluctant to inform me of my condition of which I may not have been previously aware.

4   On the other hand, others know that of course I can hear, but believe that I can't talk. Often, therefore, when my wife and I go out to dinner, a waiter or waitress will ask Kit if "*he* would like a drink" to which I respond that "indeed *he* would."

5   This point was graphically driven home to me while we were in England. I had been given a year's leave of absence from my Washington law firm to study for a diploma in law degree at Oxford University. During the year I became ill and was hospitalized. Immediately after admission, I was wheeled down to the X-ray room. Just at the door sat an elderly woman—elderly I would judge from the sound of her voice. "What is his name?" the woman asked the orderly who had been wheeling me.

6   "What's your name?" the orderly repeated to me.

7   "Harold Krents," I replied.

8   "Harold Krents," he repeated.

9   "When was he born?"

10   "When were you born?"

11   "November 5, 1944," I responded.

12   "November 5, 1944," the orderly intoned.

13   This procedure continued for approximately five minutes, at which point even my saint-like disposition deserted me. "Look," I finally blurted out, "this is absolutely ridiculous. Okay, granted I can't see, but it's got to have become pretty clear to both of you that I don't need an interpreter."

14   "He says he doesn't need an interpreter," the orderly reported to the woman.

15   The toughest misconception of all is the view that because I can't see, I can't work. I was turned down by over forty law firms because of my blindness, even though my qualifications included a cum laude degree from Harvard college and a good ranking in my Harvard Law School class.

16   The attempt to find employment, the continuous frustration of being told that it was impossible for a blind person to practice law, the rejection letters, not based on my lack of ability but rather on my disability, will always remain one of the most disillusioning experiences of my life.

17   I therefore look forward to the day, with the expectation that it is certain to come, when employers will view their handicapped workers as a little child did me years ago when my family still lived in Scarsdale.

18   I was playing basketball with my father in our backyard according to procedures we had developed. My father would stand beneath the hoop, shout, and I would shoot over his head at the basket attached to our garage. Our next-door neighbor, aged five, wandered over into our yard with a playmate. "He's blind," our neighbor whispered to her friend in a voice that could be heard distinctly by Dad and me. Dad shot and missed; I did the same. Dad hit the rim; I missed entirely; dad shot and missed the garage entirely. "Which one is blind?" whispered back the little friend.

19   I would hope that in the near future when a plant manager is touring the factory with the foreman and comes upon a handicapped and nonhandicapped person working together, his comment after watching them work will be, "Which one is disabled?"

Example Technique Questions

1. Is there a thesis statement in the essay? If you identify one, does it have an essay map?

   _____

   _____

2. The author uses humor to describe the situations that he found himself in. Point out some examples, and relate how the humorous tone affects your feelings toward the essay.

   _____

   _____

   _____

   _____

   _____

   _____

   _____

3. Examples sometimes are expressed in the form of dialogue. Explain why this is an effective method to develop Krents' main points.

   _____

   _____

   _____

Critical Reading and Thinking Questions

1. Krents expresses that there are many common misconceptions about blind people. Point out three examples.

   _____

   _____

2. Even though the author uses humor throughout the essay, how do you know his attitude about being handicapped is serious?

   _____

   _____

_____

_____

_____

Example Writing Exercises

1. In his essay "Darkness at Noon," writer Harold Krents points out a misconception that people have about blind persons: that they cannot work. Have you ever been in a situation in which you were temporarily handicapped? Have you ever been confined to a wheelchair, had an arm in a sling or a leg in a cast? Have you ever had your eyes dilated at the optometrist's so that someone else had to drive you home? Write an example paragraph about how it would feel to be disabled. Give examples of how the handicap might affect daily life and if others empathize with those that are truly handicapped.

2. Using the topic of your paragraph in Exercise 1, write an essay. Expand your ideas by including how the media and peer pressure influence how society judges the handicapped.

More Topics for an Example Essay

John Henley/Lithium/Age Fotostock

Here are some possible topics for example writing assignments. Remember, you must use examples for a purpose, so do not forget to create a thesis sentence with an appropriate attitude and controlling idea. One option is to use the essay map to organize the subtopics for your body paragraphs. Be certain that all specific information supports your topic sentences.

1. Tattooing
2. Dropping out of high school
3. Role models
4. Premarital sex
5. Violence in video games, movies, or television
6. Working for a large corporation
7. Male and female homosexuality
8. Interracial marriage
9. Fraternities and sororities
10. Body piercing
11. Charitable acts
12. Positive or negative aspects of home schooling
13. Three ethnic dishes
14. Computer programs
15. Video games

☑ Writing Checklist for an Example Essay

❑   Choose a topic.

❑   Explore the topic using one or more of the prewriting techniques you have studied to discover topics for your body paragraphs (or as your essay map items).

❏ Create the thesis statement. Do not forget to include an attitude about the topic and a controlling idea (this can be an essay map).

❏ Write a first draft of the introductory, body, and concluding paragraphs of the essay.

❏ Be sure to include examples.

❏ Remember to use transitional expressions to create rhythm and sentence variety and to show relationships between ideas.

❏ Revise the first draft.

❏ Print or type the essay and submit it.

CHAPTER REVIEW

■ In an example essay, detailed examples are used to illustrate, clarify, convince, or make concrete a general topic.

■ The topic sentence of an example paragraph states the general topic and the controlling idea that guides the development of the paragraph. The six reporters' questions can be used to focus the discussion. Transitional expressions help identify examples, connect related ideas, and add rhythm to the paragraph.

■ In an example essay, the thesis sentence states the general topic, the controlling idea, and the essay map with subtopics. All the examples given in the body paragraphs should support the controlling idea of the essay.

 Visit *The Write Start* **Online!**

For additional practice with the materials found in this chapter, visit our Student Companion Web site by going to cengagebrain.com and searching for this text. The Web site also features additional readings, quizzes, writing activities, and Internet links.

Pages 129–130: Harold Krents, "Darkness at Noon." Originally published in the *New York Times*, May 26, 1976. Copyright © 1976 New York Times. Reprinted by permission. All rights reserved.

The Classification Essay

Some topics you will be assigned to write about are very complex. A simple definition or description of these topics often is not sufficient to adequately explain them. How, then, do you approach a large, complex subject so your reader has a full understanding of the point you are trying to make? One possibility is **classification**, the separation of smaller points from a larger concept and the arrangement of these smaller concepts into easily recognized groups.

Write a paragraph classifying ships into categories based on shape, type, color, and function. Ship categories can encompass those in the preceding pictures: military, private, and commercial. Other categories represented might be: historical, experimental, police, or Coast Guard.

These groups can be based on shape, kind, color, function, or any other category your reader will understand easily. For example, you can classify chefs as specializing in regional cooking: French, Southwest American, Northern Italian, Cajun. You can categorize birds by color: blue, red, yellow. You can group geometric figures by shape: rectangles, circles, triangles, and cones.

Identifying Your Purpose

The purpose of classification, as for all writing, is either to inform, entertain, or persuade. When the subject is sufficiently complicated, classification is one method of making a complex subject easier to write about and easier for your reader to understand.

Suppose you were to write about William Shakespeare, and your focus was his genius. You would not be able to find out his IQ and his SAT scores because such testing did not exist in the sixteenth and seventeenth centuries. You could try to find out what his contemporaries and later critics said about him. Unfortunately, not many comments from his contemporaries have survived, and the analyses of later critics are too numerous for you to read.

You might look at Shakespeare's writings. He was a prolific writer, and we have plenty of his works. In fact, because so many of his plays have survived and are still produced and studied worldwide, this might give you your focus.

> **Example**
>
> William Shakespeare can be considered a genius because of his prolific writings in so many forms. Shakespeare wrote sonnets, histories, comedies, tragedies, dark comedies, and romances. Many of his plays are still produced both on the stage and in films. Courses of study in Shakespeare's writings remain a staple in colleges and universities worldwide.

In the preceding paragraph, the scope of Shakespeare's genius can be more readily understood because his works are classified into different categories.

PRACTICE 1   Creating Categories

ANALYZING

Separate each of the following topics into three classifications or groups. They can be based on shape, color, size, kind, or any other category that helps explain the topic. The first one is done as a sample.

Fish: freshwater   tropical   oceanic

Clothes: _____   _____   _____

Music: _____   _____   _____

Movies: _____   _____   _____

Storms: _____   _____   _____

Dates: _____ _____ _____

Ice cream: _____ _____ _____

Writing the Classification Paragraph

A classification paragraph should indicate the general topic being discussed as well as explain the categories into which it is divided. One or more of the pre-writing techniques you have studied can be used to focus the discussion, and transitional expressions can provide signposts for guiding the reader.

The Topic Sentence in a Classification Paragraph

In a classification paragraph, the topic sentence must state the subject, how the subject will be divided, and why classifying the subject is important. Here is an example of a topic sentence for a classification paragraph shown in Exhibit 10.1.

**Exhibit 10.1
Classification Topic
Sentence**

Topic Sentence: The negative effects of discrimination can be understood easily if its targets are classified by race, gender, and age.

Subject: discrimination

Categories: race, gender, age

**Controlling idea
and attitude:** to learn about discrimination's negative effects

PRACTICE 2   Writing Topic Sentences

W R I T I N G

Write a topic sentence for each of the subjects you classified in Practice 1. Remember, your topic sentence must state the subject, the classification categories, and why it is important to divide the topic into groups.

Using Supporting Details

To develop the controlling idea, use the subtopics you have discovered with the prewriting technique. They will help you focus on how you will develop the categories in which you have divided the subject. In Exhibit 10.1, the controlling idea and attitude that discrimination has negative effects focuses on people who most often suffer the effects of discrimination: people of color, women, and older adults. While other aspects might be expressed in the paragraph, such as events that have happened and the reasons for those occurrences, the people involved will be the main focus.

A paragraph based on the categories of race, gender, and age might look like the sample shown in Exhibit 10.2.

**Exhibit 10.2
Supporting Details**

The negative effects of discrimination can be more easily understood if

its targets are classified by race, gender, and age. Although some progress

has been made, racial discrimination is still evident in our culture. Hate

groups still march in parades on Main Street, and with the advent of the

Internet, they have filled cyberspace with their special brand of hatred against all **people of color. Women** are still expected by many men to stay home and take care of the house and the children (and of the husband's needs). In the workplace, men still get promoted faster, and men are still paid more for the same work as women. **Older adults** often are not hired because they are perceived as less dynamic and less willing to learn since they are set in their ways. Additionally, many older adults are downsized because younger workers can take their place at a lower salary rate.

Discrimination knows no limits. It can strike almost anyone, anytime, and anywhere.

PRACTICE 3   Writing a Classification Paragraph

W R I T I N G

Using one of the topics from Practice 1, write a classification paragraph. Develop the paragraph by focusing on the three categories into which you divided the subject. Use the topic sentence you created in Practice 2 as the first sentence of the paragraph.

Using Transitional Expressions to Identify Classifications

While developing each category or group helps to inform, entertain, or persuade the reader, **transitional expressions** help to connect related ideas and add rhythm to the paragraph. Use transitional expressions in your classification paragraph so that the categories do not appear merely as a list. The groups or categories should work together to develop the subject and the controlling idea.

Transitional Expressions for Classification		
can be categorized	can be classified	can be divided
can be grouped	the first/second category	the first group
the first/second kind	the first/second type	the last

See how adding transitional expressions can help make the paragraph in Exhibit 10.2 more readable and understandable.

> The negative effects of discrimination can be more easily understood if its targets **are classified** by race, gender, and age. Although some progress has been made with **the first group**, people of color, racial discrimination is still evident in our culture. Hate groups still march in parades on Main Street, and with the advent of the Internet, they have filled cyberspace with their

special brand of hatred against all people of color. **The second group** targeted by discrimination is women. Women are still expected by many men to stay home and take care of the house and the children (and of the husband's needs). In the workplace, men still get promoted faster, and men are still paid more for the same work as women. Members of **the last category**, the elderly, are often downsized because younger workers can take their place at a lower salary rate. Discrimination knows no limits. It can strike almost anyone, anytime, and anywhere.

In the preceding classification paragraph, the transitional expressions "are classified," "the first group," "the second group," and "the last category" also are used to announce that the next group to be discussed is forthcoming. The technique helps to keep the reader focused on the specific categories being used to develop the topic and the controlling idea and attitude.

PRACTICE 4   Adding Transitional Expressions to a Classification Paragraph

Using the paragraph you wrote in Practice 3, add at least three transitional expressions to connect related ideas, add rhythm, and announce upcoming categories. After you have finished, compare the two paragraphs. The paragraph containing the transitional expressions should be easier to read and understand.

Moving from Paragraph to Essay

Now that you have studied and practiced the techniques to create effective classification, it is time to expand your ideas to a larger writing unit: the classification essay. Using the techniques you learned in Part One regarding developing the essay paragraphs and the classification techniques you have just learned, you can write a classification essay. This might be a good time to return to Part One and review the techniques for developing the full essay.

Creating the Introductory Paragraph

Some writers think that once they have divided their topic into distinct categories, their job is complete. Nothing could be further from the truth. All writing has to have a purpose, and the purpose must be clearly expressed. The thesis sentence in a classification essay must state the topic, announce the writer's attitude toward the topic, and state the controlling idea that will clarify the organizational format of the essay.

The thesis in a classification essay should occur naturally as the introductory paragraph unfolds. In the following introductory paragraph, taken from the sample student essay to follow, notice how the thesis sentence announces the subject (*selecting beneficiaries in a will*), his attitude about the process (*it makes the selections easier*), the writer's controlling idea about the topic (*categorizing the beneficiaries*), and the essay map containing the categories to be developed in the body paragraphs (*the disorderly, the beggars,* and *the friends*). The thesis sentence is underlined for identification purposes.

Example

Year after year, many Americans go through the dreadful task of preparing a will. Whether using the family attorney or the family computer, the question of who gets the house and who gets the loot needs to be answered clearly in black and white. Documents of this nature can get very complex and detailed, needing a linguist for translation, but choosing kin for determining who's in and who's definitely out of the legal instrument shouldn't be difficult at all. <u>Placing relatives into three categories, the disorderly, the beggars, and the friends, eases the process of selecting beneficiaries.</u>

Using the thesis sentence with an essay map makes the contents and organizational structure clear for both writer and reader. As we shall see following, the essay will continue by developing the essay map items in their respective body paragraphs.

PRACTICE 5   Writing a Thesis Sentence for a Classification Essay

Create a thesis sentence with an attitude and controlling idea and a three-item essay map using the topic idea in the paragraph you created for Practice 3. Make certain that the three essay map items you choose will be able to develop the topic as the controlling idea suggests. (See the sections titled "The Attitude in the Thesis Sentence" and "The Controlling Idea in the Thesis Sentence" in Chapter 4 if you need to review this information.)

Creating the Body Paragraphs

For an essay on *preparing a will*, the focus of the body paragraphs will be the paragraph topics listed in the thesis sentence's essay map.

- The first body paragraph's topic will be about the *disorderly relatives*.
- The second body paragraph's topic will be about the *beggars*.
- The third body paragraph will be about *friends*.
- Each of the body paragraphs in a classification essay focuses on one of the categories into which the topic has been divided.

Remember, as you write about each of the topics, your focus should be on the attitude and controlling idea; in this case, the combined attitude and controlling idea is *classifying potential beneficiaries makes the process of writing the will easier.*

Creating the Concluding Paragraph

The approach of the concluding paragraph should flow naturally from the essay's main topic. Because the essay's focus is placing potential beneficiaries into categories in order to make the overall process of selecting the actual beneficiaries easier, an evaluation of the main points in each category would seem appropriate. You might discuss how to be more precise in the classification of the disorderly, the beggars, and the friends. You could classify them further by age, schooling, how many times they have been arrested, or how distant they are on the branches of the family tree. You could further classify them by how many family functions they have attended, how many times they have asked for money, or how many times they have sued members of the family over property, possessions, or money. (Refer to Chapter 6 for other approaches for concluding paragraphs.)

Sample Student Essay: LEFT OUT

Randy Raterman

In the essay "Left Out," student writer Randy Raterman takes a humorous and somewhat sarcastic look at making a will. The problem is not so much a question of whether to leave possessions to relatives; the problem turns out to be deciding which relatives should be mentioned in the will. Raterman divides the potential recipients into three groups, two of which are decidedly on the "left out" list, making it easier to identify those on the "in" list. Notice how many adjectives the author attaches to nouns in order to bring them to life.

Vocabulary

Before starting to read, use a dictionary to look up the definitions of the following words that appear in the essay.

amplify (5)	beneficiaries (4)	commendable (4)
linguist (1)	mendicant (3)	ominous (5)
proverbial (3)	riffraff (2)	

Left Out

1   Year after year, many Americans go through the dreadful task of preparing a will. Whether using the family attorney or the family computer, the question of who gets the house and who gets the loot needs to be answered clearly in black and white. Documents of this nature can get very complex and detailed, needing a linguist for translation, but choosing kin for determining who's in and who's definitely out of the legal instrument shouldn't be difficult at all. Placing relatives into three categories, the disorderly, the beggars, and the friends, eases the process of selecting beneficiaries.

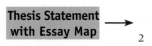

2   The first group to be eliminated from the selection of beneficiaries is the disorderly. Almost every family has individuals fitting this category. Kinfolk of this kind should include the uncontrollable creatures hanging from the branches of the family tree. This prevents the disobedient, undisciplined, unruly, rebellious, and violent souls from inheriting one red cent. If an entire branch is infested with precarious parasites, pruning is essential. Additionally, the pesky rodents burrowing in the tree roots may fill the void left by the branchless trunk. Tending to legalities is imperative because related riffraff have no problem dragging heirs through the legal system in search of a gold mine. Even though the timid and light of heart

may be hesitant, constructing this category is highly effective for excluding unworthy, vulture-like inheritors.

Topic Sentence → 3 The second category, the beggars, also needs to be eliminated from consideration. Recording names of kinfolk in this second group may be the most challenging; numerous leeches will befriend the benefactors while simultaneously desiring particular heirlooms. Nonetheless, some mendicant pests are easy to identify. If receiving inescapable phone calls from long-lost family members gives rise to the question: "What did that misfit want? We haven't heard from him in years," simply jot down the callers' names. If several members possess a needy personality that seems only satisfied if they amass more objects than those listed in the will, put them on the list. Members of the proverbial family tree exhibiting sponge-like characteristics (never losing absorbency for family possessions) appropriately fit the category as well. Consequently, individuals in this group are notorious for dragging legitimate recipients to court, so double check all legal documents for erroneous entries. Unmentioned kin clearly belong with the uncontrollable creatures, parasites, and pesky rodents, or they (and their legal team) will think they are rightful recipients.

Topic Sentence → 4 The final category of potential, worthwhile inheritors contains the names of preferable kin. When composing the list, focus on relatives having friendly traits. Jot down the names of those who are truly close and dear; immediate loved ones would be devastated if they were accidentally left out or inherited the dirty sock collection, so double check to make sure these names have been inscribed. A truly considerate benefactor would include names of kin who have come to the rescue in time of need, no questions asked. Many relatives may at first seem helpful, but excluding those who want a crispy, new Ben Franklin for a couple hours of babysitting will leave just a handful of good-natured, kindhearted, and loving souls. Obviously, the most difficult task is still at hand. Who from the roster will be the recipients, and what will the recipients receive? Nonetheless, legally protecting the beneficiaries from the leeches, sponges, parasites, pesky rodents, and uncontrollable creatures inhabiting the family tree would be commendable.

5 Unfortunately, most Americans pass away each year having not completed a will or any other legal instrument that indicates how they want their possessions distributed to family. Occasionally, the goods get turned over to the state, leaving opportunities for the unworthy, ominous family members to inherit entire estates. Unpleasant as it may be, a few affectionate, kindhearted kin will be grieving the loss of a family member, so don't amplify the grief by not having a will or estate plan. Numerous little family squabbles may break out after the departure of the benefactor if legalities haven't been resolved, so heed the warning to exclude wicked, unworthy family members from the list of recipients.

Classification Technique Questions

1. How does the writer categorize potential beneficiaries?

_____

_____

_____

2. What other categories can you think of that might fit in the essay?

_____

_____

3. Underline as many of the classification transitional expressions that you can find, and list them on the following lines.

_____

_____

_____

Critical Reading and Thinking Questions

I B W E A

ANALYZING

1. What do you think is the writer's purpose for writing the essay?

_____

_____

_____

2. How do the transitional expressions help create a more effective essay?

_____

_____

_____

3. One form of alliteration is the intentional repetition of consonant sounds at the beginning of words or in stressed syllables (*petulant puppies, withering willows*). Point out some examples of alliteration in the essay. How does Raterman's use of alliteration support the humorous aspect of the essay?

_____

_____

_____

_____

_____

Classification Writing Exercises

1. Write a paragraph about how friends and relatives might be classified at home, school, and work. Do not forget to state an attitude and controlling idea in your topic sentence.
2. Expand the ideas in the paragraph you wrote for Exercise 1, and write a classification essay. Discover categories for each subtopic by using one or more of the prewriting techniques you have studied. Use transitional expressions to create rhythm and sentence variety and to connect related ideas.

Sample Professional Essay: WHY I WANT A WIFE

Judy Brady-Syfers

The following essay, first published in *Ms.* magazine under the name Judy Syfers, is a satiric look at a woman's traditional, social role as a servant to her husband's needs. The author divides this major role into distinct categories as she comments on the female situation in respect to her husband, herself, and the society at large.

Vocabulary

Before you start reading, use a dictionary to look up the definitions of the following words that appear in the essay.

adherence (7)	dependent (3)	entail (7)
hors d'oeuvres (6)	monogamy (7)	nurturant (3)
rambling (5)	replenished (6)	

Why I Want a Wife

1 I belong to that classification of people known as wives. I am a Wife. And, not altogether incidentally, I am a mother.

2 Not too long ago a male friend of mine appeared on the scene fresh from a recent divorce. He had one child, who is, of course, with his ex-wife. He is looking for another wife. As I thought about him while I was ironing one evening, it suddenly occurred to me that I, too, would like to have a wife. Why do I want a wife?

3 I would like to go back to school, so I can become economically independent, support myself, and, if need be, support those dependent upon me. I want a wife who will work and send me to school. And while I am going to school I want a wife to take care of my children. I want a wife to keep track of the children's doctor and dentist appointments. And, to keep track of mine, too. I want a wife to make sure my children eat properly and are kept clean. I want a wife who will wash the children's clothes and keep them mended. I want a wife who is a good nurturant attendant to my children, who arranges for their schooling, makes sure that they have an adequate social life

with their peers, takes them to the park, the zoo, etc. I want a wife who takes care of the children when they are sick, a wife who arranges to be around when the children need special care, because, of course, I cannot miss classes at school. My wife must arrange to lose time at work and not lose the job. It may mean a small cut in my wife's income from time to time, but I guess I can tolerate that. Needless to say, my wife will arrange and pay for the care of the children while my wife is working.

4   I want a wife who will take care of *my* physical needs. I want a wife who will keep my house clean. A wife who will pick up after my children, a wife who will pick up after me. I want a wife who will keep my clothes clean, ironed, mended, replaced when need be, and who will see to it that my personal things are kept in their proper place so that I can find what I need the minute I need it. I want a wife who cooks the meals, a wife who is a *good* cook. I want a wife who will plan the menus, do the necessary grocery shopping, prepare the meals, serve them pleasantly, and then do the cleaning up while I do my studying. I want a wife who will care for me when I am sick and sympathize with my pain and loss of time from school. I want a wife to go along when our family takes a vacation so that someone can continue to care for me and my children when I need a rest and change of scene.

5   I want a wife who will not bother me with rambling complaints about a wife's duties. But I want a wife who will listen to me when I feel the need to explain a rather difficult point I have come across in my course of studies. And I want a wife who will type my papers for me when I have written them.

6   I want a wife who will take care of the details of my social life. When my wife and I are invited out by my friends, I want a wife who will take care of the babysitting arrangements. When I meet people at school that I like and want to entertain, I want a wife who will have the house clean, will prepare a special meal, serve it to me and my friends, and not interrupt when I talk about things that interest me and my friends. I want a wife who will have arranged that the children are fed and ready for bed before my guests arrive so that the children do not bother us. I want a wife who takes care of the needs of my guests so that they feel comfortable, who makes sure that they have an ashtray, that they are passed the hors d'oeuvres, that they are offered a second helping of the food, that their wine glasses are replenished when necessary, that their coffee is served to them as they like it. And I want a wife who knows that sometimes I need a night out by myself.

7   I want a wife who is sensitive to my sexual needs, a wife who makes love passionately and eagerly when I feel like it, a wife who makes sure that I am satisfied. And, of course, I want a wife who will not demand sexual attention when I am not in the mood for it. I want a wife who assumes the complete responsibility for birth control, because I do not want more children. I want a wife who will remain sexually faithful to me so that I do not have to clutter up my intellectual life with jealousies. And I want a wife who understands that *my* sexual needs may entail more than strict adherence to monogamy. I must, after all, be able to relate to people as fully as possible.

8   If, by chance, I find another person more suitable as a wife than the wife I already have, I want the liberty to replace my present wife with another one. Naturally, I will expect a fresh, new life; my wife will take the children and be solely responsible for them so that I am left free.

9   When I am through with school and have a job, I want my wife to quit working and remain at home so that my wife can more fully and completely take care of a wife's duties.

10   My God, who *wouldn't* want a wife?

Classification Technique Questions

A N A L Y Z I N G

1. Most sentences begin with "I want a wife." Is this repetitious form effective? Why or why not?

   _____

   _____

2. The author lists a staggering number of wife-duty categories. Are they related in any particular way? Explain.

   _____

   _____

3. What is the effect of the author's continual use of "my" in the essay?

   _____

   _____

Critical Reading and Thinking Questions

A N A L Y Z I N G

1. What is the purpose of Brady-Syfers' essay?

   _____

   _____

   _____

   _____

2. This essay was written in 1972. Is it still relevant today? Why or why not?

   _____

   _____

3. In the last line of the essay, Brady-Syfers asks, "My God, who *wouldn't* want a wife?" How would you answer this question, and why?

   _____

   _____

Classification Writing Exercises

1. Write a paragraph about the many roles that people have to assume and how those roles are perceived by others. The perceptions can be by individuals, groups, or society as a whole.
2. Examine the roles people play in their lives, such as student, friend, parent, and worker, and how the various roles make them feel. Take one person, playing three roles, and write an essay explaining how the person acts and feels in each role.

More Topics for a Classification Essay

Here are some possible topics for classification writing assignments. Remember, your essay must have a purpose, so do not forget to create a thesis statement with an appropriate attitude. Use the essay map to organize the subtopics for your body paragraphs. Be certain that all specific information supports your topic sentences.

1. Thrill-seeking activities
2. Television sitcoms
3. Sports
4. Movies
5. Pets
6. Summer jobs
7. Dates
8. Types of discipline
9. Phobias
10. Parties
11. Video games (technical, violent/action, humorous, nonviolent/action)
12. Digital cameras
13. Musical genres
14. Hairstyles (men's and women's)
15. Martial arts

Andrey Armyagov/Fotolia LLC

AP Photo/Richard Drew

Thomas Frey/imagebroker/Age Fotostock

© 2014 Wadsworth, Cengage Learning

☑ Writing Checklist for a Classification Essay

❏ Choose a topic that can be broken down into categories.

❏ Explore the topic and its categories using one or more of the prewriting techniques you have studied.

❏ Choose the categories to be used for the body paragraphs.

❏ Create the thesis sentence and essay map.

❏ Write your essay, remembering to use transitional expressions to create rhythm and sentence variety and to connect related ideas.

❏ Revise the first draft.

❏ Proofread the final draft.

❏ Print or type the essay and submit it.

CHAPTER REVIEW

■ In a classification essay, a large, complex topic is approached by breaking it into categories that the reader can easily grasp.

■ The six reporters' questions can be used to help develop the categories into which the topic is divided, and transitional expressions can identify the classifications.

■ In the five-paragraph classification essay, the introductory paragraph introduces the topic, states the categories that frame the discussion, and indicates the controlling idea and attitude. Each of the body paragraphs expands on one of the categories presented in the thesis sentence.

 ### Visit *The Write Start* Online!

For additional practice with the materials found in this chapter, visit our Student Companion Web site by going to cengagebrain.com and searching for this text. The Web site also features additional readings, quizzes, writing activities, and Internet links.

Pages 143–145: Judy Brady, "Why I Want a Wife." Originally published in *Ms. Magazine,* 1971. Reprinted by permission of the author.

The Process Essay

Have you ever had to explain how something works or how you did something? Perhaps you had to explain how to install a computer program or how you made chocolate fudge. Think about how you would explain these activities in writing. You would have to describe a step-by-step **process** to develop these topics.

Identifying Your Purpose

Explaining the steps involved in completing an operation, a procedure, or an event is called process writing. Process is an important method in developing ideas, especially for science, history, sports, medicine, and business. In a science class, you might be assigned to explain how you did a specific experiment. In a history class, you might have to explain how a historical event

UniversalImagesGroup/Getty Images

Jeff Randall/Lifesize/Getty Images

ERIC FEFERBERG/AFP/Getty Images

© 2014 Wadsworth, Cengage Learning

Write a process essay about one of the preceding activities. Consider the order of each step in the process prior to writing.

happened. In a business class, you might have to explain how a product's advertising campaign was carried out. All of these writing situations involve explaining a process. The following paragraph outlines some steps necessary to the process of becoming a better college student.

Example

In order to use time more effectively, the student should buy a schedule planner. Write the subjects for each day in the planner, and then add the time it will take to study each subject per day. Studying immediately after class can be an effective method for remembering information because it already is fresh in the mind. Do not forget to schedule a 15- to 20-minute break between studying each subject, or take a break if a particular problem or passage is difficult to understand. Studying a topic should be scheduled well in advance of the class in which it is supposed to be discussed. This allows for time to think about the assignment and formalize answers to the questions the instructor might ask. It also allows for time to prepare questions for the instructor about material not understood.

PRACTICE 1 — Drafting a Process Paragraph

Write a paragraph explaining, step by step, how one of the following activities is accomplished.

- fix a meal
- study for a test
- plant a garden
- purchase a car
- plan a party

Directional Process

There are two methods to develop a topic using process: directional and informational. **Directional process** explains how to do something: how to bake a cake, how to tune a car engine, or how to write a process essay. The intent, or goal, of directional process writing is to enable the readers to do something, to **duplicate a process**, after they have followed the directions. Recipes, assembly instructions, how-to books, and manuals are all examples of directional process writing. The following directional process paragraph explains, in part, how to plan for an inexpensive vacation.

Example

Setting a budget not only helps when planning a trip but can help to save money. Decide how much money is available, and plan the trip around places fitting the budget. Once the budget is set, look on the Internet for sites offering discounts on travel/hotel packages. If suitable package deals are not available, call hotels in the area. Inquire about seasonal discounts. Discounted tickets for events and places of interest usually are available for cities promoting tourism. Also, stop by travel agencies for brochures on the locations and other discounted packages.

Anyone planning a trip can duplicate the preceding process, adapting it as needed.

Informational Process

Informational process explains how something was made, how an event occurred, or how something works: how a treaty between two or more countries was finalized, how the Panama Canal was built, or how an industrial laser is used in medical procedures. After reading informational process writing, readers should **understand a process**, but they usually do not repeat it. *Duplication is not the intent of informational process as it is for directional process.* After all, you might understand how the Panama Canal was built, but you would never be able to duplicate its construction. Look at the following informational process paragraph that describes the process a patient suffering from gastroesophageal reflux disease (GERD) must undergo to determine if surgery is necessary.

> **Example**
>
> When the doctor suggests that an operation is necessary, a GERD sufferer may be referred to a gastroenterologist or gastrointestinal surgeon. The patient will undergo a series of upper gastrointestinal X-rays that involve swallowing a chalky substance called barium and watching the substance go down the esophagus into the stomach for diagnosis of a hiatal hernia that may demonstrate gastroesophageal reflux. The specialist may recommend endoscopy, wherein a small tube with a microscopic camera attached to the end is placed into the esophagus, helping the doctor visualize the damage done to the lining of the esophagus by gastric juices. If GERD is confirmed, the surgeon will help the patient make the decision whether or not to have the surgery.

Obviously, readers can understand the process in the preceding paragraph. However, they certainly could not duplicate it, nor should they want to!

Writing a Process Paragraph

A process paragraph introduces the process under discussion and outlines the steps in the process. Transitional expressions relate the steps in the process to one another to help connect ideas, so the steps do not seem to be merely an uncoordinated list.

The Topic Sentence in a Process Paragraph

Directional and informational process paragraphs begin with a topic sentence clearly stating what the reader should be able to do or to understand after reading the steps of the process. The topic sentence also should point out why the process is important. Read the following topic sentence for an informational process paragraph.

> **Example**
>
> A series of dubious events led to the outbreak of the Spanish-American War.

The entire paragraph might read this way.

> A series of dubious events led to the outbreak of the Spanish-American War. Cubans had long attempted to overthrow Spanish rule in their country. The rebellion began in 1885 and lasted for many years. William Randolph Hearst, owner of the *New York Journal*, falsely reported on the war; his reporters made the conflict seem as if the Spanish were massacring the Cubans. Such propaganda caused a wave of anti-Spain feelings to sweep across America. In late February 1898, the American vessel *Maine*, sent to Cuba to protect American people and property, blew up in Havana harbor, killing more than 260 people. Consequently, Americans instantly assumed that the Spanish had blown up the *Maine* by means of a submarine. War frenzy broke out in the United States, and Americans wanted war more than ever. "To hell with Spain, remember the *Maine*!" was a popular chant shouted by war enthusiasts.

In the preceding example, the process that led to the Spanish-American War is as follows: the Cubans rebel against the Spanish, the *New York Journal* prints false reports of the treatment of Cuban rebels by the Spanish, the vessel *Maine* is sent to Havana, the *Maine* blows up, Americans think the Spanish are responsible. All of these steps eventually led to the war between Spain and the United States. The reason the writer thinks the topic is important is expressed in the word *dubious*. This attitude suggests that some of the events that led to the war were less than genuine. The writer uses words such as *falsely*, *propaganda*, and *frenzy* to suggest that Americans were, in many ways, tricked into their anti-Spain attitude.

Organizing the Process Paragraph

Directional and informational process paragraphs are developed according to the order in which the steps of the process occur. Sticking to chronological order avoids confusion. For example, in describing how to save information to a travel drive using a computer, you would not give the instructions as suggested in the list on the left; rather, you would follow the chronological order as listed on the right.

Wrong

1. Click on the Save icon
2. Move cursor to down arrow
3. Click on "Travel Drive (A:)"
4. Move cursor to "Save As"
5. Open Menu by clicking on arrow
6. Click on File icon

Right

1. Click on the File icon
2. Move cursor to "Save As"
3. Click on "Save As"
4. Open Menu by clicking on arrow
5. Click on "Travel Drive (A:)"
6. Click on the Save icon

PRACTICE 2   Organizing and Rewriting a Process Paragraph

Using the paragraph you wrote for Practice 1, go through the paragraph and make a numbered list of the steps in the process. Are they out of chronological order? Are any important steps missing? If so, rewrite the paragraph so

EDITING

that all relevant steps are included in the proper chronological order. If your paragraph for Practice 1 did not need to be rewritten, choose another of the topics from Practice 1, create a numbered list of relevant steps in the process, and write a paragraph following the correct chronological order for the steps.

Transitional Expressions: Connecting the Steps

Once you have the steps of your process in the correct order, you have to connect them so that they follow each other smoothly. Using transitional expressions will help you connect the steps of the process, and they will announce to the reader that a step is forthcoming. Of course, transitional expressions will also add rhythm to the paragraph, making it easier to read.

Transitional Expressions for Process

afterwards	before	initially	to begin
as	begin by	later	until
as soon as	during	meanwhile	upon
at first	finally	next	when
at last	first, second	now	while
at this point	following	then	

PRACTICE 3 Adding Transitional Expressions to a Process Paragraph

BUILDING

Using the paragraph you wrote for Practice 1, add at least three appropriate transitional expressions. When you have finished, compare the two paragraphs. The paragraph containing the transitional expressions should be easier to understand and easier to read.

Moving from Paragraph to Essay

Now that you have studied and practiced the techniques to create effective process paragraphs, it is time to expand your ideas to a larger writing unit: the process essay. Using the prewriting and writing techniques you learned in Part One regarding developing the essay paragraphs and the process techniques you have just learned, you can write a process essay. This might be a good time to return to Part One and review the techniques for developing the full essay.

Creating the Introductory Paragraph

Because process writing uses chronological order to organize its development, writers sometimes think that they need not be concerned about overall organization and focus. But a process essay is writing, and all writing has a specific purpose. The thesis sentence in a process essay should state the essay's overall purpose, the writer's attitude toward the topic, and the organizational structure.

The thesis for directional and informational process essays should blend naturally into the introductory paragraph. The following example of an introductory paragraph was written by a student for a directional process essay. You will see the full essay a bit later in this chapter. Notice how the thesis statement announces the topic (*taking photographs using a digital camera*), the writer's combined attitude and controlling idea about the topic (*certain steps are necessary to make the process successful*), and the essay map containing the body paragraph subtopics (*how to take a picture, viewing the images taken,* and *downloading and saving the images to a computer*). The thesis sentence in the example is underlined for identification purposes.

> **Example**
>
> Using a traditional film camera can be tricky and require a lot of technical know-how that takes years to learn. In addition, developing photographs requires an expensive and space cluttering darkroom filled with equipment and chemicals. Today, with the invention of the digital camera, much of this expertise, equipment, and space is no longer needed to take quality photographs. Anyone who owns a computer can produce photographs—and even send them via the Internet—relatively easily. But first, it's necessary to master the digital camera to shoot photographs. Within a few minutes, sharp, quality photographs can be a reality—and without the expense of film and developing. <u>Taking photographs successfully using a digital camera depends on having a basic knowledge of how to take a picture, viewing the images taken, and downloading and saving the images to a computer.</u>

This essay will continue by developing each of the subtopics in the body paragraphs as outlined in the essay map. Using the thesis sentence with the essay map makes the content and organizational structure clear for both writer and reader.

PRACTICE 4 — Writing a Thesis Sentence for a Process Paragraph

Create a thesis sentence with an attitude, a controlling idea, and a three-item essay map using the topic idea in the paragraph you wrote for Practice 3. Make certain that the three essay map items you choose are suitable for developing the topic as the controlling idea and attitude suggest. (See "The Attitude in the Thesis Sentence" and "The Controlling Idea in the Thesis Sentence" in Chapter 4 if you need to review this information.)

Creating the Body Paragraphs

For a paper on the topic of *creating a successful photograph using a digital camera*, the focus of the body paragraphs will be the topics listed in the thesis sentence's essay map.

- The first body paragraph's topic will be *how to take a picture.*
- The second body paragraph's topic will be *viewing images taken.*
- The third body paragraph's topic will be *downloading and saving the images to a computer.*
- Your focus should not be on film speed, types of cameras, or lighting equipment.

Keep the focus on the attitude and the controlling idea: the steps necessary *to make taking digital photographs easier.*

Creating the Concluding Paragraph

The approach of the concluding paragraph should flow naturally from the essay's main topic. Because the essay's focus is the steps necessary to make taking digital photographs easier, an *evaluation* of the importance of the essay's subject seems appropriate. You might mention that photographic equipment and supplies such as scanners, portable wallets, and memory drives can help the digital photographer. You might remind the readers that they probably will put a lot of time and thought into the photographs they are taking, so care and patience during the shoot is critical. (Refer to Chapter 6 for other approaches for concluding paragraphs.)

Sample Directional Process Student Essay: USING A DIGITAL CAMERA SUCCESSFULLY

Jocilyn Jimenez

> Photography is a popular activity for millions of people. But with today's automatic cameras that promise to do everything but ensure a smile on the subject's face, there comes a price. The photographs taken with these technological marvels do not always live up to the expectations of the amateur picture-taker. In this essay, "Using a Digital Camera Successfully," student writer Jocilyn Jimenez explains how to produce quality photographs using a digital camera. She uses many transitional expressions to help connect relevant ideas and keep the steps in the process in chronological order.

Vocabulary

Before starting to read, use a dictionary to look up the definitions of the following words appearing in the essay.

adept (5)	designated (4)	engaged (2)
enhance (5)	expertise (1)	initially (3)
port (4)	scrolling (3)	sufficient (2)

Using a Digital Camera Successfully

1 Using a traditional film camera can be tricky and require a lot of technical know-how that takes years to learn. In addition, developing photographs requires an expensive and space cluttering darkroom filled with equipment and chemicals. Today, with the invention of the digital camera, much of this expertise, equipment, and space is no longer needed to take quality photographs. Anyone who owns a computer can produce photographs—and even send them via the Internet—relatively easily. But first, it's necessary to master the digital camera to shoot photographs. Within a few minutes, sharp, quality photographs can be a reality—and without the expense of film and developing. Taking photographs successfully using a digital camera depends on having a basic knowledge of how to take a picture, viewing the images taken, and downloading and saving the images to a computer.

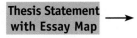

2 Before a picture can be taken, the digital camera must be set properly. Digital cameras do not use film; instead, they use a "smart disk" to hold

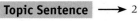

images. First, check to make certain that a smart disk is in the camera. Second, remove the LENS CAP. Next, turn the "ON/OFF" dial so it points at the "REC" dot, and press the "ON" button in the middle of the dial. Now, a picture can be taken. However, if there is not sufficient light, the flash can be engaged. Release the flash by pressing the "FLASH LEVER," usually located on either side of the lens barrel. Then, for a close-up, the ZOOM feature can be engaged. Usually the zoom is engaged by pressing a small button near the picture-taking button on the top of the camera. Now, point and shoot! It's that easy.

Topic Sentence ⟶ 3   Images can be viewed right on the camera, so a decision can be made about whether or not to keep them. That's one of the exciting features of the digital camera—no wasted film, and no paying for prints that don't turn out well for whatever reason. Initially, set the on/off dial to "PLAY." The stored images will then be shown, starting with the first image taken and scrolling to the last. Second, scroll through the images by pressing the "+" or "-" buttons. To DELETE an image, scroll until the image appears in the monitor window. Next, press the red "DELETE" button. A menu will appear asking whether or not the image is to be deleted. Press "OK" if you want to erase the image, and simply press the "DELETE" button a second time if you decide to keep the Image. Again, it's that easy.

Topic Sentence ⟶ 4   Finally, saving the images is a simple matter of downloading them to a computer. Find the IMAGE TRANSFERRING CABLE, and plug it into the designated port on the digital camera. Then, connect the other end to the proper port on the computer. Next, set the camera "ON/OFF" button to "PLAY." The system is ready to transfer images. Remember to keep the LENS CAP *on*. The system will not download if the cap is off. Now, from the START menu, select PROGRAMS. Click on "DOWNLOAD," and then select where you want to save the images. Usually, saving images to a disk or ZIP or to a DOCUMENT folder on the desktop is sufficient. Finally, click "SAVE," and the download process will begin.

5   Using the digital camera frequently, a photographer can create good but simple photographs. As the user becomes more adept, he or she can purchase many accessories to enhance the quality of the photographs. Programs that crop, frame, border, and add/delete background can be bought at almost any camera shop or on the Internet. Eventually, the user might want to buy a scanner, a portable memory drive, a creative filter system, a high performance transfer cable, a fisheye converter, and a portable digital wallet storage unit. While expensive, accessories can make photography a fun, creative, and rewarding activity. Lastly, while accessories can enhance the quality and ease of photographic development, time and patience during the shoot is critical. All the advanced technology in the world can't make up for a head out-of-frame or subjects with their eyes closed!

Process Technique Questions

1. What are the major steps in the process? List them on the lines following.

_____

_____

_____

2. Identify some of the transitional expressions the writer uses. How do they help organize the steps chronologically?

_____

_____

_____

_____

3. Identify any steps that, in your opinion, were not clearly expressed or needed more explanation. Can you suggest any additional information that would make the process clearer and more understandable?

_____

_____

Critical Reading and Thinking Questions

1. Which of the steps is explained in the most detail? Why do you think the writer chose to focus more on that step than on the others? Did this add or detract from the essay's effectiveness? Explain.

_____

_____

_____

_____

2. What is the main idea of the essay?

_____

_____

3. Does the information in the concluding paragraph make you want to run out and buy a digital camera, or does it make you leery of doing such a thing? Explain.

_____

_____

_____

Process Writing Exercises

1. Write a directional or informational process paragraph about a popular or unusual hobby. If directional, be certain to provide readers with steps to ensure their being able to duplicate the process. If informational, be

certain that the steps in the process allow readers to understand how the process was completed.

2. Now, expand the paragraph you wrote for Exercise 1 and write a full essay. Before writing, make a list of the steps in the hobby and put them in chronological order. Be sure to add appropriate transitional expressions to help order the steps, create rhythm, and create sentence variety.

Sample Informational Process Student Essay: HOW TO BE SUCCESSFUL AT KICKING THE SMOKING HABIT

Stephany K. Higgs

With the advent of so many advances in medical technology, the negative effects of smoking have been known for a long time. The depth and breadth of smoking's short- and long-term effects on the body, and even fetuses in the womb, have caused millions to quit the habit and prevented millions more from beginning the activity in the first place. Yet despite educational programs, the surgeon general's warning on each pack of cigarettes, and continual public service announcements in all the media, millions more find it next to impossible to kick the habit. In this essay, "How to Be Successful at Kicking the Smoking Habit," student writer Stephany K. Higgs outlines the steps necessary to stop smoking. Notice how she mixes both tangible activities that can help the smoker quit with the psychological motivations that must be understood to make the process of quitting effective.

Vocabulary

Before you begin reading, use a dictionary to look up the definitions for the following words appearing in the essay.

cessation (3)	cravings (2)	designated (4)
empowered (2)	induced (3)	resolve (1)
skepticism (3)	tenacity (1)	

How to Be Successful at Kicking the Smoking Habit

1   On New Year's Eve, millions of people resolve to quit smoking during the upcoming year. Unfortunately, many people fail before they even get started because smoking is both a physical and psychological addiction. Quitting will require commitment and tenacity. Quitting smoking can be done if smokers explore the reasons why they smoke, develop a plan with a method for stopping smoking, and obtain support from friends and family.

2   People smoke for many reasons; therefore, it is important for smokers to identify the reasons why they smoke. Analyzing the origin of the habit is the first positive step toward kicking the habit. For most people, smoking is a learned behavior; consequently, smokers tend to come from families where one or more of their parents were smokers. The majority of them are anxious people who started smoking because it seemed to provide a temporary release from current or future distress and uncertainties. Some tobacco users

Thesis Statement with Essay Map →

Topic Sentence →

started smoking to be cool and to fit in with the crowd; moreover, others started smoking because they enjoyed the taste of tobacco upon trying it out. While others did not necessarily enjoy the act of smoking, they felt addicted to the nicotine and needed to continue to satisfy their cravings. Now, with the origin of the habit exposed, the smoker is empowered with the knowledge of why he or she smokes and can seek out healthier alternatives to satisfy needs.

Topic Sentence ⟶ 3 Developing a plan with a method for cessation of smoking is the next important step. There are many products on the market today, available with or without prescription, which can be helpful to the smoker trying to quit. Smokers need to decide which method would be most effective for them; some methods are more costly than others although not necessarily more effective. Nicotine patches, gum, and tablets are some of the many aids available to the smoker. Therefore, discussing these aids with the smoker's physician, friends, family, and co-workers can be helpful in stopping the habit because many of them have knowledge, either directly or indirectly, about these products and how they have worked for themselves and/or friends and loved ones. Alternative methods such as hypnotism and sleep-induced behavior modification have been viewed with skepticism by the medical community and should be approached with caution and research by the smoker. Once smokers choose a method they believe will work best for them, it is important to make the commitment to stay with it. Additionally, smokers must realize there will be times when they will feel the method is not working. There will be times when they will fall off the quit-smoking-wagon and will need to climb back on again. If they expect this and have a plan to handle the climb back up, they can reach their goal.

Topic Sentence ⟶ 4 Receiving support from friends, family, and co-workers in the effort to quit smoking can be one of the deciding factors in whether or not a smoker will stop smoking and remain smoke free. Letting those closest to the smoker know that the smoker's intention is to quit smoking gives the smoker a support system. Finding someone who would also like to quit can be effective because the two can support each other by calling on one another when they feel weak in their effort to give up. Family members, friends, and co-workers should be sensitive to the ups and downs the smoker will experience by smoking only in designated areas until such time as the smoker feels strong enough to be around other smokers without joining them. Engaging the support of a former smoker can be helpful in getting smokers trying to quit over the rough spots.

5 On every package of cigarettes there is a warning by the Surgeon General: "Smoking Causes Lung Cancer, Heart Disease, Emphysema, and May Complicate Pregnancy." Health-related illnesses are the number one reason most people would like to quit smoking. Beyond that, it is a smelly, messy, and expensive addiction. Sadly, it is one of the hardest addictions to break. However, with determination and support, quitting smoking can be done, and succeeding greatly increases the chance for continued good health.

Process Technique Questions

1. Although the essay is informational, how many steps does the writer focus on in the process?

_____

_____

2. The writer does not use many transitional expressions as illustrated in this chapter. Point out some places in the essay where transitional expressions could be used. How would they make the essay more effective?

_____

_____

_____

Critical Reading and Thinking Questions

A N A L Y Z I N G

1. Why does the writer focus on smokers' motivations for smoking? Would it not be better to write a directional process essay so smokers could follow steps that would stop them from smoking? Explain.

_____

_____

_____

_____

2. The writer talks about a variety of "behavior modification" procedures and products that a smoker can use to help stop the habit. She also mentions consulting with a doctor and informing friends and family about the commitment to stop smoking. Why are these support mechanisms important?

_____

_____

_____

_____

_____

_____

_____

_____

Process Writing Exercises

1. Write an informational process paragraph about a hard-to-break habit or addiction. It can be about a dangerous addiction, such as to heroin or alcohol, or a seemingly benign one, such as being addicted to watching

W R I T I N G

soap operas or eating chocolate. Do not forget to create an attitude in the topic sentence that shows the importance of the process.

2. Now, write an informational essay about a habit or addiction. Expand your ideas by using one or more of the prewriting techniques you have studied. Remember, the intent of the informational process essay is to have the reader understand the process, not necessarily to be able to duplicate it or the results stemming from it.

Sample Professional Essay: CAT BATHING AS MARTIAL ART

Bud Herron

Not much is known about Bud Herron; in fact, surfing the Internet yields no information at all about this humorist. "Cat Bathing as Martial Art" can be found at many humor sites on the Web, but it was originally published in the *Franklin Daily Journal* (Indiana) in 1984. This rendition was found at lifestorywriting.com. This very funny essay is a good example of an informational process essay. While the essay is satirical and very humorous, especially for cat owners who have ever tried the futile and dangerous activity of the title, it is also carefully organized according to the steps in the process.

Vocabulary

Before you start to read, use a dictionary to look up the definitions for the following words appearing in the essay.

berserk (3)	contrary (2)	enzyme (1)
flak (4)	folklore (2)	latherings (8)
nonchalantly (6)	saliva (1)	

Cat Bathing as Martial Art

1   Some people say cats never have to be bathed. They say cats lick themselves clean. They say cats have a special enzyme of some sort in their saliva that works like new, improved Wisk—dislodging the dirt where it hides and whisking it away.

2   I've spent most of my life believing this folklore. Like most blind believers, I've been able to discount all the facts to the contrary: the kitty odors that lurk in the corners of the garage and dirt smudges that cling to the throw rug by the fireplace. The time comes, however, when a man must face reality, when he must look squarely in the face of massive public sentiment to the contrary and announce: "This cat smells like a port-a-potty on a hot day in Juarez." When that day arrives at your house, as it has at mine, I have some advice you might consider as you place your feline friend under your arm and head for the bathtub:

3   ■ Know that although the cat has the advantage of quickness and lack of concern for human life, you have the advantage of strength. Capitalize on that advantage by selecting the battlefield. Don't try to bathe him in an open area where he can force you to chase him. Pick a very small bathroom. If your bathroom is more than four feet square, I recommend that you get in the tub with the cat and close the sliding-glass doors as if you were about to take a shower. (A simple shower curtain will not do. A berserk cat can shred a three-ply rubber curtain quicker than a politician can shift positions.)

4   ■ Know that a cat has claws and will not hesitate to remove all the skin from your body. Your advantage here is that you are smart and know how to dress to protect yourself. I recommend canvas overalls tucked into high-top construction boots, a pair of steel-mesh gloves, an army helmet, a hockey face mask, and a long-sleeved flak jacket.

5   ■ Prepare everything in advance. There is no time to go out for a towel when you have a cat digging a hole in your flak jacket. Draw the water. Make sure the bottle of kitty shampoo is inside the glass enclosure. Make sure the towel can be reached, even if you are lying on your back in the water.

6   ■ Use the element of surprise. Pick up your cat nonchalantly, as if to simply carry him to his supper dish. (Cats will not usually notice your strange attire. They have little or no interest in fashion as a rule. If he does notice your garb, calmly explain that you are taking part in a product testing experiment for J. C. Penney.)

7   ■ Once you are inside the bathroom, speed is essential to survival. In a single liquid motion, shut the bathroom door, step into the tub enclosure, slide the glass door shut, dip the cat in the water, and squirt him with shampoo. You have begun one of the wildest 45 seconds of your life.

8   ■ Cats have no handles. Add the fact that he now has soapy fur, and the problem is radically compounded. Do not expect to hold on to him for more than two or three seconds at a time. When you have him, however, you must remember to give him another squirt of shampoo and rub like crazy. He'll then spring free and fall back into the water, thereby rinsing himself off. (The national record for cats is three latherings, so don't expect too much.)

9   ■ Next, the cat must be dried. Novice cat bathers always assume this part will be the most difficult, for humans generally are worn out at this point and the cat is just getting really determined. In fact, the drying is simple compared to what you have just been through. That's because by now the cat is semi-permanently affixed to your right leg. You simply pop the drain plug with your foot, reach for your towel and wait. (Occasionally, however, the cat will end up clinging to the top of your army helmet. If

this happens, the best thing you can do is to shake him loose and to encourage him toward your leg.) After all the water is drained from the tub, it is a simple matter to just reach down and dry the cat.

10   In a few days the cat will relax enough to be removed from your leg. He will usually have nothing to say for about three weeks and will spend a lot of time sitting with his back to you. He might even become psychoceramic and develop the fixed stare of a plaster figurine. You will be tempted to assume he is angry. This isn't usually the case. As a rule he is simply plotting ways to get through your defenses and injure you for life the next time you decide to give him a bath. But at least now he is clean.

Process Technique Questions

ANALYZING

1. Is the essay intended to be directional or informational?

_____

2. How many steps are explained?

_____

_____

_____

_____

_____

3. Identify any transitional expressions that are used. Do they help organize the information chronologically? Explain.

_____

_____

_____

_____

4. Would some transitional expressions be effective? Which ones would you add, and where would you place them? Do the bullets take the place of transitional expressions?

_____

_____

_____

Critical Reading and Thinking Questions

A N A L Y Z I N G

1. What process is being explained in the essay?

_____

_____

_____

2. Herron's humor is based largely on exaggeration (hyperbole). What examples in the essay do you find particularly effective and why?

_____

_____

_____

3. The title of the essay includes the phrase "Martial Art," but the activity is never mentioned in the text. How is bathing a cat like a martial art, and how do the owner and the cat resemble martial artists?

_____

_____

_____

Process Writing Exercises

W R I T I N G

1. Write an informational process paragraph describing an activity people do with pets. Make a list of the steps in the activity, and use transitional expressions to link them together.
2. Expand the ideas in the paragraph you wrote in Exercise 1. Write an informational process essay about the owner-pet activity. Expand your original list of steps by using one or more of the prewriting techniques you have studied. Remember to connect the steps using transitional expressions to create rhythm, order steps chronologically, and add sentence variety.

More Topics for a Process Essay

Here are some possible topics for directional and informational essay writing assignments. Remember, your process essay should have a clearly defined purpose.

1. How to repair a machine or appliance (for example, photocopier, lamp, toaster, radio)
2. How to act on a first date in order to guarantee a second date
3. How to preserve a food (for example, pickles, peaches, tomatoes)

H. Mark Weidman Photography/Alamy

4. How a camera works
5. How stars form (and/or die)
6. How a cure for a disease was discovered
7. How a bill is processed in a legislature
8. How to install computer hardware (for example, sound card, modem, or travel drive)
9. How to start a home-based business
10. How to propose marriage
11. How to appear trustworthy to others
12. How to protect the environment
13. How to establish good credit
14. How to be a good parent
15. How to prevent identity theft

☑ Writing Checklist for a Process Essay

☐ Choose a topic.

☐ Explore the topic using one or more of the prewriting techniques you have studied.

☐ Decide whether to write an informational or directional essay.

❏ Write a thesis sentence. Remember to include an attitude and a controlling idea.

❏ Choose as many of the steps in the process as you think will adequately develop the process and make it either duplicative (directional) or understandable (informational) for the reader.

❏ Include any tips or insights that will enable the reader to better comprehend the process you are describing.

❏ Write the essay, remembering to use transitional expressions to help the reader understand the order of the steps.

❏ Revise the first draft.

❏ Proofread the final draft.

❏ Print or type the essay and submit it.

CHAPTER REVIEW

■ A process essay explains how something happened, how to do or make something, or how something works. Directional process essays explain how to do something or make something, and their purpose is to enable the reader to duplicate the process. Informational process essays explain how something was done or made, and their purpose is to have the reader understand the process but not duplicate it.

■ In a process paragraph, the steps of the process are usually organized chronologically, and transitional expressions help keep the steps in sequence.

■ In a process essay, the introductory paragraph introduces the process, outlines the main steps, and explains the importance of the process. The body paragraphs develop the main steps in sequence. In the concluding paragraph, an evaluation of the process is a possible approach.

 ## Visit *The Write Start* Online!

For additional practice with the materials found in this chapter, visit our Student Companion Web site by going to cengagebrain.com and searching for this text. The Web site also features additional readings, quizzes, writing activities, and Internet links.

Pages 161–162: Howard (Bud) Herron, "Cat Bathing as Martial Art." First published in the *Franklin Daily Journal* (Indiana), 1984. Reprinted by permission of the author.

The Comparison or Contrast Essay

As your writing opportunities increase, often you will need to discuss an object, person, idea, event, or item not only in terms of its own features, but also in terms of how it relates to another object, person, idea, event, or item. This type of writing can be challenging because it forces you to think about each item independently of the other and then to think about how the items relate to each other. Are they alike? Are they different? How? Why? Developing a topic in this fashion is called **comparison or contrast**.

Write a contrast paragraph focusing on the differences between the two individuals in the preceding pictures. Also, at the end of your paragraph, comment on what you think each person does for a living.

Identifying Your Purpose

When using **comparison or contrast** to organize a paragraph or essay, you are looking for **similarities or differences**. When *comparing*, you are looking for similarities. When *contrasting*, you are looking for differences. For example, consider two computers.

In comparing them, you might notice

- the monitor screens both measure 14 inches
- the housings are made of a high-impact plastic
- the keyboards have all the same function keys
- the hard drives have the same information storage capacity

In contrasting them, however, you might notice

- one has a black housing, and the other has a blue one
- one has a combination battery and CD-ROM port, and the other does not
- one has a monitor and a CPU that stand separate from the keyboard, while the other system has the monitor, CPU, and keyboard self-contained in one housing

By comparing and contrasting, then, you know that both units are computers, but that one is a traditional desktop model while the other is a laptop. Comparison and contrast, therefore, helps you understand one person, place, feeling, idea, event, or object in relation to another. In other words, the comparison or contrast has purpose behind it. Look at the following two examples.

Example Comparison Paragraph

The occupations of cosmetologist and nurse may seem very different, but they share many common attributes. For instance, the cosmetologist makes the client's appearance better by using the proper grooming techniques. The nurse uses the latest medical procedures when treating a patient. A cosmetologist's client often feels depressed or anxious about his or her appearance. By using the coloring products appropriate to the client's complexion and age, the cosmetologist can change her appearance dramatically, making the client feel good about herself once again. The nurse makes the patient feel better by administering the proper medications or exercise appropriate for the patient's problem and age group. Both the cosmetologist and the nurse make people in their care feel better about themselves.

Even though the occupations of cosmetologist and nurse do not seem very similar on the surface, points of comparison can be found. Of course, there must be a purpose to the comparison, and in the preceding comparison, the fact that both the cosmetologist and the nurse make their patients feel better is the important consideration.

Example Contrast Paragraph

In the novel *Runaway Jury*, by John Grisham, the character development is superb because the writer alludes to certain aspects of the characters' personalities throughout the development of the plot. One of the strong points of this novel is that the reader is being fed only enough information about the characters at crucial times; therefore, a desire is created within the reader to know each character more intimately and to know how they will relate to the rest of the story. In contrast, *The Testament*, also by John Grisham, has a glaring lack of character development from the very beginning of the story. There is some confusion in the first few chapters as to who the main characters are. Instead of revealing the nature of each personality throughout the book, the author gives bland, generic, and brief descriptions of them. There also is an overabundance of characters who truly are not necessary to the development and enrichment of the plot, so the desire to know the characters better and to see how the plot relates to them is not achieved.

Although both novels are written by the same author and both novels involve lawyers and the law (John Grisham trademarks), the contrasts clearly are definable and important on several levels. First, if you are going to pay $24.95 for a novel, you certainly want its characters to be well developed and interesting. Secondly, on a technical level, you want to know that a writer you are considering investing time and money in is an accomplished artist who can bring his characters to life in a lively and compelling way that will hold your interest.

You might, at times, be called on to compare and contrast many people, places, events, or items. However, most of the time, you will be comparing or contrasting two items, and for the sake of simplicity, that is what you will learn how to do in this chapter.

PRACTICE 1   Compare or Contrast?

Look at the following pairs of topics. Indicate whether it would be better to compare or contrast each pair by putting a check mark in the space provided.

	Compare	Contrast
1. Fire and ice	_____	_____
2. Alaska and Arizona	_____	_____
3. Capitalism and communism	_____	_____
4. Men and women	_____	_____
5. Soccer and rugby	_____	_____

6. E-mail and snail mail   _____   _____

7. Swimming in a lake and swimming in a pool   _____   _____

8. Canoeing and kayaking   _____   _____

9. Thin-crust and deep-pan pizza   _____   _____

10. Being married and being single   _____   _____

Writing a Comparison or Contrast Paragraph

When you write a paragraph about two items, your first task is to decide whether to compare or contrast them. Once that is done, you can select the appropriate supporting details, write an appropriate topic sentence, and decide how to organize the points in your paragraph.

Deciding to Compare or to Contrast and Selecting Supporting Details

Sometimes, it will be obvious to you whether to compare or contrast two items. At other times, the similarities and differences may not jump out at you. After you have chosen your pair of topics to develop, what is the best method to use to help you decide if you should compare or contrast the two items? How will you know if there are enough elements between the two items to make comparing or contrasting them worthwhile? Creating a chart like the one in the following example is an easy method that helps you make such decisions.

Compare and Contrast Chart

Two items:

Humungous University	Tiny Town College

Similarities:

Great humanities departments	Exceptional fine arts
Faculty 90% PhDs	Faculty 85% PhDs
Computer-friendly campus	Each student receives laptop
In-state campus near home	Out of state but only 100 miles away

Differences:

All traditional sports teams	"Club" sports and intramurals
Federal and state financial aid	Private and government aid
50,000 students	5,000 students
Student/faculty ratio 30:1	Student/faculty ratio 11:1
Many graduate degrees	M.A. and M.F.A. degrees only

Once you have filled in the similarities and differences of the two items, it should become obvious which approach will result in the better paragraph. You will also be able to use the items in your list as supporting details as you develop the paragraph. So, using the chart can make developing your paragraph much easier.

PRACTICE 2   **Making a Compare and Contrast Chart**

Choose one of the topics from Practice 1 and complete a compare and contrast chart for it.

> **Compare and Contrast Chart**
>
> **Two items:**
>
> _____   _____
>
> **Similarities:**
>
> _____   _____
>
> _____   _____
>
> _____   _____
>
> **Differences:**
>
> _____   _____
>
> _____   _____
>
> _____   _____

The Topic Sentence in a Comparison or Contrast Paragraph

The topic sentence in a comparison or contrast paragraph clearly states the two items being developed and why comparing or contrasting them is important. The following is an example of a topic sentence for a comparison or contrast paragraph.

> When choosing between ice hockey and roller hockey for a child's participation, cost is usually the deciding factor.

This topic sentence clearly states the two items for comparison: ice hockey and roller hockey. The important reason for discussing the topic is the cost factor, which also indicates that contrast, not comparison, will be the method of development.

PRACTICE 3   **Writing a Topic Sentence**

Write a topic sentence for the subject you chose in Practice 1 and for which you completed a comparison and contrast chart in Practice 2.

Organizing a Comparison or Contrast Paragraph

Once you know whether you are comparing or contrasting and the supporting details you will use, you need to organize your thoughts and decide how to present them. There are two commonly used organizational plans for comparison and contrast paragraphs: block and point-by-point.

1. The *block method* presents all the information about one item first, then uses this information for comparison or contrast when presenting information about the second item.
2. The *point-by-point method* presents the information about both items together, creating an ongoing series of comparisons and contrasts.

In the following paragraph about ice hockey and roller hockey, the block method is used.

Block Method Example

When choosing between ice hockey and roller hockey for a child's participation, cost is usually the deciding factor. Playing roller hockey in small in-house leagues costs on average seventy-five dollars. If children show talent, they may play for a "select" tournament team, and the average cost will skyrocket to three hundred dollars. Equipment for roller hockey, although expensive, is necessary for protection against injury. Well-padded, durable skates can cost an average of two hundred dollars; helmets, on average, cost fifty dollars; and kneepads, girdle, and pants can cost one hundred and fifty dollars. This brings the total average cost of roller hockey to four hundred seventy-five dollars for an in-house league and seven hundred fifty dollars for a select tournament team. Ice hockey is considerably more expensive than roller hockey because more equipment is required. Playing ice hockey in an in-house league costs an average of three hundred fifty dollars, and playing for a select tournament team can cost six hundred dollars. As with roller hockey equipment, ice hockey equipment is expensive. In addition, ice hockey requires shoulder pads while roller hockey does not. The pads can cost upwards of seventy-five dollars. Also, ice hockey requires a thicker, heavier stick that can cost ninety to one hundred dollars. Ice hockey skates have an average cost of three hundred dollars, which is one hundred dollars more than roller hockey skates. Helmets, kneepads, girdle, and pants can cost two hundred to three hundred fifty dollars. The total average cost for playing ice hockey in an in-house league is nine hundred to twelve hundred dollars.

Notice that the cost elements of roller hockey are discussed in the first half of the paragraph (without mention of ice hockey). Then the same elements in regard to ice hockey are discussed in the second half of the paragraph. But this time as each ice hockey item is mentioned, reference is made to the corresponding roller hockey item as well. In this way, the comparison between the elements is continually made. If this were not done, then the two halves of the paragraph would seem disconnected, and the contrast would not exist.

The block method can be diagrammed in this manner.

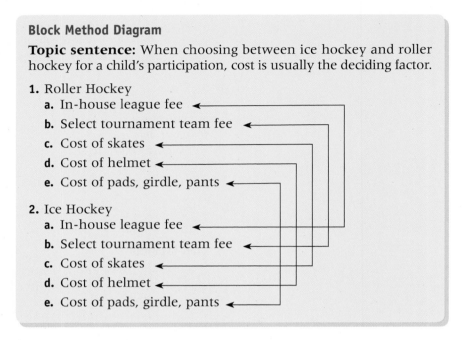

Block Method Diagram

Topic sentence: When choosing between ice hockey and roller hockey for a child's participation, cost is usually the deciding factor.

1. Roller Hockey
   a. In-house league fee
   b. Select tournament team fee
   c. Cost of skates
   d. Cost of helmet
   e. Cost of pads, girdle, pants
2. Ice Hockey
   a. In-house league fee
   b. Select tournament team fee
   c. Cost of skates
   d. Cost of helmet
   e. Cost of pads, girdle, pants

Remember, when using the block method, you discuss all the factors in the first item of comparison or contrast in the first part of the paragraph without mentioning the second item being compared or contrasted. Then, in the second half of the paragraph, you discuss each point regarding the second item in the comparison or contrast, remembering to make reference to each item that was mentioned in the first half of the paragraph. This will connect the two items so that the paragraph will not seem to be about two items that have nothing to do with one another.

In the point-by-point method, the similar point in regard to the second item in the comparison or contrast follows each point concerning the first item. The point-by-point method is diagrammed in this manner.

Point-by-Point Method Diagram

Topic sentence: When choosing between ice hockey and roller hockey for a child's participation, cost is usually the deciding factor.

First Point: a. Roller hockey in-league fee
                   b. Ice hockey in-league fee

Second Point: a. Roller hockey Select Tournament Team
                   b. Ice hockey Select Tournament Team

Third Point: a. Roller hockey skates
                   b. Ice hockey skates

Fourth Point: a. Roller hockey helmets
                   b. Ice hockey helmets

Fifth Point: a. Roller hockey pads, girdle, pants
                   b. Ice hockey pads, girdle, pants

For the point-by-point method, the paragraph contrasting ice hockey and roller hockey might be rewritten like this.

> **Point-by-Point Method Example**
>
> When choosing between ice hockey and roller hockey for a child's participation, cost is usually the deciding factor. When playing roller hockey in small in-house leagues, the average cost is seventy-five dollars. On the other hand, playing ice hockey in an in-house league costs an average of three hundred fifty dollars. If children show talent, they may play for a "select" tournament team, and the average roller hockey team cost will skyrocket to three hundred dollars. Whereas on a select ice hockey tournament team, the costs can soar to six hundred dollars. Equipment for roller hockey, although expensive, is necessary for protection against injury. Well-padded, durable roller hockey skates can cost an average of two hundred dollars, while ice hockey skates have an average cost of three hundred dollars and up. In roller hockey, helmets, on average, cost fifty dollars. Similarly, ice hockey helmets cost about fifty to sixty dollars. Knee pads, girdle, and pants for roller hockey can cost one hundred fifty dollars. However, ice hockey knee pads, girdle, and pants can cost two hundred to three hundred fifty dollars. In addition, ice hockey requires shoulder pads while roller hockey does not. The pads can cost upwards of seventy-five dollars. Also, ice hockey requires a thicker, heavier stick than does roller hockey, and the stick can cost ninety to one hundred dollars. In conclusion, the average cost for playing in a roller hockey in-house league is four hundred seventy-five dollars and nine hundred to twelve hundred dollars for playing in an ice hockey in-house league. While the cost for playing for a roller hockey select tournament team can rise to seven hundred fifty dollars, playing for an ice hockey select tournament team can be as much as fourteen hundred dollars.

PRACTICE 4   Writing Block and Point-by-Point Method Paragraphs

Using the topic sentence you wrote in Practice 3, write a comparison or contrast block method paragraph for the topic you have chosen. Then rewrite the paragraph using the point-by-point method.

Using Transitional Expressions to Connect Comparisons or Contrasts

Transitional expressions are important because they stress either comparison or contrast, depending on the type of paragraph you are writing. They also help keep the reader on track, because as we have seen, the organization of points in a comparison or contrast paragraph can be complex.

> **Transitional Expressions Showing Comparison**
>
> | | |
> | --- | --- |
> | and | in addition |
> | again | in the same way |
> | also | like |

as well as	likewise
both	neither
each	similarly
equally	similar to
furthermore	so
just as	the same
just like	too

Transitional Expressions Showing Contrast

although	on the contrary
but	on the other hand
despite	otherwise
different from	nevertheless
even though	still
except for	though
however	whereas
in contrast	while
instead	yet

PRACTICE 5   **Adding Transitional Expressions to a Comparison or Contrast Paragraph**

I B W E A
BUILDING

Add appropriate transitional expressions to one of the paragraphs you wrote for Practice 4. When you have finished, compare the two paragraphs. The paragraph with the transitional expressions should connect related ideas more effectively as well as add rhythm to the writing.

Moving from Paragraph to Essay

Now that you have studied and practiced the techniques to create effective comparison or contrast paragraphs, it is time to expand your ideas to a larger writing unit: the comparison or contrast essay. Using the techniques you learned in Part One regarding developing the essay paragraphs and the comparison or contrast techniques you have just learned enables you to write the comparison or contrast essay. This might be a good time to return to Part One and review the techniques for developing the full essay.

Creating the Introductory Paragraph

A comparison or contrast essay needs a clearly defined organization and a thesis sentence to announce to the reader just how the subject will be developed. The thesis sentence of the introductory paragraph should state the items to be compared or contrasted, the writer's attitude toward the topic, the controlling idea, and the organizational structure. By using an appropriate lead-in technique, the thesis should blend naturally into the rest of the introductory paragraph.

By using a variation of the compare and contrast chart you have already practiced to produce a comparison or contrast paragraph, you can extend and develop the ideas expressed in the chart to help you create the thesis sentence for a comparison and contrast essay.

Comparison and Contrast Essay Chart

Two items:

1. _____   2. _____

Attitude and controlling idea combined:

1. _____ (in relation to) 2. _____

Comparison and contrast points:

1. _____   _____

2. _____   _____

3. _____   _____

4. _____   _____

5. _____   _____

6. _____   _____

Thesis sentence:

_____

_____

_____

Once you have chosen your two items and have listed elements that are similar and different, choose whether you are going to compare or contrast the two topics. Next, decide on your attitude and controlling idea.

Then, choose the *three comparison or contrast points* from your list that you want to use in your essay. These will be the three subtopics for the essay map in your thesis sentence.

Finally, write the thesis sentence by following the elements you have listed in your chart.

Example

Two items:

   Sequoia Medical School   Oceana Medical School

Attitude and controlling idea combined:

   Sequoia Medical School is better than Oceana Medical School

---

Contrast points:

1. _____Faculty to student ratio_____

2. _____Tuition costs_____

3. _____Medical facilities_____

Thesis sentence:

Sequoia Medical School is better than Oceana Medical

School because of its faculty to student ratio, tuition costs,

and medical facilities.

Creating the Body Paragraphs

For an essay *contrasting two medical schools*, the focus of the body paragraphs will be the paragraph topics listed in the thesis sentence's essay map.

- The first body paragraph's topic will be *faculty to student ratio*.
- The second body paragraph's topic will be *tuition cost*.
- The third body paragraph's topic will be *medical facilities*.
- Your focus should be that these are the reasons *Sequoia Medical School is better than Oceana Medical School*.

You can develop each of the body paragraphs using either the block method or the point-by-point method, but be consistent in the method you use within a single essay.

Creating the Concluding Paragraph

The approach of the concluding paragraph should flow naturally from the essay's main topic. Because the essay's focus is that the characteristics of one medical school make it preferable to another, an *evaluation* of the main points seems appropriate. You might talk briefly about how the school's programs and features will help students gain acceptance to an area of medicine they want to specialize in or how these elements will help them grow both as a person and as a professional. You might even mention if the school has professional connections to private companies that might offer employment possibilities in research. (Refer to Chapter 6 for other approaches for concluding paragraphs.)

| PRACTICE 6 | Writing a Comparison or Contrast Essay |

Create a comparison or contrast essay chart for the topic you chose in Practice 4. After you have completed the chart, write your essay.

Sample Comparison Student Essay: COMMERCIAL VS. RESIDENTIAL REAL ESTATE SALES

Nancy Smith

Real estate sales is a popular and expanding job category. It may appear on the surface that selling commercial buildings and residential homes would be quite dissimilar. But in this essay, "Commercial vs. Residential Real Estate Sales," student writer and real estate agent Nancy Smith dispels the myth that commercial real estate sales is the more lucrative side of the business. While the essay is comparison, the writer does clarify an important difference. But by doing so, she in no way compromises the integrity of the essay's focus.

Vocabulary

Before you begin reading, use a dictionary to look up the definitions of the following words that appear in the essay.

applicant (1)	aspect (5)	commissions (4)
dwellings (3)	flexible (5)	flyers (2)
lack (4)	solicit (3)	striking (4)

Commercial vs. Residential Real Estate Sales

1 Thinking about a career in real estate? With the proper training and hard work, real estate can be a rewarding profession. Whether choosing commercial or residential sales, the decision can be easy when the applicant knows all the facts. Commercial and residential real estate are very similar in the areas of marketing, client development, and income potential.

Thesis Statement →

Topic Sentence →

2 The marketing costs for commercial real estate are paid by the real estate company; similarly, in residential real estate, costs are usually picked up by the real estate company as well. Like residential real estate agents, commercial real estate agents send out thousands of flyers that advertise property for lease or sale. For example, both commercial and residential agents announce available properties by mailing advertising brochures to area residents and to other agents. Both commercial and residential agents can act alone or share commissions with other agents when a property is sold, rented, or leased.

Topic Sentence →

3 Residential sales requires a lot of work to build up a good client base; likewise, commercial agents rely on repeat customers for fifty percent of their business. Commercial as well as residential agents also have to solicit business by "cold-calling" potential customers who may or may not be in the process of wanting to relocate. It might be surprising to find out that while businesses are looking for real estate for working space, many residential agents must provide the same characteristics for family dwellings. In families in which both parents work, "in home" office space is increasingly necessary.

Topic Sentence →

4 While there are many similarities between the two sales positions, there are some striking differences. The commercial agent usually has to make

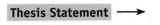

© 2014 Wadsworth, Cengage Learning

fewer sales to achieve the same commissions as does the residential agent. However, because more families relocate at any given time than do businesses, the residential agent can make up in volume what the average residential commission lacks in amount.

5   With a healthy economy and more people becoming skilled in the areas employers desire, the job market for both commercial and residential real estate agents is booming. And do not overlook the "people skills" aspect of both sales environments. Selling real estate, whether commercial or residential, is as much art as it is science. With the addition of flexible work scheduling and improved benefits, most agents are finding the world of real estate a profitable, rewarding, and fun career.

Comparison Technique Questions

1. How many points of similarity does the author use? Identify them. Is the amount enough to be convincing? Explain.

    _____

    _____

2. Although this is a comparison essay, the writer identifies a contrasting point in the last body paragraph. Why does the author provide the apparent difference?

    _____

    _____

    _____

3. What organizational pattern does the writer use, point-by-point or block?

    _____

Critical Reading and Thinking Questions

1. What is the main idea of the essay?

    _____

    _____

2. The real estate company does quite a bit to help each agent. But what personal attributes or "people skills" might an agent have to be successful?

    _____

    _____

3. Besides dedication, hard work, people skills, and industry support, what other condition must be present for a rewarding career as a real estate agent? Does this condition apply to other careers?

_____

_____

Comparison or Contrast Writing Exercises

1. Write a comparison or contrast paragraph about two jobs or two aspects of a job. Make a list of similarities and differences before deciding which paragraph to write.

2. Now, write a comparison or contrast essay following the comparison or contrast approach you used in the paragraph you wrote in Exercise 1. Use facts rather than opinion to correct a misconception that most people might have about some aspect of the job. Use the block method to organize your essay.

Sample Contrast Student Essay: TWO DIFFERENT NEIGHBORS

Tayde Cruz

> The United States and Mexico have been neighbors for over two centuries, both countries are democratic in their political makeup, and they share some economic fortunes with the North American Free Trade Agreement (NAFTA). Yet, in this essay, "Two Different Neighbors," student writer Tayde Cruz states that the two countries are not very similar at all. Born and raised in Mexico, Cruz moved to the United States with her family right after graduating from high school. She develops the essay around subtopics that are of interest to persons her age. Cruz believes that the United States is a better place for a long-term stay rather than a short-term visit.

Vocabulary

Before beginning to read, use a dictionary to look up the following words that appear in the essay.

advantages (1)	festive (3)	millennium (2)
optimistic (5)	pyramids (2)	severe (5)

Two Different Neighbors

1 Living in the United States means living in a country where there can be a good future for just about anybody; however, the United States is not the best place to vacation if the vacationer longs for activities going on all

day long, each day of the year. Mexico, on the other hand, doesn't necessarily have all the advantages of the United States when planning a future, but it has many advantages when it comes to planning a short-term vacation. In Mexico, activities begin early in the morning. For instance, there are breakfast places beside the hotel pool, so the visitor can combine swimming and pool activities with the first meal of the day. What a wake-up call! Mexico is a better vacation destination than the United States because of its historical sites, festive atmosphere, and low drinking age.

Thesis Statement →

Topic Sentence → 2   The United States has many historical sites but, in contrast to Mexico, these places are very young. For example, the Statue of Liberty is not even a century old. Another place to visit in the United States is Philadelphia. Philadelphia is an important city to visit because of its connection to the colonies winning independence from England two hundred years ago. On the other hand, in Mexico, the pyramids found at Tenochtitlan are at least a millennium old, predating the Liberty Bell by over eight hundred years. Despite its current modern architecture, Mexico City's political importance goes back to the early 16th century when the Aztec Empire fell and colonial rule was instituted by the Spanish conquerors.

Topic Sentence → 3   Festivals occur in the United States, mostly on specific weekends several times during the year. New Year's Eve happens on one night. While the evening is long and full of excitement, it is over rather quickly for such a momentous event. Mardi Gras is another popular festive event. Although it lasts for four or five days, the party is localized to one city, New Orleans. And, in the United States, fireworks are reserved for one night only, the Fourth of July. In Mexico, there's no need for a specific reason to celebrate. In Mexico, festive atmospheres are found all year long in almost any location, particularly on the coast. Puerto Vallarta has become known worldwide for its year round partying. Fireworks are exploded all year in Mexico to celebrate, well . . . anything!

Topic Sentence → 4   In most states in America, the legal drinking age is 21 years of age. Young people can die for their country in the armed forces or vote for president, but they have to wait three years to have an alcoholic drink. All summer long and during spring break on college campuses throughout the United States, young people flock to Mexico because the legal drinking age is eighteen years of age. Cancun, Mazatlan, Tijuana, and Acapulco are just a few of the cities young Americans visit to drink without worry of arrest while they celebrate graduations, a break from schoolwork, and any other rite of passage they can think of.

5   Mexico, in general, might not be the greatest place to live. It has severe financial problems, and its government is not always reliable in taking care of its citizens; whereas, it is a wonderful place to visit if only for a weekend. Mexico is a great place to get away to and forget about work, school, or the ordinary world that we all have to put up with. Still, no matter how poor Mexico's economy might be, it always has a festive and optimistic outlook on life. That is the true beauty of Mexico—its people!

Contrast Technique Questions

A N A L Y Z I N G

1. What is the writer contrasting in the essay?

_____

2. What organizational pattern does the writer use, point-by-point or block?

_____

3. Which transitional expressions does the writer use to move you smoothly from idea to idea?

_____

_____

_____

_____

Critical Reading and Thinking Questions

A N A L Y Z I N G

1. What is the main idea of the essay?

_____

_____

2. Does the writer use enough specific examples to develop and clarify the contrast? Explain.

_____

_____

_____

_____

_____

3. Although this is a contrast essay in regard to Mexico and the United States, what conclusion does the writer come to about the problems with the Mexican government and the Mexican economy and the Mexican people?

_____

_____

Comparison or Contrast Writing Exercises

W R I T I N G

1. Write a comparison or contrast paragraph about two places; they can be countries, states, regions, cities, or neighborhoods. Make a list of similarities and differences before deciding which paragraph to write.

2. Now, write a comparison or contrast essay following the approach you used in the paragraph in Exercise 1. Use personal observation rather than facts when writing the essay. Use the point-by-point method to organize your essay.

Sample Professional Essay: LIGHT SKIN VERSUS DARK

Charisse Jones

> The following essay, "Light Skin versus Dark," by Pulitzer Prize–winning *New York Times* journalist Charisse Jones, first appeared in *Glamour* magazine. In it, the author recounts a time during her high school years when she was first confronted with "colorism," a type of racism that she considers even more injurious because it comes from those of her own race. It is an unusual issue for whites because they are not confronted with this type of bias within their own race. In this regard, as you read the essay, try to decide what audience Jones is writing for, whites or blacks.

Vocabulary

Before you start reading, use a dictionary to look up the definitions of the following words that appear in the essay.

eradicated (13)	foil (13)	lexicon (4)
litany (10)	mantra (5)	notorious (6)
nuances (12)	reap (4)	smirking (2)
spectrum (8)	subtext (6)	synonymous (5)

Light Skin versus Dark

1 I'll never forget the day I was supposed to meet him. We had only spoken on the phone. But we got along so well, we couldn't wait to meet face-to-face. I took the bus from my high school to his for our blind date. While I nervously waited for him outside the school, one of his buddies came along, looked me over, and remarked that I was going to be a problem, because his friend didn't like dating anybody darker than himself.

2 When my mystery man—who was not especially good-looking—finally saw me, he took one look, uttered a hurried hello, then disappeared with his smirking friends. I had apparently been pronounced ugly on arrival and dismissed.

3 That happened nearly fifteen years ago. I'm thirty now, and the hurt and humiliation have long since faded. But the memory still lingers, reinforced in later years by other situations in which my skin color was judged by other African Americans—for example, at a cocktail party or a nightclub where light-skinned black women got all the attention.

4 A racist encounter hurts badly. But it does not equal the pain of "colorism"—being rejected by your own people because your skin is colored cocoa and not cream, ebony and not olive. On our scale of beauty, it is often the high yellows—in the lexicon of black America, those with light skin—whose looks reap the most attention. Traditionally, if someone was described that way, there was no need to say that person was good-looking. It was given that light was lovely. It was those of us with plain brown eyes and darker skin hues who had to prove ourselves.

5   I was twelve, and in my first year of junior high school in San Francisco, when I discovered dark brown was not supposed to be beautiful. At that age, boys suddenly became important, and so did your looks. But by that time— the late 1970s—black kids no longer believed in that sixties mantra, "Black is beautiful." Light skin, green eyes, and long, wavy hair were once again synonymous with beauty.

6   Colorism—and its subtext of self-hatred—began during slavery on plantations where white masters often favored the lighter-skinned blacks, many of whom were their own children. But though it began with whites, black people have kept colorism alive. In the past, many black sororities, fraternities, and other social organizations have been notorious for accepting only light-skinned members. Yes, some blacks have criticized their lighter-skinned peers. But most often in our history, a light complexion had been a passport to special treatment by both whites *and* blacks.

7   Some social circles are still defined by hue. Some African Americans, dark and light, prefer light-skinned mates so they can have a "pretty baby." And skin-lightening creams still sell, though they are now advertised as good for making blemishes fade rather than for lightening whole complexions.

8   In my family, color was never discussed, even though our spectrum was broad—my brother was very light; my sister and I, much darker. But in junior high school, I learned in a matter of weeks what had apparently been drummed into the heads of my black peers for most of their lives.

9   Realizing how crazy it all was, I became defiant, challenging friends when they made silly remarks. Still, there was no escaping the distinctions of color.

10   In my life, I have received a litany of twisted compliments from fellow blacks. "You're the prettiest dark-skinned girl I have ever seen" is one; "you're pretty for a dark girl" is another.

11   A light-complexioned girlfriend once remarked to me that dark-skinned people often don't take the time to groom themselves. As a journalist, I once interviewed a prominent black lawmaker who was light-skinned. He drew me into the shade of a tree while we talked because, he said, "I'm sure you don't want to get any darker."

12   Though some black people—like film-maker Spike Lee in his movie *School Daze*—have tried to provoke debate about colorism, it remains a painful topic many blacks would rather not confront. Yet there has been progress. In this age of Afrocentrism, many blacks revel in the nuances of the African American rainbow. Natural hairstyles and dreadlocks are in, and Theresa Randle, star of the hit film *Bad Boys*, is only one of several darker-skinned actresses noted for their beauty.

13   That gives me hope. People have told me that color biases among blacks run too deep ever to be eradicated. But I tell them that is the kind of attitude that allows colorism to persist. Meanwhile, I do what I can. When I notice that a friend dates only light-skinned women, I comment on it. If I hear that a movie follows the tired old scenario in which a light-skinned beauty is the love interest while a darker-skinned woman is the comic foil, the butt of "ugly" jokes, I don't go see it. Others can do the same.

14   There is only so much blacks can do about racism, because we need the cooperation of others to make it go away. But healing ourselves is within our control.

15   At least we can try. As a people we face enough pain without inflicting our own wounds. I believe any people that could survive slavery, that could disprove the lies that pronounced them less than human, can also teach its children that black is beautiful in all of its shades.

16   Loving ourselves should be an easy thing to do.

Comparison and Contrast Technique Questions

1. Is this a comparison or a contrast essay? Give examples.

_____

_____

_____

2. Is there a thesis sentence that clearly states the topic to be discussed? If so, identify it. If not, state what you think is the thesis of the essay.

_____

_____

_____

3. The title suggests the pair of items being contrasted. What other subtopics are contrasted or compared in the essay?

_____

_____

Critical Reading and Thinking Questions

1. How does the author distinguish between "colorism" and "racism"?

_____

_____

_____

2. The author believes that "colorism" is more harmful than "racism." Do you agree with her assessment? Explain.

_____

_____

_____

3. What examples in the essay point to the author writing for a black audience? What examples point to her writing for a white audience?

_____

_____

_____

_____

_____

Comparison or Contrast Writing Exercises

1. Write a comparison or contrast paragraph about a physical characteristic that can have a negative effect because it is not considered desirable or normal by society.
2. Now, write an essay comparing or contrasting two cultural attitudes about the physical characteristic you chose to write about in a paragraph in Exercise 1. Make a list of the negative and positive aspects of how the culture views the physical characteristic before you begin writing. Choose whether the block or the point-by-point method is the best way to organize and present the information.

More Topics for a Comparison or Contrast Essay

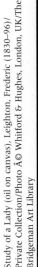

Study of a Lady (oil on canvas), Leighton, Frederic (1830–96)/ Private Collection/Photo Â© Whitford & Hughes, London, UK/The Bridgeman Art Library

Greek Police/HANDOUT/Reuters/Landov

Here are some possible topics for either comparison or contrast essay writing assignments. Remember, your comparison or contrast essay should have a clearly defined purpose.

1. Two pieces of art
2. A famous person's public image versus his or her private image
3. Two colleges
4. Two bosses or coworkers
5. Past attitudes about AIDS, lesbianism, or male homosexuality and attitudes today

6. A falsely held belief or myth and the factual reality
7. How people act in private versus public
8. How opinions have changed concerning a political issue
9. How people's thoughts about the future have changed
10. Employment opportunities in two states, countries, or regions
11. Two languages you speak or have studied (can include your native language)
12. Home schooling and traditional schooling
13. Two successful television programs (game shows, sitcoms, dramas, reality shows)
14. Two presidents of the United States or two world leaders
15. Two cultures (past or present)

☑ Writing Checklist for a Comparison or Contrast Essay

❏ Choose two things to compare or contrast.

❏ Make a list of similarities and differences using one or more of the prewriting techniques you have studied, or use a comparison and contrast chart.

❏ Choose whether you want to compare or contrast.

❏ Use the comparison and contrast chart to help write the thesis sentence.

❏ Choose either the block or point-by-point method to organize and present your ideas.

❏ Write the essay, using transitional expressions to connect related ideas, add rhythm, and add sentence variety.

❏ Revise the draft.

❏ Proofread the final essay.

❏ Print or type the essay and submit it.

CHAPTER REVIEW

■ When you compare two or more items, you are looking for similarities. When you contrast them, you are looking for differences.

■ When you write a comparison or contrast paragraph, you must first decide whether to compare or contrast the two items. In a comparison and contrast chart, you can list similarities and differences and so choose whether to compare or to contrast based on the strength of the details. The topic sentence of a comparison or contrast paragraph clearly states the items to be compared or contrasted and the controlling idea and attitude.

■ There are two basic methods for organizing a comparison or contrast paragraph. In the block method, you present all the information about one item first, and then use this information when you present information about the second item. In the point-by-point method, you present information about both items together, creating a series of comparisons or contrasts. Transitional expressions help make the organization of comparison and contrast paragraphs clear to the reader.

■ In the introductory paragraph of a comparison or contrast essay, the thesis sentence states the two items to be compared or contrasted, the controlling idea and attitude, and the subtopics that will be compared or contrasted. In the body paragraphs, either the block method or point-by-point method can be used to develop the subtopics. Finally, evaluation is a good approach to the concluding paragraph of a comparison or contrast essay because it allows you to express a judgment about the items you have been comparing or contrasting.

 Visit *The Write Start* Online!

For additional practice with the materials found in this chapter, visit our Student Companion Web site by going to cengagebrain.com and searching for this text. The Web site also features additional readings, quizzes, writing activities, and Internet links.

Pages 182–183: Charisse Jones, "Light Skin versus Dark." Originally published in *Glamour*, October 1995. Reprinted by permission of the author.

The Definition Essay

As you write, you may use concepts, terms, and words that you think your reader may not understand. You might use a term such as *black hole* or *macroeconomics*. Concepts such as *domino theory* or *Jungian psychology* may be foreign to your reader, so you may need to explain them so your reader fully understands what you are trying to communicate. Read the following short paragraph.

David Young-Wolff/PhotoEdit

Jamie McDonald/Getty Images

© 2014 Wadsworth, Cengage Learning

How we define the words we use to label the world around us can affect how we approach and interact with the world. Write two paragraphs: In paragraph 1, define the word "handicapped." Comment on how you think people see and treat people labeled "handicapped." In paragraph 2, define the term "physically challenged." Comment on how you think people see and treat people labeled "physically challenged."

> "Purple cows are purple cows because they are colored purple." The tautological reasoning embedded in the statement make its truthful wording obvious and unnecessary.

What is the paragraph trying to tell you? Is the meaning clear? Unless you know what *tautological* means, you probably will not understand the meaning of the paragraph. A better paragraph might look like this.

> "Purple cows are purple because they are colored purple." The statement contains all logical possibilities and, therefore, is always true. The statement, then, is a tautology, a needless repetition of the same, obvious concepts.

Defining the concept of *tautology* helps the reader understand why the statement regarding the purple cow is unnecessarily obvious and repetitive. The statement does not adequately explain why the cow is purple, just that it is—which is already obvious just by looking at it. A tautology, then, is considered circular reasoning.

Identifying Your Purpose

When we clearly explain the meaning of words, terms, and concepts, we are using **definition** as a method of communicating to the reader. There are two types of definition, **simple** and **extended**.

Simple Definition

Simple definitions are brief explanations such as those you might find in a dictionary. There are three types of simple definitions:

- **Synonym definition** defines a word by supplying another simpler word that means the same thing. For example, *conundrum* means *riddle* or *puzzle*, while *cacophony* means *noise*.
- **Class definition** defines a word by placing it in a broad category of similar things that readers will readily understand and then providing a specific detail that makes the original term or word different from the others in the class. For example, a *convertible* is a *car* with *a top that goes up and down*. In this definition, *convertible* is the term being defined. It is put into *a class of similar things—cars*—and then it is made different from other cars, such as sedans and coupes, because *it has a top that goes up and down*.
- **Definition by negation** begins by saying what a given word or term *is not* before saying what the word or term *actually is*. For example, a *bagel is not* just a doughnut-shaped piece of bread that is deep fried. A bagel is much more than that. It is actually *a unique type of bread that is boiled before it is baked*.

Definition is important because clear communication depends on clear understanding. Precise language is essential if you are to understand what someone else means. One word can have multiple meanings, so it is essential that you define terms for your reader.

PRACTICE 1 Writing Simple Definitions

Write a synonym, class, and negation definition for one of the following words: *freedom, rustic, malevolent, prude, shark, tomato, symbol, topography, simplicity.*

_____

_____

_____

_____

_____

_____

_____

_____

_____

Extended Definition

At times, terms such as *black hole, macroeconomics, domino theory*, and *Jungian psychology* cannot be adequately defined using a simple definition. Instead, you may need to use a few sentences or an entire paragraph or even an essay to define such terms, so they are understood clearly. This longer type of definition is called an **extended definition**. Extended definition can be accomplished by means of any one mode of development or any combination of the modes of development: description, narration, example, classification, process, comparison and contrast, and cause and effect.

Therefore, to help you define your term, you might

- describe some of its characteristics
- incorporate it into a story
- give some examples
- place it into a category
- explain its process (how it works)
- compare or contrast it to other things
- explain its causes or its effects

PRACTICE 2 Writing an Extended Definition

Write an extended definition for the word you chose in Practice 1.

_____

_____

_____

_____

_____

_____

_____

Writing an Extended Definition Paragraph

In an extended definition paragraph, you may use just one of the modes listed previously to develop your definition, or you may use as many modes in your paragraph as you find necessary. For example, if you were writing a simple definition for the term *soul music*, it might read as follows: *music relating to or characteristic of African American culture*. This definition, while informative, does not give the reader the full flavor of just how soul music represents a part of the American culture. An extended definition might expand on this idea.

> **Example**
>
> Soul music is a merging of gospel and blues, two African American musical styles. While blues praised the worldly desires of the flesh, gospel extolled the virtues of spirituality. This opposition of themes was melded into a wide-ranging and extremely diverse style, full of passions, pride, and optimism mixed with the historical emotion of pain and discrimination.

Developing a term or concept more fully allows readers to appreciate a broader set of ideas. It gives them a clearer understanding of the purpose and importance of the term or concept.

PRACTICE 3   Writing an Extended Definition Paragraph

Using one or more of the modes of development you have studied (description, example, compare or contrast, etc.), write an extended definition paragraph for a term from Practice 1 that you have not yet defined.

The Topic Sentence of an Extended Definition Paragraph

The topic sentence of an extended definition paragraph clearly states the term being defined, indicates the mode of development that will be used to define the term, and explains why defining the term is important. There are many reasons for supplying a reader with a definition and many types of terms you might need to define in your writing. Therefore, your topic sentence must clarify why you are defining a given term. For example, you may be defining

- a specialized term that is unfamiliar to most people, such as *quantum theory* or *eyelet cell transplant*
- an abstract term that can have a variety of meanings, such as *independence* or *responsibility*
- a concept that is often misunderstood, such as *free speech* or *Generation X*
- a new slang or cultural term, such as *extreme sports* or *anime*

Here is an example of a topic sentence for a definition paragraph about anabolic steroids.

> Anabolic steroids offer help in suppressing autoimmune diseases.

This topic sentence clearly states the term to be defined, *anabolic steroids*, and why it is important to define the term (*because they offer help in fighting disease*). It indicates the mode of development for defining the term, through examples of the types of diseases (autoimmune) they help to fight. The entire paragraph might read as follows.

> Anabolic steroids offer help in suppressing autoimmune diseases. Fortunately, modified steroids aid in Addison's disease by regulating fat, carbohydrate, and protein metabolism. To help overcome severe allergies and arthritis, adrenocorticotropic hormone is used as an anti-inflammatory to alleviate the symptoms. By taking prescription steroids, patients may enjoy life without having uncontrollable pains in joints as well as constant fatigue.

Using Transitional Expressions in Definition Paragraphs

Definition writing uses any and all modes of development, such as description, narration, example, classification, process, compare and contrast, and cause and effect. Therefore, you must decide how you are developing your definition as you write, and then you must use the appropriate transitional expressions to help connect related ideas and to add rhythm to your writing.

For example, the preceding paragraph regarding the use of anabolic steroids is defined primarily through example. If the writer used appropriate example transitional expressions, the paragraph might look like this.

> Anabolic steroids offer help in suppressing autoimmune diseases. **For example,** modified steroids aid in Addison's disease by **specifically** regulating fat, carbohydrate, and protein metabolism. To help overcome severe allergies and arthritis, for instance, adrenocorticotropic hormone is used as an anti-inflammatory to alleviate the symptoms. By taking prescription steroids, as a case in point, patients may enjoy life without having uncontrollable pains in joints as well as constant fatigue.

When the two paragraphs are compared, it is obvious that the one with the transitional expressions is easier to understand and easier to read because the examples are announced and the sentence variety adds rhythm to the writing.

After you have decided which mode of development to use for your definition essay, refer to the appropriate chapter in this textbook to find the list of transitional expressions for the mode you are using.

PRACTICE 4   Rewriting a Paragraph Using Transitional Expressions

Rewrite the paragraph you created for Practice 3. First, find the chapter dealing with the mode of development that you used in the paragraph. Second, select and add the appropriate transitional expressions to connect related ideas and to add rhythm to the paragraph. Finally, compare the two paragraphs when you have finished. The paragraph with the transitional expressions should be easier to understand and to read.

Moving from Paragraph to Essay

Now that you have studied and practiced the techniques to create effective definition paragraphs, it is time to expand your ideas to a larger writing unit: the definition essay. Using the techniques you learned in Part One regarding developing the essay paragraphs and the definition techniques you have just learned enables you to write the definition essay. This might be a good time to return to Part One and review the techniques for developing the full essay.

Creating the Introductory Paragraph

Like all essays, the definition essay needs a clearly defined organization at the beginning to announce to the reader just how the subject will be developed. The thesis sentence should state the item to be defined, the writer's attitude toward the topic, the controlling idea, and organizational structure. By using an appropriate lead-in technique, the thesis statement should blend naturally into the introductory paragraph.

For example, read the following introductory paragraph that would introduce the body paragraph regarding anabolic steroids you read earlier. The thesis sentence is underlined for identification purposes.

> Many believe anabolic steroids were developed to create the perfect superhuman. Searching for the perfect body eventually spawned a new breed of athlete; these athletes found steroids gave them more muscles and bulk, allowing them to enhance their performances. As time passed, athletes, in an effort to become even bigger and stronger, abused steroids. Because of this abuse, steroids have a bad reputation with the general public. However, steroids, when used properly for the right reasons, provide excellent health benefits. <u>The medical use of steroids is beneficial because they help fight autoimmune diseases, facilitate muscular development in patients with arm and leg immobility, and aid in the regeneration of dysfunctional organs.</u>

Creating the Body Paragraphs

Notice that the first item in the preceding essay map speaks to *steroids helping to fight autoimmune diseases*. As has been mentioned already, this essay would use example as its mode, or method, of developing the topic in the body paragraphs.

- The first body paragraph's topic would be how steroids *help fight autoimmune diseases*.
- The second body paragraph's topic would be how steroids *facilitate muscular development in patients with arm and leg immobility*.

- The third body paragraph's topic would be how steroids *aid in the regeneration of dysfunctional organs.*
- Your focus should be that steroid use *is beneficial.*
- Your focus should not be on the *harmful effects of steroid abuse* or on the *illegality* or the *cost* of steroids.

Keep your focus on the *beneficial* aspects of steroid use.

However, the essay about steroids could just as easily be written as a *process essay* that specifies *how steroids work* effectively to aid in the fight against disease, limb, and organ disabilities. The writer has the responsibility to choose the mode that best develops the topic.

For example, in the following paragraph regarding the definition of a "perfect store," the writer could have chosen to develop the topic through *example,* by giving examples of characteristics that define a perfect store, such as friendly employees, fast service, and fair pricing. But the writer chose to use process to define the perfect store.

> While shopping in a perfect store, customers are generally sold products at an inexpensive price. Shoppers are typically offered items that are clearly marked with price tags on each separate package. This allows customers to choose rapidly and easily the product that gives them the best buy. There are not any reasons to look for the price on the store shelf and then have to worry about whether or not the item matches the price tag. A perfect store not only honors its own sales coupons but also accepts other department store advertised prices and coupons. This gives the customers the convenience of shopping at one store instead of having to go to two or three. No matter what store shoppers patronize, these pricing policies offer them the opportunity to receive the best possible price.

Before deciding on which mode of development to use in the body paragraphs, you might try planning a paragraph using two or more modes. This technique can help you choose the mode that works best for the paragraph's topic. In other words, you might find that developing the topic *choosing a career* is clearer and more effective if you write it as an *example paragraph* rather than as a *compare or contrast paragraph.* In many definition essays, including the two sample student essays that follow, the writer uses a different mode (and sometimes combines modes) for each body paragraph.

PRACTICE 5   Rewrite a Definition Paragraph Using a New Mode

Rewrite the paragraph you wrote in Practice 4 using a different mode of development. Do not forget to use the transitional expressions appropriate to your new mode of development choice.

Creating the Concluding Paragraph

The approach of the concluding paragraph should flow naturally from the essay's main topic. Because the essay's focus is the beneficial use of steroids, a *warning* would seem an appropriate choice. Since the lead-in mentioned how some athletes abuse steroids in their search for more power and strength, you might mention some of the adverse effects that misusing steroids can have, such as brain tumors, cancer, and loss of bone mass. (Refer to Chapter 6 for other approaches for concluding paragraphs.)

Sample Definition Student Essay: THE PATCHWORK QUILT

Kathy Young

In this essay, "The Patchwork Quilt," by returning-learner Kathy Young, the author offers a sweet and nostalgic reminiscence about her children, now grown and moved away. Instead of using the first-person narrator "I" to tell her story, she uses the third-person narrator, as if someone else were watching her and telling her story to the reader. By doing so, she makes herself more of a character *in* the story rather than just a teller of the story.

Vocabulary
Before you begin reading, use a dictionary to look up the definitions of the following words that appear in the essay.

absorb (3)	awkward (3)	ballerina (3)
chronological (1)	dollops (2)	elegance (4)
impulsive (4)	peering (2)	raggedy (1)
rambunctious (2)	recipient (2)	stingy (3)

The Patchwork Quilt

1   She sat by the window and thought, "The older my child becomes, the faster time seems to pass for me, and the passage of time does not seem to be the same for her as it is for me. How unfair!" Longing to go back in time, she slowly opened the closet door. The stacks of old, raggedy, taped boxes, stored safely away on the top shelf, contained irreplaceable creations that played out like a movie of a child's life. Carefully, the pieces were pulled out one by one, and she laid them across every open space of the bedroom floor. As the pieces were neatly arranged in chronological order, a flood of memories raced through her mind as the child's art began to tell a story. The patchwork of stained-glass-like pieces spoke of her daughter's sparkling personality, displayed the path of the child growing into a young adult, and showed a youthful and innocent ignorance unfolding into mature knowledge.

2   Each piece, glowing like the sun and shimmering like the stars, reflected the child's identity. The pieces seemed to come alive and dance happily about the room without a care in the world. Peering closely, she could picture the rambunctious child hurrying to finish each project; consequently, the masterpieces appeared quite fluid, as if moving on their own. Before her eyes was a moving vision of the child hurrying about, as if there were so many more exciting treasures to be explored. The picture shone brightly in her mind like the light from a camera's flash. Most of the pieces captured the bubbling and

lively spirit born into the heart of this child. As the pieces glowed, the room was overtaken with a sense of the child's desire to please the recipient of the creations. The images displayed the unmistakable personality of the child: like a happy magnet, it would draw the images in, attaching its happy self to each one. Then, the colorful pieces attached themselves to each other like dollops of rain forming the intricate parts of a snowflake. They began to express a changing image reflecting the child's maturing spirit.

3   Because the multitude of pieces represented such a long journey, she became lost traveling down the endless line of memories echoing with bedtime giggles and late-night "talks"—those heart-to-heart confessions of self-realization. The early pieces, like a clumsy two-year old, seemed to struggle for coordination and balance. It was difficult to decide if the purple scribble was a tree or a self-portrait. Eventually, the pieces began to perform with the beauty of a ballerina gracefully dancing out a story. Moving forward, the maturing artist seemed to become stingy; the creations obviously focused more on pleasing the self rather than others. The once carefree soul, represented by unfinished summer-camp potholders and pictures of pink unicorns, began to evolve into a dramatic, confused, and awkward teenager. Albums appeared full of poems about love, pictures of Hollywood, teenage heartthrobs, and mysterious coded messages from girlfriends. The child's art had lost some of its innocent spirit, replaced by emotions that ran deeper and sometimes a bit darker.

4   As the years advanced, the creations began to unwrap themselves like a gift displaying an understanding and knowledge of the beauty of all the emotions of life. The once innocent and then impulsive imagination gathered itself into a complete quilt, all the pieces fitting together to form a whole. The mix-match of colors blended in shades of grace and layers of emotional elegance. The blobs of misshapen clay had been transformed into incredible pieces of pottery—both beautiful and functional. Colorful and playful crayon drawings gave way to delicate pencil sketches: clouds, flowers, a young man's hand; the young artist was learning new ways of expressing hidden emotions. The chipped, finger-painted clown face was exchanged for a waving field of wheat beneath a darkening blue-black sky. The journey into self was leading to unexpected locations.

5   As she replaced the pieces in their respective boxes and closed each lid, she quickly replayed the entire experience in her mind. The jiggle of the piggy bank. The reindeer ornament that reminded her of a time when Santa Claus was real. The box of seashells from a first vacation so full of the excitement and wonder. She sat on the bed, content to be frozen in time. Minutes and hours held little meaning for her now. Only years and years that seemed like minutes and hours. She took comfort in the memories that allowed her to still feel the warmth of a young girl's hug, and a kiss that was more rewarding than all the pennies in the world.

© 2014 Wadsworth, Cengage Learning

Definition Technique Questions

ANALYZING

1. What is the dominant mode of development the author uses for definition in the first body paragraph of the essay?

_____

_____

_____

2. What is the metaphor the author uses as she continues to define in the second body paragraph?

_____

_____

_____

_____

3. The essay's title is "The Patchwork Quilt." Why not just "The Quilt"? What is significant about the word "patchwork"? And, why a "quilt"? Why not a tile mosaic, or a jigsaw puzzle, or a collage?

_____

_____

_____

_____

_____

_____

_____

_____

_____

_____

Critical Reading and Thinking Questions

1. What do you think is the point of the story?

_____

_____

_____

_____

2. In paragraph 4, the author is staring at the memorabilia on the floor when she thinks to herself, "The mix-match of colors blended in shades of grace and layers of elegance." Obviously, she is not commenting on colors and layers in a stack. What do you think she is talking about?

_____

_____

I B W E A

A N A L Y Z I N G

_____

_____

3. In the second paragraph, the author defines some of the early pieces as "masterpieces." Obviously, they are not. Why do you think she refers to them as such?

_____

_____

_____

_____

_____

Definition Writing Exercises

1. Write a definition paragraph about a piece of memorabilia that is important to you. Use at least two modes of development to define it.
2. Now, write a definition essay using the object you defined in Exercise 1. However, in this essay, define the object as to its importance to someone else. To adequately expand the definition, use as many of the modes of development as you think necessary.

Sample Definition Student Essay: WHAT IS CHRISTIAN ROCK?

Mat McNeal

> In this essay, "What Is Christian Rock?" student writer Mat McNeal explores the characteristics that make Christian rock music different from other forms of rock. While the general category is *rock music*, the author narrows the definition by focusing on the specific, unique elements within Christian rock. Notice the use of technical terms and the use of more familiar examples as the definition unfolds.

Vocabulary
Before you begin reading, use a dictionary to look up the definitions of the following words that appear in the essay.

advocates (4)	blasphemy (3)	demonic (4)
enlightenment (2)	genre (3)	harmony (2)
interactive (1)	profanity (3)	symbolizing (2)
trinity (2)	vulnerable (1)	

What Is Christian Rock?

1   Teenagers and young adults seem to live in a world surrounded by music. At the same time, many are vulnerable to losing their faith. Worship leaders and pastors all around the world are seeking ways to attract more young adults to become interactive with their local church. Christian rock is one solution. Millions of people do not understand what Christian rock actually is. To do so is to understand its characteristics, to know its similarities and differences from mainstream rock, and to know how it influences listeners.

2   At first, Christian rock may sound like typical rock songs with guitars, basses, drum sets, and keyboards. However, there are slight differences. Christian rock comes in three forms: *contemporary, alternative*, and *worship*. The *contemporary* form falls along the lines of pop, pop-rock, ballads, country, rhythm and blues, folk, and southern gospel. This style is mostly polyphonic: the instruments and voices move independently of one another. These songs can have lyrics, or they can be purely instrumental. *Alternative* includes rock 'n' roll, heavy rock, punk, hip-hop, and rap. This form is mostly monophonic: the instruments and voices are performing exactly the same notes without a distinct accompanying melody or harmony. Finally, *worship* is a style combining both *contemporary* and *alternative* into songs of joy and enlightenment of God's glory. This form is more homophonic: the instruments and voices move together rhythmically even though there is a distinct melody with accompanying harmony. Harmonically, contrasting sounds dominate; consequently, the melodies of *contemporary* and *alternative* are difficult to sing along with until the lyrics are memorized. *Worship* melodies, on the other hand, are easy to sing along with. A majority of verses and choruses repeat three times, symbolizing the trinity of the Father, the Son, and the Holy Spirit.

3   Christian rock has other similarities and differences with other forms of popular music. Instrumentally, both styles use similar instruments and closely allied rhythms. Also, the vocal styles are comparable. For example, Christian singer and songwriter Paul Colman sounds similar to both Bono of U2 and John Mayer. Another Christian rock group, Building 429, sounds like Creed, Three Doors Down, and Lifehouse. However, lyrically, the songs they perform are like night and day. Christian rock lyrics are about God's love, religious enlightenment, and compassion for others; whereas, some other rock genres contain profanity, blasphemy, sexual content, and the promotion of drug use. Christian rock is not tolerant of the inclusion of such offensive elements into its praise of God's domain and purpose. For example, U2 started its career in the Christian rock family until Bono, during a Grammy Award acceptance speech, used profanity and, later, would not apologize for having done so. Since then, U2 music has been pulled from the shelves of Christian bookstores around the world.

4   In this day and age of strife and turmoil, Christian rock has many influences on people worldwide. The general reason for Christian rock's existence is to enlist young adults to live a Christian life. The concept comes from churches all around the world that are attempting to reach out to nonbelievers and also to reinforce Christian values to advocates. The outcomes have been proven in churches throughout the world; many are introducing a contemporary service which combines Christian rock and a sermon during the ministry. Many senior citizens believe that rock, even Christian rock, is demonic; therefore, some pastors allowing a contemporary rather than a traditional service are being impeached. This occurrence is astonishing because thousands of young adults are falling in love with the new style of ministry and are enjoying such services. To eliminate such services and the pastors who perform them might cause many young adults to turn away from the church and Christian ideals.

5   Even though there is some disagreement within churches about the contemporary service, it seems the future of Christian rock is promising. Perhaps, the traditional style will one day become a minority while most worshipers will favor the contemporary service. A younger audience of new believers mixed with the existing congregation could boost dramatically attendance at church services. But, more importantly, the mix of the old and the new, in both people and ministry, could solidify the Christian bonds that should unite all of us. Behind the music, Christians from around the world could come together and live in peace and the glow of God's love.

Ralf-Finn Hestoft/Redux

Definition Technique Questions

1. What is the dominant mode of development used in each of the body paragraphs?

_____

_____

_____

_____

_____

_____

2. The author uses three highly technical terms in the essay: homophonic, monophonic, and polyphonic. Do these terms help or hinder your understanding of his definition of Christian rock?

_____

_____

_____

_____

_____

_____

_____

Critical Reading and Thinking Questions

I B W E A

A N A L Y Z I N G

1. What is the main idea of the essay?

_____

_____

_____

_____

_____

_____

2. What problem do many traditional, older Christians have with the Christian rock as a religious element? Why does the author think this position is dangerous?

_____

_____

_____

3. Can you see any downside to the use of Christian rock to attract and hold young adults to Christian ideals?

_____

_____

_____

_____

_____

_____

_____

_____

Definition Writing Exercises

1. Write a definition paragraph about type of advertising or a marketing strategy aimed at young adults, and comment on why it is effective.
2. Now, write a definition essay using the advertising or marketing strategy you defined in Exercise 1. Use a variety of modes of development in the body paragraphs to expand the definition. Also, try defining by negation at least once in the essay.

Sample Professional Essay: I WAS A MEMBER OF THE KUNG FU CREW

Henry Xi Lau

> The author writes about Chinatown in New York City, one of the oldest such ethnic "ghettos" in the country. Although he writes about people and things as if he were still there, Lau was attending the prestigious Yale University at the time he wrote this essay. Look for the many definitions he uses to make his points and clarify his ideas.

Vocabulary

Meaning comes primarily from words. Before you start reading, use a dictionary to look up the meanings of the following words that appear in the essay.

amble (4)	articulate (10)	assessing (6)
asymmetrical (5)	augments (8)	bok choy (4)
crescent (2)	despaired (6)	gorge (11)
random (5)	stalemate (8)	sufficient (6)

In the essay, you will also encounter some Chinese terms:

kung fu is more than just a method of fighting. It is both a physical and mental discipline, a philosophy to help attain a considerate, healthy, and safe life.

sifu means "teacher" or "master" and is a term of honor and respect.

qigong means the skill of attracting vital energy. Its name comes from the Chinese (specifically Cantonese) *qi (chi,* "energy") and *gong (kung,* "skill"). *Qigong* is a self-healing art that combines movement and meditation.

I Was a Member of the Kung Fu Crew

1   Chinatown is ghetto, my friends are ghetto, I am ghetto. I went away to college last year, but I still have a long strand of hair that reaches past my chin. I need it when I go back home to hang with the K.F.C.—for Kung Fu Crew, not Kentucky Fried Chicken. We all met in a Northern Shaolin kung fu

class years ago. Our *si-fu* was Rocky. He told us: "In the early 1900s in China, your grand master was walking in the streets when a foreigner riding on a horse disrespected him. So then he felt the belly of the horse with his palms and left. Shortly thereafter, the horse buckled and died because our grand master had used *qi-gong* to mess up the horse's internal organs." Everyone said, "Cool, I would like to do that." Rocky emphasized, "You've got to practice really hard for a long time to reach that level."

2   By the time my friends and I were in the eighth grade, we were able to do 20-plus pushups on our knuckles and fingers. When we practiced our crescent, roundhouse and tornado kicks, we had 10-pound weights strapped to our legs. Someone once remarked, "Goddamn—that's a freaking mountain!" when he saw my thigh muscles in gym class.

3   Most Chinatown kids fall into a few general categories. There are pale-faced nerds who study all the time to get into the Ivies. There are the recent immigrants with uncombed hair and crooked teeth who sing karaoke in bars. There are the punks with highlighted hair who cut school, and the gangsters, whom everyone else avoids.

4   Then there is the K.F.C. We work hard like the nerds, but we identify with the punks. Now we are reunited, and just as in the old days we amble onto Canal Street, where we stick out above the older folks, elderly women bearing leaden bags of bok choy and oranges. As an opposing crew nears us, I assess them to determine whether to grill them or not. Grilling is the fine art of staring others down and trying to emerge victorious.

5   How the hair is worn is important in determining one's order on the streets. In the 80s, the dominant style was the mushroom cut, combed neatly or left wild in the front so that a person can appear menacing as he peers through his bangs. To gain an edge in grilling now, some kids have asymmetrical cuts, with long random strands sprouting in the front, sides or back. Some dye their hair blue or green, while blood red is usually reserved for gang members.

6   Only a few years ago, examination of the hair was sufficient. But now there is a second step: assessing pants. A couple of years ago, wide legs first appeared in New York City, and my friends and I switched from baggy pants. In the good old days, Merry-Go-Round in the Village sold wide legs for only $15 a pair. When Merry-Go-Round went bankrupt, Chinatown kids despaired. Wide-leg prices at other stores increased drastically as they became more popular. There are different ways of wearing wide legs. Some fold their pant legs inward and staple them at the hem. Some clip the back ends of their pants to their shoes with safety pins. Others simply cut the bottoms so that fuzzy strings hang out.

7   We grill the opposing punks. I untuck my long strand of hair so that it swings in front of my face. Nel used to have a strand, but he chewed it off one day in class by accident. Chu and Tom cut their strands off because it scared people at college. Jack has a patch of blond hair, while Tone's head is a ball of orange flame. Chi has gelled short hair, while Ken's head is a black mop. As a group, we have better hair than our rivals. But they beat us with their wide legs. In our year away at college, wide legs have gone beyond our 24-inch leg openings. Twenty-six- to 30-inch jeans are becoming the norm. If wide legs get any bigger, they will start flying up like a skirt in an updraft.

8   We have better accessories, though. Chi sports a red North Face that gives him a rugged mountain-climber look because of the jungle of straps sprouting in the back. Someone once asked Chi, "Why is the school bag so important to one's cool?" He responded, "Cuz it's the last thing others see when you walk away from them or when they turn back to look at you after you walk past them." But the other crew has female members, which augments their points. The encounter between us ends in a stalemate. But at least the K.F.C. members are in college and are not true punks.

9   In the afternoon, we decide to eat at the Chinatown McDonald's for a change instead of the Chinese bakery Maria's, our dear old hangout spot. "Mickey D's is good sit," Nel says. I answer: "But the Whopper gots more fat and meat. It's even got more bun." Nel agrees. "True that," he says. I want the Big Mac, but I buy the two-cheeseburger meal because it has the same amount of meat but costs less.

10   We sit and talk about ghettoness again. We can never exactly articulate what being ghetto entails, but we know the spirit of it. In Chinatown toilet facilities we sometimes find footprints on the seats because F.O.B. s (fresh off the boats) squat on them as they do over the holes in China. We see alternative brand names in stores like Dolo instead of Polo, and Mike instead of Nike.

11   We live by ghettoness. My friends and I walk from 80-something Street in Manhattan to the tip of the island to save a token. We gorge ourselves at Gray's Papaya because the hot dogs are 50 cents each. But one cannot be stingy all the time. We leave good tips at Chinese restaurants because our parents are waiters and waitresses, too.

12   We sit for a long time in McDonald's, making sure that there is at least a half-inch of soda in our cups so that when the staff wants to kick us out, we can claim that we are not finished yet. Jack positions a mouse bite of cheeseburger in the center of a wrapper to support our claim.

13   After a few hours, the K.F.C. prepares to disband. I get in one of the no-license commuter vans on Canal Street that will take me to Sunset Park in Brooklyn, where my family lives now. All of my friends will leave Chinatown, for the Upper East Side and the Lower East Side, Forest Hills in Queens and Bensonhurst in Brooklyn. We live far apart, but we always come back together in Chinatown. For most of us, our homes used to be here and our world was here.

Definition Technique Questions

ANALYZING

1. Point out an example of defining by classification. State the differences.

_____

_____

_____

_____

_____

_____

2. Although many Americans think of African Americans when they see or hear the term "ghetto," it is actually an Italian term most associated with European Jews during World War II. How does Lau use the term? Specifically comment on what he says in paragraphs 1, 10, and 11. Use specific examples from other paragraphs to support your answer.

_____

_____

_____

3. Point out an example of definition by negation.

_____

_____

_____

Critical Reading and Thinking Questions

1. What is the main idea of the essay?

_____

_____

_____

_____

2. Dialogue is used in paragraphs 8 and 9. How does this affect the essay?

_____

_____

_____

_____

_____

_____

3. With the exception of the dialogue in paragraphs 8 and 9, the essay is written in what is called Standard American English. Why do you think the author chose not to write it in a ghetto dialect?

_____

_____

_____

_____

_____

Definition Writing Exercises

1. Write a definition paragraph using a term that defines the group you hang with or are associated with. Use locations, activities, clothes, and other personal aspects (hair, tattoos, etc.) to help define the term.
2. Now, write a definition essay using the term you defined in Exercise 1. Use a variety of modes of development in your essay to expand the definition. Also, try to define by negation in one of the body paragraphs where appropriate.

More Topics for a Definition Essay

Kirsty McLaren/Alamy

Here are some possible topics for extended definition essay writing assignments. Remember, your definition essay should have a clearly defined purpose.

1. Reality television programs
2. Pornography
3. Democracy
4. Heroism or cowardice
5. Talk show
6. Success or failure
7. A fanatic
8. Stand-up comedian
9. A new term from an extreme sport
10. The perfect sandwich (or pizza, dessert, barbecue, etc.)
11. "Life, liberty, and the pursuit of happiness"
12. A slang term
13. A bully
14. Family values
15. Political correctness

☑ Writing Checklist for a Definition Essay

❑   Choose a concept, term, or word to define.

❑   Write simple definitions for the topic: synonym definition, class definition, and definition by negation. Consult a dictionary or other references if necessary.

❑   Explore other definitions used by specific groups or by society as a whole. Use one or more of the prewriting techniques you have studied.

❑   Define your purpose by writing a thesis sentence.

❑   Choose which mode or modes of development you want to use to define the topic.

❑   Draft the essay, remembering to use transitional expressions as needed.

❑   Revise the first draft.

❑   Proofread the final draft.

❑   Print or type the essay and submit it.

CHAPTER REVIEW

■ A definition clearly explains the meaning of words, terms, and concepts. Definitions can be simple, as in a dictionary definition, or extended, in which a term is described at length.

■ An extended definition paragraph uses one or more of the modes of development to describe its topic. The topic sentence states the term and explains why it is important and is being defined. Transitional expressions help the reader follow as the topic is developed.

■ In a definition essay, the thesis sentence states the topic to be defined, the controlling idea or attitude toward the topic, and the main points that are going to be made. The thesis sentence should suggest the mode or modes that will be used in the body paragraphs. In a definition essay, the body paragraphs often vary in mode, and sometimes modes are blended within a single body paragraph. The concluding paragraph's approach should flow from the content of the previous paragraphs.

 ## Visit *The Write Start* Online!

For additional practice with the materials found in this chapter, visit our Student Companion Web site by going to cengagebrain.com and searching for this text. The Web site also features additional readings, quizzes, writing activities, and Internet links.

Pages 202–204: Henry Han Xi Lau, "I Was a Member of the Kung Fu Crew." Originally published in *The New York Times Magazine*, October 19, 1997. Reprinted by permission of the author.

The Cause or Effect Essay

When attempting to persuade others about a belief or point of view you hold, often you try to convince them by pointing out special relationships that different things or events share. By doing this, you are using a powerful tool that focuses on a strong logical method of developing a topic: **cause** or **effect**. This mode of development analyzes **causal relationships**, the connection between cause and effect.

AP Photo

REBECCA COOK/Reuters/Landov

Scott Gries/Getty Images

© 2014 Wadsworth, Cengage Learning

Organizations such as Habitat for Humanity construct low-cost housing for the homeless. It has received international attention thanks to famous people such as rock musician and actor Bon Jovi's involvement, as well others such as former president Jimmy Carter. Write two paragraphs: In the first paragraph, write about why you think people volunteer their time and effort to work for such charitable and socially responsible organizations. In the second paragraph, write about what you think the benefits are for people in particular and the nation in general.

Identifying Your Purpose

Cause or effect development explains the reasons or results associated with some thing or event: *cause* analysis develops *why* something happens, and *effect* analysis explains *the results and consequences* stemming from causes. Causal relationships help us understand why things happen in the world around us and the possible consequences that may result from actions or events.

For example, a writer might ask the question, "Why did President Bill Clinton lie to the American public about the Monica Lewinsky affair?" as a way of finding out the possible causes of his action.

Possible Causes

He did not define his actions with Monica Lewinsky as "having sex."

He did not want the first lady, Hillary Rodham Clinton, to find out about the affair.

He did not want to be embarrassed publicly in the press.

He did not want history to focus on this aspect of his presidency.

The writer also might ask, "What might happen because President Clinton lied to the American public?" as a way of figuring out the events that might occur as a result of the lying.

Possible Effects

He might have been impeached for "high crimes and misdemeanors."

History books might focus on this aspect of his presidency rather than his successes with domestic and foreign affairs.

Democratic candidates might find it difficult to get elected or reelected to office.

As we know, President Clinton was impeached in the U.S. House of Representatives. Although the U.S. Senate voted against removing him from office, his reputation took quite a few hits, and many believe his vice president, Al Gore, lost the 2000 presidential election to George W. Bush because of the effects of President Clinton's activities.

Another possible effect was that First Lady Hillary Rodham Clinton gained the sympathy of many people. She subsequently won election to the Senate and wrote a best-selling book about her time as first lady. She was also seen by many, at the time, as a possible Democratic candidate for the presidency. Subsequently, after not garnering the Democratic candidacy for President, she was appointed and confirmed as President Barack Obama's Secretary of State.

Writing a Cause or Effect Paragraph

Obviously, the search for cause or effect answers can be a complex undertaking. More than one explanation usually can be found, and often many of the answers are possible. This complexity can be helpful in achieving thorough development of an issue. Thoroughly developing your point of view can help you persuade your reader that your view of an issue has been both logically and reasonably stated. Look at the following two examples of paragraphs focusing on cause and effect.

Example Cause Paragraph

Obtaining money and managing money are common causes of stress, especially for those who have little. For students, and those hoping to attend college, securing funds is a top priority. Of course, there are grants, loans, and scholarships, but sometimes those resources are not enough. Getting a job or obtaining a loan does not ease any of the tension and, more likely, will cause even more stress. Knowing how to manage money is very important. A poor expenditure plan can cause shortfalls affecting payment of bills and tuition. Being in debt not only means needing money to pay bills, but extra money will be necessary to pay penalties and interest. Money is not the root of all evil—poor planning is!

In the preceding paragraph, *obtaining money* and *money management* are the twin *causes* of stress. The link between the two causes is that once you do get the money, you must manage the funds properly or more troubles can occur.

Example Effect Paragraph

The possibility of health risks is extremely high for a prescription drug addict. Every medication that is taken has side effects, such as headache, nausea, and sleep problems. Constipation results from many potent prescription drugs. High emotional and physical feelings, followed by correspondingly low emotional and physical states, are effects that often occur when prescription drugs are abused. The addict usually takes different types of drugs to counteract this emotional roller coaster. The effect of this new addiction is potential heart problems. Other effects stemming from prescription drug abuse are dental problems and poor immunity against diseases because prescribed drugs can remove essential vitamins and minerals from the body.

In the preceding paragraph, health risks, such as *headache, nausea, sleep deprivation, emotional highs and lows*, and *potential heart problems* are the effects of prescription drug abuse. The link between the effects is that new drugs to counteract one set of effects can lead to other negative effects.

Causal Chains

Whether you are focusing on cause or on effect, it is helpful, before you begin writing, to develop a **causal chain**. A causal chain demonstrates the series of events that can develop, and it helps clarify the relationships that exist between events.

Cause and Effect Diagram 1

Causes		*Effects*
Too many unpaid bills	can lead to	increased physical tension.
Increased physical tension	can lead to	severe headaches.
Severe headaches	can lead to	nausea and loss of appetite.
Nausea and loss of appetite	can lead to	physical and mental fatigue.
Physical and mental fatigue	can lead to	health problems.

In the preceding example, notice how an effect can become a cause for the next effect. Things and events do not exist in a vacuum isolated from the other things and events around them. Yes, you can focus on cause, and you can focus on effect, but to be most persuasive, you should share with readers the special insights you have learned from the causal chain.

Another method for identifying causes and effects is to use the following diagram.

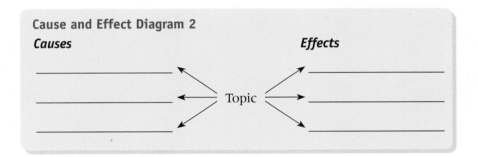

By filling in the spaces under Causes and Effects, you can separate the links in the causal chain. By doing so, you can decide which elements you want to be the focus of your essay.

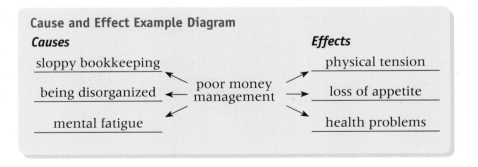

Once readers know *why* something has happened (causes) and the consequences that might stem from the causes (effects), they are much more likely to be receptive to your conclusions about the topic. In other words, they understand your view of a topic, and understanding an issue is often half the battle to accepting the writer's ideas concerning the issue.

PRACTICE 1   Creating Causal Chains

B U I L D I N G

Create a causal chain for each of these topics:

■ road rage
■ overbuilding houses
■ ozone depletion

While you can make the chain as long as you want, try to have at least three causes and effects in the chain. Use both techniques illustrated in Diagrams 1 and 2 to develop your chain and then to separate the causes from the effects.

Problems to Avoid

When using cause and effect reasoning, do not confuse **chronological order** and **coincidence** with true cause and effect relationships. Do not assume that because one event follows another in time, the first event causes the second to occur. No true causal relationship exists between two events just because one follows the other.

> **Example**
>
> Every time a black cat crosses my path, something bad happens to me.

Bad things indeed may happen to you, but the proverbial black cat as a cause of bad luck is a superstition that has no basis in reality. Your bad luck is probably due to your not being properly prepared for the events in your life or possibly just being at the wrong place at the wrong time—coincidence. Do not assume that because two or more events occur around the same time, one causes the other and that a cause and effect relationship exists between them.

> **Example**
>
> After I attended a movie, several days later I came down with a cold. Someone in the theater must have been ill, and I must have caught it from them. Therefore, my going to the movies caused me to catch a cold.

Many people that you come in contact with each day may have colds. You could catch a cold from any one of them. Cause and effect is posited in the example, but there is no proof of a link. In this case, coincidence is just as likely a possibility.

| PRACTICE 2 | Analyzing Chronological Order and Coincidence |

Explain why the following events do not have a causal relationship, either because of *chronological order* or *coincidence*.

1. The successful field goal, passing through the uprights just as the final gun sounded, won the game by a score of 17 to 14.

_____

_____

_____

_____

_____

_____

2. I always get sick the day after Thanksgiving. I need to stop eating so much, and I guess I'll have to stop going on those brisk, long walks that my family always takes after dinner.

_____

_____

_____

_____

_____

_____

_____

_____

The Topic Sentence in a Cause or Effect Paragraph

The topic sentence in a cause or effect paragraph clearly states the topic and why the topic's causes or effects are being developed.

■ After choosing your subject, create your causal chain to identify the causes and effects stemming from the topic.

■ When this step is completed, decide whether you are going to focus on causes or effects.

The topic sentence will announce your purpose to the reader, and it will clarify the paragraph's development.

Examples

Focus on Causes
Proper nutrition can lead to a long, healthful life. (This paragraph will develop *proper nutrition* as a cause of a *long, healthful life*.)

Focus on Effects
A long, healthful life can increase earnings potential. (This paragraph will develop *earnings potential* as an effect or result of a *long, healthful life*.)

PRACTICE 3   **Developing a Paragraph about Causes**

B U I L D I N G

This practice will help you develop a paragraph that focuses on causes.

1. Pick one of the following topics.

a phobia (an unreasonable fear, such as fear of heights, spiders, open spaces, flying)

looking for a new job

a good relationship

2. List as many causes of your topic choice as you can think of.

a. _____

b. _____

c. _____

d. _____

e. _____

3. If any of the causes in your list are merely chronological or coincidental, draw a line through them.

4. Write a topic sentence that focuses on causes.

_____

_____

_____

_____

_____

5. Write a sentence for each of the causes in your list that is not merely chronological or coincidental.

_____

_____

_____

_____

_____

6. On a separate sheet of paper, rewrite your sentences into paragraph form.

PRACTICE 4   **Developing a Paragraph about Effects**

This practice will help you develop a paragraph that focuses on effects.

1. Pick one of the following topics.
having a child out of wedlock
children watching too much television violence
using a cell phone while driving

2. List as many effects of your topic choice as you can think of.

a. _____

b. _____

c. _____

d. _____

e. _____

3. If any of the effects in your list are merely chronological or coincidental, draw a line through them.

4. Write a topic sentence that focuses on effects.

_____

_____

_____

_____

5. Write a sentence for each of the effects in your list that is not merely chronological or coincidental.

_____

_____

_____

_____

_____

6. On a separate sheet of paper, rewrite your sentences into paragraph form.

Using Transitional Expressions in Cause and Effect Writing

There are several transitional expressions you will find useful when writing about causes or effects.

Cause	*Effect*
because	as a consequence of
causes, caused by	as a result (of)
the reason	consequently
since	resulting in
therefore	then

PRACTICE 5   Adding Transitions to Cause and Effect Paragraphs

Add appropriate transitional expressions to the cause paragraph you created for Practice 3 and the effect paragraph you created for Practice 4. When you have finished, compare the paragraphs pairs. The paragraphs containing the transitional expressions should be easier to read and understand.

BUILDING

Moving from Paragraph to Essay

Now that you have studied and practiced the techniques to create effective cause and effect paragraphs, it is time to expand your ideas to a larger writing unit: the cause or effect essay. Using the techniques you learned in Part One regarding developing the essay paragraphs and the cause or effect techniques you have just learned, you can create the cause or effect essay. This might be a good time to return to Part One and review the techniques for developing the full essay.

Creating the Introductory Paragraph

A cause or effect essay needs a clearly defined organization in the introductory paragraph to announce to the reader just how the subject will be developed. The thesis sentence indicates whether the essay will focus on cause or effect, the writer's attitude toward the topic, the controlling idea, and the organizational structure. By using an appropriate lead-in technique, the thesis should blend naturally into the rest of the introductory paragraph.

Using one of the causal chain techniques you have studied can help you identify causes and effects. You then can extend and develop the ideas expressed in the diagrams to create the thesis sentence for a cause or effect essay.

> **Example Cause Thesis Sentence**
>
> Sloppy bookkeeping, lack of organization, and mental fatigue can lead to poor money management.

> **Example Effect Thesis Sentence**
>
> Poor money management can lead to physical tension, loss of appetite, and health problems.

Although both essays are concerned with poor money management, the focus of each essay is different: The first essay will focus on causes of poor money management, while the second essay will focus on the effects of poor money management.

Creating the Body Paragraphs

For an essay on the *causes of poor money management*, the focus of the body paragraphs will be the paragraph topics listed in the thesis statement's essay map.

- The first body paragraph's topic will be *sloppy bookkeeping*.
- The second body paragraph's topic will be *lack of organization*.
- The third body paragraph's topic will be *mental fatigue*.
- As you write about each of the topics, your focus should be that these are *causes for poor money management*.
- Your focus should not be on how reading the *Wall Street Journal* can help you be more successful in picking stocks or how reading *GQ* magazine can help you dress more like a businessperson.

Keep your focus on the controlling idea or attitude: *the three causes can lead to poor money management*.

For an essay on the *effects of poor money management*, the focus of the body paragraphs will be the paragraph topics listed in the thesis statement's essay map.

- The first body paragraph's topic will be *physical tension*.
- The second body paragraph's topic will be *loss of appetite*.
- The third body paragraph's topic will be *health problems*.
- Your focus should be that these are the *negative effects caused by poor money management*.
- Your focus should not be *how poor money management can reduce the value of your stock portfolio* or *how it can cause your plans to buy a house to be put on hold*.

Keep your focus on the controlling idea: *that poor money management can lead to health-related problems*.

Creating the Concluding Paragraph

The approach of the concluding paragraph should flow naturally from the essay's main topic. Because the first essay's focus is the causes leading to poor money management, a *call to action* would seem an appropriate choice. You might suggest some actions businesspeople can take to help correct sloppy bookkeeping practices. You might even suggest that they survey some bookkeeping services that will handle their accounts for a reasonable fee. You might suggest that they take a workshop on enhancing organization skills or that they enroll in a yoga or tai chi class to get rid of unwanted, destructive tension.

Because the second essay's focus is the effects caused by poor money management, a *warning* would seem an appropriate choice. You might warn the reader that there are other negative consequences that might come from poor money management: negative credit reports, relationship problems (with spouses, business partners, and friends), and inadequately funded short- or long-term business plans. Remember to keep the focus connected to the essay's idea of importance or attitude: the negative effects caused by poor money management. (Refer to Chapter 6 for other approaches for concluding paragraphs.)

Sample Cause Student Essay: PROBLEMS IN PARENTING

Mark Collom

> Raising a family is a challenging endeavor no matter what the age or socioeconomic status of the parents. Literally thousands of books and articles have been written about parenting. In this essay, "Problems in Parenting," student writer Mark Collom, speaking from his own experiences as a parent, focuses on the rewarding but difficult aspects of raising children.

Vocabulary

Before you begin reading, use a dictionary to look up the definitions of the following words that appear in the essay.

abstract (1)	baton (5)	bestow (2)	commendable (1)
conversely (1)	depict (2)	endeavors (5)	enterprises (1)
extravagances (4)	intrinsic (5)	precedence (4)	pungent (2)

Problems in Parenting

1   Think for a moment or two, and recall the name of some commendable young man or woman. If the background of the admirable person were known, more often than not, they would be considered the product of a good mother and father. Conversely, all quickly can point to some delinquent character and assess that poor parenting was the cause of that person's problems. Good parenting might appear to be an easy skill, perhaps, even an art. But good parents are made, not born. Being a proper Mom and Dad is one

Thesis Statement with Essay Map →

of life's most challenging enterprises and one of its most rewarding, as well. The abstract mixture of love, discipline, and sacrifice make good parenting a difficult task.

Topic Sentence → 2   When the first newborn is proudly brought home from the hospital, life makes an almost complete change for the parents. The new child, with helpless innocence, is the focus of all the love the parents can bestow. "Precious Moments" figurines are likely to depict parental love as a baby being cradled in the arms of the mother; however, the parent's love is also represented in many other not so pleasant events. Volumes of stained, pungent diapers in need of attention, equally offensive vomit upon Mother's newest blouse, and months of "yo-yo" nights of interrupted sleep are all taken in stride. Countless adversities are magically reduced by love into mere inconveniences.

Topic Sentence → 3   Good parenting relies upon the conscience of the adults making decisions for the welfare of the youngsters. Although limitations upon the children are easy to point out, usually such judgments also result in restrictions on the mother and father. With the children sprawled about the family-room floor, Mom and Dad opt for *Sabrina the Teenage Witch* and *Boy Meets World* because the movie on another station carries the "R" rating. Even though both grown-ups would prefer to watch the "other" movie, good parenting dictates the more suitable program. The weather may be stormy, and the bed warm and comfortable, but Mom and Dad will rise to get the kids ready so the family can make it to church on Sunday. Parental obligations confront the adults at every turn.

Topic Sentence → 4   Yes, Mom does deserve the Caribbean cruise she's always wanted. No, Dad's aged sedan is not a classic, yet he's not shopping for a new car. The Caribbean will wait; the old Buick can make another winter or two, for children inhabit a home, and extravagances are not high on the parental agenda. Decisions are made with offspring in mind, for the parents realize years pass quickly and the young will soon be grown and gone. New bicycles on birthdays, hockey trips with the team, and Christmas trees buried in a mound of Santa's gifts all take precedence in the eyes of Mom and Dad. Soon enough, the two will cruise the southern seas.

5   Parenting is a swirl of all the emotions. It is pride in seeing a little pitcher strike out an opponent, yet sorrow when they cannot find the strike zone any longer, and the midget hurler walks in the winning run. It is a delight when a little child joyfully speeds to Daddy's arms after making a first successful twirl on new skates; however, a sadness overcomes the father when, years later, the teenager runs out the door to be with friends without even saying goodbye. With all the intrinsic difficulties, being a good parent is the most challenging of all endeavors. The role is also the most fulfilling; therefore, every generation will continue to accept the passing of the baton.

Design Pics/Ron Nickel/Jupiter Images

Cause Technique Questions

A N A L Y Z I N G

1. What causes does the writer focus on that make parenting difficult?

_____

_____

_____

_____

2. Does the writer use many transitional expressions? If not, which ones would be appropriate, and where would you place them?

_____

_____

_____

_____

3. Identify some of the specific sacrifices that parents often have to make.

_____

_____

_____

_____

_____

Critical Reading and Thinking Questions

A N A L Y Z I N G

1. What is the main idea of the essay?

_____

_____

2. What does the writer mean by "yo-yo" nights of interrupted sleep?

_____

_____

3. Point out some of the other "yo-yo" elements in the life of parents raising children. How do these examples support the "yo-yo" nights of interrupted sleep idea? Is there a deeper significance than just for the day-to-day routine?

_____

_____

_____

_____

Cause Writing Exercises

1. Write a paragraph about what causes a couple to be defined as "good parents." Before you begin writing, create a causal chain, and pick out at least three cause elements to use in your paragraph.
2. Write a cause essay based on the cause elements you used in Exercise 1. For your essay, speak to some foreign students to get their opinions about what makes "good parents." Add their ideas to your essay.

Sample Effect Student Essay: GIVING OUT

Yvonne Olsen

Most people would think that a person applying for a volunteer position would be doing so only because the effects of helping others would bring the charitable person a great measure of satisfaction and personal growth. In this essay, "Giving Out," just the opposite happens. Student writer Yvonne Olsen relates how a friend took a position for a somewhat selfish reason, but that some unforeseen, beneficial effects became a part of the total equation.

Vocabulary

Before you begin to read, use a dictionary to look up the definitions to the following words that appear in the essay.

anticipated (3)	discourteous (2)	eager (2)
energetic (4)	gourmet (2)	interact (3)
miraculously (5)	mumble (3)	volunteer (1)

Giving Out

1 Cindy left the interview feeling undecided about the job she had just gotten. She did not interview for a paying job; rather, she had sought a volunteer position at a local hospital. Cindy wanted to volunteer at the hospital because she wanted to see what the medical profession was all about. She

was a good science student, so she thought going to medical school might be an option. She wasn't all that excited about getting up at 5:30 in the morning each day, and the thought of having to do a lot of work without pay wasn't high on her list, either. She thought it was going to be a long summer. Instead, the volunteer position turned out to be very rewarding mentally, socially, and educationally.

Thesis Statement with Essay Map →

Topic Sentence → 2   The first day at the hospital was a mental shock. Cindy was working on the full admit floor where the patients were very ill. Most of them had spent weeks in the hospital. Most were elderly, depressed, or bored. Some of them looked lifeless, for all hope of leaving the hospital had been delayed when a physician scheduled them for another set of tests or for another surgery. When Cindy saw that most of the patients were hooked to oxygen, she learned to appreciate her own good health. The first few times at the hospital were depressing for her, as well, but soon she began to focus on some positive aspects. A feeling of happiness ran through her mind when she got to take discharged patients out of the hospital to meet their families. These patients, seemingly in the depths of despair only days earlier, now were all smiles because they knew that soon they would be home. The patients were eager to see their families, and they would tell her about what they were going to do once they left the hospital. Of course, not all of the discharged patients were going home; some would be going to nursing homes or to other extended care facilities. Positive feelings rose in her chest when she was helping nurses run specimens to the lab, picking up prescriptions from the pharmacy, and serving patients their breakfast. When patients wanted a newspaper or fresh gourmet coffee, she would go to the lobby and return to smiling faces and outstretched hands. They often were grateful for such small things, while people on the outside of the hospital were often discourteous or accepted such favors without thanks. Cindy's self-esteem began to rise.

Topic Sentence → 3   Besides all of the mental benefits, there were also social benefits that she hadn't anticipated. Cindy had always been a bit shy, but being with so many patients and co-workers helped her to become more talkative. She talked to elderly patients about their families and illnesses. She listened to endless love stories of when they were her age. They liked the fact that there was someone to listen to their stories. Of course, not all of the patients were easy to talk to. The younger patients would not want to speak to anyone because they were angry at being stuck in a hospital away from friends and video games. Cindy could not understand all of her patients, particularly those who were heavily sedated and could only mumble. She learned that even if she could not understand the patient, she could pretend to just to make them feel important. At times, she would assure nervous patients that the tests or the surgeries were not as serious as they seemed. As it became easier to relate to the patients, it became easier to interact with her co-workers. Questions became easier to ask, and thoughts became easier to express. As the weeks went by, Cindy lost most of her shyness.

Topic Sentence → 4   Volunteering also turned out to be a great educational experience. After all, the hospital does have many nursing and medical students. She learned the structure of the hospital from the maintenance crew to the kitchen personnel to the neurosurgeons. She learned about the different medical tools that were used in the various departments. Cindy heard of many medical conditions that she never knew existed. Speaking to doctors and nurses helped her to see what their professions were like. Nurses worked hard to make the patients comfortable and assist the doctors in curing the patients. Volunteering taught her about good, energetic life and about weak, dying life. These educational experiences helped Cindy decide that a career in medicine was going to be her life's calling.

5   The volunteer position helped Cindy in many ways. Being around people less fortunate taught her to be grateful that her family and friends were

© 2014 Wadsworth, Cengage Learning

healthy, which she used to take for granted. After her volunteer experience, she realized that illness could strike at any time. But most of all, she got a sense of how she wanted to direct her life. Cindy decided to go to medical school because she saw how a good physician could help a patient recover miraculously. Even though she was not paid for her services, Cindy felt that volunteering in the hospital earned her more than she could ever calculate.

Effect Technique Questions

1. What effects does the writer focus on that finally made Cindy's experience worthwhile?

   _____

   _____

   _____

   _____

   _____

   _____

2. Did the writer use many transitional expressions? If not, which ones would be appropriate, and where would you place them?

   _____

   _____

Critical Reading and Thinking Questions

1. How did Cindy's expectations differ from the reality she found at the hospital?

   _____

   _____

   _____

   _____

2. How does the title "Giving Out" provide additional meaning now that you have read the essay?

   _____

   _____

   _____

   _____

Effect Writing Exercises

1. Write a paragraph about the effects of a particular experience: a job, boot camp, attending college, moving away from home. Before starting to write, create a causal chain, and choose at least three effects to use in your paragraph.
2. Write an essay based on the topic and effect elements you used in Exercise 1. Expand the list of effects by focusing on the initial expectations prior to the experience and how those expectations eventually changed.

More Topics for a Cause or Effect Essay

Here are some possible topics for cause or effect essays. Remember, cause or effect writing must have a purpose, so do not forget to create a thesis sentence. Use the essay map to organize the topics for your body paragraphs.

Causes

1. The causes of drug abuse
2. The causes of the increasing high school dropout rate
3. The causes of test anxiety
4. The causes of high taxation
5. The causes of road rage or for being relaxed behind the wheel
6. The causes of divorce or for a long-lasting, happy marriage
7. The causes of spousal abuse or for diffusing tension in a relationship
8. The causes of a high teen pregnancy rate
9. The causes of low unemployment
10. The causes of high prison populations
11. The causes of pollution
12. The causes of prejudice
13. The causes of cheating in college
14. The causes for low voter turnout
15. The causes of low or high self-esteem

Effects

1. The effects of a large corporation leaving a small town
2. The effects of pollution
3. The effects of a week's vacation
4. The effects of overprescribing antibiotics
5. The effects of high speed limits
6. The effects of owning a pet
7. The effects of international trade agreements
8. The effects of reading a popular book or seeing a movie
9. The effects of a tornado
10. The effects of prejudice
11. The effects of drug abuse
12. The effects of road rage
13. The effects of a high teen pregnancy rate
14. The effects of spousal abuse (include children if you want)
15. The effects of high unemployment

☑ Writing Checklist for a Cause or Effect Essay

- ❏ Choose a topic.
- ❏ Create a causal chain to discover both causes and effects.
- ❏ Decide whether to write a cause or an effect essay.
- ❏ Choose an appropriate number of either causes or effects to fit the assignment.
- ❏ Create a thesis sentence.
- ❏ Draft the essay. Do not forget to use transitional expressions.
- ❏ Revise the first draft.
- ❏ Proofread the final draft.
- ❏ Print or type the essay and submit it.

CHAPTER REVIEW

- ■ A cause or effect essay explains the reasons associated with some thing or event: cause analysis develops *why* something happens, and effect analysis explains *the results and consequences* stemming from the causes.
- ■ Developing a causal chain is a prewriting activity that can help you focus on important causes and effects.
- ■ While developing cause or effect writing, avoid seeing a causal relationship when either coincidence or simple chronology is at work.
- ■ In a cause or effect paragraph, the topic sentence announces the topic and indicates whether causes or effects will be discussed. Transitional expressions help show cause and effect relationships.
- ■ In a cause or effect essay, the thesis sentence in the introductory paragraph indicates the topic, attitude, controlling idea, and the causes or effects that will be discussed in the remainder of the essay.

 ### Visit *The Write Start* Online!

For additional practice with the materials found in this chapter, visit our Student Companion Web site by going to cengagebrain.com and searching for this text. The Web site also features additional readings, quizzes, writing activities, and Internet links.

The Persuasive Essay

When you try to convince someone else that your point of view or belief is correct, you are using **persuasion**. Persuasion is one of the most common types of writing in college. Persuasive writing attempts to convince the reader that a particular point of view is justifiable because of the evidence used to explain and support the topic. For your writing to be persuasive, you must have a clearly stated position and specific support that make your opinion believable.

Image Source/Jupiter Images

Image Source/Jupiter Images

We live in a society in which it seems everyone is suing or being sued, even for something as simple as spilled coffee (Patron vs. McDonald's—the patron won).
Write two paragraphs:
In the first paragraph, pretend you are a defense attorney. Use two or three pieces of evidence to persuade a judge or jury that your client (the defendant) is innocent of the crime he or she is accused of committing (you choose the crime).
In the second paragraph, using the same defendant and crime you used in paragraph 1, pretend that you are the prosecuting attorney. Use two or three pieces of evidence (they can be the same or different from the ones in paragraph 1) to persuade the judge or jury that the defendant is guilty of the crime.

Identifying Your Purpose

Persuasive writing can be *informal, semiformal,* or *formal.* Think of *informal persuasion* as when you and your friends or family try to convince one another about the rightness of your opinions on issues ranging from which college basketball team should be number one to which fast-food restaurant serves the best pizza. Commercials on radio and television also are types of informal persuasion, as are public service ads for nonprofit organizations and most political advertisements.

Formal persuasion is usually called **argumentation**. This type of persuasion requires not only that you argue for your own beliefs, but also that you argue directly against someone else's beliefs. Argumentation uses evidence from primary and secondary sources (information often found in the library) that are cited using a formal documentation process (such as the one used by the Modern Language Association or by the American Psychological Association, for example). Research papers, analytical essays, and certain business reports fall into this category. You will be introduced to the argument research essay in Chapter 16.

In this chapter, we are interested in *semiformal persuasion*—a type of persuasion that falls somewhere between the two mentioned previously. Semiformal persuasion requires a bit more logical thought and organization than is needed around the kitchen table in informal arguing but not quite the rigid structure that is made necessary by the quotations and accompanying documentation of formal argumentation.

Writing a Persuasive Paragraph

In quizzes, papers, and exams, you will be required to argue for and against ideas. Therefore, knowing how to use the fundamentals of persuasive writing is one of the most important skills you can learn. Exhibit 15.1 shows a persuasive paragraph that tries to convince the reader that the author has a well-thought-out point of view.

**Exhibit 15.1
The Persuasion
Paragraph**

Mandatory drug testing will help eliminate poor job performance. Workers will do better quality work to meet the standards of the company. The company will be more successful because of the quality of the product the workers will produce. Additionally, the workers' job performance will improve because of a better attitude. Mandatory drug testing also will reduce the number of job-related accidents; that, in turn, will enhance performance. A safe work environment promotes better performances as employees will feel safer and more secure as they do their jobs. Workers having more confidence in the employer, fellow employees, and the workplace will complete tasks more confidently and successfully.

In the preceding paragraph, the writer's conclusion that "mandatory drug testing will help eliminate poor job performance" is supported by statements suggesting that mandatory drug testing will create a safer workplace and a safer employee. A safer atmosphere creates a better attitude on the part of the worker who, in turn, will perform better on the job. The ideas that support the conclusion are not outlandish or overblown; rather, they are reasonably expressed and developed in a convincing manner.

The Topic Sentence in a Persuasive Paragraph

In a persuasive paragraph, the topic sentence states the writer's conclusion or point of view about a particular topic. The writer's conclusion either can be for or against (pro or con) the idea concerning the topic. Therefore, the topic sentence is the key to a successful persuasive paragraph. The verbs used in a persuasive topic sentence are usually *should/should not* or *must/must not*.

Examples

The pending legislation on the right of citizens to carry concealed handguns should be defeated.

This paragraph will argue against (con) citizens having the right to carry concealed handguns.

Employers should provide day care for their employees.

This paragraph will argue for (pro) companies providing day care for the children of their employees.

Euthanasia should be legalized because of our constitutional rights of personal freedom.

This paragraph will argue for (pro) physician-assisted suicide.

Athletics should not receive more funding than academics.

This paragraph will argue against (con) sports receiving more money than academics.

PRACTICE 1 — Writing Persuasive Topic Sentences

B U I L D I N G

For the following ten topics listed, write either a pro (for) topic sentence or a con (against) topic sentence. Try to write five pro sentences and five con sentences.

1. Topic: Selling cigarettes to teens under eighteen years of age

_____

_____

_____

2. Topic: Regulation of sexually explicit material on the Internet

_____

_____

_____

3. Topic: Organized prayer in public schools

_____

_____

_____

4. Topic: Lower speed limits on federal highways

_____

_____

_____

5. Topic: Military draft for eighteen-year-old males and females

_____

_____

_____

6. Topic: Adoption of children by gay and lesbian couples

_____

_____

_____

7. Topic: Safety inspections for automobiles

_____

_____

_____

8. Topic: Elimination of athletic scholarships

_____

_____

_____

9. Topic: Increasing the income tax

_____

_____

_____

10. Topic: Legalization of marijuana

_____

_____

_____

The Pro and Con List

Once you have decided on a topic, it is vital that you know the major argument points on both sides of the issue, whether or not you know which side you are going to take. First, list as many points for each side that you can think of in a pro and con list, as shown in Exhibit 15.2.

**Exhibit 15.2
The Pro and Con List**

Topic: Nuclear Energy

Pro (For) List	**Con (Against) List**
Cheaper fuel costs	Radioactive waste
Less dependence on foreign oil	Unemployment in fossil-fuel industries
Creates high-tech jobs	Environmental pollution
Saves natural resources	Nuclear power plant accidents
Ensures strong nuclear arsenal	Nuclear weapons proliferation

Once you have listed as many points as you can think of, consider the points on both sides of the argument, and choose the side you wish to argue for. Decide which points you will use in your paragraph to support your topic.

PRACTICE 2   **Creating Pro and Con Lists**

Create a pro and con list for each of the following topics. Think of as many items for each list as you can.

1. Topic: Teaching sex education in mixed-gender classes

Pro	**Con**
_____	_____
_____	_____
_____	_____
_____	_____
_____	_____

2. Topic: Gays serving in the military

Pro	Con
_____	_____
_____	_____
_____	_____
_____	_____
_____	_____

3. Topic: Smoking in public places

Pro	Con
_____	_____
_____	_____
_____	_____
_____	_____
_____	_____

4. Topic: Foreign language requirements in high school and college

Pro	Con
_____	_____
_____	_____
_____	_____
_____	_____
_____	_____

5. Topic: Affirmative action in employment

Pro	Con
_____	_____
_____	_____
_____	_____
_____	_____

Techniques to Support the Argument

To persuade the reader that a particular position is convincing, writers use a variety of support techniques in the persuasive paragraph: answering the opposition, referring to an authority, predicting consequences, stating facts, and providing examples. While you probably will never use all of them in one paragraph, you will use them when you write persuasively.

Answering the Opposition

At times, the best way to persuade your reader is to respond directly to an opponent's point. This also shows your reader that you are aware of your opponent's side of the issue, not just your own.

Referring to an Authority

An authority is a person or a group that is considered an expert on the subject under discussion and will give an unbiased but knowledgeable opinion.

Predicting Consequences

Predicting consequences can strengthen an argument and persuade your reader to agree with your point of view and disagree with your opponent's.

Stating Facts

Facts are those things that actually exist or have existed, such as people, places, things, and events. A *fact* differs from an *opinion* in a quite significant way. An opinion is how we think about, or interpret, facts. For instance, it is a *fact* that in 1978 the U.S. Congress removed our currency from the gold standard (the dollar amount of paper money and coins in circulation could not exceed the dollar amount of gold stored at Fort Knox in Kentucky). That fact cannot be argued. However, whether or not you think it was a good idea to remove the gold standard is your *opinion*, and that can be argued. Whether your *opinion* or your opponent's *opinion* is the more persuasive, the *fact* remains that the gold standard was removed in 1978.

Providing Examples

Good examples can develop an idea quickly and clearly and help convince your reader of your point of view. Examples also are used to clarify, illustrate, or make concrete a general idea about the subject. Therefore, be certain that your examples support your position or convincingly argue against your opponent's.

| PRACTICE 3 | Drafting Pro and Con Paragraphs |

Select one of the pro and con lists you created in Practice 2. Write a sentence for each of the pro items you listed, and write a sentence for each of the con items you listed. Next, write a topic sentence for the group of pro sentences, and write a topic sentence for the group of con sentences. Finally, rewrite your sentences into standard paragraph form. These are your rough drafts for your persuasive paragraphs on both sides of an issue.

Logical Fallacies

When choosing the supportive evidence that proves your point, keep in mind that some ideas will sound good at first but might have flaws on closer inspection. Some support information might be irrelevant, misleading, oversimplified, unfair, or lead to erroneous conclusions. These proofs actually prove nothing, and they can destroy an otherwise good argument.

It is very important that you recognize statements that exhibit false logic. These statements are known as *logical fallacies*. If readers catch you using logical fallacies as proof, they will think you are a poor arguer or that you are an unethical arguer because you are purposely trying to be deceptive.

Although there are many logical fallacies, a few of the more common ones are listed as follows.

- **Ad hominem** (Latin: "to the man") arguments attack the person's character rather than the person's ideas. Example (politics): *My opponent is an avowed atheist; therefore, he cannot lead this country out of the economic disaster we find ourselves in.* While many voters may not like the fact that a particular candidate does not believe in God, such a spiritual position probably has little if anything to do with the candidate's ability to handle economic problems. The ad hominem argument shifts the focus away from the argument and to the person.

- **Bandwagon** arguments suggest that because everyone else is doing something, so should you. Example (advertising): *Millions of people are using Ampheta-cal to lose weight. So what are you waiting for?* Even if the claim were true, an amphetamine-based product that overstimulates the central nervous system may be medically dangerous. The bandwagon argument tries to persuade you to be like everyone else.

- **Either-or** arguments state that there are only two ways of dealing with a problem. Example (law): *Abortions should either be permitted in all situations or be illegal under any circumstances.* This argument does not allow for alternative choices, such as allowing abortions when the mother's life is in danger or the pregnancy is due to rape, or disallowing abortions when one of the parents is willing to raise the child or adoptive parents are available. The either-or argument does not allow for compromise.

- **Hasty generalization** arguments jump to conclusions using too little evidence. Example (education): *Inner-city students do not do well on standardized tests because they do not study enough.* Inner-city students may study as much as students in the suburbs or rural locales. Standardized tests often are biased against inner-city students because of the language and examples used in developing questions. Also, how is "inner-city" being defined? What population must a city have to qualify for the study? Do the inner-city students come from various ethnic groups or a particular ethnic group? What are the boundaries of the "inner city" as opposed to the "outer city"? Has such a distinction been made, and if so, what is the rationale for making the distinction? The hasty generalization argument often jumps to a conclusion based on too few examples or unfairly designed definitions.

- **Non sequitur** (Latin: "it does not follow") arguments have a conclusion that does not follow from the evidence. Example (business): *Women should not own businesses because they do not play golf as well as men.* While it may be true that some business is conducted on golf courses, the vast majority of successful business transactions have nothing whatsoever to do with the game of golf. In fact, most businessmen and businesswomen do not play golf at all. The non sequitur argument is not an argument. In fact, the evidence does not provide for a logical, reasonable conclusion.

- **Red herring** arguments create false issues that lead the reader away from the real argument. (The term *red herring* comes from the practice of English dog trainers dragging a sack of dead herring across the scent of a fox in an attempt to distract the dogs.) Example (sports): *Our football team is not playing well because the owners never come to the games.* The real reason for the team not playing well probably has little to do with owners attending or not attending games. Poor coaching, play calling, player selection, and conditioning are more likely to be the reasons for the team's poor play. The red herring argument makes use of misleading information to divert the reader's attention from the real issue.

PRACTICE 4   Identifying Logical Fallacies

I D E N T I F Y I N G

Write the name of the logical fallacy in the space provided after each of the following argument statements.

1. It is not safe to swim in the ocean because there have been several shark attacks over the past few years in Australia and South Africa.

_____

2. Are we going to increase the number of mounted police in the park, or are we going to abandon it to the homeless, to the drug dealers, and to robbers and rapists?

_____

3. I am sure Raoul's parents are wealthy because he drives a new car to school.

_____

4. Mom, I need a Palm Pilot because all the kids at school have them.

_____

5. She would not make a good governor because her husband has never been involved in politics, his business takes him out of town a lot, and he was not even born in this country.

_____

6. My opponent does not support handgun legislation because he is a coward interested more in his own safety than the well-being of defenseless women and children.

_____

Organization Patterns

Once you have made your pro and con list and have chosen the types of evidence you want to use to support your topic, you will need to organize your paragraph for an effective presentation. There is no defined pattern that a writer has to use when writing persuasively. However, there are several patterns that will logically organize your points into a convincing persuasive paragraph.

Pattern 1: Arguing Only Your Own Points

In the first organizational pattern, you use only support points that argue for your point of view. Therefore, you use only pro list items if you are arguing for a point of view, or you use only con list items if you are arguing against a point of view.

Example: Arguing Only Your Own Points

Nuclear energy should not be more widely used because of radioactive waste disposal problems and the possibility of a nuclear reactor accident. One of the problems with nuclear energy is waste management. Radioactive waste can remain dangerous for thousands of years; therefore, disposal sites must meet rigid safety standards to keep the public safe. Sites must be deep in the ground to shield the public from possible radiation exposure, and they must be immune to earthquake damage. Such sites are hard to find and expensive to maintain. In addition to the waste disposal problem, nuclear accidents pose a real danger to people living near nuclear reactors. In 1986, in the Ukrainian town of Chernobyl, a nuclear reactor accident put thousands at risk of radioactive poisoning. A radiation cloud spread over northern Europe and Great Britain. Thirty-one Soviet citizens died, and over 100,000 had to be evacuated from surrounding areas. The risks involved in the long-term control and management of such a volatile substance as radioactive materials makes it a very risky proposition. Until more trustworthy safeguards can be developed in both the use and disposal of radioactive substances, we should not increase our use of nuclear energy.

Pattern 2: Arguing against Your Opposition's Points

Another way to organize a persuasive paragraph is to state only your opposition's support points (either pro or con) and then argue against them.

Example: Arguing against the Opposition

Despite the possible benefits to society, nuclear energy should not be more widely used as a fuel source. Many scientists and researchers claim nuclear energy is desirable as an energy source because it creates enormous amounts of power from small resources. While this may be true, other costs outweigh the purely monetary. In 1986, in the Ukrainian town of Chernobyl, a nuclear reactor accident killed 31 Soviet citizens and caused 100,000 people to be evacuated. A radioactive cloud covered much of northern Europe and Great Britain. Military leaders in Washington, D.C., state that a nuclear energy industry will also ensure a continuous source of radioactive material necessary to maintain our nuclear weapons arsenal for the defense of the nation. However, every year there are reports of nuclear by-products missing from government inventories. Enemies of the United States could use this material to build nuclear weapons with which to threaten us. Also, unfriendly nations could steal the technology for nuclear reactors that could be used to produce materials for making nuclear weapons. The potential for disaster far outweighs the potential benefits coming from the nuclear energy industry. Nuclear energy is not a safe or practical energy source.

Pattern 3: Alternating Your Points with Arguing against the Opposition

The third pattern of organization is alternating use of support points for your side of the argument and listing your opponent's points and arguing against them. Note that this is a hybrid or mixing of Patterns 1 and 2.

> **Example: Alternating Your Points with Arguing against the Opposition**
>
> Despite the possible benefits to society, nuclear energy should not be more widely used as a fuel source. One of the problems with nuclear energy is waste management. Radioactive waste can remain dangerous for thousands of years; therefore, safe deposit sites must meet rigid safety standards to keep the public safe. Sites must be deep in the ground to shield the public from possible radiation exposure, and the sites must be immune to earthquake damage. Many scientists and researchers claim nuclear energy is desirable as an energy source because it creates enormous amounts of power from small resources. While this may be true, other costs outweigh the purely monetary. In 1986, in the Ukrainian town of Chernobyl, a nuclear reactor accident killed 31 Soviet citizens and caused 100,000 people to be evacuated. A radioactive cloud covered much of northern Europe and Great Britain. Nuclear weapons proliferation is another problem if nuclear energy production is increased. Every year there are reports of nuclear by-products missing from government inventories. Enemies of the United States could use this material to build nuclear weapons with which to threaten our security. Economists like to say that increasing the nuclear energy industry will create more high-tech jobs, but the same industry will cause widespread unemployment in traditional fossil-fuel industries like coal, oil, and gas. The potential for both disaster and a negative impact on the economy should convince lawmakers to not increase our use of nuclear energy as a fuel source.

Once you have chosen an organization pattern for your paragraph, select several points from the appropriate list or lists and write sentences for each. Arrange the sentences according to the organization pattern you have chosen.

PRACTICE 5   **Using the Organizational Patterns of Persuasion**

Using the rough draft persuasive paragraph you created in Practice 3, rewrite the paragraph three times, using the three organizational patterns you have just studied.

Using Transitional Expressions in the Persuasive Paragraph

Transitional expressions are useful for connecting related ideas and adding rhythm to a paragraph so that it reads more smoothly. Although transitional expressions can be used anywhere they are appropriate, writers often use them to signal the types of evidence they are using in persuasive paragraphs.

Example: Alternating Your Points with Arguing against the Opposition

Despite the possible benefits to society, nuclear energy should not be more widely used as a fuel source. According to some authorities, one of the problems with nuclear energy is waste management. Radioactive waste can remain dangerous for thousands of years; therefore, safe deposit sites must meet rigid safety standards to keep the public safe. Consequently, sites must be deep in the ground to shield the public from possible radiation exposure, and the sites must be immune to earthquake damage. However, many scientists and researchers claim nuclear energy is desirable as an energy source because it creates enormous amounts of power from small resources. While this may be true, other costs outweigh the purely monetary. In 1986, in the Ukrainian town of Chernobyl, a nuclear reactor accident killed 31 Soviet citizens and caused 100,000 people to be evacuated. A radioactive cloud covered much of northern Europe and Great Britain. Nuclear weapons proliferation is another problem if nuclear energy production is increased. Thus, every year there are reports of nuclear by-products missing from government inventories. Enemies of the United States could use this material to build nuclear weapons with which to threaten our security. Economists like to say that increasing the nuclear energy industry will create more high-tech jobs, but the same industry will cause widespread unemployment in traditional fossil-fuel industries like coal, oil, and gas. The potential for both disaster and a negative impact on the economy should convince lawmakers to not increase our use of nuclear energy as a fuel source.

Transitional Expressions for Persuasive Writing

Answering the Opposition and Referring to Authority	Predicting Consequences and Stating Conclusions	Facts and Examples
according to	consequently	another, next
although	in conclusion	because, since
nevertheless	therefore	finally, last
of course	thus	first, second
on the other hand		for
others may say		

Go back and read the paragraph example in Exhibit 15.1. Then, read that same paragraph as illustrated following with transitional expressions included. The transitional expressions are in boldface for identification purposes.

> Mandatory drug testing will help eliminate poor job performance. **Consequently,** workers will do quality work to meet the standards of the company. The company, **therefore,** will be more successful because of the quality of the product the workers will produce. **Next,** the workers' job performance will increase **because** of a better attitude. Mandatory drug testing also will reduce the number of job-related accidents; that, **of course,** will enhance performance. **Thus,** a safe work environment promotes better performances as employees will feel safer and more secure as they perform their jobs. **Lastly,** workers having more confidence in the employer, fellow employees, and the workplace will complete tasks more confidently and successfully.

PRACTICE 6　　Rewriting Paragraphs Using Transitional Expressions

Using appropriate transitional expressions, rewrite the three persuasive paragraphs you wrote for Practice 5. After you have finished, compare the two sets of paragraphs. The ones exhibiting the transitional expressions should be easier to understand and easier to read.

Moving from Paragraph to Essay

Now that you have studied and practiced the techniques to create effective persuasion paragraphs, it is time to expand your ideas to a larger writing unit: the persuasive essay. Using the techniques you learned in Part One regarding developing the essay paragraphs and the persuasion techniques you have just learned, you can write a persuasive essay. This might be a good time to return to Part One and review the techniques for developing the full essay.

Creating the Introductory Paragraph

Like all essays, the persuasive essay needs a clearly defined organization and a thesis sentence to announce to the reader just how the subject will be developed. The thesis sentence should state the topic, the writer's attitude toward the topic, the controlling idea, and the organizational structure. By using an appropriate lead-in technique, the thesis sentence should blend naturally into the rest of the introductory paragraph.

Using the Pro and Con Lists to Create the Thesis Statement for a Pro Essay

Before writing an essay about *students working while in college* (reprinted as follows), one student created pro and con lists. After examining both lists, he chose the pro position and constructed a thesis statement with an essay map consisting of three of the five items on the pro side of the list. Notice that the pro and con lists, when used as the basis for the essay map, act both as an organizational tool and a working outline. The pro and con lists and thesis are illustrated as follows.

© 2014 Wadsworth, Cengage Learning

Topic: Working While in College

Pro	*Con*
1. Working compels students to pursue education more seriously.	1. Working would have a negative impact on the students' grade point average.
2. Working teaches students responsibility.	2. Parents created the students, so parents ought to pay for college.
3. Working removes the financial burden from parents.	3. Going to college teaches students to be responsible, whether they work or not.
4. Working causes students to appreciate college.	4. Working takes away from study time.
5. Working gives students extra money for living expenses and extracurricular activities.	5. Working would make students tire easily at college.

Using the numbers 1, 2, and 3 in the Pro list, the writer constructed the following thesis sentence.

Thesis Sentence: Students should work their way through college because doing so compels the students to pursue education more seriously, teaches the students responsibility, and removes the financial burden from parents.

The topic of the essay is *students working while attending college*, and the writer's combined attitude and controlling idea is *students should work while attending college* (pro) as opposed to a paper that might argue *students should not work while attending college* (con). Notice that the essay map in this thesis sentence comes as a series at the end of the sentence. The three items in the series will be the topics of the first, second, and third body paragraphs, respectively.

Creating the Body Paragraphs

In the sample student essay on *working while in college*, the three items in the essay map form the basis of the three body paragraphs.

- The first body paragraph will focus on *students pursuing education more seriously*.
- The second body paragraph will focus on *students learning responsibility*.
- The third body paragraph will focus on *easing the parents' financial burden*.
- You cannot focus on *studying abroad, athletics,* or *joining fraternities or sororities*.

Keep your focus on the *benefits of working while in college* and on the items in the essay map.

Creating the Concluding Paragraph

As in all types of essays, the concluding paragraph should grow out of the introductory and body paragraphs. All of the approaches to the concluding paragraph work well in persuasive essays. For example, *evaluation* is a good approach, especially if you have chosen the pattern in which you answer the opposition or use a mix of arguing your own points and answering the opposition. With evaluation, you can emphasize the strength of your position and the weakness of the opposition's position. If you have chosen simply to argue for your own position, you might take the *prediction* approach to the concluding paragraph, indicating the future benefits if your point of view prevails. If you have chosen to argue primarily against the opposition, *warning* would be a good technique to use. You can indicate the dire consequences that may come to pass if your opposition's point of view prevails. Finally, a *call to action* in the concluding paragraph works well to persuade the reader to join you in working to see that your point of view is adopted.

Sample Student Essay: WORKING PAYS OFF

Randy Raterman

In this essay, "Working Pays Off," student writer Randy Raterman favors students working while in college. Notice how well the author develops each topic in the body paragraphs. His attention to detail makes the reader feel that he has thought about the issues thoroughly and that he probably worked during his college career.

Vocabulary

Before you begin reading, use a dictionary to look up the following words that appear in the essay.

altered (1)	compels (1)	convey (3)	diligently (2)
excel (2)	excursions (2)	fathom (5)	imposes (1)
paraphernalia (3)	perseverance (3)	shebang (4)	tedious (2)

Working Pays Off

1   Many students have argumentative perspectives toward working their way through college. Some students feel working would have a negative impact on the grade point average. As far as being responsible, numerous students believe going to lectures every day, taking notes, and cramming for exams imposes enough responsibility in itself; additionally, others feel the parents ought to pay for college because it was Mom and Dad who created them. Somehow, the attitude of students not working needs to be altered so that the students better appreciate college education. **Students should work their way through college because doing so compels the students to pursue education more seriously, teaches the students responsibility, and removes the financial burden from parents.**

Thesis Statement with Essay Map →

Topic Sentence → 2   Many working class students experience firsthand what it's like to have backbreaking, monotonous jobs with no particular ladder to climb. The main goals of these individuals are to do everything humanly possible to excel in college, graduate, and quit their dead-end, tedious, everyday jobs. Consequently, several students argue grade points averages would be substantially lower if they had to work. Being concerned about a lower G.P.A. is a good point, but one having no leg to stand on. True, the extra load of working along with going to school robs time from social activities and family excursions; however, working students labor diligently on scholastics knowing failure leads nowhere and climbs no ladders. Unemployed students never experience the level of gratification gained by employed students with high G.P.A. s. Yes, employment may consume a little of the students' study time; although time can be regained by reevaluating priorities, numerous students will continue searching for excuses not to work. While nobody will ever proclaim working their way through college was easy, the experience is truly rewarding and compels the student to be responsible.

Topic Sentence ⟶ 3   Being a responsible adult is another admirable trait hard work leaves ingrained in your personality. Numerous unemployed students lack perseverance and have carefree attitudes originating from parents paying the bills for tuition, books, and other paraphernalia. A majority of the jobless enrolled for classes only fear being kicked off of their parents' insurance or losing various funds provided by Uncle Sam if they flunk out. Nevertheless, employed students convey to others, after having finished the process, that paying for college teaches responsibility. True, nonworking students attending classes and achieving good grades show signs of a responsible nature, but the high magnitude of responsibility is much more prevalent in working students. Many employed students maintain a high G.P.A. along with raising a family. Children add an enormous amount of additional responsibility to a student's daily grind. Yes, working can make anyone tire easily, but the hard work, long hours, and high level of responsibility are extremely gratifying when college is completed and the students can quit their dead-end, fatiguing, tedious jobs.

Topic Sentence ⟶ 4   The employed students also can be proud of keeping their financial burden off their parents, or at least of keeping monetary setback to a minimum. Many loving parents go to their wits end trying to support their offspring though college. While mortgaging the family residence, working two and three jobs, and depleting life savings, parents become overwhelmed by the cost of education. Stress, due to insufficient funds for the children's education, can sometimes cause major difficulties between the parents. There have even been divorces caused by such financial problems. The responsible, working students pay their own way through school or at least pay a significant portion of the tuition, easing the stress and monetary problems of the parents. Proud parents of children working their way through college will have enough funds to help out and enough to help with their own retirement. In the future, this can be a blessing to both parents and children. Unfortunately, a few students believe that since their parents brought them into the world, the parents owe them everything. After all, they didn't ask to be born! Such attitudes may stem from a lack of responsibility during the development stage when they were young. Although it is true that the parents did bring the children into the world, they should not pay for the whole shebang; no, such thinking on the part of the children is not socially or morally acceptable.

5   Many working students simultaneously envy and despise the nonworking student. Although most students wish they were born with a silver spoon in their mouths, few ever are; as a result, many college goers are employed and do work their way through college. Working also provides students with money for living expenses and extracurricular activities, so going to a movie theater is not a financial dilemma. Nevertheless, students working their way through college can be proud of scholastic accomplishments while carrying high levels of responsibility from day to day. The enormous level of gratification and satisfaction students experience while working their way through college is one which nonworking students will never fathom.

Persuasion Technique Questions

1. What organization pattern does the writer use?

_____

_____

_____

_____

2. Can you think of any pro points the author could have considered that might have made his argument even stronger?

_____

_____

_____

_____

3. The writer uses many transitional expressions. Pick out one or two in each body paragraph, and explain how it helps make the writer's position more believable.

_____

_____

_____

_____

Critical Reading and Thinking Questions

1. What is the main idea of the essay?

_____

_____

_____

2. Does the writer use mostly opinion, or does he use mostly facts? Point out sentences that support your answer.

_____

_____

_____

3. How convincing is the support evidence? Does the writer make any claims that seem too extreme or opinionated? Point out examples.

_____

_____

_____

Persuasive Writing Exercises

W R I T I N G

1. Write a persuasive paragraph either for or against parents supporting their adult children who come back home to live, perhaps because of a divorce or sudden unemployment. Before writing, create a pro and con list to discover points of view of both children and the parents.
2. Now, write a persuasive essay by expanding the ideas you created in Exercise 1. Do not forget to use transitional expression to order your ideas logically and to create rhythm within the essay.

Creating the Introductory Paragraph and Thesis Statement for a Con Essay

Before writing an essay about mixed-gender training in the military (re-printed as follows), one student created pro and con lists. After examining both lists, he chose the con position and constructed a thesis statement with an essay map consisting of three of the four items in his con list. Notice that the pro and con lists, when used as the basis for the essay map, act both as an organizational tool and a working outline. The pro and con lists and thesis are illustrated as follows.

Topic: Men and Women Training Together in the Military

Pro	*Con*
1. Men and women have to work together at some point, so let them train together.	1. There would be more sexual harassment cases.
2. If you separate by sex, then why not by race and religion. It is the same concept.	2. It would increase complaints of favoritism.
3. Good manners and behavior are a part of military custom whether women are around or not.	3. Men would be concentrating on whether they might say or do something offensive to women rather than concentrating on duties.
4. There would still be complaints of being separate but not equal.	4. Mixed-sex units would cause less unit cohesion.

Using numbers 1, 2, and 4 in the Con list, the writer constructed the following thesis sentence.

> **Thesis Sentence:** Training men and women in same-sex units would lead to a breakdown in unit cohesion, more complaints of sexual harassment, and increased complaints of favoritism.

The first, second, and third body paragraphs, then, will develop the topics of a breakdown in unit cohesion, more sexual harassment complaints, and increased favoritism.

Sample Student Essay: GUYS AND GALS

Bryan Kemper

> In his essay "Guys and Gals," student writer Bryan Kemper, a military veteran, explains why he is against men and women training together in the same military units. Kemper is neither against women being in the military, nor is he against women receiving equal training. His conclusion is that, if they were trained separately, both men and women would be better trained and, therefore, the military's effectiveness would be increased.

Vocabulary

Before you begin reading, use a dictionary to look up the following words that appear in the essay.

cohesion (1)	comply (1)	designated (3)
favoritism (3)	harassment (1)	integration (1)
preferential (1)	reprimanded (4)	stereotypes (4)

Guys and Gals

1   The integration of women and men has become an increasing problem in the American military. There are concerns about women being sexually harassed in the workplace, and concerns about men receiving preferential treatment. Other issues include women having easier standards to comply with, and men having to attend time-consuming sensitivity training. Both men and women should receive the same opportunities and fair treatment. **Thesis Statement with Essay Map** → Training men and women in same-sex units would lead to more complaints of sexual harassment, a breakdown in unit cohesion, and increased complaints of favoritism.

Topic Sentence → 2   Sexual harassment is a problem that will not go away, and the problem will not get any better as long as men and women are being trained together. Some advocates of same-sex training units believe that men and women will have to work together at some point in their military careers. Because the military is about discipline and teamwork, men and women should be trained together so they will learn to get along with each other. However, when there are men and women working together, there is the potential for sexual harassment to occur. Training in two separate units can insure that men and women are given equal amounts of quality training. Separate male and female units would also afford women the opportunity to prove their abilities to perform the same duties as any male unit in the military after the proper amount of training, without the added pressure of performing in front of their male counterparts before they are ready.

Topic Sentence → 3   Under the current system, women are not allowed the same opportunities for duty assignments as men. The different job assignments allowed for women, especially in combat units, are very limited. Separation of male and female units would not lessen the opportunity of duty assignments for women; separate units would increase women's opportunity for different duty positions made available. Female training units should be specially designated for the performance of certain combat duty assignments; moreover, units should be set aside to perform exactly the same duties as a male unit. Women should be given the same training as men, using the same standards. Because of equal opportunity for separate male and female units, there would be no complaints of favoritism or preferential treatment. Separate units would be more beneficial for women and men alike; in the end, each unit would be more cohesive, and the military, as a whole, would become more effective in succeeding in its missions.

Topic Sentence → 4   Women and men are not judged by the same standard in today's military; consequently, there are complaints that women receive preferential treatment. Often men are reprimanded for incidents involving sexual harassment or misconduct; the man's side of the story often is not taken into consideration. Men are given more opportunity for job promotion or advancement than women, and there are more men in leadership positions. Because of gender stereotypes, women are excused from performing required duties. Favoritism can be argued for either side. If trained separately, men and women would be evaluated among their peers based solely on merit and job performance. If evaluated with peers of the same sex, neither men nor women would receive favoritism according to their gender.

5   Men and women are still going to have to work together in the military. Not all units and job assignments should be separate, but there are many combat units where they should be segregated. If there are separate units for men and women, they still should be trained to work together; however, the units should be kept separate as much as possible. Perhaps a block of training hours could be set aside every week for just such a purpose. But, for the most part, men and women should be trained in separate units for real equal opportunity employment conditions to exist.

Persuasion Technique Questions

ANALYZING

1. What organizational pattern does the writer use?

_____

_____

_____

_____

_____

2. Does the writer use mostly opinion or mostly facts? Point out sentences that support your answer.

_____

_____

_____

3. Did the writer use many transitional expressions? If not, which ones would be appropriate, and where would you place them?

_____

_____

_____

Critical Reading and Thinking Questions

A N A L Y Z I N G

1. What is the main idea of the essay?

_____

_____

_____

2. How convincing is the support evidence? Does Kemper make any claims that seem too extreme or opinionated? Point out examples.

_____

_____

_____

3. What techniques does the writer use in the concluding paragraph? How does it support the writer's point of view put forward in the body paragraphs?

_____

_____

_____

Persuasive Writing Exercises

1. Write a persuasive paragraph either for or against women participating with men in a traditionally all-male sport, such as wrestling, baseball, football, ice hockey, soccer, or basketball. You can use facts, opinions, or a combination of both to support your thesis.

WRITING

2. Write a persuasive essay about a behavior that in the past was considered unacceptable for women but today is considered permissible, such as women asking men out on a date, women working as mechanics or race car drivers, or single women having or adopting children to raise on their own. Before writing your essay, make a pro and con list that reflects both sides of the issue. Choose which side you wish to defend, and then write your essay using transitional devices to connect your ideas.

Sample Professional Essay: LAST RITES FOR THE INDIAN DEAD

Suzan Shown Harjo

This essay, "Last Rites for the Indian Dead," was written by Suzan Shown Harjo, a Native American of Cheyenne descent, and it first appeared in the *Los Angeles Times*. In her essay, Harjo identifies a problem that affects Native Americans, but she also argues that the issue poses an ethical conflict for all Americans.

Vocabulary

Before you begin reading, use a dictionary to look up the definitions for the following words that appear in the essay.

abhorrent (7)	archaeological (2)	cranial (3)	curation (11)
decapitated (3)	desecration (8)	exhumed (3)	funerary (15)
macabre (10)	mastodons (6)	pseudo- (4)	relic (7)
rummaging (8)	strewn (8)		

Last Rites for the Indian Dead

1 What if museums, universities, and government agencies could put your dead relatives on display or keep them in boxes to be cut up and otherwise studied? What if you believed that the spirits of the dead could not rest until their human remains were placed in a sacred area?

2 The ordinary American would say there ought to be a law—and there is, for ordinary Americans. The problem for American Indians is that there are too many laws of the kind that make us the archaeological property of the United States and too few of the kind that protect us from such insults.

3 Some of my own Cheyenne relatives' skulls are in the Smithsonian Institution today, along with those of at least 4,500 other Indian people who were violated in the 1800s by the U.S. Army for an "Indian Cranial Study." It wasn't enough that these unarmed Cheyenne people were mowed down by the cavalry at the infamous Sand Creek massacre; many were decapitated and their heads shipped to Washington as freight. (The Army Medical Museum's collection is now in the Smithsonian.) Some had been exhumed only hours after being buried. Imagine their grieving families' reaction on finding their loved ones disinterred and headless.

4 Some targets of the Army's study were killed in noncombat situations and beheaded immediately. The officer's account of the decapitation of the Apache chief Mangas Coloradas in 1863 shows the pseudoscientific nature of the exercise. "I weighed the brain and measured the skull," the good doctor

wrote, "and found that while the skull was smaller, the brain was larger than that of Daniel Webster."

5   These journal accounts exist in excruciating detail, yet missing are any records of overall comparisons, conclusions, or final reports of the Army study. Since it is unlike the Army not to leave a paper trail, one must wonder about the motive for its collection.

6   The total Indian body count in the Smithsonian collection is more than 19,000, and it is not the largest in the country. It is not inconceivable that the 1.5 million of us living today are outnumbered by our dead stored in museums, educational institutions, federal agencies, state historical societies, and private collections. The Indian people are further dehumanized by being exhibited alongside the mastodons and dinosaurs and other extinct creatures.

7   Where we have buried our dead in peace, more often than not the sites have been desecrated. For more than 200 years, relic hunting has been a popular pursuit. Lately, the market in Indian artifacts has brought this abhorrent activity to a fever pitch in some areas. And when scavengers come upon Indian burial sites, everything found becomes fair game, including sacred burial offerings, teeth, and skeletal remains.

8   One unusually well-publicized example of Indian grave desecration occurred two years ago in a western Kentucky field known as Slack Farm, the site of an Indian village five centuries ago. Ten men—one with a business card stating "Have Shovel, Will Travel"—paid the landowner $10,000 to lease digging rights between planting seasons. They dug extensively on the 40-acre farm, rummaging through an estimated 650 graves, collecting burial tools, tools, and ceremonial items. Skeletons were strewn about like litter.

9   What motivates people to do something like this? Financial gain is the first answer. Indian relic-collecting has become a multimillion-dollar industry. The price tag on a bead necklace can easily top $1,000; rare pieces fetch tens of thousands.

10   And it is not just collectors of the macabre who pay for skeletal remains. Scientists say that these deceased Indians are needed for research that someday could benefit the health and welfare of living Indians. But just how many dead Indians must they examine? Nineteen thousand?

11   There is doubt as to whether permanent curation of our dead really benefits Indians. Dr. Emery A. Johnson, former assistant surgeon general, recently observed, "I am not aware of any current medical diagnostic or treatment procedure that has been derived from research on such skeletal remains. Nor am I aware of any during the 34 years that I have been involved in American Indian . . . health care."

12   Indian remains are still being collected for racial biological studies. While the intentions may be honorable, the ethics of using human remains this way without the full consent of relatives must be questioned.

13   Some relief for Indian people has come on the state level. Almost half of the states, including California, have passed laws protecting Indian burial sites and restricting the sale of Indian bones, burial offerings, and other sacred items. Representative Charles E. Bennett (D–Fla.) and Sen. John McCain (R–Ariz.) have introduced bills that are a good start in invoking the federal government's protections. However, no legislation has attacked the problem head-on by imposing stiff penalties at the marketplace, or by changing laws that make dead Indians the nation's property.

14   Some universities—notably Stanford, Nebraska, Minnesota, and Seattle—have returned, or agreed to return, Indian human remains; it is fitting that institutions of higher education should lead the way.

15   Congress is now deciding what to do with the government's extensive collections of Indian human remains and associated funerary objects. The secretary of the Smithsonian, Robert McAdams, has been valiantly attempting

to apply modern ethics to yesterday's excesses. This week, he announced that the Smithsonian would conduct an inventory and return all Indian skeletal remains that could be identified with specific tribes or living kin.

16   But there remains a reluctance generally among collectors of Indian remains to take action of a scope that would have a quantitative impact and a healing quality. If they will not act on their own—and it is highly unlikely that they will—then Congress must act.

17   The country must recognize that the bodies of dead American Indian people are not artifacts to be bought and sold as collectors' items. It is not appropriate to store tens of thousands of our ancestors for possible future research. They are our family. They deserve to be returned to their sacred burial grounds and given a chance to rest.

18   The plunder of our people's graves has gone on too long. Let us rebury our dead and remove this shameful past from America's future.

Persuasion Technique Questions

ANALYZING

1. Does Harjo use mostly opinion or mostly facts in the essay? Point out some examples.

_____

_____

_____

_____

_____

_____

_____

_____

_____

2. Is the evidence that Harjo uses effective in convincing you that her ideas should be taken seriously by Congress and by average Americans? Explain.

_____

_____

_____

_____

_____

3. Did the writer use many transitional expressions? If not, which ones would be appropriate, and where would you place them?

_____

_____

_____

_____

_____

Critical Reading and Thinking Questions

ANALYZING

1. What kind of conclusion does Harjo use to end the essay? Why is this an effective choice?

_____

_____

_____

_____

_____

_____

_____

2. Harjo clearly points out that desecrating Indian graves is a problem. But what is the ethical issue she raises that confronts the entire nation?

_____

_____

_____

_____

_____

_____

_____

Persuasive Writing Exercises

1. Write a persuasive paragraph either in support of or against the U.S. government having made reparation payment to the families of Japanese Americans whose homes, possessions, and businesses were confiscated and who were interned in American concentration camps during World War II.
2. Write a persuasive essay either for or against the U.S. government making reparation payments to the families of African Americans who were held as slaves up until the end of the Civil War. To complete the assignment, you may have to consult an encyclopedia or do some research at the library or on the Internet.

More Topics for a Persuasive Essay

Here are possible topics for persuasive essay writing assignments. Remember, your essay should have a clearly defined purpose. Pick either a pro or a con position for your essay.

1. Organized prayer in public schools should (not) be allowed.
2. Parents on welfare should (not) be required to work.
3. Controversial organizations (Communist Party, Ku Klux Klan) should (not) be allowed to advertise in campus publications.
4. Two years of studying a foreign language should (not) be required in high school.
5. Parents should (not) be held legally responsible for their minor children's actions.
6. Affirmative action should (not) be implemented for college enrollment.
7. The legal drinking age should (not) be 18 years of age.
8. Marijuana should (not) be legalized for medical purposes.
9. English should (not) be legally designated as the official language of the United States.
10. Single adults should (not) be allowed to adopt children.
11. Gays and lesbians should (not) be allowed to legally marry.
12. Assisted suicide should (not) be legalized.
13. Separation of church and state should (not) be upheld constitutionally.
14. Illegal immigrant workers should (not) be given permanent legal status.
15. Congress should (not) have to officially declare war before troops can be sent to fight in a foreign country.

☑ Writing Checklist for a Persuasive Essay

- ❏ Choose an issue.
- ❏ Make a pro and con list to explore both sides of the issue.
- ❏ Choose a side to argue.
- ❏ Create a thesis sentence.
- ❏ Choose an organizational pattern for the body paragraphs.
- ❏ Draft the essay using transitional expressions to connect related ideas.
- ❏ Make sure you support your point of view with sound evidence.
- ❏ Check for logical fallacies.

❏　　Revise the first draft.

❏　　Proofread the final draft.

❏　　Print or type the essay and submit it.

CHAPTER REVIEW

■ A persuasive essay attempts to convince the reader that a particular point of view is correct. Persuasive writing can be informal, semiformal, or formal (also called argumentation).

■ In a persuasive paragraph, the topic sentence states the writer's point of view about a topic—pro or con. In developing such a paragraph, it is useful first to list the pros and cons about the topic. The pro and con list can help you adopt a position and choose supporting points for the paragraph.

■ Techniques to support an argument include answering the opposition, referring to an authority, predicting consequences, using facts, and using examples. Transitional expressions help signal which technique is being used.

■ A persuasive paragraph has three basic patterns of organization: arguing only your own points, arguing against your opposition's points, and alternating arguing your own points and arguing against the opposition.

■ When you write a persuasive essay, you can use the pro and con list to develop your controlling attitude (pro or con) and to select the items for the essay map and, consequently, the body paragraphs.

■ The four approaches to the concluding paragraph—evaluation, warning, prediction, and call to action—can all be used effectively in a persuasive essay.

 Visit *The Write Start* Online!

For additional practice with the materials found in this chapter, visit our Student Companion Web site by going to cengagebrain.com and searching for this text. The Web site also features additional readings, quizzes, writing activities, and Internet links.

Pages 247–249: Suzan Shown Harjo, "Last Rites for Indian Dead." Originally published in the *Los Angeles Times*, September 16, 1989. Reprinted by permission of the author.

PART THREE

Special Writing Situations

As you progress in your academic life, you will encounter special writing situations on numerous occasions: the **research paper** and **timed in-class writing**. Although all writing relies on the principles and skills you have developed in your basic writing classes, these special writing situations call for additional approaches and techniques if you are to complete them successfully.

The Undergraduate Research Paper

You will be required to write research papers in many of your classes. Research papers give you the opportunity to dig deeply into a topic. You will find information about the topic through many sources in the library and on the Internet. In your essay, you will document your sources. More times than not, you will argue against a point of view that you have discovered by offering your own conclusions on the subject. You will use the source material you have found to support your conclusions.

Timed In-Class Writing

One of the most common types of writing you will encounter in college is the in-class essay exam. Because you will have a limited amount of time to answer, there is an added dimension to this type of writing experience: time pressure. To be successful, you must have a method to organize your thoughts quickly in order to effectively construct a developed essay in a short amount of time.

In the following two chapters, you will be introduced to the elements and techniques that will enable you to write successfully in these two of the major areas of your college work.

16

The Undergraduate Research Paper

The research paper is an extended essay. Because you will be using documented sources to support, clarify, and exemplify your observations and conclusions, the research paper is generally longer than other types of essays, normally from 7 to 20 pages. The work involved in writing a research paper is considerable, so you should allow yourself as much time as you need—usually a month or more—to research, write, and proofread the paper.

The research paper writing process can be divided into distinct steps.

1. Select a topic that you know you can find information about in the library or on the Internet.
2. Limit the topic by stating the paper's purpose.
3. Research the topic and take notes.
4. Outline your paper.
5. Select the quotations and citations you have on your note cards and printouts that you will use to support your stated purpose.
6. Arrange the quotations and citations in the order in which they will be used in your paper.
7. Write the paper.
8. Document the paper using the appropriate format.
9. Proofread the paper for grammatical, spelling, and documentation format errors.
10. Revise the paper for submission by making the necessary changes you found while proofreading.

Following these basic steps can save you a lot of time and energy as you make your way through the research process. For a thorough understanding of the research writing process, you should read the detailed explanations that follow.

© 2014 Wadsworth, Cengage Learning

Select a Topic

It is of vital importance that the subject you choose to write about can be researched. Generally speaking, this means that the subject must have books, articles, and critical essays written about it. If it does not, then you will not be able to find sources written by others that agree with your point of view to use as support for your conclusions.

A lack of source material is not usually a problem when you are doing research about famous people, places, and events of the past. However, when writing about current people, places, and events, you must be careful that there is enough information from which to draw your support material.

Before you do anything else, go to the library and make certain that there are enough books, articles, and critical essays about your topic to make continuing the process worthwhile. If you can find a minimum of 10 to 20 books, articles, and critical essays about your topic, you should be able to find enough material to support your views. If you cannot, you should probably select another topic.

Limit the Topic

Research papers, like all writing, must have a clearly defined purpose. Use the techniques you studied in Chapter 4 regarding constructing a thesis sentence to clearly define the parameters of your paper's approach.

The thesis sentence with essay map will automatically limit your paper to the stated subtopics, and it will clearly define your attitude toward the topic and the paper's organization. Using the thesis sentence with essay map also will help you bring into focus those specific areas (the essay map subtopics) for which you will collect your support material. This will save you a lot of time and effort because you will use only 5 to 10 percent of all the material you find. The more focused the research, the less time you will waste.

Before finalizing your thesis sentence, however, you might want to do some research and reading to gain a clear perspective on your final subtopics.

Research the Topic and Take Notes

To find information in a library regarding your topic, you can use the following sources to focus your research:

- the general online catalog
- *The Reader's Guide to Periodical Literature*
- *The Bibliographic Index*
- the specific indexes for such disciplines as the humanities and the social sciences

Your library, in all probability, also uses *NewsBank*, which you can use to access over one thousand newspapers for information. Or your library may subscribe to other computerized databases of periodicals and journals. Most libraries also have source information on microfilm, microfiche, and CD-ROM.

You also can use a variety of encyclopedias to find information regarding your topic. Many instructors will not allow you to use information from encyclopedias in your formal research paper, but they are good sources in which to find general background information that can lead you to other sources and ideas.

You can search for information on the Internet by doing a simple *keyword search*. Ask the reference librarian for assistance if you are not familiar with this process.

As you gather information related to your stated purpose, you need to save citations and quotations to use in your paper. You can use index cards or computer printouts for keeping such information. It is best to use a separate index card for each citation or quotation.

Using Online (Internet) Sources

The Internet is a valuable resource for quickly gathering material from which to choose the information you will use to support your ideas in the research paper. However, you need to know that not all Internet sources are necessarily reliable, relevant, or proper to use in a formal, college-level researched paper.

There are many online source guides you can use that will explain why you need to evaluate Internet material.

■ You can simply type *"Evaluating Internet Sources"* into your search engine box, and you will find a list of links that you can use to help you evaluate online sources that you might consider using for material to include in your paper, such as www.studygs.net or www.virtualsalt.com/evalu8it.htm.

The information you will find in these guides includes, but is not limited to, the following:

■ **How did you locate the Web sites?** Did your instructor or a librarian refer you to the Web sites? Did you find the Web site in a reputable journal? (This most likely means that the Web sites are reliable.)

■ **What is the Web site's domain?** Is it a *.com (a business site); an .org (usually an organization that is nonprofit and may/may not advocate for certain causes); a .net (a network organization or Internet provider); an .edu (usually a college or university academic site); or a .gov (federal government sites).*

These domain names often can clarify the Web site's mission, point of view, or whether or not it has no particular bias. Web sites with strong biases for or against a particular issue or cause are often not proper source material for your paper unless you clearly make these positions clear to the reader. How the material and the biased way it is presented can affect how your reader judges your opinions in the paper.

■ **What is the material's authority?** In other words, who is the author of the material? Is it a single person or a group? Is the author's name clearly identified? What are the author's credentials? Is the author a recognized authority in the field under discussion? What is the author's background, and is the author published in credible journals?

■ **Is the material found in the Web site accurate and objective?** *Accuracy* is the most difficult aspect of material to qualify, online or otherwise. The best method is to compare the material to that found on other Web sites to find discrepancies or similarities. Also, how old is the information? Many types of information change, often very quickly, depending upon the discipline. For example, in the fields of medicine, astrophysics, and law, what is considered as "factual" or "up-to-date" often changes from day to day depending on new research, new findings, and new legal decisions. Even in fields such as history and literature, new discoveries and interpretations can change old, tried-and-true beliefs into new and accepted ideas. *Objectivity* also is an important consideration when deciding to use information found on the Web. While there is no such thing as pure objectivity, an author should be able to control biases to some degree. However, as was stated earlier, many individuals and organizations have very strong beliefs(biases) toward particular issues. Some individuals and organizations will purposely distort information to try and convince others that their point of view is true.

■ **The writer's responsibilities are many.** As a writer, you must figure out if the information you are using to support your ideas is authoritative, reliable, relevant, accurate, and objective.

Outline the Paper

Follow whatever outlining method you are comfortable with or that your instructor has required. Some instructors require you to submit an outline, and some do not. There are *essay map outlines, sentence outlines, paragraph outlines,* and *topic outlines.* Your instructor will explain which one he or she wants you to use. Whichever outline you use, begin fleshing out your ideas in the order that your outline suggests, and incorporate your support materials where appropriate.

Select the Researched Support Material

Before you use any support material in your paper, you must decide whether or not it will actually support your points and conclusions. To do this, ask a series of questions about the material.

- Does the material support your attitude toward the topic as stated in the thesis sentence?
- How current is the information? This may not be important if you are dealing with a historical subject, such as the Spanish Inquisition or World War II. However, if you are writing about a new medical procedure such as Lasik eye surgery or a new photographic technique such as a CCD (charged coupled device), information that is only a few years old may be out of date.
- Does the information come from an objective or biased source? The best sources for gathering information are those that are not published or written by people having a particular political, social, or monetary reason for publishing the information. In other words, if they have a lot to gain personally by persuading people with the information, then the material might be too biased to be convincing. On the other hand, if you use material from persons or groups who do not stand to gain personally by convincing others to support their position, then the information is usually more objective. Using support material that is objective usually is considered more convincing.
- What kind of material should you look for to support your ideas and conclusions? The most convincing evidence to support your claims will appeal to reason, not emotion. To persuade the reader that a particular position is convincing, use the following support evidence: *answering the opposition, referring to an authority, predicting consequences, stating facts,* and *providing examples.* See Chapter 15 for information regarding these types of evidence.

Arrange the Quotations

With the outline completed, you should arrange your index cards and computer printouts in the order in which you will use them in the paper. You can identify their placement in the paper by marking them with numbers or letters corresponding to those of your outline sections.

Write the Paper

Remember to include your thesis sentence in the introductory paragraph, and develop your subtopics in the body paragraphs. The research paper, because of its length, has more body paragraphs than the short essay model you have been studying so far in this textbook. In addition, the thesis sentence with essay map may be too short for this type of paper. You can use several sentences or short paragraphs to introduce the paper's overall topic and the topics of the body paragraphs.

Finish the essay by using one of the techniques you have studied for concluding paragraphs. See Chapters 4, 5, and 6 to review the basic elements of the introductory, body, and concluding paragraphs.

As you write your paper, try to use transitional expressions you have studied in this textbook to connect related ideas, add sentence variety, and create rhythm within the paper.

Document the Paper

When using the work of others in your paper, you must tell the reader from what source you quoted or cited the source of the quotation or idea. The borrowed information must be cited within the text of the paper and at the end of the paper in the Works Cited section.

Use the Appropriate Format

Different disciplines use different documentation formats. For example, in the humanities (English, speech, communication, theater, foreign language, and art), the Modern Language Association (MLA) is commonly used. In the sciences (biology, botany, psychology, nursing, and chemistry), the American Psychological Association (APA) documentation format is commonly used.

Because this is a textbook for an English course, the MLA documentation format will be explained later in this chapter. You will also see examples of documentation in a student-written research paper, as well as a research paper written by a professional writer.

Avoid Plagiarism

Beware of plagiarism. It can cause your paper to receive a failing grade, and it can cause you other academic problems, such as suspension or expulsion from school. **Plagiarism** occurs when you use someone else's ideas as if they were your own and do not give the other person credit. Plagiarism also includes buying a paper or letting someone else substantially write or edit your work for you.

Plagiarism can arise because of poor note-taking. Misquoting or inaccurately summarizing or paraphrasing can also cast suspicion on the integrity of your writing. When you take notes for a quotation or citation, be certain you copy the information carefully. If you put someone else's idea into your own words by summarizing or paraphrasing, you are still required to document the information. Failure to do so is considered plagiarism.

Plagiarism is the worst kind of academic dishonesty because it degrades our ability to trust that others are writing honestly and with integrity about their own thoughts and ideas and about the thoughts and observations of others.

Proofread the Paper

Submitting a paper that is substantially free of errors will create a positive impression in your instructor's mind. A paper free of misspelled words, grammatical errors, and documentation errors tells the reader that the writer cares about the writing and the reader's experience in reading it.

Conversely, a paper full of errors reflects poorly on the writer and the assignment. Errors reduce the pleasure of the reading experience, sidetrack the reader's attention from the paper's purpose, and create the impression that the writer is either careless, uneducated, or both.

Proofreading is the process of eliminating mechanical and content errors. *Mechanical errors* encompass misspelled words (including typos), punctuation, capitalization, and spacing. *Content errors* include incorrect facts or inaccurate or misleading information that makes the expressed ideas difficult or confusing to understand. It is the writer's responsibility, with minor assistance from others, such as tutors and writing lab staff, to find and correct both types of errors. Generally, proofreading is more effective if you do it at least twice: once for content errors and again for mechanical errors.

Prepare the Paper for Submission

Instructors often have their own preferences, but there are some standard guidelines for preparing research papers for submission. Needless to say, a research paper should not be handwritten. It should be prepared on a computer or word processor using the following guidelines.

- Use bright, white, unlined computer paper. Do not use gray or colored paper.
- Use 20- or 25-lb. paper. This paper weight is substantial enough to resist creases and tears.
- Use black ink.
- Set margins at 1 inch to 1½ inches.
- Double-space. Your instructor has to read many papers, and double-spacing makes them easier to read. In addition, the double-spacing leaves room for the instructor's comments.
- Anchor the pages with a staple in the upper left corner of the paper.
- Look through the paper. If it is not professional in appearance, make the necessary changes before submitting the paper to your instructor.
- Hand the paper in flat, not folded.

The Modern Language Association (MLA) Documentation Format

This section illustrates just a few of the many entry examples for documenting citations from sources such as books, periodicals, and electronic media. You can find complete guides to documenting in a variety of formats in any bookstore, library, or on the Internet.

When documenting sources from which you have used information, you must cite the material in two places in your research paper: within the narrative of the paper and at the end in the Works Cited section.

Citing within the Paper

MLA uses a parenthetical documentation method to cite sources when they are quoted or paraphrased. When citing a source, the borrowed material is followed by parentheses ( ) containing the last name of the author, a space, and then the page number where the information can be found. If the quotation or paraphrase is introduced with a statement containing the author's name, the name is not repeated in the parentheses. Two examples follow.

> "There is no truth to the rumor that the chemical formula tested by the company did not answer the problem that had surfaced," stated Dr. Angela Washington (28).
>
> A prominent chemist stated, "There is no truth to the rumor that the chemical formula tested by the company did not answer the problem that had surfaced" (Washington 28).

To find the full citation information, the reader can consult the entry for "Washington" in the Works Cited list at the end of the paper.

Some points to remember regarding citations in the text:

■ Use only the last name of the author in the parentheses. If you quote from two different people having the same last name, include the initial of the first name to distinguish between the two authors.

■ Do not use a comma to separate the author's name from the page number.

■ Place the parentheses immediately after the quotation. If it is at the end of a sentence, place it before the period.

■ Parentheses usually do not follow citations taken from the Internet because these sources rarely have page numbers, and MLA suggests mentioning the author's name in the text, or frame (frames will be discussed later in this chapter). If you do not place the author's name in the frame or a page number is available, then you do place this information in parentheses. Do not place the URL (online address) after the quotation. At present, MLA considers URLs too long and cumbersome for inclusion in either the text or in the Works Cited section. However, your instructor may want you to include them, particularly in the Works Cited section. Clarify with your instructor what they want you to do.

■ If a quotation is taken from an article that appears only on one page of a magazine or journal, it is not necessary to duplicate the page number in the parentheses following the quotation.

In-Text and Block Citations

If your quotation is short, no more than three or four typed lines, provide an **in-text citation**. An in-text citation incorporates the material into the text. Place quotation marks around the quoted material. Be certain that your finished sentence is grammatically correct.

> **In-Text Citation**
>
> According to a well-documented theory, "the most likely reason the dinosaurs became extinct was a large meteor struck the earth throwing up enough dust to block out sunlight for months" (Smith 74). The theory has been supported by evidence from around the world. A thin layer of iridium has been found at the K-T boundary in Europe, North and South America, Asia, and Africa.

If your quotation is five or more typed lines, separate it from the text by using a **block citation**. Indent the entire quotation ten spaces from the left margin. Leave the right margin alone. Do not put quotation marks at the beginning and end of the quoted material as you do for an in-text quotation. Be certain to follow the quotation with the parenthetical citation.

> **Block Method Citation**
>
> A child's performance in school has a lot to with his home environment. According to Dr. Gerald Gaines, an expert in elementary education issues,

(continued)

> However well-meaning advocates of testing and standards are, the current plan does not factor in the changing composition of American families and how these changes have affected a child attending school today. Children coming through the schoolhouse doors may have just left a home that would have been largely unrecognizable thirty years ago. The phenomenal increase in single-parent families, poverty level income families, and families in which child abuse occurs on a regular basis has changed how these children face their day in school. (143)

The government needs to take a closer look at how welfare money and services are interfacing with the educational models that have been poor predictors as to how children will fare in their formative educational years.

Framing or Signaling the Quotation

You should never put a quotation into your writing without introducing it to the reader. You can introduce the quotation by stating the name of the person you are quoting, along with his or her title, or expertise. You can even offer a brief comment on the quotation's content. This information is called a **frame** or **signal phrase**, and it can be placed before the quotation, after the quotation, or in the middle of the quotation.

In a *front frame* or *front signal phrase*, the punctuation (a comma or colon) is placed *after* the final word of the introductory phrase, but always *before* the opening quotation mark.

> **The Front Frame or Front Signal Phrase**
>
> Company spokesperson Ashonti Mekela said, "Marketing expertise can guarantee good sales over a short period of time even though the product has no real perceived value to the consumer" (12).

In the *end frame* or *end signal phrase*, the punctuation (comma) is placed *after* the final word of the quotation and is always *before* the closing quotation mark.

> **The End Frame or End Signal Phrase**
>
> "Marketing expertise can guarantee good sales over a short period of time even though the product has no real perceived value to the consumer," said company spokesperson Ashonti Mekela (12).

In the *middle frame* or *middle signal phrase*, the first punctuation (comma) is placed after the last word in the first part of the quotation, but always *before* the first closing quotation mark. The second punctuation (comma) is placed after the last word of the frame, but always *before* the second opening quotation mark.

Middle Frame or Middle Signal Phrase

"Marketing expertise," according to company spokesperson Ashonti Mekela, "can guarantee good sales over a short period of time even though the product has no real perceived value for the consumer" (12).

Try not to use the same framing or signaling style repeatedly. Like all other characteristics of good writing, variety shows maturity of content and style.

Citing at the End of the Paper—The Works Cited Section

As stated earlier, when you use someone else's information, you must cite the information in two places in your paper. You have just studied the first place, in the text of the paper using a parenthetical citation. The second place you must cite the borrowed information is at the end of the paper in the **Works Cited** section. The parenthetical citation in the text of your paper indicates to the reader where in the Works Cited section the full citation information can be found.

The Works Cited section lists only those works that you cited in your paper. Do not list any sources that you did not quote from or paraphrase. When constructing your Works Cited list, adhere to the following criteria.

- Entries in the list appear alphabetically according to the author's last name.
- Entries are not numbered.
- Entries without an author appear alphabetically by the first word in the title.
- The first line of an entry extends to the left margin. Subsequent lines of the entry are indented five spaces.
- Double-space the entries.

See the Works Cited pages of the student and professional research papers at the end of this chapter for examples of how this section should be set up.

Examples of Works Cited Entries

Use the following models to guide you as you construct your Works Cited section.

Books
Book by One Author

Rodriquez, Mario. *The Middle Child.* New York: Century, 1999.

The author's last name is placed first, followed by the first name. Titles of books are italicized. The city where the publishing company is located comes next, followed by a full colon and then the name of the publishing company. A comma follows the name of the publisher, and the publication date follows the comma.

Book by Two or More Authors

Han, Yichuan, and Mel Simons. *The Black Hole: Galaxy-Eater.* London: Yorkshire,
2000. Print.

The first author's name appears as it did for the Book by One Author entry, but all subsequent authors' names appear first name first, followed by the last name.

Book by Unknown Author

Growing Flowers in an Apartment. Phoenix: Piaget, 1998. Print.

If the author is not known, the title of the book comes first.

Periodicals

Periodicals are publications that come out on a regular basis: daily, weekly, monthly, quarterly, semiannually, and annually. They include journals, magazines, and newspapers. Journal, magazine, and newspaper article entries use the following order:

1. Author(s)
2. Article's title
3. Name of the periodical
4. Series number, if available
5. Volume number (usually for journals)
6. Issue number, if available
7. Publication date
8. Page numbers of the entire article

Article with One Author

Washington, Pervis. "The Black Experience." Personal Life Digest 16 (1999):
31–47.

Titles of articles are enclosed by quotation marks. The publication in which they appear is underlined. The series or volume number is followed by the publication date in parentheses to separate it from the series or volume number (to avoid confusion). Use a full colon after the date of publication, followed by the page numbers for the entire article.

Article with Unknown Author

"Computers and You." Computer Journal 4 (Winter 2000): 118–24.

If the author is not known, the title of the article comes first.

Article in a Weekly Magazine

Bigtree, Watasha. "Climate for Change in the Industrial Regions in the United
States." Social Issues 10 Sept. 2000: 13–36.

"10 Sept." is the indicator that this is a weekly periodical. Note that the day date is given before the month and year.

Article in a Monthly Magazine

Miller, Judy. "Attention to Detail in the Boardroom: Planning for an Effective
Meeting." Female Executive Jan. 1999: 57–62.

"Jan." is the indicator that this is a monthly periodical.

Article in a Newspaper with Numbered Sections

Edwards, Connie. "Parenting in the Millennium." <u>Globe-Sentinel</u> 8 Aug.

2000, sec. 7: 3.

The first number after "sec." is the section, followed by the specific page number.

Article in a Newspaper with Lettered Sections

Achiba, Kwazi. "Using Filers in Astrophotography." <u>Daily Gazette</u> 3 May

1999: C2.

"C" is the section heading, followed by the specific page number—in this entry, "2."

Electronic Sources: Internet and CD-ROM

Entries for Internet sources look just like entries for periodicals with one major exception: the Universal Resource Locator (URL—the online address). The URL always follows the information in the entry. MLA style is to enclose URLs in angle brackets, as shown in the examples that follow. The URL should not be underlined, nor should it be a different color from the rest of the text. However, when you type a URL using a computer, most programs automatically change the address to a hyperlink. If your printer has a color cartridge, the address will print in blue and will be underlined. If your printer has a black ink cartridge, the URL will print in black and will be underlined. Most instructors are used to seeing these URLs in student papers. Unless your instructor tells you to do otherwise, leave it alone. Or you can ask what format your instructor prefers.

Online Journal Article

Bahamma, Rahal. "Some New Thoughts about Pi." <u>Math-Mavin</u> 3 (2000). 4 Sept.

2000 <http://www.mathmavin.org/journals.html>.

Online Magazine Article

Sahad, Ahmad. "Genetic Mutations in Genome Sequences." <u>Genome</u> Feb. 1999.

15 Mar. 2003 <http://www.genseqpro.com/1999/html>.

When there are two dates in the source, the first date indicates when the information was placed online. It is followed by a period. The second date indicates when you accessed the information. It is not followed by a period.

Article on CD-ROM

Mirinakov, Mikail. "Political Reformation in Former Russian Satellite Coun-

tries." <u>Soviet Daily Citizen</u> 21 Oct. 2000: 7. <u>Soviet Daily Citizen Ondisc.</u>

CD-ROM. Infoquest. Dec. 2000.

CD-ROMs, like other electronic sources, do not always have complete publication information. In such cases, provide the information that is available.

Sample Student Research Paper with Documentation: SIX-YEAR-OLD HARASSERS?

Jennifer Staggs

> This research paper, "Six-Year-Old Harassers," by student writer Jennifer Staggs, argues against an idea that six-year-old children cannot be held responsible for acts defined as sexual harassment and that school districts may be exempt from being sued over adolescent sexual misconduct. Staggs uses material from a variety of secondary sources to support her conclusions, and she documents it using the MLA format. Although paragraph numbers appear in the margins of the research paper that follows, these are provided for reference purposes within this text only and are not a standard element in the MLA format. In the paper itself, the pages would have running heads, and the Works Cited section would begin on a new page.

Jennifer Staggs

English 102.01

Professor Checkett

January 5, 2009

Six-Year-Old Harassers?

1 The words "sexual harassment" may give individuals mental pictures of one adult harassing another in the corporate world or even in the military. However, in George F. Will's article, "Six-Year-Old Harassers?" printed in <u>Newsweek</u> magazine, sexual harassment is now affecting school-aged children. Will claims normal adolescent behavior should not provoke lawsuits and disrupt school districts from receiving federal aid funds. Furthermore, he points out the Supreme Court's poor interpretation of a 1972 law sending school districts across the nation into "defensive silliness" due to the lawsuit between a fifth-grader named LaShonda and a Georgia school district. Since the lawsuit became publicized, other children, including a six-year-old boy, have been suspended for kissing girls on the cheek or for other "normal" adolescent behaviors. Although Will's point sounds reasonable, he does not use substantial evidence to back his claim that school districts should not be held responsible, and he does not state any of the effects that so-called "normal" adolescent behavior or "sexual harassment" has on the accused or the victim.

2 G. F., the fellow fifth-grade boy accused of sexually harassing LaShonda, continued harassing LaShonda and other students for five months. His sexual misbehavior included sexually explicit language, groping, and other crudities; however, Will justified G. F.'s actions by stating that G. F. "was no more vulgar than many

fifth-grade boys occasionally are" (88). George Will believes others are overreacting to typical adolescent behavior. Because accusing a young boy of sexual harassment is very serious, we must first understand what normal adolescent sexual behavior is before dismissing the behavior as typical. William N. Friedrich, a pediatrician, stated in an article:

> Sexual intrusiveness has captured considerable concern of late, particularly with our increasing awareness that preteens can behave in sexually coercive ways with other children. . . . More normative manifestations of this behavioral domain could include the mutual touching of another child's sex parts, self-stimulating behaviors, and exhibitionism. Sexual knowledge is a child's basic understanding of sexual acts and varies with the child's age. (10)

Although G. F.'s behavior may seem normal to Will, the fifth-grader's excessive sexual bullying continued for a long five months, evoking anxiety in a young girl offended by this behavior.

3   Another problem related to sexual harassment in schools is that school districts are being held responsible. In the 1994 case of LaShonda and her Georgia school district, she had the right to hold the school liable due to a 1972 federal law prohibiting any form of sexual discrimination in any educational program receiving federal funds. LaShonda is seeking $500,000 from her school district, which only received $679,000 in federal aid in the 1992–93 school year. George Will blames the Supreme Court for misinterpreting the law and allowing such a lawsuit that may diminish funding for schools. However, in an interview with Caroline Konieczka, an elementary school teacher for twenty years, she stated, "Students must feel safe in the classroom. School is a place of learning, and teachers must do what is in the best interest of their students. If a child comes to a teacher for help, the teachers must take certain steps necessary to help that child." Mrs. Konieczka feels five months is too long for any type of misbehavior to go on, and the school district and parents should be held responsible for such negligence. Most parents want their children to feel safe and secure in school. After all, school is a home away from home for children.

4   Today, teachers have a lot more responsibility than the teachers of yesterday. Not only do they teach children how to read, write, and do arithmetic, they fill the roles of parent, sociologist, and psychologist, all the while expected to create a safe learning environment. Parents and communities expect teachers to mold children into healthy, happy, functional learners. Teachers are expected to keep up with new learning techniques, keep order in the classroom, and develop personal relationships with students to better monitor each child's learning style.

"Handling sexual harassment is just one more task confronting today's teachers. And lest elementary teachers think they are exempt, this episode [the LaShonda/ Georgia case] makes it clear that sexual harassment presents a challenge to teachers at all grade levels," declares Tish Raff, an elementary school assistant principal (1). Because parents are not as accessible during the day due to work schedules and more mothers entering the workplace, teachers have difficulty making contact with a child's parents to discuss matters like sexual harassment or any other type of behavior. Therefore, more responsibility is put on educators' shoulders to monitor and interpret questionable or abnormal adolescent behavior. And teachers may not pick up on certain type of behaviors. Who should be held responsible then? According to a study by the American Psychological Association, "It is estimated that four out of five students report that they have been the target of sexual harassment, but only seven percent told a teacher what happened" (Finks 122). Programs should be set up in all schools to stress communication between the teacher, parent, and student. Children should be able to communicate with teachers, so they can respond properly.

5   In recent years, it has been a school's responsibility to conduct sex education in the classroom; however, a change is due. Parents should be heavily involved in the process. Not only is sex education very important, children are catapulted into an adult subject that may make them feel insecure about themselves and others of the opposite sex. Moms and dads with school-aged children need to be sensitive in addressing the subject of sex and should address what is being taught in the class-room. "Children may show excessive modesty or anxiety at displays of affection between parents or other individuals. Alternatively, children may be very curious and open regarding sexual matters, including interest in the opposite sex and interest in more mature television shows or videos," states pediatrician and mother-of-two Dr. Naomi Neufeld, Director of UCLA's Kidshape Program (12). Therefore, a parent's involvement and sensitivity in the sex education of their child is remarkably impor-tant. The mother and father may then instruct the child on appropriate behavior between two individuals of the opposite sex and validate the material being taught in the classroom.

6   As George Will suggests, school districts may be protected from sexual harass-ment lawsuits under the Individuals With Disabilities Education Act of 1994. The 1994 Act limits disciplinary actions against students with "behavior-disorder dis-abilities," even if the child was not diagnosed before committing any crime or unac-ceptable behavior. Consequently, most children who behave badly from time to time may end up with the label "disabled." It is understandable that a school district would not want to be held liable for sexual harassment in the classroom and

jeopardize losing federal funding, but to pass the buck to children by insisting they have a disability is not solving the problem. A better solution is for the school district to accept responsibility, move in, and prevent such bad behavior from escalating in the future. Assistant Superintendent Beverly Lydiard has developed a program that stresses communication where "teachers are trained in an intervention technique which uses a letter from the victim to the harasser as a communication document, rather than as an accusation." She also says, "If the problem behavior does not change, the situation is then handled more traditionally." This intervention technique allows the victim to express their feelings on paper rather than the potentially intimidating circumstance of a face-to-face confrontation, and the harasser can read the letter to better understand and reflect on how the victim is feeling. The harasser may then write an apology to the victim. Cases of harassment have dwindled since this process has been instituted.

7   In his article, George Will challenges the victims of sexual harassment. He claims if every adolescent claimed their grades suffered and were unable to concentrate, schools across the nation could be held accountable. The evidence Will uses is the 1994 study by the American Association of University Women. The study indicated that 81% of the students report having experienced some form of sexual harassment during their school years. Yet, he attacks the study by saying it was "hysteria mongering" conducted by "victimization feminists." There is a major flaw in his article's thesis; he is notably insensitive toward victims. Victims of any sexual harassment encounter can undergo extreme amounts of stress and anxiety. Just like LaShonda, many adolescents should not have had to endure harassment or bullying that can affect the quality of life. It clearly states in *The Merck Manual* [a well-respected manual that provides information on the diagnosis and therapy for a wide array of medical and psychological afflictions] that anxiety makes "decision-making difficult, and concentration is burdensome" (Berkow et al. 1499). Anxiety can create many other side-effects including sleeplessness, depression, irritability, fearfulness, and vomiting. It is crucial to keep in mind that anxiety does not just fade away. Victims like LaShonda may take a long time to heal, and it is possible that their outlook on sex and the opposite sex can be damaged forever.

8   If LaShonda had never filed suit against her school district, she, as well as others, would probably still be easy targets of sexual harassment. Since the lawsuit, schools across the nation have increased awareness of improper behavior. Hopefully, parents also will become more involved with the sex education of their children to promote open communication with school faculty to intervene in such situations

before any lasting damage is done. Again, normal adolescent behavior should be expected and allowed, but the difference between normal and abnormal should be explored and understood. Children are sacred. The nation must use the law to protect them from harm and to promote positive self-esteem.

Works Cited

Berkow, Robert, et al. *The Merck Manual*. 13th ed. West Point: Merck Sharp and Dome, 1973. Print.

Finks, Rosie. "Sexual Harassment: Myths and Realities." American Psychological Association 4 Apr. 1996: 2. Web. 1 Dec. 1999.

Friedrich, William N. "Normative Behavior in Children." Pediatrics 9 (1991): 5–7.

Konieczka, Caroline. Personal Interview. 10 Nov. 1999.

Lydiard, Beverly. "Intervention." Prevention Oct. 1996: 2.

Neufeld, Naomi. "Sex Education." Redbook Aug. 1997: 11–15.

Raff, Tish. "Sexual Harassment: A Guide for Faculty, Staff, and Students." University of Tennessee 5 Sept. 1996: 1–2. Web. 1 Dec. 1999.

Will, George F. "Six-Year-Old Harassers?" Newsweek 7 June 1999: 88.

Research Paper Technique Questions

I B W E A

A N A L Y Z I N G

1. What is the main idea of the essay?

_____

_____

_____

_____

_____

_____

2. Do you agree more with Staggs or with George Will? Explain.

_____

_____

_____

_____

3. In the essay's second paragraph, there is a block quotation containing [. . .] markings. What does this indicate has happened to the original quotation?

_____

_____

_____

4. In paragraph 6, the writer did not include the author's name or a page number in a parenthetical reference marker at the end of the quotation beginning "Teachers are trained [. . .]." Is this proper MLA formatting?

_____

_____

_____

_____

_____

_____

CHAPTER REVIEW

■ A research paper is an extended essay that uses documented sources to support, clarify, and exemplify your observations and conclusions.

■ There are ten steps in writing a research paper: (1) Select a topic that you know you can find information about in the library or on the Internet. (2) Limit the topic by stating the paper's purpose. (3) Research the topic and take notes. (4) Outline your paper. (5) Select the quotations and citations that you will use to support your stated purpose. (6) Arrange the quotations and citations in the order they will be used. (7) Write the paper. (8) Document the citations using the appropriate format. (9) Proofread the paper for grammatical, spelling, and documentation format errors. (10) Prepare the paper for submission by making the necessary changes you found while proofreading.

■ The documentation format used in a research paper depends on the subject area of the paper. Two frequently used formats are the Modern Language Association format and the American Psychological Association format.

© 2014 Wadsworth, Cengage Learning

 ## Visit _The Write Start_ Online!

For additional practice with the materials found in this chapter, visit our Student Companion Web site by going to cengagebrain.com and searching for this text. The Web site also features additional readings, quizzes, writing activities, and Internet links.

17

The Essay Exam

It is one thing to write an essay when you have time to plan your approach and organization, do research, write a rough draft, and seek the advice and counsel of teachers and tutors. It is quite another when you have to write an in-class essay, most often without benefit of notes and with the added pressure of a very short time in which to accomplish the task.

Time and Grade

How you prepare quickly to answer a prompt for an essay exam rests largely on three elements:

1. The exam's time frame.
2. Whether the exam comprises one essay question, multiple short-answer essay questions, or a mix of essay and other types of questions.
3. How much grading weight has been given to the various parts of the exam.

A one-hour exam might include the following:

- true-or-false questions
- fill-in-the-blank questions
- one or more short essay questions
- one long essay question

It is important to know how much the test is worth as part of the semester grade, and it is also important to know how much each part of the test is worth. How much time and effort you spend on any one part of an exam ultimately depends on the value of each section of the test.

For instance, suppose the exam period is one hour. The exam consists of a single essay prompt and some true or false questions, and the essay is worth 75 points out of 100 for the entire exam. You should certainly spend 30–45 minutes out of the hour on the essay question, with 10–15 minutes given to the other questions. Or if you have 90 minutes to answer three short-answer essay questions, then you would want to give 30 minutes to each question because they surely will be given equal weight when graded by the instructor.

It goes without saying that you should always try to do your best on any exam. But you should take into account time frames and weight of grade when you allot the time necessary to finish an essay exam or the essay portion of an exam with a variety of questions.

Key Terms in Essay Questions

Essay questions are *prompts*. The prompt either identifies one topic or a list from which you can choose one or more topics to write about. After receiving the prompt, never begin writing immediately. Take a few minutes to make a plan. Before making a plan, however, you need to be certain what the prompt is asking you to do. Understanding the key terms of the prompt will go a long way in helping you figure out how to respond. Study the following steps.

1. Read the prompt several times to identify the key terms in the prompt. These key terms will often tell you the approach (the kind of response) the instructor is looking for.

   ■ *analyze/explain:* explain how a process works and why the process is important.
   ■ *argue/discuss:* take a stand or have a definite point of view supported by evidence (such as facts, statistics, examples, and quotations from experts).
   ■ *cause/effect:* if cause, identify the reasons for something occurring; if effect, identify the results of something occurring. Some questions will want you to explain both the causes and effects.
   ■ *classify:* divide the topic idea into categories and relate why the categories are important.
   ■ *compare/contrast:* if comparison, discuss how two or more items are similar; if contrast, discuss how two or more items are different from one another.
   ■ *define:* write an extended definition in which you choose examples to illustrate the concept's meaning.
   ■ *evaluate:* discuss the pros and cons of an issue, and make a judgment.
   ■ *illustrate:* give specific examples of a general topic.
   ■ *narrate:* describe something that happened.
   ■ *summarize:* briefly present the main ideas from a list of many ideas, some major and some minor.

2. Once you have the topic and the approach identified, select those specific ideas that will support your thesis concerning the topic. Because you have studied the thesis sentence with essay map in this book, we suggest using it to organize your response. The essay map is a multiple-item series that identifies the subtopics you will use to explain your response to the overall topic. The essay map allows you to state your conclusion and organizational approach to a topic quickly and clearly. It is an outline in sentence form.
3. Use each of your essay map items (we suggest two or three) as the topic of each corresponding body paragraph in which you will develop your ideas concerning the overall topic.
4. Try to save a few minutes to check your essay for sentence fragments (incomplete ideas) and spelling errors. Neatly write in corrections.

Prompts with Thesis Statement and Essay Map Examples

Following are examples of prompts that could be asked in a variety of college courses. Also provided are possible thesis statements that are mini outlines for the essay to be written.

Sociology

Prompt: Explain the meaning of "class stratification" in relation to education and employment.

Key term: meaning The approach is to define the term by showing how it relates to two aspects of society.

Possible thesis: <u>Class stratification negatively affects poor people by making it more difficult for them to go to college and to get meaningful employment.</u>

History

Prompt: Analyze the reasons for the rise of Germany's militarism prior to World War II.

Key term: analyze The approach will be to explain how the events after World War I led to the rise of Hitler and his military forces.

Possible thesis: <u>The stringent terms placed on Germany by the Treaty of Versailles, coupled with the worldwide economic depression, led to the rise of Hitler's military machine prior to World War II.</u>

Business

Prompt: Discuss the causes of the 1982 economic stagnation in the United States.

Key term: causes The approach will be to identify and discuss those economic policies and events that led to the economic downturn.

Possible thesis: <u>High interest rates, soaring fuel costs, and high unemployment led to the 1982 economic crisis in America.</u>

Art

Prompt: Summarize the history of Modern Art from the mid-nineteenth century until the present using three specific "schools" as your reference points.

Key term: summarize The approach will be to divide Modern Art into three parts and briefly explain why each of three "schools" represents modern artistic evolution.

Possible thesis: <u>The history of modern art can be traced to the elements of three schools of painting: Impressionism, Surrealism, and Cubism.</u>

Criminology

Prompt: Defend the position that the insanity defense should be abolished.

Key term: defend (argue) The approach will be to use evidence to support the idea that the insanity defense should be eliminated.

> *Possible thesis:*
> <u>The insanity defense should be abolished because "insanity" is a legal term not a psychological one, incarceration in a mental institution is not punishment, and parole boards do not have control over when the "prisoner/patient" is released.</u>
>
> **Literature**
>
> *Prompt:* Compare two symbols in Frost's poems "Stopping by Woods on a Snowy Evening" and "Desert Places."
>
> *Key term: compare* The approach is to choose two symbols in each poem and discuss their similarities.
>
> *Possible thesis:* <u>The snow and the woods in Frost's poems "Stopping by Woods on a Snowy Evening" and "Desert Places" represent loneliness.</u>

Remember, before you can write about a topic, you must understand the question's focus regarding the topic. Identify the key term in the prompt, and then write your thesis.

PRACTICE 1 — Writing Timed Essays

Your skill and confidence in taking essay exams will increase the more you practice timed essay writing. Over the next few weeks, practice by writing essays for the following prompts. Be certain to use only the amount of time stated in each prompt.

1. *The prompt:* In any discussion, the participants must define terms to avoid misunderstanding and confusion. Pick one of the following terms and write an essay clarifying what you mean when you use it in a specific context: freedom, conservative, maturity, intelligence, liberal, beauty, success, independent, wealth.

   Time: 15 minutes.

   Grade value: 25% of exam.

   Key term: _____

2. *The prompt:* Scientists have been cloning sheep, mice, and other animals for a number of years. Now, however, scientists are exploring cloning a human. Write an essay in which you evaluate the pros and cons of cloning a human.

   Time: 30 minutes.

   Grade value: 50% of exam.

   Key term: _____

3. *The prompt:* Although a few young people from poor backgrounds find success in movies such as *Good Will Hunting* and *Finding Forrester*, poor economic environments cause many young people to fail in school and in

their personal lives. Write an essay about poverty's devastating effects on young people.

Time: 60 minutes.

Grade value: 100% of exam.

Key term: _____

4. *The prompt:* Imagine you live next to a small, beautiful park. The park consists of a pond, a walking trail, a gazebo, and stands of shade trees and flowering shrubs. You find out that there is a plan being put before the city council to build a mega-store and parking lot where the park is located. The mega-store will mean 200 full- and part-time jobs and tens of thousands of tax dollars for the community. Write an essay in which you contrast the value of the new mega-store versus that of the park for the people of the community.

Time: 2 hours.

Grade value: 25% of total semester grade.

Key term: _____

Introductory and Concluding Techniques

While you may not be able to quote statistics or famous people in the introduction or conclusion of your exam essay (unless the exam is open-book or one for which you can bring prepared notes), you can construct a good introduction and conclusion. Refer to Chapter 4, "The Introductory Paragraph," and Chapter 6, "The Concluding Paragraph," to review the techniques for effectively introducing your thesis and for giving your essay a sense of completeness. Try to memorize the various types of techniques. Often the prompt will suggest an idea that will help you create a few interesting lead-in sentences in the introductory paragraph and a relevant concluding remark.

CHAPTER REVIEW

- Writing an essay exam always involves the added pressure of limited time and usually involves the added challenge of relying on your memory for ideas and facts. It is a good idea to pace yourself on an essay exam, allowing time in proportion to the essay question's value in the exam or semester grade.
- Essay questions are prompts, and they contain key terms that indicate the approach that you should take in your answer.
- Use an essay map to plan your essay before writing it.

 Visit *The Write Start* Online!

For additional practice with the materials found in this chapter, visit our Student Companion Web site by going to cengagebrain.com and searching for this text. The Web site also features additional readings, quizzes, writing activities, and Internet links.

PART FOUR

The Writer's Resources

Part Four of this text offers a complete guide to correct grammar, punctuation, and usage. It also contains information and helpful techniques for students whose first language is not English. The chapters in Part Four are grouped into three sections:

- Sentence Elements (Chapters 18–20) covers nouns, pronouns, verbs, adjectives, and adverbs.
- Basics of Sentence Structure (Chapters 21–28) looks at combining sentence elements into complete sentences, including working with clauses and phrases, prepositions, and punctuation. Additionally, the chapters cover Articles and Interjections (Ch. 24), gives practice in Common Errors made by students (Ch. 25), provides practice in Sentence Combining (Ch. 26), and covers rules for Capitalization and Numbers (Ch. 28).
- Words and Meaning (Chapters 29–30) provides advice on problem areas such as commonly misspelled words, Articles and Interjections, Common Sentence Errors, Sentence Combining, and editing practice for appropriate word choice.

Nouns and Pronouns

Nouns, the building blocks of English sentences, are words that stand for people, places, or things. They are most often the subject of the sentence as well as the object of phrases.

Nouns

Nouns are words that stand for people, places, or things. Nouns can be *singular* or *plural*.

Nouns

	Singular	Plural
Person	man	men
	woman	women
	child	children
Place	cave	caves
	beach	beaches
	forest	forests
	yard	yards
	mountain	mountains
Thing	ring	rings
	computer	computers
	discussion	discussions
	truth	truths
	sport	sports
	idea	ideas
	vacation	vacations
	conversation	conversations

To form the plural of most nouns, you simply add an *-s* or *-es* to the end of the word. However, there are some exceptions.

1. Nouns ending in *-f* or *-ve* form the plural by adding *-ves*.

half	halves
shelf	shelves

2. Hyphenated nouns (nouns that are formed by joining several short words with hyphens) form plurals by adding *-s* or *-es* to the main word in the phrase.

mother-in-law	mothers-in-law
sergeant-at-arms	sergeants-at-arms

3. Some nouns form plurals in other ways, such as by changing the spelling of the plural form. These are sometimes called irregular forms of plural nouns.

foot	feet
child	children
criterion	criteria
woman	women
man	men

4. Other nouns do not change at all when forming the plural. These exceptions must simply be memorized.

fish	fish
deer	deer
shrimp	shrimp

Nouns can also be classified as *proper* or *common*. *Proper nouns* are the specific names or titles of people, places, or things, and they are capitalized. Common nouns are general terms for people, places, or things, and they are not capitalized.

Common Nouns	Proper Nouns
singer	Sheryl Crow
beach	Corona Del Mar
magazine	*Time*
student	Julianne

PRACTICE 1   Finding Nouns

Underline the nouns (not pronouns) in the following sentences. *(Note: Sentences for the Writer's Resources exercises are often based on the professional and student essays used in the text.)*

Example: The <u>family</u> travels to the <u>mountains</u> every <u>weekend</u>.

1. I was twelve, and in my first year of junior high school.

2. I discovered black was not supposed to be beautiful.

3. At that age, boys suddenly became important.

4. But by that time, black kids no longer believed in that sixties mantra, "Black is beautiful."

5. Light skin, green eyes, and long, wavy hair were once again synonymous with beauty.

6. Colorism—and its subtext of self-hatred—began during slavery on plantations.

7. Some social circles are still defined by hue.

8. Some African Americans, dark and light, prefer light-skinned mates, so they can have a "pretty baby."

9. In my family, color was never discussed, even though our spectrum was broad—my brother was very light; my sister and I much darker.

10. But in junior high, I learned in a matter of weeks what had apparently been drummed into the heads of my black peers for most of their lives. (Jones, "Light Skin versus Dark")

PRACTICE 2   Singular and Plural Nouns

In the following paragraph from the student essay "Two Different Neighbors" by Ms. Cruz, (in Chapter 12) find and correct the errors in singular and plural noun use.

Example: Living in the United States means living in a ~~countries~~ **country** where there can be a good ~~futures~~ **future** for just about anybody.

However, the United States is not the best places to vacation if you are looking for a place with activity going on all days long, each day of the years. Mexico, on the other hands, doesn't necessarily have all the advantage when it comes to planning a short-term vacations. In Mexico, one can be active from the moment when one awakes. For instance, there are breakfast place beside the hotel pool, so the visitor can combine swimmings and pool activity with the first meal of the days. What a wake-up calls!

PRACTICE 3   Correcting Errors in Noun Use

Find and correct the errors in noun use (singular/plural, common/proper nouns) in the following paragraphs by Ms. Cruz ("Two Different Neighbors").

The united states has many historic sites but, in contrast to mexico, these place are very young. For example, the statue of liberty is not even a centuries old. Another places to visit in the united states is Philadelphia. Philadelphia is an important cities to visit because of its connection to the colonie's winning independence from england two hundred year ago. On the other hand, in mexico the Pyramids found at tenochitlan are at least a millennium old, predating the liberty bell by over eight hundred years. Despite its current modern architectures, mexico city's political importance goes back to the early 16th Century when the aztec empire fell, and colonial rule was instituted by the Spanish conqueror.

Pronouns

A pronoun is a word that takes the place of, or refers to, a noun. The noun that the pronoun refers to is known as the antecedent of the pronoun.

> **Example**
>
> Fariba said that she did not understand the question. (The pronoun is *she*, and *Fariba* is its antecedent.)

Pronouns can be divided into several categories. The most common categories are *personal pronouns, relative pronouns, demonstrative pronouns, indefinite pronouns,* and *reflexive pronouns.*

Personal Pronouns

Personal pronouns refer to a specific person or thing *(I/me, you, he/him, she/her, it, we/us, they/them)*. Personal pronouns are divided into three forms, depending on how they are used in a sentence. These forms are subjective (pronoun used as a subject), objective (pronoun used as an object), and possessive (pronoun used to indicate possession/ownership).

Subjective Pronouns

	Singular	Plural
1st person	I	we
2nd person	you	you
3rd person	he, she, it	they

Objective Pronouns

	Singular	Plural
1st person	me	us
2nd person	you	you
3rd person	him, her, it	them

Possessive Pronouns

	Singular	Plural
1st person	my (mine)	our (ours)
2nd person	your (yours)	your (yours)
3rd person	his (his)	their (theirs), its
	her (hers)	
	its (its)	

The following examples demonstrate the uses of these three types of personal pronouns.

I frequently listen to music when *I* drive. (Subjective pronoun; the pronoun is used as a subject)

They enjoy decorating their home. (Subjective pronoun)

Dave is starting to annoy *you.* (Objective pronoun; the pronoun is the object of the sentence)

He gave the same gift to *him.* (Objective pronoun)

That is *my* sweater. (Possessive pronoun; the pronoun shows ownership or possession)

He borrowed *her* keys. (Possessive pronoun)

PRACTICE 4   Using Personal Pronouns

In the following paragraph, underline subjective pronouns once, objective pronouns twice, and possessive pronouns three times. Some sentences may contain more than one type.

A racist encounter hurts badly. But it does not equal the pain of "colorism"—being rejected by your own people because your skin is colored cocoa and not cream, ebony and not olive. On our scale of beauty, it is often the high yellows—in the lexicon of black America, those with light skin—whose looks reap the most attention. Traditionally, if someone was described that way, there was no need to say that person was good-looking. It was a given that light was lovely. It was those of us with plain brown eyes and darker skin hues who had to prove ourselves. (Jones, "Light Skin versus Dark")

Pronoun-Antecedent Agreement

Pronouns take the place of other nouns or pronouns. The word or words to which a pronoun refers is the *antecedent*. It is important that pronouns agree with their antecedents. For example, the singular antecedent *everyone* must be used with the singular pronouns *he* or *she*.

The following examples illustrate sentences in which pronouns agree with the antecedent.

> If *someone* works late at night, *he* or *she* may not be able to concentrate in class the next morning.
>
> Or
>
> When *Adam* works late at night, *he* is not able to concentrate in class the next morning.
>
> *Each ticket holder* stood in line waiting for *his or her* refund.
>
> *Many* were angry that *their* efforts had not been rewarded.

PRACTICE 5   Using Correct Pronoun-Antecedent Agreement

In the following sentences, underline the antecedent and fill in the correct pronoun.

1. Louisa referred to a social crisis in _____ sociology project.

2. Anyone can learn to paint if _____ has effective instruction and patience.

3. Each baseball player gave _____ best effort in the tournament.

4. Elena and Marguerita gave _____ suggestions to Hoda.

5. She grows peppers and squash; _____ taste best fresh from the garden.

6. The graphic art students turned in _____ portfolios.

7. Someone left _____ towels all over the locker room.

8. The managers want us to attend _____ budget meeting next week.

9. The average consumer wants the best price, but _____ may not shop carefully enough to find one.

10. The faculty of the college argued over _____ grading policies all year.

Relative Pronouns

Relative pronouns introduce a qualifying or explanatory clause.

Relative Pronouns

who	Used as a subject in reference to people
whom	Used as an object in reference to people
which	Used as a subject in reference to things
that	Used as a subject in reference to things
whoever	Used as a subject in reference to an uncertain number of people
whichever	Used as a subject in reference to an uncertain number of things

The following examples illustrate the use of relative pronouns.

<u>Who</u> made the phone call? (*Who* is used as the subject)

The phone call was made by <u>whom</u>? (*Whom* is used as the object)

<u>Which</u> movie shall we watch tonight? (*Which* is used as a subject referring to things)

I don't like <u>that</u>! (*That* is used as the object referring to a thing)

Demonstrative Pronouns

Demonstrative pronouns point out or specify certain people, places, or things.

Demonstrative Pronouns

Singular	Plural
this	these
that	those

Indefinite Pronouns

Indefinite pronouns refer to general or indeterminate people, places, or things.

Indefinite Pronouns

These pronouns do not refer to specific people, places, or things.

Singular

each	another	anybody	neither
everybody	somebody	anyone	nobody
everyone	someone	anything	no one
everything	something	either	nothing

Singular or plural			
all	more	none	
any	most	some	
Plural			
both	few	many	several

Reflexive Pronouns

Reflexive pronouns are formed by adding *-self* or *-selves* to certain pronouns. They are used to indicate action performed to or on the antecedent.

Reflexive Pronouns

	Singular	Plural
1st person	myself	ourselves
2nd person	yourself	yourselves
3rd person	himself	themselves
	herself	
	itself	

The following sentences illustrate the use of the reflexive pronoun.

We gave *ourselves* a party to celebrate the end of the school year.
Vinh found *himself in* an impossible situation.

The reflexive pronoun form can also be used to intensify meaning. This is called an *intensifier*.

The instructor *herself* found the concepts confusing.
Raoul *himself had* made the engine.

PRACTICE 6   Using Correct Pronoun-Antecedent Agreement

Fill in the blanks with the correct pronouns. Underline the antecedent of each pronoun.

Example: <u>All students</u> must do _____**their**_____ assigned reading before class.

1. Dr. Brenda Izen washed _____ car on a rainy afternoon.

2. Janet and Wayne are remodeling _____ basement.

3. The bankers and the insurance agents met today; _____ discussed many problems facing the elderly.

4. The highway looks slick because _____ is covered with a layer of black ice.

5. Everyone should be responsible for _____ behavior.

6. Anyone failing the test today must do well on _____ test at midterm.

7. Each lawyer presented _____ argument.

8. Have Ramona and Luis paid for _____ concert tickets?

9. Most of the exercises in this book have _____ specific objectives.

10. Each child left _____ home early for school.

PRACTICE 7   Using Pronouns Correctly

Correct the following paragraphs for pronoun use. The first pronoun has been done for you; the correct answer is in parentheses. Some sentences are correct.

My mother, Rita Ann, suffered from a mental illness called *manic-depressive bipolar disorder*. **Her** Its illness had damaging effects on his life throughout the years. The differences in them from 1987 to 2001 showed the horrific conclusion to a life hardly lived. Their disease took it life from him and her away from his family. Manic depression adversely affected your mother's appearance, comprehension, and its family. (Kate Smith, "Short—Yet Not Sweet")

PRACTICE 8   Using Pronouns Correctly

Edit the following paragraph for pronoun usage. The first incorrect pronoun has been done for you; the correct answer is in parentheses. Some pronouns in the passage may be correct.

Your (my) mother had been a beautiful woman. He was fashion-model-thin with black shiny hair that fell like a waterfall of smooth, shiny oil. It was tall and athletic. Perhaps that was due to her love of exercise. You can remember him waking every morning, jogging and stretching, rain or shine or snow, then taking a shower and putting on its makeup. Not that he had anywhere to go, but she was very important for him to look attractive. It didn't do anything out of the ordinary; in fact, you did what any ordinary housewife and mother would do each day. He appeared to be a vital woman. It wasn't until 1995 that manic depression made her endure several changes. He was no longer full of life as she once proved himself to be. It stopped waking at a reasonably early hour each day. He stopped exercising, and, when he did awaken, he did not comb its hair, nor did he even bother to dress which, at one time, had been a very important and popular activity for him. You no longer had a routine. Because exercise became a chore for him, It became unhealthy and overweight. Your mother was no longer the vital woman they had known and loved. (Kate Smith, "Short—Yet Not Sweet")

Verbs and Verbals

 A verb is a word indicating action, feeling, or being. Verbs can be divided into three classes: **action verbs**, **linking verbs**, and **helping verbs**. Additionally, the form of the verbs can indicate the time of the action: **present**, **past**, or **future** (also known as **tense**). Each of these tenses has many forms that we use every day. The most commonly used tenses are *simple present* and *simple past*.

Present Tense

Use an *-s* or *-es* ending on the verb when the subject is *he, she,* or *it,* or the equivalent.

Verbs in the Simple Present Tense
Sample verb: dance

	Singular	Plural
1st person	(I) dance	(we) dance
2nd person	(you) dance	(you) dance
3rd person	(he, she, it) dances	(they) dance

Past Tenses for Regular Verbs

Regular verbs are those verbs that form the past tense by adding *-ed* or *-d*. The simple past tense is used to refer to an action that began and ended at one time period in the past.

Simple Past Tense of Regular Verbs
Sample verb: dance

	Singular	Plural
1st person	(I) danced	(we) danced
2nd person	(you) danced	(you) danced
3rd person	(he, she, it) danced	(they) danced

PRACTICE 1   Using the Present and Past Tense of Regular Verbs

Use each of the following regular verbs in a sentence, using the present tense. Then, change the sentence to the past tense. The first sentences are done for you.

1. (dance)   present tense: She dances every day for exercise.

   past tense: She danced every day for exercise.

2. (walk)   present tense: _____

   past tense: _____

3. (bake)   present tense: _____

   past tense: _____

4. (talk)   present tense: _____

   past tense: _____

5. (shop)   present tense: _____

   past tense: _____

6. (follow)   present tense: _____

   past tense: _____

7. (trip)   present tense: _____

   past tense: _____

8. (travel)   present tense: _____

   past tense: _____

9. (evaluate)   present tense: _____

   past tense: _____

10. (predict)   present tense: _____

   past tense: _____

Past Tenses for Irregular Verbs

Many irregular verbs (more than 100 in English) do not form the past tense by adding -ed or -d. Some verbs do not change forms at all. Some verbs form the past tense by changing the spelling of the entire word (these are called *stem-changing verbs*). The Alphabetical List of Irregular Verbs included here shows the most commonly used irregular verbs in the English language.

The **past participle** is the form of the verb used with the "perfect" tenses (the verb tense requiring *has/have* showing ongoing action from the past up to or including the present, as in the following sentence: He *has gone* to the store, but he will be back soon).

Alphabetical List of Irregular Verbs

Simple Form	Simple Past	Past Participle
arise	arose	arisen
be	was, were	been
bear	bore	borne/born
beat	beat	beaten/beat
become	became	become
begin	began	begun
bend	bent	bent
bet	bet	bet
bid	bid	bid
bind	bound	bound
bite	bit	bitten
bleed	bled	bled
blow	blew	blown
break	broke	broken
breed	bred	bred
bring	brought	brought
broadcast	broadcast	broadcast
build	built	built
burst	burst	burst
buy	bought	bought
cast	cast	cast
catch	caught	caught
choose	chose	chosen
cling	clung	clung
come	came	come
cost	cost	cost
creep	crept	crept
cut	cut	cut
deal	dealt	dealt
dig	dug	dug
do	did	done
draw	drew	drawn
eat	ate	eaten
fall	fell	fallen
feed	fed	fed
feel	felt	felt
fight	fought	fought

(continued)

Simple Form	Simple Past	Past Participle
find	found	found
fit	fit	fit
flee	fled	fled
fling	flung	flung
fly	flew	flown
forbid	forbade	forbidden
forecast	forecast	forecast
forget	forgot	forgotten
forgive	forgave	forgiven
forsake	forsook	forsaken
freeze	froze	frozen
get	got	gotten
give	gave	given
go	went	gone
grind	ground	ground
grow	grew	grown
hang	hung	hung
have	had	had
hear	heard	heard
hide	hid	hidden
hit	hit	hit
hold	held	held
hurt	hurt	hurt
keep	kept	kept
know	knew	known
lay	laid	laid
lead	led	led
leave	left	left
lend	lent	lent
let	let	let
lie	lay	lain
light	lit/lighted	lit/lighted
lose	lost	lost
make	made	made
mean	meant	meant
meet	met	met
mislay	mislaid	mislaid
mistake	mistook	mistaken
pay	paid	paid
put	put	put
quit	quit	quit
read	read	read
rid	rid	rid

Simple Form	Simple Past	Past Participle
ride	rode	ridden
ring	rang	rung
rise	rose	risen
run	ran	run
say	said	said
see	saw	seen
seek	sought	sought
sell	sold	sold
send	sent	sent
set	set	set
shake	shook	shaken
shed	shed	shed
shine	shone/shined	shone/shined
shoot	shot	shot
show	showed	shown/showed
shrink	shrank/shrunk	shrunk
shut	shut	shut
sing	sang	sung
sit	sat	sat
sleep	slept	slept
slide	slid	slid
slit	slit	slit
speak	spoke	spoken
speed	sped/speeded	sped/speeded
spend	spent	spent
spin	spun	spun
spit	spit/spat	spit/spat
split	split	split
spread	spread	spread
spring	sprang/sprung	sprung
stand	stood	stood
steal	stole	stolen
stick	stuck	stuck
sting	stung	stung
stink	stank/stunk	stunk
strive	strove	striven
strike	struck	struck/stricken
string	strung	strung
swear	swore	sworn
sweep	swept	swept
swim	swam	swum
swing	swung	swung
take	took	taken

(continued)

Simple Form	Simple Past	Past Participle
teach	taught	taught
tear	tore	torn
tell	told	told
think	thought	thought
throw	threw	thrown
thrust	thrust	thrust
understand	understood	understood
undertake	undertook	undertaken
upset	upset	upset
wake	woke/waked	woken/waked
wear	wore	worn
weave	wove	woven
weep	wept	wept
win	won	won
wind	wound	wound
withdraw	withdrew	withdrawn
wring	wrung	wrung
write	wrote	written

Some irregular verbs do not follow the stem-changing pattern.

Irregular Verbs That Do Not Change Their Form
(All end in -*t* or -*d*.)

Present Form	Past Form	Past Participle
bet	bet	bet
cost	cost	cost
cut	cut	cut
fit	fit	fit
hit	hit	hit
hurt	hurt	hurt
quit	quit	quit
spread	spread	spread

Because the verb *be* is used so often as a helping verb, as a linking verb, and to form verb tenses, it is useful to see how irregular the form is.

To be **(infinitive form)**

	Present Tense		Past Tense	
	Singular	*Plural*	*Singular*	*Plural*
1st person	I am	we are	I was	we were
2nd person	you are	you are	you were	you were
3rd person	he, she, it is	they are	he, she, it was	they were

PRACTICE 2   Using the Past Tense of Irregular Verbs

Supply the correct form of the past tense of the irregular verbs in the following sentences. The first one has been done for you.

1. (go) All winter we _____**went**_____ to the nearby resort to ski.

2. (be) They _____ alone for hours before they joined the rest of the group.

3. (win) The members of the band _____ the competition, even though their uniforms had burned in a fire.

4. (lie) The homework _____ on the kitchen counter instead of the teacher's desk.

5. (be) Why _____ you absent for more than a month?

6. (withdraw) He _____ the funds necessary for the remodeling project.

7. (weave) The woman _____ the basket in a pattern passed down from generation to generation.

8. (string) He had the racquet _____ before the tournament.

9. (throw) Shelley _____ the first pitch, terrifying the batter.

10. (shrink) The new blouse _____ the first time she washed it.

Progressive Tenses and the Present Participle

The verb *be* is used to form the progressive tenses. To form the present progressive, past progressive, and future progressive tenses, combine the appropriate form of *be* + a verb + *-ing*.

Present Progressive	**Past Progressive**	**Future Progressive**
I am talking	I was talking	I will be talking
They are dancing	They were dancing	They will be dancing

PRACTICE 3   Choosing the Correct Verb Form

Supply the missing past tense or present participle in the following paragraphs.

Example: For her recital, the soprano _____**sang**_____ (sing) a variety of arias.

Since the days of early cinema, Latin men _____ (portray) some of the most virile, passionate, and forbidden characters on the screen. With their swarthy good looks and smoldering eyes, these "Latin lovers" _____ (cause) female moviegoers to swoon for decades. But unlike his blond counterpart, the Latin lover was generally not _____ (cast) in the leading role. He _____ (play) the rogue to the Anglo gentleman. He _____ (be), however, suave and more than able to captivate even the strongest screen siren. Early screen actors such as Rudolph Valentino, Ramon Novarro, and Gilbert Roland invariably _____ (set) the stage for today's Latino film roles.

While the Latin lover stereotype seems like a whimsical characterization that only _____ (to exist) on the big screen decades ago, its effects _____ (seep) into the American psyche, _____ (force) Latinos, especially those in the film industry, into a smothering, tight mold. Although no stereotype should _____ (to be, deem) acceptable, some argue that the Latin lover image is just a step above the other stereotypes today's Latin actors have to play—drug runners, gang members, and crime lords. ("The Don Juan Syndrome" by Chapa)

PRACTICE 4　　Correcting Verb Errors

Correct the errors in verb forms in the following paragraph. The first sentence has been done for you.

My mother **had been** (had been) a beautiful woman. She _____ (to be) fashion-model thin with black, shiny hair that _____ (to fall) like a waterfall of smooth, shiny oil. She was tall and athletic. Perhaps this was due to her love of exercise. I can remember her _____ (to wake) every morning, _____ (to jog) and

_____, (to stretch) rain or shine or snow, then _____

(to take) a shower and _____ (to put) on her makeup. Not that

she had anywhere to go, but it was very important for her to look attractive.

She didn't do anything out of the ordinary; in fact, she _____ (to

do) what any ordinary housewife and mother _____ (to do) each

day. (Kate Smith, "Short—Yet Not Sweet")

Complex Verb Forms

In addition to simple forms, there are more complex verb forms. The following chart illustrates the most commonly used verb tenses. Each tense expresses a specific time or duration. Students for whom English is a foreign language need to practice the use of each tense in spoken and written English.

Common Verb Tenses
Sample verb: talk

Tense	First Person Singular	Sample Sentence
present	I talk	I like to talk in a group.
present progressive	I am talking	I am talking on the phone now!
present perfect	I have talked	I have talked about this often.
present perfect progressive	I have been talking	I have been talking since dawn!
past	I talked	I talked to him last night.
past progressive	I was talking	I was talking about my car.
past perfect	I had talked	I had talked before I decided.
past perfect progressive	I had been talking	I had been talking before they sang.
future	I will talk	I will talk to you tomorrow.
future progressive	I will be talking	I will be talking all morning tomorrow.
future perfect	I will have talked	I will have talked enough by then.
future perfect progressive	I will have been talking	I will have been talking for three hours by the time the meeting is over.

The present perfect and past perfect tenses are formed by combining the appropriate form of the verb *have* with the **past participle** form of a verb. The past participle form of a verb usually ends with -*d*, -*ed*, or -*en*.

> **Present Perfect Tense**
>
> *has* or *have* + past participle of the main verb
>
> | **Singular** | **Plural** |
> |---|---|
> | He has talked | They have talked |
>
> **Past Perfect Tense**
>
> *had* + past participle of the main verb
>
> | **Singular** | **Plural** |
> |---|---|
> | He had talked | They had talked |

The **present perfect tense** is used to describe an action that started in the past and continues to the present time. It can also be used to describe an action that has recently taken place or an action for which the exact past time is indefinite.

> Julia *has played* with the symphony for five years.

This sentence means that Julia began playing with the orchestra five years ago and is still playing with the symphony today.

> Asim *has traveled* to Pakistan several times recently.

This sentence indicates no specific time for the travel mentioned. If a specific time is mentioned, the simple past would be used.

> Asim *traveled* to Pakistan last December.

The **past perfect tense** is used to describe an action that occurred in the past before another point in time in the past or before another past activity.

> Julia *had played* with the symphony for five years before she retired.

This sentence means that Julia played in the symphony for five years, and then she retired. All of this activity took place in the past.

PRACTICE 5   Using the Present Perfect and Past Perfect Tenses

> *Read All About It . . .* To read the full essay from which these sentences are excerpted, see page 405.

Change the verb tenses from present to past, changing perfect tenses as needed. The first sentence has been done for you.

A volatile inner-city drama is ~~taking~~ **took** place in New York where blacks ~~have~~ **had** ~~been~~ **been** boycotting Korean groceries for four months. The recent attack on three Vietnamese men by a group of blacks who mistook them for Koreans has brought this long-simmering tension between two minority groups to the world's attention. Korean newspapers from San Francisco to Seoul have been running front-page stories. Non-Asian commentators around the country, whose knowledge of Korea may not be much more than images from the Korean war and the ridiculous television series *M.A.S.H.*, are making all sorts of comments. (Kang, "A Battle of Cultures")

Passive Voice

Most writing is done in the **active voice** for direct, concise expression. The **passive voice** is chosen when the actor of the sentence is not important or when the writer wishes to avoid naming the subject.

In the passive voice, the object of an active verb becomes the subject of a passive verb. The form of the verb becomes *be + past participle*.

> | | | S | V | O |
> |---|---|---|---|---|
> | **Active:** | | Carol | tells | the story. |
> | | | S | V | O |
> | **Passive:** | | The story | was told | by Carol. |

The Active Voice Compared to the Passive Voice

In the *active voice,* the subject of the sentence does the acting (action verb/transitive verb).

> In the *passive voice*, the subject is acted upon.
> The students finished the project.
> (subject = *students*; active verb = *finished*)
> The project was finished by the students.
> (subject = *project* [acted upon by students]; passive verb = *was finished*)

The following list shows the conversion of the active to the passive voice for the important verb tenses.

	Active	**Passive**
present	Carol tells the story.	The story is told by Carol.
present progressive	Carol is telling the story.	The story is being told by Carol.
present perfect	Carol has told the story.	The story has been told by Carol.
past	Carol told the story.	The story was told by Carol.
past progressive	Carol was telling the story.	The story was being told by Carol.
past perfect	Carol had told the story.	The story had been told by Carol.
future	Carol will tell the story.	The story will be told by Carol.
future progressive	Carol will be telling the story.	The story is going to be told by Carol. (*going to* is often used instead of *will*)
future perfect	Carol will have told the story.	The story will have been told by Carol.

PRACTICE 6　　Using the Active Voice

The following sentences are written in passive voice. Rewrite each in active voice.

1. The house was destroyed by the earthquake.

_____

2. The garden was planted by my mother.

_____

3. Creative recipes were developed by the chefs.

_____

4. Our mortgage payment was increased by the bank.

_____

5. The cake was devoured by the children.

_____

PRACTICE 7　　Using the Passive Voice

The following sentences are written in active voice. Rewrite each in passive voice.

1. The fire almost destroyed Yellowstone National Park.

_____

2. The insurance company did not raise their rates.

_____

3. Tiger Woods broke the tournament record.

_____

4. The thief mugged his grandfather in the park.

_____

5. The new skiers finally mastered the bunny slope.

_____

PRACTICE 8 | **Using Correct Verb Forms and Tenses**

Change the verb tense in the following paragraph from present to past. Next underline all the verbs in the paragraph. The first sentence has been done for you.

I __**am/was**__ playing basketball with my father in our backyard according

to procedures we _____. My father would stand

beneath the hoop, shout, and I would shoot over his head at the basket attached

to our garage. Our next-door neighbor, aged five, _____

over into our yard with a playmate. "He's blind," our neighbor

_____ to her friend in a voice that could be heard

distinctly by Dad and me. Dad _____ and _____;

I did the same. Dad _____ the rim; I missed entirely; dad shot and

missed the garage entirely. "Which one is blind?" _____

back the little friend. (Harold Krents, "Darkness at Noon")

PRACTICE 9 | **Using Correct Verb Forms and Tenses**

Read All About It ... To read the full essay from which these sentences are excerpted, see page 386.

In the following paragraph, supply the correct form or tense of the verbs in the spaces provided. The first sentence has been done for you. Be careful to use the perfect tenses when appropriate.

One day when I was 35 or thereabouts I _____ (hear) about

an Indian powwow. My father _____ (attend) them and so with

great curiosity and a strange joy at _____ (discover) a part of my heritage, I _____ (decide) the thing to do to get ready for this big event was to have my friend make me a spear in his forge. The steel _____ (be) fine and blue and iridescent. The feathers on the shaft _____ (be) bright and proud.

In a dusty state fairground in southern Indiana, I _____ (find) white people dressed as Indians. I _____ (learn) that they were "hobbyists," that is, it was their hobby and leisure pastime to masquerade as Indians on weekends. I _____ (feel) ridiculous with my spear, and I _____ (leave).

It was years before I _____ (tell) anyone of the embarrassment of this weekend and _____ (see) any humor in it. But in a way it was that weekend, for all its silliness, that was my awakening. I _____ (realize) I didn't know who I was. I didn't have an Indian name. I didn't speak the Indian language. I didn't know the Indian customs. Dimly I _____ (remember) the Ottawa word for dog, but it was a baby word, *Kahgee*. . . . Even more hazily I remembered a naming ceremony (my own). I remembered legs dancing around me, dust. Where _____ that _____ (be)? What _____ I _____ (be)? "Sawaquat," my mother _____ (tell) me when I asked, "where the tree _____ (begin) to grow." (Lewis Sawaquat, "For My Indian Daughter")

20 Adjectives and Adverbs

ESL Adjectives

An **adjective** is a word that modifies (or describes) a noun or pronoun. Although adjectives usually come before the nouns they describe, they can also follow the noun (in the predicate of the sentence).

> The *glistening* ocean sparkled in the sunset.
> The coffee tasted *hot*.

Adjectives can be *objective* (describing nouns with sensory details) or *subjective* (describing concepts, feelings, or ideas in more general terms that are open to personal interpretation). Both are useful in good writing and enhance meaning, especially in combination.

Objective Adjectives	Subjective Adjectives
glowing	beautiful
crashing	harsh
stabbing	painful
twisted	ugly
strident	persistent
tender	loving

Adverbs

An **adverb** is a word that modifies (describes) a verb, an adjective, or another adverb. Often adverbs end in *-ly*. Another test to identify an adverb is if it answers one of the questions *where*, *how*, or *when*. Adverbs describe the action of a passage. In some cases they refer to other adverbs to intensify meaning. As with adjectives, the careful use of effective adverbs can improve the style of your writing.

Lisa stormed *angrily* up the stairs. (modifies the verb)

He was *very* cold. (modifies the adjective)

The guests were *too* early to dinner. (modifies the adverb)

Commonly Used Adverbs

carefully	loudly	poorly	softly	rudely
happily	perfectly	sadly	quickly	very
harshly	politely	slowly	quietly	

Comparative and Superlative Forms

The **comparative** and **superlative** forms of modifiers are used to compare more than two people or things; this forms a comparison in a matter of degree: as in tall, taller (*comparative*), tallest (*superlative*); complex, more complex (*comparative*), most complex (*superlative*).

To Form Comparatives

Add *-er* to single-syllable adjectives and adverbs: big/bigger

Add the word *more* to adjectives and adverbs with more than one syllable: happily/more happily

To Form Superlatives

Add *-est* to adjectives and adverbs of one syllable: short/shortest

Add the word *most* before adjectives and adverbs that have two or more syllables: pleasant/most pleasant

*Exception: With two-syllable adjectives ending in *-y,* change the *y* to *i* and add *-est*: silly/silliest

---

PRACTICE 1   **Using Adjectives and Adverbs**

In the blanks provided, write an appropriate adjective or adverb from the preceding lists of adjectives and adverbs. Use some superlative forms when possible. The first answer has been done for you.

1. It was a _____**beautiful**_____ night. The colors of the sunset burned in the west as the sun slowly descended.

2. The _____ limbs of the tree grew up harshly into the winter sky.

3. The view from the bridge was the most _____ view she had ever seen!

4. The wound was very _____ to the touch.

5. The _____ bellow of the car's horn blared in front of the house.

6. The _____ player on the basketball team was also the most clumsy.

7. Demands of course work often interfere with _____ made plans.

8. The cacophony of sound from the orchestra room was the most _____ noise the principal had heard all day.

9. His evaluation was the _____ the employees had ever received.

10. The cartoon characters encouraged the _____ behavior among the watching children.

PRACTICE 2   **Writing a Paragraph with Adjectives and Adverbs**

Construct a descriptive paragraph of five to eight sentences, using at least one adjective and one adverb in each sentence.

_____

_____

_____

_____

_____

_____

_____

_____

_____

_____

PRACTICE 3   Expanding Sentences with Adjectives and Adverbs

In the following sentences, add creative adjectives and adverbs to improve the basic sentence. Identify the words that you add as adjectives or adverbs. The first sentence has been done for you.

1. The mockingbird chirped.

The agitated (adjective) mockingbird chirped persistently (adverb).

2. The intruder glared at the inhabitants of the cottage.

_____

3. She sang during the Christmas concert.

_____

4. The school bus full of children rocked back and forth in the parking lot.

_____

5. The students left the classroom before the instructor could assign more homework.

_____

6. Fans jeered at the referee when he overlooked the foul.

_____

7. The ceremony dragged on for hours.

_____

8. Melodies drifted from the practice rooms.

_____

9. Art students attempted to create a life drawing.

_____

10. The woman did not know where she had left her keys.

_____

PRACTICE 4   Adding Adverbs and Adjectives

Using one of the sentences in the previous exercise as a topic sentence, create an eight-sentence paragraph narrating the events to tell a more complete story. Be sure to continue to select vivid and creative adjectives and adverbs in the subsequent sentences. Underline and identify the adjectives and adverbs used in the paragraph.

_____

_____

_____

_____

_____

_____

_____

_____

_____

21

Clauses

An understanding of the basic sentence is essential when writing and revising. The **basic sentence** is composed of a *subject* and a *verb*; the sentence must have "sufficient meaning." In other words, it must make sense!

When a sentence is combined with another sentence or clause, it is called an **independent clause** within the sentence. In the following sections, elements within the basic sentence—**independent clauses**, **dependent clauses**, and **conjunctions** that combine clauses—will be discussed.

Independent and Dependent Clauses

A **clause** is a group of related words containing both a subject and a verb. Clauses can be *independent* or *dependent*. An **independent clause** can stand alone as a complete sentence. A **dependent clause** (or subordinate clause) begins with a subordinating conjunction or relative pronoun and cannot stand alone as a sentence.

> We went shopping during the holidays. *independent clause* (subject = *we*; verb = *went*)
>
> although we went shopping during the holidays. *dependent clause* (subordinate conjunction = *although*; subject = *we*; verb = *went*)
>
> Carl and Louisa were often late to class. *independent clause* (subject = *Carl and Louisa*; verb = *were*)
>
> because Carl and Louisa were often late to class. *dependent clause* (subordinate conjunction = *because*; subject = *Carl and Louisa*; verb = *were*)

Combining Clauses

Often, clauses are combined using **conjunctions**. Independent clauses are combined using a comma and any of the following **coordinating conjunctions**.

Coordinating Conjunctions

for	and	nor	but
or	yet	so	

Example

The parents speak, *but* the children refuse to listen.

Independent clauses may also be joined with a semicolon (*The parents speak; the children refuse to listen*) or with a semicolon and an **adverbial conjunction**. These conjunctions may also serve as transition words.

Common Adverbial Conjunctions

accordingly	hence	nonetheless
additionally	however	now
also	incidentally	otherwise
anyway	indeed	similarly
besides	likewise	still
certainly	meanwhile	then
consequently	moreover	thereafter
finally	nevertheless	thus
furthermore	next	undoubtedly

Example

The team practiced in the morning; *furthermore,* they practiced again in the evening.

Dependent clauses are joined to independent clauses with the addition of a **subordinate conjunction**.

Common Subordinate Conjunctions

after	even though	when
although	if (as if)	whenever
as	since	wherever
because	though	whether
before	unless	while
during	until	

Example

The ship returned to port *because its propeller was broken.*

When a dependent clause precedes an independent clause, a comma follows the dependent clause.

> *Because its propeller was broken,* the ship returned to port.

PRACTICE 1 — Combining Sentences

Combine the following pairs of sentences to avoid repetition. Use coordinating conjunctions, adverbial or subordinate conjunctions, or semicolons. Label the type of conjunction you have used in your answer.

Example: I could see lumps of charcoal in the fireplace.
They were glowing red-hot.

Answer: <u>**I could see lumps of charcoal in the fireplace, and (coordinating**</u>
<u>**conjunction) they were glowing red hot.**</u>

1. We lay in our sleeping bags.

2. Our father read stories by the firelight.

Answer: _____

_____

3. It was dark inside and out.

4. The air raids seemed more eerie.

Answer: _____

_____

5. The night planes flew very low.

6. They shook the whole earth.

Answer: _____

_____

7. I am proud of my mother and father.

8. Both are taking ESL classes at the community college.

Answer: _____

_____

9. My parents work over fifty hours a week.

10. It is not easy to work and go to school at the same time.

Answer: _____

_____

PRACTICE 2   **Combining Clauses**

Read All About It . . .   To read the full essay from which these sentences are excerpted, see page 386.

Combine the following groups of sentences, from the essay by Lewis Sawaquat, using the correct conjunctions and the correct punctuation. Underline the conjunctions you choose to use.

Example: **1.1** My little girl is singing herself to sleep upstairs.
              1.2 Her voice mingles with the sounds of the birds.
              1.3 The birds are outside.
              1.4 The birds are in the old maple trees.

My little girl is singing herself to sleep upstairs, and her voice mingles

with the sounds of the birds outside in the old maple trees.

2.1 My daughter is two.

2.2 I am nearly fifty.

2.3 I am very taken with her.

_____

_____

3.1 She came along late in my life.

3.2 She was unexpected.

3.3 She is a gift.

3.4 The gift is startling.

_____

_____

4.1 My wife and I laughed watching her.

4.2 We heard behind us a low guttural curse.

4.3 Then we heard an unpleasant voice.

4.4 The voice was raised in a guttural war whoop.

_____

_____

5.1 I turned to see a fat man in a bathing suit.

5.2 He covered his mouth.

5.3 He prepared to make the Indian war cry again.

6.1 He was middle-aged.

6.2 He was younger than I was.

6.3 He had three little children lined up next to him.

6.4 They were grinning foolishly.

7.1 My wife suggested we leave the beach.

7.2 I agreed.

8.1 His beach behavior might have been socially unacceptable to more civilized whites.

8.2 His basic view of Indians is expressed daily in our small town.

8.3 These views are frequently on the editorial pages of the county newspaper.

9.1 It doesn't matter to them.

9.2 We were here first.

9.3 The United States Supreme Court has ruled in our favor.

10.1 It matters that we have something that they want.

10.2 They hate us for it.

---

22 Phrases

A phrase is a group of related words without a subject, verb, or both subject and verb. Phrases are used in sentences to complete thoughts or add descriptive detail. To avoid problems with ambiguous meaning or errors in punctuation, phrases must be placed near the noun, verb, or other part of speech to which the phrase refers.

Several types of phrases are used as modifiers in sentences: appositives, prepositional phrases, participial phrases, gerund phrases, infinitive phrases, and absolute phrases.

Appositives

Appositives are words or phrases that rename the preceding words or phrases. Appositives are often identified as *noun phrases*.

> My friend *Mary* loves to cook with chocolate. (appositive as single word)
>
> Mary, *a chocolate lover*, shops carefully for the best chocolate in town. (appositive as a phrase)
>
> The novel *The Grapes of Wrath* is often studied in college English classes.

The punctuation of appositive words and phrases follows the rules for restrictive and nonrestrictive clauses.

Prepositional Phrases

A **prepositional phrase** contains a **preposition** (for example, *in, on, over, before, after*) and its object.

> He waited *for the train*.
>
> The cat prefers to stay *in the house*.
>
> They enjoy going out *for pizza after the football games*.

Participial Phrases

A **participial phrase** is a group of words consisting of a **participle** and its completing words. All verbs have present participle and past participle forms.

> *Staring at the blank computer screen,* Martin found himself unable to finish his essay. (present participle form)
>
> *Interrupted by the demands of his hungry two-year-old,* he could not finish reading the paper. (past participle form)
>
> *Walking down the hall,* she was hit by the door as it flew open at the end of class.
>
> *Bewildered by the question,* the student could not finish the test.

Gerund Phrases

A **gerund** is the *-ing* form of a verb that functions as a noun in a sentence. A **gerund phrase** includes a gerund and its completing words.

> *Dancing* is her favorite activity. (*Dancing* functions as the subject of the sentence.)
>
> *Writing a collection of poems* remains Sophia's secret hobby. (The gerund phrase functions as the subject of the sentence.)
>
> Employees will not be paid without *completing the weekly projects.* (The gerund phrase functions as the object of the preposition *without*.)

In some cases, the possessive form of a noun or pronoun precedes a gerund.

> The parents were not thrilled with their *son's tattooing a snake on his arm.*
>
> *Her dancing in the moonlight* amazed the children.

Infinitive Phrases

An **infinitive phrase** is a group of words consisting of *to* plus a verb and its completing words. An infinitive phrase can function as a noun, adjective, or adverb.

> *To read* is the best way to study grammar. (The infinitive phrase functions as a noun, the subject of the sentence.)
>
> Disneyland is one of the best places *to visit while on vacation.* (The infinitive phrase functions as an adjective and modifies the noun *places*.)
>
> Her daughter was too nervous *to play the piano in front of an audience.* (The infinitive phrase functions as an adverb, modifying the adjective *nervous*.)

Absolute Phrases

An **absolute phrase** consists of a noun or pronoun and a **participle** plus any other completing words. Absolute phrases modify the entire sentence and cannot be punctuated as a complete sentence.

> *Their project nearly completed,* the painters began to clean their equipment. (The past participle *completed* is used in the phrase.)
>
> The violinist, *her arms and shoulders aching with pain,* practiced long hours every night. (The present participle *aching* is used in this verb phrase.)

PRACTICE 1   Identifying Clauses and Phrases

In the blank to the side of each group of words, write *IC* if the group of words is an independent clause, *DC* if the group of words is a dependent clause, and *P* if the group of words is a phrase. If the group of words is a phrase, identify the type of phrase.

Example: P (prepositional) Under the floor

1. _____ From the center of downtown Tucson

2. _____ the ground sloping gently away to Main Street.

3. _____ Here lies the section of the city

4. _____ known as El Hoyo.

5. _____ In no sense it is a hole

6. _____ as its name would imply.

7. _____ Its inhabitants are Chicanos

8. _____ who raise hell on Saturday night

9. _____ listening to Padre Estanislao

10. _____ on Sunday morning. (Suarez, "El Hoyo")

PRACTICE 2   Identifying Clauses and Phrases

In the blank to the side of each group of words, write *IC* if the group of words is an independent clause, *DC* if the group of words is a dependent clause, and *P* if the group of words is a phrase. If the group of words is a phrase, identify the type of phrase.

1. _____ In other respects

2. _____ living in El Hoyo has its advantages.

3. _____ If one is born with a weakness for acquiring bills

4. _____ El Hoyo is where the collectors are less likely to find you.

5. _____ When Teofila Malacara's house burned to the ground

6. _____ with all her belongings

7. _____ a benevolent gentleman carried through the gesture

8. _____ that made tolerable her burden.

9. _____ He made a list of 500 names

10. _____ soliciting from each a dollar. (Suarez, "El Hoyo")

PRACTICE 3   Sentence Combining with Phrases

Combine the following pairs of sentences by turning one of them into one of the types of phrases defined previously. This is an excellent sentence combining technique to reduce repeated words and extra pronouns. Underline and identify the type of phrase you have used.

Read All About It . . . To read the full essay from which these sentences are taken, see the San Francisco essay in Chapters 4, 5, and 6.

Example: The Pacific Ocean is a boater's paradise. It is like an unbelievable expanse of blue glass.

Answer: <u>**The Pacific Ocean, like an unbelievable expanse of blue glass, (preposition) is a boater's paradise.**</u>

1. Boating enthusiasts can participate in activities in and out of the water.

2. This is in San Francisco.

Answer: _____

_____

3. The San Francisco Maritime National Historical Park contains four national landmark ships.

4. This includes the famous square-rigger *Balclutha* and the ferry boat *Eureka*.

Answer: _____

_____

5. Alcatraz Island offers guided tours, a self-guided hiking trail, and a slide show.

6. It is the former maximum-security prison.

Answer: _____

_____

7. Tourists can sail or motor out into the bay to see the view.

8. The view is of an enormous expanse of the Pacific Ocean and the incredible Golden Gate Bridge.

Answer: _____

_____

9. The fog rolls over the 1.2-mile-long bridge.

10. The sight of the fog is both spectacular and haunting.

Answer: _____

_____

Two-Word and Three-Word Verb Phrases

Two-word and three-word verb phrases are often difficult for nonnative speakers of English. Many of them are idiomatic expressions, and they need to be studied or memorized.

Phrasal Verbs (Two-Word and Three-Word Verbs)

The term *phrasal verb* refers to a verb and preposition that together have a special meaning. For example, ***put*** + ***off*** means "postpone." Some phrasal verbs consist of three parts. For example, ***put*** + ***up*** + ***with*** means "tolerate." Phrasal verbs are also called *two-word verbs* or *three-word verbs*.

A phrasal verb may be either *separable* or *nonseparable*.

Separable Phrasal Verbs

(a) I *handed my paper in* yesterday. (b) I *handed in my paper* yesterday.	With a separable phrasal verb, a noun may come either between the verb and the preposition or after the preposition, as in (a) and (b).
(c) I *handed it in* yesterday. 　　(Incorrect: I handed in it yesterday.)	A pronoun comes between the verb and the preposition if the phrasal verb is separable, as in (c).

Nonseparable Phrasal Verbs

(d) I *ran into* an old friend yesterday. (e) I *ran into* her yesterday. 　　(Incorrect: I ran an old friend into.) 　　(Incorrect: I ran her into yesterday.)	With a nonseparable phrasal verb, a noun or pronoun must follow the preposition, as in (d) and (e).

(continued)

Phrasal verbs are especially common in informal English. Following is a list of common phrasal verbs and their usual meanings. The phrasal verbs marked with an asterisk (*) are nonseparable.

A	ask out	*ask someone to go on a date*
B	bring about, bring on.............	*cause*
	bring up	*(1) rear children; (2) mention or introduce a topic*
C	call back	*return a telephone call*
	call in	*ask to come to an official place for a specific purpose*
	call off	*cancel*
	* call on.....................................	*(1) ask to speak in class; (2) visit*
	call up	*call on the telephone*
	* catch up (with)......................	*reach the same position or level*
	* check in, check into	*register at a hotel*
	* check into..............................	*investigate*
	check out	*(1) take a book from the library; (2) investigate*
	* check out (of)	*leave a hotel*
	cheer up.................................	*make (someone) feel happier*
	clean up	*make clean and orderly*
	* come across	*meet by chance*
	cross out	*draw a line through*
	cut out	*stop an annoying activity*
D	do over	*do again*
	* drop by, drop in (on)	*visit informally*
	drop off...................................	*leave something/someone at a place*
	drop out (of)	*stop going to school, to a class, to a club, etc.*
F	figure out................................	*find the answer by reasoning*
	fill out	*write the completions of a questionnaire or official form*
	find out...................................	*discover information*
G	* get along (with)	*exist satisfactorily*
	get back (from)	*(1) return from a place; (2) receive again*
	* get in, get into	*(1) enter a car; (2) arrive*
	* get off	*leave an airplane, a bus, a train, a subway, a bicycle*
	* get on	*enter an airplane, a bus, a train, a subway, a bicycle*

*Indicates a nonseparable phrasal verb.

* get out of	....	(1) *leave a car;* (2) *avoid work or an unpleasant activity*
* get over	....	*recover from an illness*
* get through	....	*finish*
* get up	....	*arise from bed, a chair*
give back	....	*return an item to someone*
give up	....	*stop trying*
* go over	....	*review or check carefully*
* grow up (in)	....	*become an adult*
H hand in	....	*submit an assignment*
hang up	....	(1) *conclude a telephone conversation;* (2) *put clothes on a hanger or a hook*
have on	....	*wear*
K keep out (of)	....	*not enter*
* keep up (with)	....	*stay at the same position or level*
kick out (of)	....	*force (someone) to leave*
L * look after	....	*take care of*
* look into	....	*investigate*
* look out (for)	....	*be careful*
look over	....	*review or check carefully*
look up	....	*look for information in a reference book*
M make up	....	(1) *invent;* (2) *do past work*
N name after, name for	....	*give a baby the name of someone else*
P * pass away	....	*die*
pass out	....	(1) *distribute;* (2) *lose consciousness*
pick out	....	*select*
pick up	....	(1) *go to get someone (e.g., in a car);* (2) *take in one's hand*
point out	....	*call attention to*
put away	....	*remove to a proper place*
put back	....	*return to original place*
put off	....	*postpone*
put on	....	*put clothes on one's body*
put out	....	*extinguish a cigarette or cigar*
* put up with	....	*tolerate*
R * run into, *run across	....	*meet by chance*
* run out (of)	....	*finish a supply of something*

(continued)

*Indicates a nonseparable phrasal verb.

S * show up .... *appear, come*

    shut off .... *stop a machine, light, faucet*

T * take after .... *resemble*

    take off .... *(1) remove clothing; (2) leave on a trip*

    take out .... *(1) take someone on a date; (2) remove*

    take over .... *take control*

    take up .... *begin a new activity or topic*

    tear down .... *demolish; reduce to nothing*

    tear up .... *tear into many little pieces*

    think over .... *consider carefully*

    throw away, throw out .... *discard; get rid of*

    throw up .... *vomit; regurgitate food*

    try on .... *put on clothing to see if it fits*

    turn down .... *decrease volume or intensity*

    turn in .... *(1) submit an assignment; (2) go to bed*

    turn off .... *stop a machine, light, faucet*

    turn on .... *begin a machine, light, faucet*

    turn out .... *extinguish a light*

    turn up .... *increase volume or intensity; arrive*

Source: The material on verb phrases is from Betty S. Azar, *Understanding and Using English Grammar* (Englewood Cliffs, NJ: Prentice Hall Regents). Used with permission.

*Indicates a nonseparable phrasal verb.

PRACTICE 4　Using Phrasal Verbs

Select from the following list of phrasal verbs and complete the following sentences.

call in	figure out
pick out	put up (with)
get back (from)	pick up
look up	takes after
keep out (of)	turn in

1. Please _____ the toys after you are finished playing.

2. _____ the edge of the canyon!

3. The students will _____ their assignments at the beginning of class.

4. The young man examined all of the flowers as he tried to _____ a corsage for his date.

5. _____ the poison ivy!

6. I cannot _____ the answer to this problem!

7. The child _____ his father in looks but after his mother in personality.

8. While you are on vacation, please try not to _____ to the office too often.

9. The teacher would no longer _____ the rudeness of the students.

10. If you are unsure about your project, _____ your topic on the online database at the library.

PRACTICE 5   **Using Phrasal Verbs**

In the following sentences, circle the correct verb phrase from each pair in parentheses. The first one has been done for you.

1. Please (turn in / turn out) your homework on the assigned date.

2. You'll have to (look over / look after) Grandmother; she's not well.

3. If you don't succeed this time, will you (give back / give up)?

4. Can you (get back from / get along with) her now that you agree on something?

5. James Rojas III was (named after / named to) his father and grandfather.

6. Don't forget to (pick out / pick up) milk on the way home from school.

7. He (tore into / tore up) her note to destroy the evidence.

8. (Think up / Think over) your plans to drop out of school; you may regret your decision.

9. You need to (check out / check up) the facts before you make accusations!

10. Did you (bring on / bring up) that he missed three practice sessions?

Prepositions and Preposition Combinations

ESL Prepositions

Prepositions and **prepositional phrases** provide important details within sentences, yet they are often difficult to identify. A preposition connects a noun or pronoun to the rest of the sentence, often showing location or time. Learning the most common prepositions is necessary to be able to understand the structure and punctuation needed for most sentences.

Common Prepositions

about	before	despite	of	to
above	behind	down	off	toward(s)
across	below	during	on	under
after	beneath	for	out	until
against	beside	from	over	up
along	besides	in	since	upon
among	between	into	through	with
around	beyond	like	throughout	within
at	by	near	till	without

           S   **V**

(a) The student studies *in the library.*

                        PREP O of PREP
                              (NOUN)

       S   **V**

(b) We enjoyed the party *at your house.*

                     PREP   O of PREP
                              (NOUN)

(c) We went **to the zoo** **in the afternoon.**

              (place)   (time)

(d) **In the afternoon**, we went to the zoo.

An important element of English sentences is the prepositional phrase. It consists of a preposition (**PREP**) and its object (**O of PREP**). The object of a preposition is a noun or pronoun.

In (a): *in the library* is a prepositional phrase.

In (c): In most English sentences, place comes before time.

In (d): Sometimes a prepositional phrase comes at the beginning of a sentence.

PRACTICE 1   Identifying Prepositional Phrases

Find the subjects (S), verbs (V), objects (O), and prepositional phrases (PP) in the following sentences.

<pre>
          S   V   O   PP
</pre>

Example: Jack put the letter in the mailbox.

1. The children walked to school.

2. Beethoven wrote nine symphonies.

3. Mary did her homework at the library.

4. Bells originated in Asia.

5. Chinese printers created the first paper money in the world.

6. He wrote poetry until the day he died.

7. He waited for the train.

8. The cat prefers to stay under the bed.

9. They enjoy going out for ice cream after the T-ball games.

10. Because of the stress, he was unable to sleep.

Preposition Combinations

The following list of preposition combinations is important for ESL students to study and practice because these phrases can be unusual and idiomatic.

Prepositional Combinations with Adverbs and Verbs

A
be absent from
accuse of
be accustomed to
be acquainted with
be addicted to
be afraid of
agree with
be angry at, with
be annoyed with
apologize for
apply to, for
approve of
argue with, about
arrive in, at
be associated with
be aware of

B
believe in
blame for
be blessed with
be bored with

C
be capable of
care about, for
be cluttered with
be committed to
compare to, with
complain about
be composed of
be concerned about
be connected to
consist of
be content with
contribute to
be convinced of
be coordinated with
count (up)on
cover with
be crowded with

D
decide (up)on
be dedicated to
depend (up)on
be devoted to

be disappointed in, with
be discriminated against
distinguish from
be divorced from
be done with
dream of, about
be dressed in

E
be engaged to
be envious of
be equipped with
escape from
excel in
be excited about
excuse for
be exposed to

F
be faithful to
be familiar with
feel like
fight for
be filled with
be finished with
be fond of
forget about
forgive for
be friendly to, with
be furnished with

G
be grateful to, for
be guilty of

H
hide from
hope for

I
be innocent of
insist (up)on
be interested in
be involved in

J
be jealous of

K
be known for

L
be limited to
look forward to

M	be made of, from		rescue from
	be married to		respond to
O	object to		be responsible for
	be opposed to	S	be satisfied with
P	participate in		be scared of
	be patient with		stare at
	be polite to		stop from
	pray for		subscribe to
	be prepared for		substitute for
	prevent from		succeed in
	prohibit from	T	take advantage of
	protect from		take care of
	be proud of		be terrified of
	provide with		thank for
	be provided with		be tired of, from
R	recover from	U	be upset with
	be related to		be used to
	be relevant to	V	vote for
	rely (up)on	W	be worried about
	be remembered for		

PRACTICE 2 Using Preposition Combinations

Fill in the blanks with the correct preposition combination. The verb has been indicated. Supply the correct form of the verb *to be* (if necessary) and the preposition. The first one has been done for you.

1. Denise could not (decide) __**decide upon**__ her classes for next semester.

2. Midwesterners must (be prepared) _____ severe storms.

3. She (be scared) _____ driving in a thunderstorm.

4. Students must (be responsible) _____ preparing for class.

5. Katherine could not (be content) _____ her new life in retirement.

6. Many students continue to (be discriminated) _____ in college admission policies.

7. Don't (hide) _____ the truth!

8. The neighbors (be known) _____ their outrageous parties.

9. You must not (forget) _____ the exams next week.

10. The young man was found (guilty) _____ breaking and

entering.

PRACTICE 3   Using Prepositions

Write an eight- to twelve-sentence paragraph describing your favorite holiday. Underline all prepositions, prepositional phrases, and preposition combinations. Be sure that you have chosen the correct preposition or phrase combination.

_____

_____

_____

_____

_____

_____

_____

_____

_____

24

Articles and Interjections

 **Articles**

An **article** is a type of word that introduces a noun and indicates whether it is specific or countable. The most frequently used articles are *a*, *an*, and *the*.

> **Using Articles: Generic Nouns**
>
> Ø means no article is used.
>
> **Singular Count Noun**   (a) A *banana* is yellow.*
>
> A speaker uses generic nouns to make generalizations. A generic noun represents a whole class of things; it is not a specific, real, concrete thing but rather a symbol of a whole group.
>
> **Plural Count Noun**   (b) Ø *Bananas* are yellow.
>
> In (a) and (b): The speaker is talking about any banana, all bananas, bananas in general. In (c): The speaker is talking about any and all fruit, fruit in general.
>
> **Noncount Noun**   (c) Ø *Fruit* is good for you.
>
> Notice that no article (Ø) is used to make generalizations with plural count nouns and noncount nouns, as in (b) and (c).
>
> *Usually **a** or **an** is used with a *singular generic count noun.*
>   A *window* is made of glass.
>   A *doctor* heals sick people.
>   Parents must give *a child* love.
>   A *box* has six sides.
>   An *apple* can be red, green, or yellow.
>
> **The** is sometimes used with a singular generic count noun (not a plural generic count noun, not a generic noncount noun). Generic **the** is commonly used with, in particular:
>   **1.** Species of animals
>   The *whale* is the largest mammal on earth.
>   The *elephant* is the largest land mammal.
>   **2.** Inventions
>   Who invented the telephone? The wheel? The refrigerator? The airplane?
>   *The computer* will play an increasingly large role in all our lives.
>   **3.** Musical instruments
>   I'd like to learn to play the piano.
>   Do you play *the guitar*?

Using A or *Some*: Indefinite Nouns

Singular Count Noun   (d) I ate *a banana*.

Indefinite nouns are actual things (not symbols), but they are not specifically identified.

Plural Count Noun   (e) I ate *some bananas*.

In (d): The speaker is not referring to "this banana" or "that banana" or "the banana you gave me." The speaker is simply saying that she or he ate one banana. The listener does not know nor need to know which specific banana was eaten; it was simply one banana out of that whole group of things in this world called bananas.

Noncount Noun   (f) I ate *some fruit*.

In (e) and (f): *Some* is often used with indefinite plural count nouns and indefinite noncount nouns. In addition to *some*, a speaker might use *two, a few, several, a lot of* with plural count nouns, or *a little, a lot of* with noncount nouns.

Using *The*: Definite Nouns

Singular Count Noun   (g) Thank you for *the banana*.

A noun is definite when both the speaker and the listener are thinking about the same specific thing.

Plural Count Noun   (h) Thank you for *the bananas*.

In (g): The speaker uses *the* because the listener knows which specific banana the speaker is talking about, i.e., that particular banana that the listener gave to the speaker.

Noncount Noun   (i) Thank you for *the fruit*.

Notice that *the* is used with both singular and plural count nouns and with noncount nouns.

General Guidelines for Article Usage

(a) ***The** sun* is bright today.
   Please hand this book to *the teacher*.
   Please open *the door*.
   Jack is in *the kitchen*.

GUIDELINE: Use *the* when you know or assume that your listener is familiar with and thinking about the same specific thing or person you are talking about.

(b) Yesterday I saw *some dogs*.
   ***The** dogs* were chasing a *cat*.
   ***The** cat* was chasing a *mouse*.
   ***The** mouse* ran into a *hole*.
   ***The** hole* was very *small*.

GUIDELINE: Use *the* for the second mention of an indefinite noun.*
In (b): First mention = *some dogs, a cat, a mouse, a hole.* Second mention = *the dogs, the cat, the mouse, the hole.*

(c) Incorrect: *The apples* are my favorite fruit.
   Correct: *Apples* are my favorite fruit.

*****The** is not used for the second mention of a generic noun. Compare:
   1. What color is *a banana* (generic noun)? *A banana* (generic noun) is yellow.
   2. Tom offered me *a banana* (indefinite noun) or an apple. I chose *the banana* (definite noun).

© 2014 Wadsworth, Cengage Learning

GUIDELINE: Do not use **the** with a plural count noun (e.g., apples) or a noncount noun (e.g., gold) when you are making a generalization.

(d) Incorrect: *The gold* is a metal.
Correct: *Gold* is a metal

(e) Incorrect: I drove *car*
Correct: I drove *a car*
I drove *the car*
I drove *that car*
I drove *his car*

GUIDELINE: Do not use a singular count noun (e.g., *car*) without:
  1. an article (*a/an* or *the*); or
  2. *this/that*; or
  3. a possessive pronoun.

Source: The material on prepositions and articles was adapted from Betty S. Azar, *Understanding and Using English Grammar* (Englewood Cliffs, NJ: Prentice Hall Regents). Used with permission.

PRACTICE 1   Using Articles

In the following dialogues, try to decide whether the speakers would probably use *a/an* or *the*. The first example has been done for you.

1. A: I have _____**an**_____ idea. Let's go on _____**a**_____ picnic Saturday.

   B: Okay.

2. A: Did you have fun at _____ picnic yesterday?

   B: Sure did. And you?

3. A: You'd better have _____ good reason for being late!

   B: I do.

4. A: Did you think _____ reason Jack gave for being late was believable?

   B: Not really.

5. A: Where's my blue shirt?

   B: It's in _____ washing machine. You'll have to wear _____ different shirt.

6. A: I wish we had _____ washing machine.

   B: So do I. It would make it a lot easier to do our laundry.

7. A: What happened to your bicycle? _____ front wheel is bent.

    B: I ran into _____ parked car when I swerved to avoid _____ big pothole in the street.

    A: Did you damage _____ car?

    B: A little.

    A: What did you do?

    B: I left _____ note for _____ owner of _____ car.

    A: What did you write on _____ note?

    B: My name and address. I also wrote _____ apology.

8. A: Can you repair my car for me?

    B: What's wrong with it?

    A: _____ radiator has _____ leak, and one of _____ windshield wipers doesn't work.

    B: Can you show me where _____ leak is?

9. A: Have you seen my boots?

    B: They're in _____ closet in _____ front hallway.

PRACTICE 2   Using Articles

Complete the sentences with *a/an, the,* or Ø (Ø means no article).

1. _____ beef is a kind of _____ meat.

2. _____ beef we had for dinner last night was excellent.

3. Jack is wearing _____ straw hat today.

4. Jack likes to wear _____ hats.

5. _____ hat is _____ article of clothing.

6. _____ hats are _____ articles of clothing.

7. _____ brown hat on that hook over there belongs to Mark.

8. Everyone has _____ problems in _____ life.

9. My grandfather had _____ long life.

10. That book is about _____ life of Helen Keller.

11. Tommy wants to be _____ engineer when he grows up.

12. The Brooklyn Bridge was designed by _____ engineer.

13. John Roebling is _____ name of _____ engineer who designed the Brooklyn Bridge. He died in 1869 from _____ infection. He died before _____ bridge was completed.

14. _____ people wear _____ jewelry to make themselves more attractive.

15. _____ jewelry Diana is wearing today is beautiful.

16. Mary is wearing _____ beautiful ring today. It is made of _____ gold and _____ rubies. _____ gold in her ring was mined in Canada. _____ rubies came from Burma.

17. One of the first things you need to do when you move to _____ new city is to find _____ place to live. Most _____ newspapers carry _____ advertisements (called "want ads") for _____ apartments that are for rent. If you find an ad for a furnished apartment, _____ apartment will probably contain _____ stove and _____ refrigerator. It will also probably have _____ furniture such as _____ beds, _____ tables, _____ chairs, and maybe _____ sofa.

18. My wife and I have recently moved to this city. Since we're going to be here for only _____ short time, we're renting _____ furnished apartment. We decided that we didn't want to bring our own furniture with us. _____ apartment is in _____ good location, but that's about the only good thing I can say about it. Only one burner on _____ stove works. _____ refrigerator is noisy, and _____ refrigerator door won't stay closed unless we tape it shut. _____ bed sags in the middle and creaks. All of the rest of _____ furniture is old and decrepit too. Nevertheless, we're still enjoying living in this city. We may have to look for _____ another apartment, however.

PRACTICE 3 More Practice with Articles

Fill in the blanks in the following paragraph with the appropriate article or Ø.

Fisherman's Wharf offers the visitor _____ wide array of fascinating attractions. _____ fishing fleet docks along _____ Jefferson Street promenade. _____ early morning stroll along "Fish Alley" will allow you to see fishermen at work. Jefferson Street has _____ host of _____ specialty shops and _____ entertainment for _____ entire family. _____ Wharf has its share of museums, but they are _____ bit out of _____ ordinary. There's _____ wax museum, _____ Ripley's Believe It or Not! Museum, and _____ museum in _____ guise of _____ medieval dungeon. If you're not too claustrophobic, you can visit _____ Pier 45 and tour _____ USS *Pampanito*, _____ retired WWII submarine. Also, you might want to visit Ghirardelli Square and pick _____ souvenir or two from _____ many specialty shops located there. Finally, before you leave _____ Wharf, make certain you take with you _____ loaf or two of San Francisco's famous sourdough bread. You'll probably want to visit Fisherman's Wharf several times before your vacation is over. (from "San Francisco or Bust!")

Interjections

Interjections are words that express intense or sudden feelings or reactions. These words are often expressed forcefully, as in *Help!* or *Watch Out!* and are followed by exclamation points if they are the entire sentence. If the words are attached to a sentence, they are followed by a comma.

These expressions, however, are rarely used in formal expository writing. They are most often used in narrative or creative writing in which there is realistic dialogue.

> **Examples**
> *Wait!* You forgot your receipt!
> *Well*, now what should I do?

PRACTICE 4   Using Interjections

Interjections are usually used at the beginning of the sentence.
Fill in the blanks with correct INTERJECTIONS. Look up the definitions of the following words. Then complete the exercise. Some answers could fit more than one sentence! Try to use all of the interjections given.
Eek!, Wait!, Oops!, Wow!, Hey!, Oh no!, Ouch!, Ah!, Well, Sorry!

1. _____ He stole my computer!

2. _____ You hurt me.

3. _____ I have to go.

4. _____ I can't stand snakes.

5. _____ That is an adorable puppy.

6. _____ I lost my violin.

7. _____ Don't leave without us!

8. _____ How wonderful.

9. _____, I guess you can have some of my popcorn

10. _____ I tripped over the rug.

PRACTICE 5   Using Interjections

Fill in the blanks with an interjection that fits the meaning.
Here are some suggested Interjections to choose from:
Hurry, Wow, Hey, Ouch, Oops, Alas, Shh, Well (followed by a comma), Ah

1. _____ Don't leave without me!

2. _____ That coffee is hot.

3. _____ My favorite mug broke.

4. _____ I guess I'll buy the car.

5. _____! We won the ping pong game.

6. _____ Albert hit the baseball out of the park!

7. _____ there is something scary in the cave.

8. _____ cannot attend the family reunion.

9. _____ What is that sound?

10. _____ now I understand what you mean.

25

Correcting Common Errors

Sentence fragments, comma splices, run-on sentences, dangling or misplaced modifiers, restrictive/nonrestrictive clauses, words that are confused or words that sound alike and contractions are among the most common errors that writers make when drafting sentences or when combining independent and dependent clauses.

Sentence Fragments

Sentence **fragments** are dependent clauses or phrases punctuated as if they are complete sentences.

> Because the propeller was broken.
> Running up the stairs.

To correct a fragment, attach the dependent clause to an independent clause or add a subject or verb to the phrase.

> Because the propeller was broken, the ship returned to port.
> She tripped as she was running up the stairs.

Comma Splices

A **comma splice** occurs when a comma is used instead of a semicolon to combine independent clauses.

> **Comma Splice**
> Brian studies the cello, David studies the piano.

> **Corrected Versions**
>
> Brian studies the cello, and David studies the piano.
>
> Brian studies the cello; David studies the piano.

Run-on Sentences

A **run-on sentence** (or fused sentence) occurs when a sentence contains two or more independent clauses with nothing joining them together.

> **Run-on Sentence**
>
> Brian plays the cello David plays the piano.

> **Corrected Versions**
>
> Brian plays the cello; David plays the piano.
>
> Brian plays the cello, and David plays the piano.

COMMON ERROR

PRACTICE 1   **Correcting Fragments and Run-on Sentences**

Read All About It ... | Edwin Bliss, "Managing Your Time" (paragraph 5)

Identify the following examples as fragments (*F*), run-on sentences (*RO*), comma splices (*CS*), or independent clauses (*IC*). Some sentences will be correct (*IC*).

1. To work for longer periods without taking a break. _____

2. Is not an effective use of time. _____

3. Energy decreases, boredom sets in, and physical stress and tension accumulate. _____

4. Switching for a few minutes from a mental task to something physical can provide relief. _____

5. Isometric exercises, walking around the office, even changing from a sitting position to a standing position for awhile. _____

6. Merely resting, however, is often the best course and you should not think of a "rest" break as poor use of time. _____

7. Not only will being refreshed increase your efficiency but relieving tension will benefit your health. _____

8. Anything that contributes to health, is good time management. _____

PRACTICE 2	Sentence Combining to Correct Fragments and Run-ons

Combine the sentences in Practice 1 into a paragraph, avoiding fragments, comma splices, and run-ons.

_____

_____

_____

_____

_____

_____

_____

_____

_____

_____

Restrictive and Nonrestrictive Clauses/Modifiers

Clauses can be *restrictive* or *nonrestrictive*. **Restrictive clauses** are essential to identify nouns or to complete the meaning. These clauses simply follow the nouns or ideas they are modifying. No commas are used to offset restrictive clauses.

> In the line, the young woman *who was wearing a red bandana and hoop earrings* needed a ticket. (This relative clause is essential to identify which woman needed a ticket.)

Most clauses beginning with *that* are restrictive clauses and are not set off with commas.

> Where is the report *that he left on the desk this morning?*

Nonrestrictive clauses are not essential to complete the meaning of the sentence. You can remove them from the sentence, and the basic meaning of the sentence will remain clear. Because they are nonessential, these clauses are always offset by commas.

> Linda and Burt, *who just returned from Alaska,* would go on another vacation tomorrow. (This relative clause is not essential because it just adds interesting details to the sentence; without it, the meaning of the sentence is still clear.)

> The cockatiels, *which were chirping loudly to the music of the nearby television*, should live for up to twenty years. (This clause is nonessential, supplying interesting details but not essential information.)

Misplaced or Dangling Clauses/Modifiers

Misplaced or dangling modifiers are clauses or phrases that are misleading because they are in the wrong place in the sentence. To fix this error, make sure the clause or phrase is next to the subject or verb that it describes. Dangling modifiers are phrases that begin the sentence, but do not describe or refer to the subject at the beginning of the sentence. This error can be fixed by placing the phrase or clause in the correct place or by rewriting the sentence to clarify the word order and structure.

> The movers packed the furniture, *tired and angry*, and drove the truck to the wrong city. (This is a misplaced phrase because the adjective phrase "tired and angry" describes the movers, not the furniture).
>
> Correction: Tired and angry, the movers packed the furniture and drove the truck to the wrong city.
>
> *Flying over the roof*, the family watched the planes. (This is a misleading dangling modifier because the planes were flying over the roof, not the family!)
>
> Correction: The family watched the planes flying over the roof.

PRACTICE 3   **Correcting Restrictive, Nonrestrictive, Misplaced or Dangling Clauses or Phrases**

The following sentences have restrictive/nonrestrictive, misplaced or dangling modifying phrases. Underline the misplaced or dangling phrase in each sentence, and rewrite the sentence so that the meaning is clear and accurate.

Example: David fed the birds <u>in his robe and slippers</u>.

     In his robe and slippers, David fed the birds.

1. The storekeeper did not sell the book to the customer with the cover missing.

_____

_____

_____

2. Walking down the hall, the VCR cart nearly pushed her into the wall.

_____

_____

_____

3. The mail carrier delivered the package to the woman who was wrapped in holiday wrapping paper.

_____

_____

_____

4. To lift the exercise equipment up the stairs, a great deal of strength is required.

_____

_____

_____

5. After losing her job, her parents encouraged her to move back home with them.

_____

_____

_____

6. Singing in the basement, the dog began to whine, and the cat dashed up the stairs.

_____

_____

_____

7. The teacher gave the class a lecture which consisted of only five students.

_____

_____

_____

8. The salesman answered the angry customer's accusations smiling.

_____

_____

_____

9. Driving past the house, the signs of a forbidden party were suddenly obvious.

_____

_____

_____

10. Testing the samples, the lab suddenly filled with smoke.

_____

_____

_____

COMMON ERROR

PRACTICE 4   **Using Correct Subject-Verb Agreement**

In the following sentences, choose the correct form of the verb in the parentheses. First, underline each subject and decide whether it is singular or plural. Next, underline the verb form that correctly agrees with the subject. The tense must also be accurate.

Example: He always (carry, carries) a credit card in his wallet.

1. One of the fundamental features of our legal system (is, are) that we (is, are) presumed innocent of any wrongdoing unless and until the government (prove, proves) otherwise.

2. Random drug testing of student athletes (turn, turns) this presumption on its head, telling students that we (assume, assumes) they are using drugs until they (prove, proves) to the contrary with a urine sample.

3. The overwhelming majority of student athletes in Ridgefield Park, and throughout New Jersey, (is, are) law abiding citizens, and there (is, are) no basis in law or logic to presume otherwise or to treat them worse than accused criminals.

4. An equally cherished constitutional command (is, are) the rule that government officials may not (search, searches) us without an adequate reason.

5. Thus, for example, even though we (know, knows) there is a drug problem in our society, we do not (allow, allows) the police to randomly stop us on the street to see if we are carrying drugs.

6. The constitutional prohibition against "unreasonable" searches also (embody, embodies) the principle that merely belonging to a certain group is not a sufficient reason for a search, even if many members of that group (is, are) suspected of illegal activity.

7. Thus, for example, even if it were true that most men with long hair (was, were) drug users, the police would not be free to stop all long-haired men and search them for drugs.

8. Unfortunately, many school officials concerned about drug use by students (seem, seems) willing to ignore these principles.

9. There is no doubt that the concern (is, are) well placed, and it (is, are) one we share.

10. Drug use (is, are) a scourge on our society, exacting a terrible toll in lost lives. ("Just Say No to Drug Testing" by Rocah)

Compound Subject-Verb Agreement

Some sentences contain a compound subject. A **compound subject** is formed by two or more simple subjects joined with a coordinating conjunction. The verb form *must agree in number with the subject*. If the coordinating conjunction is *and,* the verb is usually plural.

> Fredric and Elise *are* working together on the project.

However, if the compound subject is thought of as a unit, a singular verb is used.

> Macaroni and cheese *is* a favorite dish for children.

If the compound subject is preceded by a singular term such as *each* or *every,* the verb is singular.

> After the storm, *every* person, plant, and animal *was* drenched.

If the compound subject is connected with the correlative conjunctions *either/or, neither/nor, not only/but also*, the verb must agree with the following rules.

If both subjects are singular, the verb is singular.

> Either Fredric or Elise *is* going to turn in the project to the boss.

If both subjects are plural, the verb is plural.

> Neither the violins nor the cellos *need* to rehearse their parts with the conductor.

If one subject is singular and the other is plural, the verb agrees with the subject closest to the verb.

> Either my sisters or my friend *is* going to help plan the reception.

| PRACTICE 5 | Using Correct Compound Subject-Verb Agreement |

In each sentence, underline the verb that agrees with the compound subject.

Example: During the summer, parents and children (<u>look</u>, looks) forward to vacations.

1. The top of the slalom course and the bottom (appear, appears) far apart.

2. Every mountain and ocean (is, are) indicated on the new map.

3. The sea lion and her cub (stands, stand) on the dock near Fisherman's Wharf.

4. Each gymnast and coach (congratulate, congratulates) the winner of the competition.

5. The costume on the mannequin and the one on my child (fit, fits) differently.

6. Each towel, sheet, and pillow case (turns, turn) pale in the bleach-filled water.

7. Members of the anniversary party or the guests (is, are) in the pictures in the album.

8. Either exhaustion or procrastination (delay, delays) my progress.

9. Neither a calculator nor a dictionary (was, were) available in the bookstore.

10. My sisters or my mother (are, is) going to join me for a vacation.

| PRACTICE 6 | Editing to Correct Subject-Verb Agreement |

Read All About It ...

To read the full essay from which these sentences are excerpted, see page 411.

Edit the following paragraph for subject-verb agreement. The first sentence has been done for you. Some sentences may be correct.

We ~~knows~~ **know** we have friends; at least I know my friends ~~is~~ **are** with me, if not always, at least most of the time. And most of the time I needs them, and they me. We reaches over the phone lines for that word of comfort, the encouragement we needs to go on when our own store of willpower have become depleted. (Franco, "A Magic Circle of Friends")

| PRACTICE 7 | Editing to Correct Subject-Verb Agreement |

Read All About It ...

To read the full essay from which these sentences are excerpted, see page 411.

Edit the following paragraph for subject-verb agreement. The first verb has been done for you.

We will do it instead at a slower pace, because, along the way, we ~~has~~ **have** learned lessons both small and big: for example, that the world are in no hurry to be changed and that we will has a better shot at it after a good night's sleep. We may not complete our plans by tomorrow, or even by the end of the week, because the details of our lives may interferes, such as a child home from college, or a neighbor's emergency. (Franco, "A Magic Circle of Friends")

COMMON ERROR

| PRACTICE 8 | Editing to Correct Subject-Verb Agreement |

Read All About It ...

To read the full essay from which these sentences are excerpted, see page 411.

Edit the following passage for subject-verb agreement. The first sentence has been done for you.

         call
They ~~calls~~ us "late bloomers," they call us "returnees." We is sought by schools, thanks to the sheer numbers we represent, not to mention the life experience and the common sense that even the least bright among us bring to the classroom. We feels flattered and surprised, and our ego is bolstered by the realization that we is indeed quite capable. . . .

    We may just be beginning to feel a few arthritic pangs in our toes and fingers, but with our hair neatly streaked and some expensive dental work, we knows we still look good. We know we are still strong, smart, vital and, most especially, ready to work. This time around we will makes a big difference. We knows, because for sure, we already was different. (Franco, "A Magic Circle of Friends")

COMMON ERROR

| PRACTICE 9 | Editing for Verb Use |

Edit the following paragraph for any mistakes in verbs and subject-verb agreement. The first and second sentences have been done for you; the corrections appear in parentheses.

    I really loved our mobile home. I enjoy (enjoyed) it most during the summer when our family drived (drove) around the country visiting beaches, mountains, or deserts. In the afternoon we would pulled into a state park, chosed the shadiest parking space, and plugged in for the night. We have a small home away from home with clean beds, a stove, and a refrigerator. My sisters and brothers and I play on beaches, mountain paths, or wild rivers, and come back to the campsite ready to eats our favorite meals. At night, after sitting around the fire, we would climbed into our small cozy beds and listened to our father tell us stories until we falled asleep. The next day we would unplugged our mobile house and drived to another adventure.

Words That Sound or Look Almost Alike

Writers sometimes have trouble with words that sound very much alike and are similar in appearance yet have minor but significant exceptions in spelling and meaning. These are particularly difficult spelling challenges for all writers.

Words	Definition	Example
accept/except		
accept (verb)	to acknowledge as true; to receive	She *accepted* his explanation.
		They *accepted* the wedding gifts.
except (prep.)	other than	All of the assignments *except* one were easy.
advice/advise		
advice (noun)	suggestions about solutions to a problem	He never listens to *advice*.
advise (verb)	to make suggestions; to give advice	The counselor *advises* the confused freshmen.
affect/effect		
affect (verb)	to influence	The weather will *affect* your mood.
effect (noun)	end product; result	The *effect* of the accident was obvious for years.
breath/breathe		
breath (noun)	air inhaled or exhaled	The swimmer held his *breath*.
breathe (verb)	to exhale or inhale	The cat *breathes* silently.
choose/chose		
choose (verb)	to pick or select (present tense)	They could not *choose* a restaurant.
chose (verb)	picked or selected (past tense)	They *chose* to order pizza.
conscience/conscious		
conscience (noun)	thought process acknowledging right and wrong	He has no *conscience*.
conscious (adj.)	aware of existence; capable of thinking	The students were not *conscious* after lunch.
council/consul/counsel		
council (noun)	group that meets/plans/governs	The city *council* meets each month.

(continued)

Words	Definition	Example
consul (noun)	government official in foreign service	The German *consul* met with the president.
counsel (verb)	to advise	The department chair *counseled* the frustrated student.

desert/dessert

desert (noun)	dry, barren land	The sunsets on the *desert* are spectacular.
desert (verb)	to leave alone; abandon	His friends *deserted* him.
dessert (noun)	last dish of a meal, often sweet	They decided to avoid sweet, fattening *desserts*.

diner/dinner

diner (noun)	a narrow type of restaurant with counters and booths; a person who is eating	At the *diner*, they have an old juke box. The *dinners* enjoy listening to oldies from the juke box.
dinner (noun)	the large, important meal at mid-day or evening	The fried chicken is for *dinner*.

emigrate/immigrate

emigrate (verb)	to leave a country	They *emigrated* from China.
immigrate (verb)	to enter a new country	Lila *immigrated* to the United Kingdom.

farther/further

farther (adv.)	greater distance (physically)	The sprinter ran *farther* than he had to.
further (adv.)	greater distance (mentally)	Most arguments can be *further* developed.
further (verb)	to advance an ideal or goal	The protesters *further* the cause of equality.

loose/lose

loose (adj.)	not tight	*Loose* fitting clothing has been in style recently.
lose (verb)	to misplace or be unable to find; to fail to win	I always *lose* my earrings. He *lost* the tennis match.

personal/personnel

personal (adj.)	pertaining to the individual	*Personal* information should remain confidential.

© 2014 Wadsworth, Cengage Learning

Words	Definition	Example
personnel (noun)	employees	*Personnel* should be aware of their benefits.

quiet/quit/quite

quiet (adj.)	without noise; peaceful	The class is too *quiet*.
quit (verb)	to stop; to give up	The employee *quit* suddenly.
quite (adv.)	definitely	You were *quite* right.

special/especially

special (adj.)	unique	Their anniversary was a *special* event.
especially (adv.)	even more; very	Final exams can be *especially* difficult.

than/then

than (conj.)	word to make comparison	Sale prices are better *than* original prices.
then (adv.)	at that time	First they studied; *then* they took the exam.

thorough/though

thorough (adj.)	detailed, complete, accurate	Social attitudes changed after several *thorough* studies were made.
though (conj.)	despite	*Though* the trees are changing colors, the temperature is warm.

through/threw

through (prep.)	in one side and out the other	The ball crashed *through* the window.
threw (verb)	past tense of *throw*	The president *threw* the first pitch.

COMMON ERROR

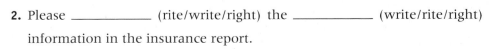

PRACTICE 10   **Frequently Confused Words**

Fill in the blanks of the following sentences with the correct word.

1. He was not telling her the _____ (hole, whole) story about the _____ (hole, whole) in the bay window.

2. Please _____ (rite/write/right) the _____ (write/rite/right) information in the insurance report.

3. The doctor will _____ (sight/cite/site) statistics to his patients about the necessity of protecting their _____ (site/sight/cite).

4. The boys want _____ (to, too, two) see _____ (to, too, two) movies tonight and hope you want to see them, _____ (to, too, two).

5. The school _____ (principal, principle) would never ask a teacher to betray her most basic _____ (principle, principal).

6. Do not _____ (except, accept) excuses from the students, _____ (accept, except) for me!

7. During his _____ (rain, reign, rein), the King would never appear in public in the _____ (rain, reign, rein).

8. Do not _____ (waist, waste) my time by boasting about the effect of the new equipment on the size of the model's _____ (waist, waste).

9. _____ (weather, whether) or not we attend the party depends on the _____ (whether, weather).

10. The swimmer cannot _____ (breath, breathe) under water; therefore, he takes several deep _____ (breaths, breathes) before he dives.

COMMON ERROR

PRACTICE 11   **Frequently Confused Words**

Edit the following paragraph for correct word choice. Circle the errors, then write the correct words in the spaces provided. The first error has been circled for you.

(Buy) the time they reached the state capital, the students were very restless from the long bus ride. They jumped off of the bus quickly and formed a line in front of the tour guide. The tour guide greeted the fifth graders and complemented them on there exceptable behavior. She quickly gulped down an aspirin as she guided her charges up the steps to the state senate chambers. The students whispered and shuffled their feet as they past the halls where the lawmakers were working. They admired the portraits of famous governors and stared up into the domed ceilings. After the tour was over,

they ran down the plane cement steps and gathered, laughing and shout-

ing, in the park to eat lunch.

_____   _____

_____   _____

_____   _____

_____

PRACTICE 12   Using Words That Sound or Look Almost Alike

Write a sentence for each of the following words, demonstrating the difference in meaning from similar words.

1. accept: _____

_____

2. advise: _____

_____

3. affect: _____

_____

4. conscience: _____

_____

5. consul: _____

_____

6. dessert: _____

_____

7. diner: _____

_____

8. emigrate: _____

_____

9. loose: _____

_____

10. personnel: _____

_____

Confusing Verbs That Sound Alike

The verbs *lie/lay*, *rise/raise*, and *sit/set* are often confused. In order to understand how to use them correctly, it is important to understand the difference between *reflexive verbs*, which *do not* take an object (the verb needs no noun to complete the meaning of the sentence), and *transitive verbs*, which *do* take an object. *Lie*, *rise*, and *sit* are reflexive; *lay*, *raise*, and *set* are transitive.

Reflexive Verbs: Lie, Rise, Sit

	Present Tense	Present Participle	Past Tense	Past Participle
lie (to rest or recline)	lie	lying	lay	has/have lain
rise (to move upward)	rise	rising	rose	has/have risen
sit (to move body into sitting position)	sit	sitting	sat	has/have sat

The family dog loves *to lie* by the front door.

Let the bread dough *rise* on the warm kitchen counter.

She *sits* in front of a computer for eight hours every day.

Reflexive verbs are often followed by a prepositional phrase, not a stand-alone noun.

Transitive Verbs: Lay, Raise, Set

	Present Tense	Present Participle	Past Tense	Past Participle
lay (to put an object down)	lay	laying	laid	has/have laid
raise (to lift or move something up)	raise	raising	raised	has/have raised
set (to carefully place something)	set	setting	set	has/have set

She *lay* the flowers carefully on the table.

Please *raise* the window shades.

He *set* the chair by the window.

The object (underlined) is necessary to complete the meaning of these sentences.

| **PRACTICE 13** | **Using Lie/Lay, Rise/Raise, Sit/Set** |

Determine if the verbs are used correctly in the following sentences. Change those that are incorrect. The first one has been done for you.

1. _____ He is lying on the couch, watching *Survivor*.

2. _____ You do not have to rise your hand at the dinner table!

3. _____ She spent the day laying on the sand or sitting by the shore.

4. _____ Set the table, and sit up straight!

5. _____ At the end of the paintball tournament, the losing team raised a white flag.

6. _____ Tatyana has set in the front row all semester because she lost her glasses.

7. _____ Her empty purse lay on the desk all day yesterday.

8. _____ The moon is raising (rising) slowly this evening.

9. _____ The vase was setting on the table.

10. _____ You have lain on your bed all afternoon!

| **PRACTICE 14** | **Using Lie/Lay, Rise/Raise, Sit/Set** |

Write your own sentences using each of the following verbs.

1. Lie

_____

_____

_____

2. Lay

_____

_____

_____

3. Rise

_____

_____

_____

4. Raise

_____

_____

_____

5. Sit

_____

_____

_____

6. Set

_____

_____

_____

Contractions That Sound Like Other Words

Another type of word that causes problems with revision and editing is contractions. Often contractions, a shortened form of a noun and verb, indicated by the insertion of an apostrophe, can be confused with other words, particularly possessive pronouns. Note the differences in the spelling and punctuation of the following words, which are spoken with the same pronunciation.

Contraction	Definition	Example
it's/its		
it's	contraction: _it is_	_It's_ going to rain.
its	belonging to it	_Its_ wings were broken.
they're/their/there		
they're	contraction: _they are_	_They're_ ready for any adventure.
their	belonging to them	_Their_ pets run their home.
there	at that place	The library is over _there,_ not here.
we're/were/where		
we're	contraction: _we are_	_We're_ going to the beach for vacation.
were	past tense of _are_	We _were_ ready for a week.
where	in which location	_Where_ is the map?

Contraction	Definition	Example
who's/whose		
who's	contraction: *who is*	*Who's* going to the party?
whose	belonging to whom	*Whose* socks are on the sofa?
you're/your		
you're	contraction: *you are*	*You're* in the way.
your	belonging to you	*Your* gift is in the mail.

PRACTICE 15   **Using Contractions That Sound Like Other Words**

Underline the correct word in the parentheses based on the meaning of the sentence. The first one has been done for you.

1. The leaves (we're / <u>were</u> / where) turning colors as autumn approached.

2. (It's / Its) engine overheated in the hot, arid Nevada desert.

3. Exactly (we're / were / where) did you think the restaurant was located?

4. (Their / There / They're) is a trail that (their / there / they're) supposed to follow.

5. Are you certain that (you're / your) ready to take the driving test?

6. (It's / Its) not a good idea to wait until the last minute to start an essay.

7. Do you know (whose / who's) socks these are?

8. (Your / You're) luck is about to change!

9. (Who's / Whose) going to go with us to the ball game?

10. The cat howled for (it's / its) dinner every night at five o'clock.

PRACTICE 16   Using Contractions Correctly

Use each of the following contractions correctly in a sentence.

1. it's: _____

_____

2. they're: _____

_____

3. we're: _____

_____

4. who's: _____

_____

5. you're: _____

_____

26

Sentence Combining Practice

Sentence combining can provide an opportunity to practice editing skills: correcting punctuation, using clauses and phrases, polishing style, and creating sentence variety.

In the following groups of sentences, combine the shorter groups of sentences to avoid repetition, reduce wordiness, and use punctuation and sentence structure correctly.

COMMON ERROR

PRACTICE 1   **Sentence Combining**

Combine the following groups of sentences from "Cat Bathing as Martial Art" into one sentence. Then put the revised sentences into one paragraph.

1.1 Some people say cats never have to be bathed.
1.2 They say cats lick themselves clean.
1.3 They say cats have a special enzyme of some sort in their saliva.

_____

_____

2.1 This enzyme works like new, improved Wisk.
2.2 This enzyme dislodges dirt where it hides.
2.3 This enzyme whisks dirt away.

_____

_____

Combine the sentences into a paragraph.

_____

_____

_____

_____

_____

_____

PRACTICE 2   Sentence Combining

Combine the following groups of sentences from "Cat Bathing as Martial Art" into one sentence. Then put the revised sentences into one paragraph.

1.1 I've spent most of my life believing this folklore.
1.2 I am like most blind believers.
1.3 I have been able to discount all the facts to the contrary.
1.4 The facts are the kitty odors that lurk in the corners of the garage and the dirt smudges that cling to the throw rug by the fireplace.

_____

_____

_____

_____

2.1 The time comes when a man must face reality.
2.2 The time comes when a man must look squarely in the face of massive public sentiment to the contrary.
2.3 The time comes when he must announce: "This cat smells like a port-a-potty on a hot day in Juarez."

_____

_____

_____

_____

3.1 That day arrives at my house.
3.2 I have some advice.
3.3 You might consider this advice.
3.4 The advice is valuable when you place your feline friend under your arm and head for the bathtub.

_____

_____

_____

_____

Combine the sentences into a paragraph.

_____

_____

_____

_____

_____

_____

_____

_____

COMMON
ERROR

PRACTICE 3   Combining Sentence

Combine the following groups of sentences from the student essay "How to Be Successful at Kicking the Smoking Habit" by Stephanie Higgs. First combine the sentences to avoid repetition and to use sentence variety with correct grammar and punctuation. Then combine the new sentences into a paragraph.

1.1 People smoke for a variety of reasons.
1.2 It is important for smokers to identify the reasons why they smoke.

_____

_____

2.1 Analyzing the origin of the habit is the first step.
2.2 This step is toward kicking the habit.

_____

_____

3.1 This is for most people.
3.2 Smoking is a learned behavior.
3.3 Smokers tend to come from families where one or more of their parents were smokers.

_____

_____

4.1 The majority of them are anxious people.
4.2 These are people who started smoking.
4.3 It seemed to provide a temporary release from current or future distress and uncertainties.

_____

_____

5.1 Some tobacco users started smoking to be cool.
5.2 Some started to fit in with the crowd.
5.3 Others enjoyed the taste of tobacco upon trying it out.

_____

_____

6.1 Others did not necessarily enjoy the act of smoking.
6.2 They felt addicted to the nicotine.
6.3 They needed to continue to satisfy their cravings.

_____

_____

7.1 The origin of the habit is exposed.
7.2 The smoker is empowered with the knowledge of why he or she smokes.
7.3 The smoker can seek out healthier alternatives to satisfy needs.

_____

_____

Combine the sentences into a paragraph.

_____

_____

_____

_____

_____

_____

_____

_____

_____

Punctuation and Other Rules of Style

http://grammar.ccc.comnet.edu/grammar/marks/marks.htm

End Punctuation

The end of a complete sentence is signaled by using a **period.** However, sentences can also end with an **exclamation mark (!)** or, when the sentence is a question, a **question mark (?).** (See page 365 for more information on question marks.)

COMMON
ERROR

| PRACTICE 1 | Using Correct End Punctuation |

Read All About It . . .

To read the full essay from which these sentences are excerpted, see page 398.

In the following sentences select the correct end punctuation. The first one has been done for you.

1. I call Forough to find out when I can bring by the clothes, which she will take to Iran for me ___.___

2. We make a date, then compare notes on Norooz parties _____

3. "How was your party _____" Forough wants to know.

4. "I thought it was great _____" I tell her, surprised _____

5. Before we say good-bye, she asks me if I'm going to the Sizda-bedar picnic _____

6. "The Sizdah-bedar picnic _____" I say enthusiastically _____

7. "I'd like to go, but I'm not sure _____ I'll have to talk to Neil."

PRACTICE 2 Punctuating Nonrestrictive Modifiers

Punctuate the phrases or clauses in the following sentences correctly, putting commas only around nonessential phrases and clauses. If a sentence is correct, write "C." The first one has been done for you.

1. The football players**,** who looked impressive in their new uniforms, marched in the homecoming parade.C

2. The technical building which had been built in 1960 was now in need of renovation.

3. Emeralds that are artificially created appear brighter than natural emeralds.

4. The mortgage which was a large part of their budget was due to be paid off in one more year.

5. The committee that I have been requested to join meets twice a week.

6. The gift basket we received for Christmas included gifts for the entire family.

7. The snowstorm descending from the northern states threatened to cancel the first week of spring semester.

8. Professor Wilson gave the test to her new group of students who refused to read homework assignments.

9. We avoided only the speakers who presented outdated information.

10. The investments that were successful the previous year were less successful in the new year.

PRACTICE 3 Using Commas Correctly

Read All About It ...
To read the full essay from which these sentences are excerpted, see page 417.

Combine the following groups of sentences into one sentence each, using a variety of phrases and clauses, and using commas correctly.

1.1 I think that we're all mentally ill.

1.2 Those of us outside the asylums only hide it a little better.

1.3 We may not hide it all that much better, after all.

_____

_____

_____

_____

2.1 We pay four or five bucks.

2.2 We seat ourselves at tenth-row center in a theater.

2.3 The theater is showing a movie.

2.4 The movie is a horror movie.

2.5 This is daring the nightmare.

_____

_____

_____

_____

3.1 We also go to reestablish our feelings.

3.2 The feelings are of essential normality.

3.3 The horror movie is innately conservative.

3.4 It is even reactionary.

_____

_____

_____

_____

4.1 We are all insane.

4.2 Sanity becomes a matter of degree.

_____

_____

_____

_____

5.1 The potential lyncher is in almost all of us.

5.2 This excludes saints.

5.3 The saints are past and present.

5.4 Most saints have been crazy in their own ways.

5.5 This occurs every now and then.

5.6 The potential lyncher has to be let loose.

5.7 He must scream and roll around in the grass.

This sentence may need the judicious use of semicolons as well as commas!

_____

_____

_____

_____

(King, "Why We Crave Horror Movies")

Semicolons

As indicated earlier (see "Clauses and Phrases" on pages 308–321), writers can combine simple sentences or independent clauses to create compound sentences by using a **semicolon (;)**. A semicolon is not a substitute for a comma and is not used with a coordinating conjunction. The semicolon joins two complete sentences; additionally (as in this sentence) it can combine one independent clause with a second independent clause introduced with an adverbial conjunction. The semicolon is used sparingly and only to connect very closely related ideas. The semicolon can add sentence variety to your writing but should not be overused. The following sentences illustrate the correct use of the semicolon.

> **Semicolon to Combine Two Sentences or Two Independent Clauses**
>
> The anaconda is the world's largest snake; it can grow to 30 feet or more in length. ("size" is the relating idea)
>
> The nurse measured the patient's blood pressure; she also took a blood sample. ("blood" is the relating idea)
>
> **Semicolon to Combine Two Sentences (Independent Clauses), the Second of Which Is Introduced by an Adverbial Conjunction and a Comma**
>
> The team practiced in the morning; furthermore, they practiced again in the evening.
>
> Aunt Louisa stopped at the baker; meanwhile, her niece waited in the car.

Colons

To add sentence variety and to emphasize particular information, you can use a **colon (:)**. Use a colon to introduce a list, when telling time, in the salutation of a business letter, and to separate titles of a book. See the following examples of the correct use of a colon.

1. Use a colon after an independent clause to introduce a list.

> **Example:** Preparing a soufflé requires four ingredients: milk, eggs, butter, and cheese.
>
> The pharmacy technician ordered popular items sold most often: aspirin, gauze, bandages, and antacid.
>
> Making chocolate chip cookies can be a sensory delight: the smooth combination of butter, eggs, and sugar; the light, fluffy addition of flour; and, finally, the sinful addition of dark, bittersweet chocolate chips.
>
> (*Notice the use of the semicolon to separate the topics of the list, when those topics include items separated by commas.)
>
> *Note*: Do not use a colon before a list if the list immediately follows a verb or a preposition.
>
> ***Improper use***
>
> The most popular condiments are: catsup, mustard, and mayonnaise. (omit the colon after the verb)

2. Use a colon when telling time.

> **Example:** The train arrives at 4:15 p.m.
>
> My 2:30 p.m. doctor's appointment was changed to 5:00 p.m.

3. Use a colon for the salutation of a business letter.

> **Example:** Dear Mrs. Howard:
>
> To whom it may concern:
>
> Sirs:

4. Use a colon to separate the title and subtitle of a book.

> **Example:** *Accounting in Context: A Business Handbook*
>
> *Writing Made Easy: A Plain Language Rhetoric*
>
> *Washington: The First Leader of the Nation*

PRACTICE 4	Using Commas, Semicolons, and Colons

In the following sentences add a colon and/or semicolon or comma when appropriate.

Example: The teacher taught using a variety of methods: lecturing, using an overhead projector, and facilitating cooperative group projects.

1. The surgeon dressed in a green surgical gown she wore a protective cap covering her hair.

2. The falling leaves covered the ground consequently the golfers had a difficult time finding their golf balls.

3. The submarine dove to a depth of 300 fathoms it hovered silently at that depth for two hours.

4. Jerry enjoyed many activities while vacationing boating, fishing, and hiking.

5. Sheila hit the ball however she was thrown out at first base.

6. The offices workers ate lunch in a variety of places out by the lake in the cafeteria or at the nearby park.

7. The crew chief made out the weekly shift schedule subsequently she hired several new workers.

8. The two falcons found a tree gathered twigs and built a nest.

9. Joseph prefers to stay home and watch TV his wife longs to go out dancing.

10. The man's hidden career dreams were baseball-related to pitch a no-hitter and hit a home run in the World Series.

Apostrophes

The **apostrophe** is used to indicate contractions or possession/ownership.

1. Some words can be combined, usually in informal writing, by using an apostrophe. This is a contraction.

> *Isn't* this strange? (is + not)
> We *couldn't* drive any farther. (could + not)

© 2014 Wadsworth, Cengage Learning

2. Add an apostrophe plus "*s*" to a noun to indicate possession.

> *Anna's* papers were left in the office.

3. To a plural noun ending in "*s*" add only an apostrophe to indicate possession.

> *Parents'* advice often is ignored.

4. For some words, an apostrophe plus "*s*" should be added to a singular word ending in "*s*." This is most often true for a proper name.

> *Tom Billings's* recipe book

5. An apostrophe plus "*s*" can be used to form the plural of figures, letters, and words being treated as words in isolation. (It is also acceptable to leave out this apostrophe.)

> Many students are not satisfied with *C's*.
> He scored *98's* on both tests.
> Don't use so many *"okay's"* when you speak.

Quotation Marks

1. Use **quotation marks** to set apart words that are quoted or the spoken words in dialogue.

> My mother wrote, "We will be travelling in our mobile home."
> Jung said, "I need to change my grammar text."

2. Periods and commas are placed inside the quotation marks, whereas semicolons and colons are placed outside the quotation marks. If the quoted material is a question, place the question mark inside the quotation marks. However, if the quoted material is part of a longer sentence that asks a question, put the question mark outside the quotation marks.

> "Do the bats fly at night?" he asked.
> Did I hear you say, "The bats fly at night"?
> He politely remarked, "I would like tea"; however, his wife asked for coffee.
> In the short story "Hills Like White Elephants," the male character makes several references to a "simple operation" as a solution to an inconvenient pregnancy.

3. Use quotation marks to set apart titles of essays, magazine articles, short stories, short poems, songs, and chapter headings that you refer to in your writing.

> The class discussed "The House on Mango Street" for two days.
>
> "Music of the Night" is her favorite song in *Phantom of the Opera*.
>
> The poem "Fire and Ice" by Frost illustrates two types of anger and destruction.
>
> "Letter from a Birmingham Jail" is an essay that effectively illustrates argumentation.

4. Quotation marks or italics can be used to set apart a word, phrase, or letter being discussed.

> Do not follow the conjunction *although* with a comma.
>
> Descriptive words such as "brilliant," "glowing," and "illuminating" support the dominant impression of "light."

5. Uncommon names or nicknames and words used in irony or sarcasm should be surrounded by quotation marks.

> James "Melon Ball" McCarthy prefers to shave his head.
>
> His crime of adultery almost made him "public enemy number one."

6. Single quotation marks should be used to indicate a quotation within a quotation.

> Tasha said, "My favorite song is 'Layla' performed by Eric Clapton."

Parentheses

1. **Parentheses** are used to set off specific details giving additional information, explanations, or qualifications of the main idea in a sentence. This would include words, dates, or statements.

> Many students name famous athletes as heroes (Sammy Sosa, Mark McGwire, and Maurice Green, for example).
>
> *Tom Sawyer* (1876) is one of Mark Twain's most enduring works.

2. The period for the sentence is placed outside the parenthesis when the enclosed information occurs at the end of the sentence and is not a complete sentence itself. If the enclosed information is a complete sentence, the period is placed inside the parenthesis.

> Many students name famous athletes as heroes (for example, Sammy Sosa).
>
> Many students name famous athletes as heroes. (One example is Sammy Sosa.)

Brackets

1. Brackets are used in quoted material to set apart editorial explanations.

> "The tenor sang 'Angel of Music' [original version sung by Michael Crawford] for his encore."

2. Brackets are also used to indicate editorial corrections to quoted material. The word "*sic*" (which means "thus") placed in brackets next to an error in quoted material means that the mistake appeared in the original text and that it is not the writer's error.

> The dean wrote, "All faculty must teach sumer [sic] school."

Dashes

1. The **dash** is used to set apart parenthetical information that needs more emphasis than would be indicated by parentheses.

> Irina's new teacher—a dynamic sociology teacher—helped her to understand American society.

2. Use a dash before a statement that expands on or summarizes the preceding statement (this could also include ironic or humorous comments).

> He studied for the exam for two days—then fell asleep before he finished!

Hyphens

1. Hyphens are used to form compound adjectives before a noun.

> a well-written play
> a forty-year-old woman

2. Do not use a hyphen after an adverb that ends in -*ly*.

> a quickly changed opinion
> a beautifully designed home

3. Check the dictionary for compound words that always require a hyphen.

> compound numbers (twenty-five, fifty-six)
> good-for-nothing
> father-in-law, mother-in-law
> president-elect

4. Some words with prefixes use a hyphen; check your dictionary if you are unsure.

> ex-husband
> non-English-speaking

5. Use a hyphen at the end of a line if you have to break a word into syllables. Do not divide a one-syllable word.

> Do not forget to review dependent clauses and subordinate conjunctions.

Underlining and Italics

1. The titles of books, magazines, journals, movies, works of art, television programs, CDs, plays, ships, airplanes, and trains should be either underlined if handwritten or formatted in *italic* type. Underlining is equivalent to or a symbol for italics.

> The Sun Also Rises
> *Good Housekeeping*
> The New York Times
> *The Last Supper*
> Tapestry
> *Buffy the Vampire Slayer*
> H.M.S. Queen Mary

2. There are some exceptions to this rule. For example, the Bible, titles of legal documents (including the U.S. Constitution), and the title of your own essay on your title page would not be underlined or italicized.

| PRACTICE 5 | Using Correct Punctuation |

Add the correct punctuation, including correct comma usage and end punctuation, to the following paragraphs. The first sentence has been done for you.

The newest move to bash immigrants in the United States has arrived with

English-only

the resurgence of the ~~English only~~ movement. The type of legislation called

for by this movement is sure to have negative repercussions for American

society at large.

In 1996 the Supreme Court agreed to review a lower courts invalida-

tion of Arizonas 1988 constitutional amendment making English the official

language of that state This law mandates that voting ballots be in English

only and that English be the official language of all government functions

and actions including government documents Government officials and

employees are to conduct business in English only additionally schools are

not allowed to teach in any other language unless the class is specifically

geared toward teaching a foreign language. (Rivera, "Why English-Only Laws

Are Useless")

| PRACTICE 6 | Using Punctuation and Correct Format for Titles in a Works Cited List |

Using the following information, make a correct "Works Cited" page for the following sources. Use correct punctuation according to MLA format. Be sure to rearrange the entries in alphabetical order.

Lawrence Thompson (author)
Robert Frost's Theory of Poetry (title of essay)
Robert Frost: A Collection of Critical Essays (title of work)
James Cox (editor)
Prentice-Hall (publisher)
Englewood Cliffs (place of publication)
1962
16–35 (pages)

Alvan S. Ryan (author)
Frost and Emerson: Voice and Vision (title of article)
Phillip Gerber (editor)
Critical Essays on Robert Frost (title of work)

Boston (place of publication)

1982

124–37 (pages)

Jane Bakerman (author)

American Literature 52 (title of work and volume)

Failure of Love: Female Initiation in the Novels of Toni Morrison (title of essay)

1981 (date)

541–63 (pages)

_____

_____

_____

_____

_____

_____

_____

_____

_____

28

Capitalization and Numbers

Correct capitalization and use of numbers is important to final editing and revision. Capitalization signals the beginning of sentences as well as marking proper nouns and the pronoun "I." Learning when to use numbers and when to spell them out with letters requires learning some basic rules as well.

Capitalization

1. Capitalize proper nouns: for example, the names of specific people, places, and products. Capitalize proper adjectives (formed from proper nouns).

> Fredric Chopin
> Sacramento, California
> Fords
> German class

2. Capitalize the days of the week, names of months and holidays, and the titles of "works" such as books, movies, artwork, poems, and songs.

> Saturday, August 28
> Friday the 13th
> Christmas holiday
> *The Painted House*

3. Capitalize the first word of every sentence.

> The dog, cat, and birds all began to bark, growl, and chirp at once.

PRACTICE 1 Correcting Capitalization Errors

In the following paragraph from the essay "Why Blame TV," by John Leonard, correct the errors in capitalization. The first sentence has been done for you.

A
a̲ctually, watching television, unless it's **C** c̲span, is usually more interesting

than the proceedings of **C** c̲ongress. Or what we read in hysterical books like

jerry mander's *four arguments for the elimination of television*. Or george

gilder's *life after television*, or marie winn's *the plug-in drugs* or neal

postman's *amusing ourselves to death* or bill mckibben's *the age of*

missing information. Or what we'll hear at panel discussions on censorship,

where right-wingers worry about sex and left-wingers worry about violence.

Or just lolling around an academic deepthink-tank, trading mantras like

"violence profiles" george gerbner), "processed culture" (Richard hoggart),

"narcoleptic joys" (michael sorkin), and "glass teat" (harlan Ellison).

Numbers

1. Numbers (instead of words) should be used for dates, street addresses, page numbers, and time stated in terms of a.m. and p.m. (but words are used with the phrase "o'clock").

> August 29, 1998
> 321 Walnut St.
> page 34
> 12:00 a.m. (twelve o'clock)

2. For formal writing in the humanities (MLA style), spell out numbers one through one hundred, and use numbers for 101 and above. (Some authorities also tell us to spell out numbers that can be expressed in one or two words.) For informal writing and for writing in the social sciences (APA style), spell out numbers one through nine, and use numbers for 10 and above.

> 1,000 pages to be completed
> twenty-four hours
> $15.99 per ticket
> $20,000 (or twenty thousand dollars)

3. Use numbers in a short passage in which several numbers are used.

> On the initial placement test, Julia scored 75, Celia scored 60, and Luis scored 85.

4. Never begin a sentence with a number.

> 25 students filled the course. (Incorrect)
> Twenty-five students filled the course. (Correct)

COMMON
ERROR

PRACTICE 2   **Correcting Number Errors**

Correct the mistakes in numbers in the following sentences. The first one has been done for you.

sixteen

1. In the egg eating contest at the local bar, Fredric ate ~~16~~ **sixteen**, Sarah ate ~~20~~ **twenty**, but John could only eat ~~12~~ **twelve** before he gagged and ran off stage.

2. 100 guests visited the Washington Monument last year.

3. The marathon dancers had been on the floor for 24 hours.

4. She bought 4 Cornish game hens for the elegant dinner party.

5. The new house was built at three hundred West Nineteenth Street.

6. Tickets for the performance of *The Lion King* cost sixty-five dollars each.

7. Pauline picked up 34 tour tickets, even though there were 50 tourists in her group.

8. At 1 p.m. the exam began; the students fled the building at two twenty.

9. 70 employees walked out when the strike vote was passed unanimously.

10. The poem "After Apple-Picking" begins with an unusual image: "My long two-pointed ladder's sticking through a tree/Toward heaven still" (Frost cited in Checkett, two hundred and forty six).

PRACTICE 3   Editing Practice

Correct the following paragraph for errors in capitalization and number use. The first sentence has been done for you.

The <u>Y</u>ukon <u>T</u>erritory is located in northwestern <u>C</u>anada. The vast area (one hundred and eighty six thousand, three hundred square miles) is bordered by alaska and british columbia. its mineral wealth and scenic vistas are 2 of its main attractions. Forests cover about forty percent of the total land area. A subarctic climate prevails with severe winters and hot summers, and the annual precipitation ranges from nine to thirteen inches.

Words and Meaning

T he Words and Meaning chapter provides advice on the problem area of commonly misspelled words.

ESL ## Commonly Misspelled Words

In English the spelling system does not follow a consistent system of spelling rules. Very often it is necessary to memorize the spelling of words that violate rules of double letter, or phonetic sounds.

The following is a list of words that are frequently spelled incorrectly.

across	grammar	possible
address	height	prefer
answer	illegal	prejudice
argument	immediately	privilege
athlete	important	probably
beginning	integration	psychology
behavior	intelligent	pursue
calendar	interest	reference
career	interfere	rhythm
conscience	jewelry	ridiculous
crowded	judgment	separate
definite	knowledge	similar
describe	maintain	since
desperate	mathematics	speech
different	meant	strength
disappoint	necessary	success
disapprove	nervous	surprise
doesn't	occasion	taught
eighth	opinion	temperature

(continued)

environment	optimist	thorough
embarrass	particular	thought
exaggerate	perform	tired
familiar	perhaps	until
finally	personnel	weight
government	possess	written

COMMON ERROR

PRACTICE 1 Identifying Correctly Spelled Words

Circle the correctly spelled word in each of the following pairs. The first one has been done for you.

1. arguement (argument)

2. separate   seperate

3. judgment   judgement

4. privelege   privilege

5. written   writen

6. jewelery   jewelry

7. success   sucess

8. desparate   desperate

9. occasion   ocaision

10. embaras   embarrass

COMMON ERROR

PRACTICE 2 Using Challenging Words in Sentences

Write a paragraph of 8 to 12 sentences using 10 of the difficult words in the previous chart of commonly misspelled words. Revise your paragraph carefully for spelling.

_____

_____

_____

_____

_____

_____

_____

30

Editing Practice for Appropriate Word Choice

(ESL) One of the final difficult stages of writing is polishing and revising for the best diction, or word choice. The wording in preliminary drafts can be monotonous and uninspiring. As you revise, using the most specific words possible will not only communicate meaning more effectively, but it will also add spirit, tone, color, and images to your work.

When revising for diction, writers need to consider the tone or voice of the work. Choose words that are accurate and specific, yet still fit the tone of the work. Words have great power, and meanings must be considered carefully. There are two levels of meaning: the dictionary definition (denotation) and the emotions and ideas associated with the word (connotation). For example, the word "*slender*" has a pleasant connotation, while the word "*scrawny*" is negative, even unhealthy. This level of meaning takes practice for nonnative speakers especially. To work on word choice, use a dictionary and a thesaurus to help expand your vocabulary options.

In the following exercises, you will stretch your vocabulary skills while practicing revision skills.

COMMON ERROR

PRACTICE 1   Practicing Effective Word Choice

In the following paragraphs, specific words have been left out. Using context clues for meaning, fill in the blanks. The first one has been done for you.

Brisk New England winds ____tumble____ into the coffee shop as I open the

back door. The warm _____ of cranberry scones and dark roast beans

_____ the frigid air. Mary, already _____ over a mixing bowl

of poppy seed muffin mix, greets me. Quietly rattling, the old oven read-

ily accepts its gooey inhabitants for baking. Newly delivered newspapers

_____ patiently against the wall waiting to _____ their stories, or to become _____ with spilled cappuccinos. I fold a green apron around the waistband of my jeans; after three years as an employee at the Hopkinton Gourmet, I know too well the _____ and stains capable from steaming coffee. With a warm cup of tea, my six A.M. _____ transforms into a more _____ familiarity; the day begins.

PRACTICE 2   Practicing Effective Word Choice

COMMON ERROR

In the following paragraphs, fill in the blanks with an appropriate word. You can use a dictionary or thesaurus to help you make word choices.

Moths that fly by day are not properly to be call moths; they do not excite that _____ sense of dark autumn nights and ivy-blossom which the commonest yellow-underwing asleep in the _____ of the curtain never fails to _____ in us. They are _____ creatures, neither gay like butterflies nor _____ like their own species. Nevertheless the present specimen, with his narrow hay-colored wings, _____ with a tassel of the same color, seemed to be _____ with life. It was a pleasant morning, mid-September, mild, _____, yet with a _____ breath than that of the summer months. The plough was already _____ the field opposite the window, and where the share had been, the earth was pressed flat and _____ with moisture. Such vigor came rolling in from the fields and the down beyond that it was difficult to keep the eyes strictly turned upon the book. The rooks, too, were keeping one of their annual festivities; _____ round the tree tops until it looked as if a vast net with thousands of black knots in it had been _____ up into the air; which, after a few moments _____ slowly down upon the trees until every twig seemed to have a knot at the end of it. Then, suddenly, the net would be _____ into the air again in a wider circle this time, with the utmost clamor and _____ , as though to be thrown into the air and _____ down upon the tree tops were a tremendously _____ experience.

Additional Readings

All the readings in this section are written by professional writers. Before reading these essays, review the brief comments about the differences between professional essays and college essays in the introduction to Part Two: "Beyond the College Essay," "Form Follows Function: The Form of Professional Essays," and "As You Become a Better Writer: Good Things to Come." Reviewing this material will help you understand why professional essays often look different from those you are writing in college. The information also will help you understand the possibilities that exist for your writing style as you become a better, more experienced writer.

The Flesch-Kincaid Grade Reading Level score follows the title of each essay in the Additional Readings section. The score is in a bracket with a corresponding letter indicating the difficulty level in reading and comprehension for that essay. For instance, a [7.0 A] score means that the essay should be read and understood by a seventh grader, and it is designated as "Accessible." A score of [9.2 I] indicates the essay should be read and understood by a ninth grader, and it is designated "Intermediate." A score of [12.3 C] indicates that the essay should be read and understood by a twelfth grader, and it is designated as "Challenging." Use the Flesch-Kincaid assessment with other tests at your school to assist in providing the students in your classes with essays that can help them in achieving writing success.

DESCRIPTION

HAVE YOU EVER MET AN ASIAN MAN YOU THOUGHT WAS SEXY?

Eric Kim

In this essay, the writer talks about stereotypes, an oversimplified opinion or conception based on conventional characteristics (for example, Asians are good at math; blondes are dumb). Think of some stereotypes that you might hold. Keep them in mind as you read the essay.

Vocabulary: Before you begin reading, look up the definitions of the following words that appear in the essay. The number in parentheses after each word refers to the paragraph number of the essay.

affront (3)	asexual (2)	caricatures (7)
chauvinist (4)	diatribes (5)	nonentity (6)
retrospect (2)	shun (4)	spewing (7)
waylaid (7)		

Have You Ever Met an Asian Man You Thought Was Sexy?

1   "Yo, Bruce Lee! Hey, whatzaah happening?" That's what a group of teenage guys shouted at me a couple of years ago as I walked down the street with a friend. They followed that up with a series of yelps and shrieks that I took to be their attempts at kung fu sounds. As I was about to turn and respond, my friend quickly pointed out that it would be better, and safer, to ignore these guys.

2   In retrospect, though, I wonder if rising above it was the best response. Sometimes I don't believe I can change people's stereotypes about Asians without confronting them. At least Bruce Lee, the late martial arts expert, is at the macho end of the spectrum, along with the stereotype of the greedy, wealthy businessmen who are invading America. At the other end of the spectrum, Asian men in America are seen as geeks—short, nerdy, passive, and somewhat asexual "Orientals."

3   As a six-foot, 180-pound, Korean American guy, I always hated that people would assume I was a wimpy bookworm who couldn't play sports. It pleased me to see how upset non-Asians would get after a few Asian friends and I whipped them in a game of full-court basketball. Before we hit the court, the other guys would snicker and assume we'd be easy to beat. Afterward, they'd act as if being outdone in sports by an Asian was an affront to their masculinity.

4   It's different for Asian women, who are usually stereotyped as exotic, passive, sensual, the ultimate chauvinist fantasy. The reality of these stereotypes is played out on the street: Look around and you'll see an Asian woman with a Caucasian man a lot sooner than you'll see a white woman with an Asian date. Even Asian women sometimes shun Asian men as being either too wimpy or too dominating. I was born and grew up in Seoul, South Korea, and went to an international high school there. The student body was about

80 percent Asian and 20 percent Caucasian. I think being in the majority gave me a certain social confidence. I never thought twice about dating or flirting with non-Asian girls. If I felt nervous or awkward, it was because I was shy, not because I wasn't white.

5   When I started college in the United States, I promised myself that I'd meet people of all races, since most of my friends in Seoul had been Asian. Yet when I arrived here, for the first time in my life I felt like a minority. For the first time in my life, I was told to "go back home" and had to listen to strangers on the bus give me their diatribes on Vietnam and Korea. Feeling I was a minority affected how I approached other people.

6   Even though there were a lot of attractive non-Asian women at school, I hesitated to approach them, because I imagined that they were only interested in Caucasian guys. I assumed that non-Asian women bought the Asian stereotypes and saw me as a nonentity. It wasn't that I kept trying and getting shot down; I simply assumed they would never consider me. The frustrating mix of my own pride and the fear of getting rejected always managed to keep me from approaching a non-Asian woman I was attracted to.

7   My girlfriend now is Asian American. There are many things I love about her, and it strengthens our relationship that we have a cultural bond. Relationships are about trust, vulnerability, and a willingness to open up. That can be hard for an Asian man to achieve with a non-Asian woman; though he may find her attractive, his emotions may be blocked by fear, waylaid by the caricatures of Asian men as paranoid deli owners, Confucius-spewing detectives, or kung fu fighters with fists of fury.

8   These images say little about what it means to be a twenty-four-year-old Asian man. These images don't reflect our athleticism, our love of rap, or our possible addiction to ESPN. Because of these images, Asian men are rarely seen for what we are—and so we may look at a non-Asian woman with interest, then tuck that interest away.

9   It's not easy to confess that I know many women don't find me attractive. But for me, the very process of facing down Asian stereotypes makes them less meaningful. Most of all, I try to keep a sense of humor about it. After all, when my friends and I whip some unsuspecting non-Asians on the basketball court, *they* are the ones who are victims of the stereotypes, not us.

Descriptive Technique Questions

1. Identify paragraphs in which the writer uses objective description and those in which he uses subjective description.

_____

_____

_____

2. How does the author describe the Asian male when perceived as the antithesis of Bruce Lee?

_____

_____

_____

3. How does the writer describe the stereotypical Asian female?

_____

_____

_____

Critical Reading and Thinking Questions

1. What is the main idea of the essay?

_____

_____

_____

2. What does the author mean in the last paragraph when he says *"they [non-Asians] are the ones who are victims of the stereotypes, not us"*?

_____

_____

3. According to the author, what are the negative consequences of stereotyping?

_____

_____

_____

Descriptive Writing Opportunities

1. At the beginning of the essay, Kim recounts something a group of teenagers shouted at him. Write a paragraph describing a variety of people by the stereotypical things they say or believe.

2. Inspect another's outward appearance, clothing, and physical features. Write an essay about how others might describe that person in stereotypical terms.

NARRATION

FOR MY INDIAN DAUGHTER

Lewis Sawaquat

Prejudice, cultural awareness, and ethnic pride are three basic elements involved in any racial minority's world. In this essay, the author focuses on the problems caused by ethnicity, ancestry, and heritage.

Vocabulary Before you begin to read, look up the definitions of the following words that appear in the story. The number in parentheses after each word refers to the paragraph number of the essay.

affluent (5)	backlash (4)	comeuppance (7)
forge (9)	guttural (2)	iridescent (9)
masquerade (10)	mingling (1)	unbidden (1)

For My Indian Daughter

1   My little girl is singing herself to sleep upstairs, her voice mingling with the sounds of the birds outside in the old maple trees. She is two and I am nearly 50, and I am very taken with her. She came along late in my life, unexpected and unbidden, a startling gift.

2   Today at the beach my chubby-legged, brown-skinned daughter ran laughing into the water as fast as she could. My wife and I laughed watching her, until we heard behind us a low guttural curse and then an unpleasant voice raised in an imitation war whoop.

3   I turned to see a fat man in a bathing suit, white and soft as a grub, as he covered his mouth and prepared to make the Indian war cry again. He was middle-aged, younger than I, and had three little children lined up next to him, grinning foolishly. My wife suggested we leave the beach, and I agreed.

4   I knew the man was not unusual in his feelings against Indians. His beach behavior might have been socially unacceptable to more civilized whites, but his basic view of Indians is expressed daily in our small town, frequently on the editorial pages of the county newspaper, as white people speak out against Indian fishing rights and land rights, saying in essence, "Those Indians are taking our fish, our land." It doesn't matter to them that we were here first, that the U.S. Supreme Court has ruled in our favor. It matters to them that we have something they want, and they hate us for it. Backlash is the common explanation of the attacks on Indians, the bumper stickers that say, "Spear an Indian, Save a Fish," but I know better. The hatred of Indians goes back to the beginning when white people came to this country. For me it goes back to my childhood in Harbor Springs, Mich.

5   *Theft.* Harbor Springs is now a summer resort for the very affluent, but a hundred years ago it was the Indian village of my Ottawa ancestors. My grandmother, Anna Showanessy, and other Indians like her, had their land there taken by treaty, by fraud, by violence, by theft. They remembered how whites had burned down the village at Burt Lake in 1900 and pushed the Indians out. These were the stories in my family.

6   When I was a boy my mother told me to walk down the alleys in Harbor Springs and not to wear my orange football sweater out of the house. This way I would not stand out, not be noticed, and not be a target.

7   I wore my orange sweater anyway and deliberately avoided the alleys. I was the biggest person I knew and wasn't really afraid. But I met my come-uppance when I enlisted in the U.S. Army. One night all the men in my barracks gathered together and, gang-fashion, pulled me into the shower and scrubbed me down with rough brushes used for floors, saying, "We won't have any dirty Indians in our outfit." It is a point of irony that I was cleaner than any of them. Later in Korea I learned how to kill, how to bully, how to hate Koreans. I came out of the war tougher than ever and, strangely, white.

8   I went to college, got married, lived in La Porte, Ind., worked as a surveyor and raised three boys. I headed Boy Scout groups, never thinking it odd when the Scouts did imitation Indian dances, imitation Indian lore.

9   One day when I was 35 or thereabouts I heard about an Indian powwow. My father used to attend them and so with great curiosity and a strange joy at discovering a part of my heritage, I decided the thing to do to get ready for this big event was to have my friend make me a spear in his forge. The steel was fine and blue and iridescent. The feathers on the shaft were bright and proud.

10   In a dusty state fairground in southern Indiana, I found white people dressed as Indians. I learned they were "hobbyists," that is, it was their hobby and leisure pastime to masquerade as Indians on weekends. I felt ridiculous with my spear, and I left.

11   It was years before I could tell anyone of the embarrassment of this weekend and see any humor in it. But in a way it was that weekend, for all its silliness, that was my awakening. I realized I didn't know who I was. I didn't have an Indian name. I didn't speak the Indian language. I didn't know the Indian customs. Dimly I remembered the Ottawa word for dog, but it was a baby word, *kahgee,* not the full word, *muhkaghee,* which I was later to learn. Even more hazily I remembered a naming ceremony (my own). I remembered legs dancing around me, dust. Where had that been? What had I been? "Sawaquat," my mother told me when I asked, "where the tree begins to grow."

12   That was 1968, and I was not the only Indian in the country who was feeling the need to remember who he or she was. There were others. They had powwows, real ones, and eventually I found them. Together we researched our past, a search that for me culminated in the Longest Walk, a march on Washington in 1978. Maybe because I now know what it means to be Indian, it surprises me that others don't. Of course there aren't very many of us left. The chances of an average person knowing an average Indian in an average lifetime are pretty slim.

13   *Circle.* Still, I was amused one day when my small, four-year-old neighbor looked at me as I was hoeing in my garden and said, "You aren't a real Indian, are you?" Scotty is little, talkative, likable. Finally I said, "I'm a real Indian." He looked at me for a moment and then said squinting into the sun, "Then where's your horse and feathers?" The child was simply a smaller, whiter version of my own ignorant self years before. We'd both seen too much TV, that's all. He was not to be blamed. And so, in a way, the moronic man on the beach today is blameless. We come full circle to realize other people are like ourselves, as discomfiting as that may be sometimes.

14   As I sit in my old chair on my porch, in a light that is fading so the leaves are barely distinguishable against the sky, I can picture my girl asleep upstairs. I would like to prepare her for what's to come, take her each step of the way saying, there's a place to avoid, here's what I know about this, but much of what's before her she must go through alone. She must pass through pain and joy and solitude and community to discover her own inner self that is unlike any other and come through that passage to the place where she sees all people are one, and in so seeing may live her life in a brighter future.

Narrative Technique Questions

1. Which sentence sums up the point of the story?

_____

_____

_____

_____

2. Which of the six reporter's questions does the writer use most often to develop the story? Give examples.

_____

_____

_____

3. Identify at least five transitional expressions used by the author. How do they help order the events chronologically?

_____

_____

_____

Critical Reading and Thinking Questions

1. What do you think is the purpose behind Sawaquat writing this story?

_____

_____

_____

2. The author writes about an event that involved his daughter. Why does his memory of her stir within him remembrances of his own identity crises?

_____

_____

_____

3. What does the author learn about himself after attending his first powwow?

_____

_____

_____

Narrative Writing Opportunities

1. Write a paragraph about a particular cultural heritage. Focus on an event or celebration of that heritage.

2. Write an essay about a person arriving in a new country. How would the person describe his or her cultural and ethnic identity to new friends and explain how that culture and ethnicity affect his or her life?

IN THE SHADOW OF MAN

Jane Goodall

In this essay, famed naturalist Jane Goodall tells a story of a personal encounter with several chimpanzees in Africa and the extraordinary behavior she witnessed.

Vocabulary Before you begin reading, look up the definitions of the following words that appear in the essay. The number in parentheses after each word refers to the paragraph number of the essay.

discarded (6)   squatting (2)
fronds (5)   strewn (4)
mandibles (4)   wandered (4)
modifying (7)   weary (1)

In the Shadow of Man

1   I had had a frustrating morning, tramping up and down three valleys with never a sign or sound of a chimpanzee. Hauling myself up the steep slope of Mlinda Valley I headed for the peak, not only weary but soaking wet from crawling through dense undergrowth. Suddenly I stopped, for I saw a slight movement in the long grass about sixty yards away. Quickly focusing my binoculars I saw that it was a single chimpanzee, and just then he turned in my direction. I recognized David Graybeard.

2   Cautiously I moved around so that I could see what he was doing. He was squatting beside the red earth mound of a termite nest, and as I watched I saw him carefully push a long grass stem down into a hole in the mound. After a moment he withdrew it and picked something from the end with his mouth. I was too far away to make out what he was eating, but it was obvious that he was actually using a grass stem as a tool.

3   I knew that on two occasions casual observers in West Africa had seen chimpanzees using objects as tools: one had broken open palm-nut kernels by using a rock as a hammer, and a group of chimps had been observed pushing sticks into an underground bees' nest and licking off the honey. Somehow I had never dreamed of seeing anything so exciting myself.

4   For an hour David feasted at the termite mound and then he wandered slowly away. When I was sure he had gone I went over to examine the mound. I found a few crushed insects strewn about, and a swarm of worker termites sealing the entrances of the nest passages into which David had obviously been poking his stems. I picked up one of his discarded tools and carefully pushed it into a hole myself. Immediately I felt the pull of several termites as they seized the grass, and when I pulled it out there were a number of worker termites and a few soldiers, with big red heads, clinging on with their mandibles. There they remained, sticking out at right angles to the stem with their legs waving in the air.

5   Before I left I trampled down some of the tall dry grass and constructed a rough hide—just a few palm fronds leaned up against the low branch of a tree and tied together at the top. I planned to wait there the next day. But it was another week before I was able to watch a chimpanzee "fishing" for termites again.

* * *

6   On the eighth day of my watch David Graybeard arrived again together with Goliath, and the pair worked there for two hours. I could see much better: I observed how they scratched open the sealed-over passage entrances with a thumb or forefinger. I watched how they bit the ends off their tools when they became bent, or used the other end, or discarded them in favor of new ones. Goliath once moved at least fifteen yards from the heap to select a firm-looking piece of vine, and both males often picked three or four stems while they were collecting tools, and put the spares beside them on the ground until they wanted them.

7   Most exciting of all, on several occasions they picked small leafy twigs and prepared them for use by stripping off the leaves. This was the first recorded example of a wild animal not merely *using* an object as a tool, but actually modifying an object and thus showing the crude beginnings of tool *making*.

Narrative Technique Questions

ANALYZING

1. What introductory paragraph technique does the author use? How does this technique lend authenticity to the essay?

_____

_____

_____

_____

2. Point out four or five descriptive details in the essay. How do these details make the essay more interesting for the reader?

_____

_____

_____

3. How does the author make it easier for the reader to connect with David Graybeard and Goliath?

_____

_____

_____

Critical Reading and Thinking Questions

ANALYZING

1. What is the point of the story?

_____

_____

_____

2. Does the author use mostly fact or opinion in the essay?

_____

_____

_____

Narrative Writing Opportunities

WRITING

1. Write a paragraph about an animal you have observed exhibiting "human-like" behavior.

2. Have you ever taken a trip or visited a place that amazed you? In an essay, describe the details that struck you as unusual and how they affected your life experiences.

EXAMPLE

OPEN SEASON ON KOREANS?

Elaine H. Kim

Professor Kim teaches Asian American Studies at the University of California-Berkeley and publishes books and articles on the subject. In this essay, she focuses on Korean stereotypes as portrayed in movies. Pay particular attention to how the author expands the scope of her essay to include other ethnic groups.

Vocabulary Before you begin reading, look up the definitions of the following words that appear in the essay. The number in parentheses after each word refers to the paragraph number in the essay.

contextualized (10)	culmination (3)	decimated (1)
garishly (2)	grotesque (3)	inscribe (10)
legitimacy (5)	milieu (2)	retribution (1)

Open Season on Koreans?

1   A new film *Menace II Society,* directed by Allen and Albert Hughes, describes a community decimated by poverty and violence, where African-American youth fight for day-to-day survival amid guns, drugs, friendship and rivalry, retribution killings, God-fearing grandparents and earnest young Muslims.

2   As a Korean American, I was horrified by one element in this milieu. In what one reviewer called the "riveting" opening scene of this newest "inner-city" film, an African-American youth blows out the brains of a greedy Korean merchant who has urged him to "Hurry up and buy! Pay and get out." The youth also kills the merchant's garishly made-up wife, who had been eyeing the youths as if they were going to steal something.

3   It seems that rude and greedy Korean merchants are movies' "bad guys" of the moment. The shopkeepers who deserve to be blown away, to no one's regret, are becoming the newest Asian stereotype. *Menace II Society* is the culmination of the racial slurs in *Do the Right Thing* and the mayhem in *Falling Down.* Besides a few other grotesque caricatures of ragged war orphans, horny prostitutes, fanatical Moonies and robotic nerds, there aren't any other images of Koreans in American culture. The Korean merchant stereotype joins the ranks of other stereotypes of Asians as Fu Manchu-style sinister villains, dragon ladies, and faceless hordes, all threatening the kind of "yellow peril" takeover Korean merchants are supposedly accomplishing in today's inner cities. The difference is that unlike the other stereotypes, which are rooted in fantasy, the Korean merchant can be encountered on the corner in our own neighborhoods.

4   Even if they are rude and greedy, Korean merchants don't deserve to be blown away any more than the African-American characters in *Menace II Society* deserve their violent deaths. But the fact is, these types of killings are part of daily life in South Central Los Angeles. During the past six months 16 Korean-American merchants have been shot in Southern California; seven of them are dead. Last year there were 800 gang-related homicides in L.A. County. The people who live and work in the inner city are under-protected by police, under-represented by politicians and under-served by larger-scale businesses.

5   Korean Americans have been inserted into the public dialogue as part of a new buzz phrase in radical politics: the "black-Korean conflict." However, they have importance only as they can illuminate (or obscure) African-American experiences or the experiences of ethnic white Americans. They have no legitimacy as subjects in their own right.

6   Not all Korean Americans are merchants. And not all Korean-American merchants are rude and greedy, just as 99 percent of African-American customers would never shoot a Korean shopkeeper. The Koreans who lost their livelihoods in the violence in Los Angeles last year were people who spent the past decade or longer working 12 to 14 hours a day, six to seven days a week, in pursuit of brave and often humble dreams that were reduced to ashes in the space of a few hours. The merchants begging and crying or standing on rooftops with guns were not there because they cared only about their money and property; they were there because their stores were the sum total of their American lives.

7   Last summer, every African American I talked with in South Central knew that the media distorted images of their own community as nothing but a bunch of crack houses and drive-by shootings. At the same time, their knowledge about Korean Americans was also limited by the media, which portrayed Koreans mostly as rude and greedy grocers. Let's face it, what source of information do people of color have about one another other than what the dominant culture presents?

8   Thus Korean immigrants talk about how the "Mexicans" looted their stores, although most of the Latino looters were identified by the press as Central American refugees. I have rarely heard Korean immigrants use the term "Latino," let alone "Central American" or even "Chicano."

9   I know of a Korean grocer named "Chin Ho" who was proud that his Latino customers called him by his first name. In fact they were calling him Chino, or "Chink." Mike Davis, author of *City of Quartz*, a book about the development of Los Angeles, told me that some Crips in Las Vegas bragged to him that they had burned down a Japanese store because they understood that Japan was causing job shortages in the U.S. The "Japanese" store was actually a Korean-American shop.

10   The Hughes brothers, Spike Lee, or any other African-American filmmaker, are not responsible for presenting a fully contextualized picture of Korean merchant life. Korean Americans need to tell their own story. So far, these immigrants have minded their own business and worked hard, sacrificing themselves to the hope that their children will become engineers or attorneys. But what we need now are cultural historians and novelists and filmmakers who can inscribe Korean Americans in images and words full of creativity and compassion.

Example Technique Questions

I B W E A

A N A L Y Z I N G

1. Is there a thesis statement in the essay? If so, identify it. If not, what do you think is the author's thesis?

_____

_____

_____

_____

_____

2. The author talks about the negative consequences of stereotyping. What real-life examples does she use to support her ideas?

_____

_____

_____

_____

3. What other stereotypes does the author point out as portrayed in the movies?

_____

_____

_____

Critical Reading and Thinking Questions

1. The author gives three examples of movies that generate stereotypes: _Menace II Society_, _Do the Right Thing_, and _Falling Down_. Have you seen any of these movies? If so, how do they help you understand Kim's thesis? If not, how does this weaken the essay?

_____

_____

_____

2. Kim does not limit her essay to Asian Americans. What other examples of ethnic groups does she mention, and how are they labeled?

_____

_____

_____

3. Kim uses examples from her own personal experience and from media sources. Which kind of example affects you the most?

_____

_____

_____

Example Writing Opportunities

1. Write a paragraph about an ethnic stereotype you have seen in a movie or on television. Give examples of how the group was stereotyped.

2. Using the ethnic group you wrote about in Exercise 1, write an essay about a member of that group who is a newly arrived immigrant in America. Give examples of how you think the person would feel about seeing his or her ethnic group portrayed as you described in Exercise 1.

CLASSIFICATION

SINGLE WHITE FEMALE

Viet D. Dinh

> Relationships are difficult enough without opposition from parents and friends because a partner is a different race. In this essay, Dinh expresses his dismay that race is often still an objection where marriage is concerned.

Vocabulary Before you begin reading, look up the definitions of the following words that appear in the essay. The number in parentheses after each word refers to the paragraph number of the essay.

absolved (23)	bequeathed (21)	conflagration (23)
innocuous (17)	opprobrium (16)	proxy (18)
talisman (21)	surreptitiously (12)	

Single White Female

1   Mary and I met in my senior year of high school at a weekend speech and debate tournament in northern California. By chance, I stopped at an afternoon storytelling competition and listened to her recite passages from *Jonathan Livingston Seagull*. We fell in love—quickly, foolishly. Each day after watching each other compete, we'd sneak into San Francisco for dinner in Chinatown (my choice) or Ghirardelli Square (hers) and a stroll through North Beach to Coit Tower.

2   About a week later, Mary's mother asked about her new boyfriend on the drive to school.

3   "I hear you've met a new boy."

4   "Yes."

5   "Is he Catholic?"

6   "Yes."

7   "College?"

8   "Yes, he's going to Harvard."

9   Her mother smiled, "Well, good. What's his name?"

10   "Viet," Mary answered, wittily adding a pronunciation tip, "as in Vietnam."

11   "I'm sorry, Mary, tell him you can't see him anymore."

12   That was the end. I saw Mary only a few times after she told me this story, mostly to talk about what happened. She wondered why we didn't continue surreptitiously; I tried to understand what motivated her mother's response. Mary offered (inexplicably) that her mother was from Indiana, and argued that she really was not racist, that if I were to apply for a job at her real estate office she probably would hire me.

13   I met Mary's mother once, years later. I worked as a real estate developer and wanted to buy some land in the area. More as an excuse than out of necessity, I called up to schedule a tour of her listings. She never placed me, and

after an hour in her car, I began to accept that Mary was right. Her mother was not a racist—at least not in the sense that I had imagined in high school. She was comfortable with me. Nothing in her manner betrayed nervousness or artificial cordiality.

14   That revelation only made my question harder to answer. What motivates an otherwise intelligent person to inflict such pain on such a seemingly irrational basis? She is not racist, yet cannot tolerate her daughter dating an Asian. Why is love, or sex, so special?

15   The question presents itself frequently. Open any magazine to the personal ads and one finds exposed on every page the impulse that Mary's mother displayed. Single White Female seeking same; Divorced Black Male, professional, seeking compatible companion; Gay White Male seeking mate; Asian Woman seeking a gentleman. The open invitation to judge based on race extends shamelessly across all social barriers, from *New York Review of Books* intellectuals to *Village Voice* bohemians to *Washingtonian* power brokers.

16   Such open reliance on racial qualifications is hard to reconcile with moral and social opprobrium accorded to racism and the suspicion of racial classifications in the post–Civil Rights era. In most cases, race cannot legally be a factor in hiring or firing, in buying or selling, in admission or rejection. Even an acknowledgment that one's friends or associates are only of a particular race gives pause and sometimes has derailed otherwise promising public careers. Yet romantic race-typing persists, explicitly and pervasively, not noticed and hardly questioned.

17   Maybe the designation of one's race in a personal ad is innocuous. The ad, after all, attempts to convey a full (maybe even inflated) picture of its owner, and race is simply part of the picture, like a glimpse of someone walking down the street or eating in a restaurant. But to offer race as part of that verbal picture is to recognize, and approve, that race matters when one judges a stranger for compatibility and attraction. Why?

18   For one thing, the racial designation may be shorthand for a number of cultural and ethnic traits that cannot be fully captured in a short ad or a quick glimpse. But to accept race as proxy for personal characteristics is to succumb to exactly the impulse that one finds reprehensible in racism: the blind acceptance of generalized biases without regard to individual qualities. It is not justifiable (both factually and morally) to assume that a black man likes jazz or that an Asian woman is petite any more than to say that black men are muggers or Asian women are submissive.

19   Moreover, race is just one arbitrary level of generalization. If it is a "package" of personal characteristics that one is looking for, that mix need not be determined by race. Asian Male describes very little of who I am, the differences among Asian cultures being large. Southeast Asian is closer, but then why not Vietnamese, or South Vietnamese? Better yet, why not simply Male?

20   When I told my sister that I don't discriminate in my romantic decisions, she replied, "Maybe you're just not very discriminating." Race-typing, she argued, flows from the natural desire to preserve one's culture in a pluralistic society. She feared that in searching for an American, I would stop being Vietnamese.

21   But this argument assumes that culture is something timeless, a never-changing talisman that has been begotten and bequeathed and is to be passed on forever. That is hardly the case. Any immigrant who returns to his native country can readily observe the chasm that only a few years' absence has forged between him and the culture that he had nostalgically and unrequitedly loved. People change, traditions evolve, and institutions adapt.

Saffron Sky

April 1, 1998 (Farvardin 12, 1377)

1   My friend Forough is going to Tehran on Saturday.

2   I rush down to the outlet mall near Sarasota. After an hour in the dressing room of Westport Woman, I emerge with a cobalt blue outfit for my cousin Maryam and a red one for my cousin Soodi. This is no easy feat, finding long-sleeved clothes (short sleeves are not permitted in Iran in public) in Florida in Spring.

3   I call Forough to find out when I can bring by the clothes, which she will take to Iran for me. We make a date, then compare notes on Norooz parties. Forough and her husband, Ali, went to the one at the University of South Florida in Tampa—a less formal affair than the dinner my family and I chose to attend. "How was your party?" Forough wants to know. "I heard it was dreadful."

4   "I thought it was great," I tell her, surprised. "There were some problems with the mike and the dancing started too late for us, but I was impressed. So were my parents. They're used to pretty fancy parties in Toronto."

5   "I heard the *tar* player had a real attitude," Forough says, launching into the list of criticisms she heard from friends who attended our party. We keep talking, trying to reconcile these differing reports of the same event. We conclude that the problem is the tendency toward infighting that so often exists among exiles. I'm not sure what causes it, but suspect it has something to do with feeling threatened. I've noticed that groups under stress tend to pull apart—the losing side in a game of Pictionary, the passengers of the *Titanic*, the underclass in any society. Perhaps this is why the two Iranian cultural groups in Tampa Bay have devoted a fair bit of time, and a couple of mailings, to putting each other down.

6   Ali is trying to get the two groups to meet and work together, maybe even merge, Forough tells me. "I can't see it," I say. "Their styles are totally opposite. Besides, there's nothing wrong with having two groups, two events, two choices. If only they could get along."

7   Before we say good-bye, she asks me if I'm going to the Sizdah-bedar picnic. "The Sizdah-bedar picnic!" I say enthusiastically. "I'd like to go but I'm not sure. I'll have to talk to Neil."

8   I hang up the phone, vaguely ashamed. I know in my heart that we will not go to the picnic. Although our reasons vary from event to event, Neil and I rarely attend the picnics, concerts, and poetry nights sponsored by Iranians here.

9   Years ago, it dawned on me that just because someone was Iranian did not mean I had much in common with them. We have little enough leisure time as a family that we guard our weekends closely. But there is more to my reclusiveness.

10   Iranians in America, like many immigrants, are a troubled group. Take away the financial problems, language barriers, and emotional challenges of immigration, take away the political schisms that cause mutual distrust, and you are still left with the central dilemma of assimilation. The need to belong is a powerful thing. It pits those of us who are children of other worlds against ourselves and one another.

11   It made the Iranian clerk I encountered a few years ago at Bloomingdale's, in Rockville, Maryland, stare coldly when I spoke to her in Farsi. She rang up my sale without a word. A few months later, when an Iranian handed me the numbered tag I took into the dressing room of another department store, I was careful to thank her in English. I pretended that I did not recognize the almond skin, arched eyebrows, and glossy hair of a countrywoman.

12   A memory surfaces, one I haven't summoned in years. I am twenty-something, working at the *Miami Herald*. I fly up to Washington, D.C., to get a new passport. I stay at the Kalorama Guesthouse, near the zoo, and wake early in the morning to go to the Iranian Interests Section on Wisconsin Avenue. The Interests Section requires that applicants wear Islamic dress. Waiting on the steps of the guesthouse for a cab, I am painfully conscious of the scarf on my head. I try to catch the eyes of people passing by, hungry for an opportunity to show them that, despite my appearance, I am not one of *them*. Let me speak a sentence loaded with colloquialisms. See, I am fluent in English! I have no accent! I'm like *you*. Don't consign me to the trash heap, where the unforgivably different belong. Don't look at me as if I were an animal at the zoo, an object of curiosity and spurious compassion.

13   This inner dialogue fills me with shame, yet I am helpless against it. I have become a party to my own disenfranchisement. The worst part of being told in a thousand ways, subtle and not, that one is inferior is the way that message worms itself into the heart. It is not enough to battle the prejudice of others, one must also battle the infection within.

14   I have struggled for years with my own ambivalence. Socializing with other Iranians invokes my angst in painful ways. Yet despite my discomfort, in every city I have lived I have sought out my countrymen and tried to establish meaningful connections with them.

15   Only in St. Petersburg, with our children as a common bond, have I succeeded. Only in Iran—or in Toronto, where relationships are cemented by family ties—is it easy to be with other Iranians. My closest friends, including my husband, are American.

16   Sometimes I get tired of the struggle.

17   So it is that each year I go to great lengths to travel to Iran. Each week I spend hours preparing our Farsi lesson.

18   Yet I won't make the effort to go to a picnic half an hour away in Clearwater.

Classification Technique Questions

I B W E A

A N A L Y Z I N G

1. The author divides the Iranians in Tampa Bay into two groups. What characteristics does she use to show differences between them?

_____

_____

_____

_____

_____

2. How does the writer classify Iranian immigrants from other Americans?

_____

_____

_____

Critical Reading and Thinking Questions

ANALYZING

1. From a personal standpoint, what does Asayesh say is the negative outcome from being classified as different? In other words, how does it make her feel?

_____

_____

_____

_____

_____

2. What do you think is the author's thesis? If you cannot find a specific idea in a sentence or two, express it in your own words.

_____

_____

_____

Classification Writing Opportunities

WRITING

1. Write a paragraph about an ethnic group living in your city. Classify them by their outward appearance and their speech.

2. Now, expand on the topic you wrote about in Exercise 1. Classify the ethnic group by including other characteristics, such as employment, education, and religion. Also, comment on the kinds of problems and conflicts they have to confront because of their ethnic and cultural differences.

PROCESS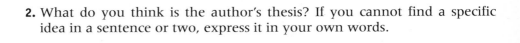

TWO WAYS TO BELONG IN AMERICA

Bharati Mukherjee

Mukherjee's "Two Ways to Belong in America" was originally published in the *New York Times*, September 22, 1996. Like much of her writing, this work involves immigrants. As you read the essay, notice how she engages your interest by moving you through a process that moves from particular events to the general as she relates personal observations and universal beliefs.

Vocabulary Before you begin reading, look up the definitions of the following words that appear in the essay. The number in parentheses after each word refers to the paragraph number of the essay.

ancestral (12)	curtailing (8)	expatriate (11)
hysteria (10)	looming (6)	mongrelization (5)
mythic (7)	opting (5)	quota (5)
referendum (13)	renouncing (5)	scrutiny (7)
subtext (9)		

Two Ways to Belong in America

1   This is a tale of two sisters from Calcutta, Mira and Bharati, who have lived in the United States for some 35 years, but who find themselves on different sides in the current debate over the status of immigrants. I am an American citizen and she is not. I am moved that thousands of long-term residents are finally taking the oath of citizenship. She is not.

2   Mira arrived in Detroit in 1960 to study child psychology and preschool education. I followed her a year later to study creative writing at the University of Iowa. When we left India, we were almost identical in appearance and attitude. We dressed alike, in saris; we expressed identical views on politics, social issues, love and marriage in the same Calcutta convent-school accent. We would endure our two years in America, secure our degrees, then return to India to marry the grooms of our father's choosing.

3   Instead, Mira married an Indian student in 1962 who was getting his business administration degree at Wayne State University. They soon acquired the labor certifications necessary for the green card of hassle-free residence and employment.

4   Mira still lives in Detroit, works in the Southfield, Mich., school system, and has become nationally recognized for her contributions in the fields of pre-school education and parent-teacher relationships. After 36 years as a legal immigrant in this country, she clings passionately to her Indian citizenship and hopes to go home to India when she retires.

5   In Iowa City in 1963, I married a fellow student, an American of Canadian parentage. Because of the accident of his North Dakota birth, I bypassed labor-certification requirements and the race-related "quota" system that favored the applicant's country of origin over his or her merit. I was prepared for (and even welcomed) the emotional strain that came with marrying outside my ethnic community. In 33 years of marriage, we have lived in every part of North America. By choosing a husband who was not my father's selection, I was opting for fluidity, self-invention, blue jeans and T-shirts, and renouncing 3,000 years (at least) of caste-observant, "pure culture" marriage in the Mukherjee family. My books have often been read as unapologetic (and in some quarters overenthusiastic) texts for cultural and psychological "mongrelization." It's a word I celebrate.

6   Mira and I have stayed sisterly close by phone. In our regular Sunday morning conversations, we are unguardedly affectionate. I am her only blood relative on this continent. We expect to see each other through the looming crises of aging and ill health without being asked. Long before Vice President Gore's "Citizenship U.S.A." drive, we'd had our polite arguments over the ethics of retaining an overseas citizenship while expecting the permanent protection and economic benefits that come with living and working in America.

7   Like well-raised sisters, we never said what was really on our minds, but we probably pitied one another. She, for the lack of structure in my life, the

© 2014 Wadsworth, Cengage Learning

erasure of Indianness, the absence of an unvarying daily core. I, for the narrowness of her perspective, her uninvolvement with the mythic depths or the superficial pop culture of this society. But, now, with the scapegoating of "aliens" (documented or illegal) on the increase, and the targeting of long-term legal immigrants like Mira for new scrutiny and new self-consciousness, she and I find ourselves unable to maintain the same polite discretion. We were always unacknowledged adversaries, and we are now, more than ever, sisters.

8   "I feel used," Mira raged on the phone the other night. "I feel manipulated and discarded. This is such an unfair way to treat a person who was invited to stay and work here because of her talent. My employer went to the I.N.S. and petitioned for the labor certification. For over 30 years, I've invested my creativity and professional skills into the improvement of *this* country's pre-school system. I've obeyed all the rules, I've paid my taxes, I love my work, I love my students, I love the friends I've made. How dare America now change its rules in midstream? If America wants to make new rules curtailing benefits of legal immigrants, they should apply only to immigrants who arrive after those rules are already in place."

9   To my ears, it sounded like the description of a long-enduring, comfortable yet loveless marriage, without risk or recklessness. Have we the right to demand, and to expect, that we be loved? (That, to me, is the subtext of the arguments by immigration advocates.) My sister is an expatriate, professionally generous and creative, socially courteous and gracious, and that's as far as her Americanization can go. She is here to maintain an identity, not to transform it.

10   I asked her if she would follow the example of others who have decided to become citizens because of the anti-immigration bills in Congress. And here, she surprised me. "If America wants to play the manipulative game, I'll play it too," she snapped. "I'll become a U.S. citizen for now, then change back to Indian when I'm ready to go home. I feel some kind of irrational attachment to India that I don't to America. Until all this hysteria against legal immigrants, I was totally happy. Having my green card meant I could visit any place in the world I wanted to and then come back to a job that's satisfying and that I do very well."

11   In one family, from two sisters alike as peas in a pod, there could not be a wider divergence of immigrant experience. America spoke to me—I embraced the demotion from expatriate aristocrat to immigrant nobody, surrendering those thousands of years of "pure culture," the saris, the delightfully accented English. She retained them all. Which of us is the freak?

12   Mira's voice, I realize, is the voice not just of the immigrant South Asian community but of an immigrant community of the millions who have stayed rooted in one job, one city, one house, one ancestral culture, one cuisine, for the entirety of their productive years. She speaks for greater numbers than I possibly can. Only the fluency of her English and the anger, rather than fear, born of confidence from her education, differentiate her from the seamstresses, the domestics, the technicians, the shop owners, the millions of hard-working but effectively silenced documented immigrants as well as their less fortunate "illegal" brothers and sisters.

13   Nearly 20 years ago, when I was living in my husband's ancestral homeland of Canada, I was always well-employed but never allowed to feel part of the local Quebec or larger Canadian society. Then, through a Green Paper that invited a national referendum on the unwanted side effects of "nontraditional" immigration, the Government officially turned against its immigrant communities, particularly those from South Asia.

14   I felt then the same sense of betrayal that Mira feels now. I will never forget the pain of that sudden turning, and the casual racist outbursts the Green

Paper elicited. That sense of betrayal had its desired effect and drove me, and thousands like me, from the country.

15   Mira and I differ, however, in the ways in which we hope to interact with the country that we have chosen to live in. She is happier to live in America as an expatriate Indian than as an immigrant American. I need to feel like a part of the community I have adopted (as I tried to feel in Canada as well). I need to put roots down, to vote and make the difference that I can. The price that the immigrant willingly pays, and that the exile avoids, is the trauma of self-transformation.

Process Technique Questions

ANALYZING

1. Is the essay directional or informational process?

_____

_____

_____

2. What are the two ways to belong in America? Point out at least two aspects in each process?

_____

_____

_____

Critical Reading and Thinking Questions

ANALYZING

1. What is the essay's thesis?

_____

_____

_____

2. Why does the author say that she and her sister stayed "sisterly," but really probably pitied each other?

_____

_____

_____

_____

Process Writing Opportunities

1. Write a paragraph about a situation in which you were the "outsider." This could be a trip to another country, your first day in a foreign language class, or spending time with someone who speaks both English and native language. How did you feel in the situation?

2. Now, using the topic in question 1, write an essay expanding on the topic. What about the process made you uncomfortable, comfortable, or both? Be specific, and use transitional expressions to link ideas and to create coherence, which is particularly important in writing about process.

COMPARISON AND CONTRAST

A BATTLE OF CULTURES

K. Connie Kang

America is a multicultural nation, yet people from varying backgrounds still find it hard to communicate with each other even though we speak a common language. In this essay, Kang suggests that for a multicultural nation to work, we need "cultural insight."

Vocabulary Before you begin reading, look up the definitions of the following words that appear in the essay. The number in parentheses after each word refers to the paragraph number of the essay.

bicultural (3)	bilingual (3)	brusque (4)
chided (10)	ethos (16)	gregarious (9)
inclination (10)	interethnic (5)	orientation (15)
prestigious (12)	retort (10)	sporadic (4)
volatile (1)		

A Battle of Cultures

1 A volatile inner-city drama is taking place in New York where blacks have been boycotting Korean groceries for four months.

2 The recent attack on three Vietnamese men by a group of blacks who mistook them for Koreans has brought this long-simmering tension between two minority groups to the world's attention. Korean newspapers from San Francisco to Seoul have been running front-page stories. Non-Asian commentators around the country, whose knowledge of Korea may not be much more than images from the Korean war and the ridiculous television series *M.A.S.H.*, are making all sorts of comments.

3 As I see it, the problem in the Flatbush area of Brooklyn started with cultural misunderstanding and was compounded by a lack of bilingual and bicultural community leaders to intervene quickly.

4 Frictions between Korean store owners in New York and blacks had been building for years. Korean merchants have been complaining about thefts.

On the other hand, their black customers have been accusing immigrant store owners of making money in their neighborhoods without putting anything back into the community. They have also complained about store owners being brusque. Over the past eight years, there have been sporadic boycotts but none has lasted as long as the current one, which stemmed from an accusation by a black customer in January that she had been attacked by a store employee. In defense, the store owner has said the employee caught the woman stealing.

5   The attack on the Vietnamese on May 13 wasn't the first time one group of Asians has been mistaken for another in America. But the publicity surrounding the case has made this unfortunate situation a case study in inter-ethnic tension.

6   What's missing in this inner-city drama is cultural insight.

7   What struck me more than anything was a recent remark by a black resident: "The Koreans are a very, very rude people. They don't understand you have to smile."

8   I wondered whether her reaction would have been the same had she known that Koreans don't smile at Koreans either without a reason. To a Korean, a smile is not a facial expression he can turn on and off mechanically. Koreans have a word for it—"mu-ttuk-ttuk-hada" (stiff). In other words, the Korean demeanor is "myu-po-jung"—lack of expression.

9   It would be an easy thing for blacks who are naturally friendly and gregarious to misunderstand Korean ways.

10   As a Korean American I've experienced this many times. Whenever I'm in Korea, which is often, I'm chided for smiling too much. "Why do you smile so easily? You act like a Westerner," people tell me. My inclination is to retort: "Why do you always have to look like you've got indigestion?" But I restrain myself because I know better.

11   In our culture, a smile is reserved for people we know and for a proper occasion. Herein lies a big problem when newcomers from Korea begin doing business in America's poor inner-city neighborhoods.

12   Culturally and socially, many newcomers from Korea, like other Asian immigrants, are ill-equipped to run businesses in America's inner cities. But because they are denied entry into mainstream job markets, they pool resources and open mom-and-pop operations in the only places where they can afford it. They work 14 and 15 hours a day, seven days a week, dreaming of the day when their children will graduate from prestigious schools and make their sacrifices worthwhile.

13   From the other side, inner-city African Americans must wonder how these new immigrants find the money to run their own businesses, when they themselves can't even get a small loan from a bank. Their hope of getting out of the poverty cycle is grim, yet they see newcomers living in better neighborhoods and driving new cars.

14   "They ask me, 'Where do you people get the money to buy a business?'" Bong-jae Jang, owner of one of the grocery stores being boycotted, told me. "How can I explain to my neighbors in my poor English the concept of our family system, the idea of 'kye' (uniquely Korean private money-lending system), our way of life?"

15   I think a little learning is in order on both sides. Korean immigrants, like other newcomers, need orientation before they leave their country as well as when they arrive in the United States. It's also important for Korean immigrants, like other Asians who live in the United States, to realize that they are indebted to blacks for the social gains won by their civil rights struggle. They face less discrimination today because blacks have paved the way. Instead of looking down on their culture, it would be constructive to learn their history, literature, music, and values and see our African American brothers and sisters in their full humanity.

16   I think it is also important to remind ourselves that while the Confucian culture has taught us how to be good parents, sons and daughters and how to behave with people we know, it has not prepared us for living in a democracy. The Confucian ethos lacks the value of social conscience, which makes democracy work.

17   It isn't enough that we think of educating our children and send them to the best schools. We need to think of other peoples' children, too. Most of all, we need to be more tolerant of other peoples' cultures. We need to celebrate our similarities as well as our differences.

18   Jang, the grocer, told me this experience has been painful but he has learned an important lesson. "We Koreans must learn to participate in this society," he said. "When this is over, I'm going to reach out. I want to give part-time work to black youths."

19   He also told me that he has been keeping a journal. "I'm not a writer but I've been keeping a journal," he said. "I want to write about this experience someday. It may help someone."

20   By reaching out, we can make a difference. The Korean grocer's lesson is a reminder to us all that making democracy work in a multicultural society is difficult but we have no choice but to strive for it.

Compare and Contrast Technique Questions

A N A L Y Z I N G

1. Point out several cultural differences that make it difficult for African Americans and Korean Americans to get along.

_____

_____

_____

_____

_____

_____

_____

2. What type of cultural misunderstandings does the author give as reasons for the long-standing problems between Korean Americans and African Americans?

_____

_____

_____

Critical Reading and Thinking Questions

A N A L Y Z I N G

1. What is the essay's purpose?

_____

_____

_____

2. Why are Korean Americans indebted to African Americans? How does Kang suggest that comparing the two cultures would help the two communities get along better?

_____

_____

_____

_____

_____

_____

_____

Comparison and Contrast Writing Opportunities

W R I T I N G

1. Write a paragraph comparing the similarities or contrasting the differences between two ethnic groups living in the same community. As you write, comment on how those similarities or differences affect relationships within the community.

2. Many families or groups (associations, clubs, churches, etc.) are composed of people of more than one ethnic background. Write an essay comparing the similarities and contrasting the differences of the cultural characteristics within a family or group. As you write, comment on how the similarities and differences cause harmony and dissension between the members.

DEFINITION

 IN ALL WAYS A WOMAN

Maya Angelou

In this essay, noted writer and poet Maya Angelou explores the many definitions of a woman. Some of the definitions are negative, and the definitions vary from group to group and change throughout the years. Despite these definitional roadblocks, the author offers a definition for women that will help them attain success in life.

Vocabulary Before you begin reading, look up the definitions of the following words that appear in the essay. The number in parentheses after each word refers to the paragraph number of the essay.

aloof (1)	amiability (9)	fickle (1)	frivolous (1)
imperative (8)	inane (2)	misnomer (6)	parlance (5)
rectitude (5)	rectoress (5)	therapeutic (9)	unabated (10)

In All Ways a Woman

1 In my young years I took pride in the fact that luck was called a lady. In fact, there were so few public acknowledgments of the female presence that I felt personally honored whenever nature and large ships were referred to as feminine. But as I matured, I began to resent being considered a sister to a changeling as fickle as luck, as aloof as an ocean, and as frivolous as nature.

2 The phrase "A woman always has the right to change her mind" played so aptly into the negative image of the female that I made myself a victim to an unwavering decision. Even if I made an inane and stupid choice, I stuck by it rather than "be like a woman and change my mind."

3 Being a woman is hard work. Not without joy and even ecstasy, but still relentless, unending work. Becoming an old female may require only being born with certain genitalia, inheriting long-living genes and the fortune not to be run over by an out-of-control truck, but to become and remain a woman command the existence and employment of genius.

4 The woman who survives intact and happy must be at once tender and tough. She must have convinced herself, or be in the unending process of convincing herself, that she, her values, and her choices are important. In a time and world where males hold sway and control, the pressure upon women to yield their rights-of-way is tremendous. And it is under those very circumstances that the woman's toughness must be in evidence.

5 She must resist considering herself a lesser version of her male counterpart. She is not a sculptress, poetess, authoress, Jewess, Negress, or even (now rare) in university parlance a rectoress. If she is the thing, then for her own sense of self and for the education of the ill-informed she must insist with rectitude in being the thing and in being called the thing.

6 A rose by any other name may smell as sweet, but a woman called by a devaluing name will only be weakened by the misnomer.

7 She will need to prize her tenderness and be able to display it at appropriate times in order to prevent toughness from gaining total authority and to avoid becoming a mirror image of those men who value power above life, and control over love.

8 It is imperative that a woman keep her sense of humor intact and at the ready. She must see, even if only in secret, that she is the funniest, looniest woman in her world, which she should also see as being the most absurd world of all times.

9 It has been said that laughter is therapeutic and amiability lengthens the life span.

10 Women should be tough, tender, laugh as much as possible, and live long lives. The struggle for equality continues unabated, and the woman warrior who is armed with wit and courage will be among the first to celebrate victory.

Definition Technique Questions

1. How many definitions of "woman" does the author give as examples?

_____

_____

_____

2. Is there an identifiable thesis statement? If so, identify it, and give reasons to support your choice.

_____

_____

_____

3. In several paragraphs, the author defines through the technique of comparison/contrast. Identify the paragraphs, and explain whether she is using comparison or contrast.

_____

_____

_____

Critical Reading and Thinking Questions

1. How does the title help support the variety of definitions given in the essay?

_____

_____

_____

2. What definition of a woman does the author offer that will help women succeed in whatever endeavor they attempt?

_____

_____

_____

_____

Definition Writing Opportunities

1. Write a paragraph defining the type of people living in a particular area of a city or a larger area, such as a region of the country. Use the labels others give them, and explain the negative meanings of those labels.

2. Angelou suggests that negative labels given to women can be used by women in a positive way. Write an essay defining how the terms you used in the paragraph you wrote in Exercise 1 might be used positively by the groups given those labels.

A MAGIC CIRCLE OF FRIENDS

Elvira M. Franco

> You might think that a forty-year-old returning to school would stand out like a sore thumb amid the twenty-somethings. But the author of this essay found a group of students her own age with similar backgrounds and with similar fears. Instead of forcing their new school environment to conform to their own experiences, the group allows their experience to help establish new ideas about life and friendships.

Vocabulary Before you begin reading, look up the definitions of the following words that appear in the essay. The number in parentheses after each word refers to the paragraph number of the essay.

abrading (9)	bolstered (12)	brash (7)
cajole (14)	camaraderie (7)	depleted (3)
exhilarating (7)	ignited (5)	multifaceted (11)
orthopedic (5)	pangs (15)	prominent (5)
unique (1)		

A Magic Circle of Friends

1   Older than forty and starting from scratch: I thought I was a unique item, but as soon as I peeked out of my shell I found a sea of women in similar positions.

2   The little child in us has grown mature and middle-aged, almost to our surprise. We share a fear that sits in the back of the mind like a spider ready to pounce, but we've also developed determination, almost like a religion.

3   We know we have friends; at least, I know my friends are with me, if not always, at least most of the time. And most of the time I need them, and they me. We reach over the phone lines for that word of comfort, the encouragement we need to go on when our own store of willpower has become depleted.

4   Returning to school, I found my friends were my best fans. In spite of their own insecurities, they never failed to offer me the cheering I often needed to rewrite a paper one more time or to stay up one last half-hour to re-read a difficult chapter.

5   After classes we would go to a diner, a bunch of over-forty classmates. Working together on a project that we felt strongly about ignited a part of us we did not know existed. While we were quite far from orthopedic shoes, bifocals were prominent. Underneath the artful makeup, we would measure the wrinkles on each other's cheeks across the table, almost as if these lines could form a cord to link us.

6   It was a good time. For years, in a locked-up corner of our minds, we had held the unspoken fear that we might actually be brain-dead. We were finally giving ourselves permission to celebrate our minds.

7   For some, it was a return to the carefree years of college. For others, a first-time discovery that learning can be both fun and exhilarating. Besides the intellectual surprises, we found joy in each other's company, and we delved in this new-found camaraderie with an intensity we did not know we could achieve outside of love and pregnancies. We were, and are, proud of our ages. The only woman in the group who was under thirty struck most of us as brash, angry, and, frankly, quite inappropriate. We were probably insensitive to her needs, but somehow we failed to find out how she felt in our midst and were almost relieved when she found excuses for not joining our study sessions.

8   We ended up treating her almost like a daughter, and doing for her what most of us have been doing for our own daughters: that is, picking up the slack. The hidden bonus was that now we could continue to do things our way, which, we all knew, was the best anyway. Things were smoother when she was not around: the rest of us would always agree, and even our dis-agreements were somehow smooth and enjoyable.

9   We had, in fact, created a sort of bubble around us, a magic circle that fol-lows us still and says we are bright, successful, caring, ambitious, and, finally, ready to change the world. We will not do it, as we might have been ready to do at twenty, pushing and fighting and abrading.

10   We will do it instead at a slower pace, because, along the way, we have learned lessons both small and big: for example, that the world is in no hurry to be changed and that we will have a better shot at it after a good night's sleep. We may not complete our plans by tomorrow, or even by the end of the week, because the details of our lives may interfere, such as a child home from college, or a neighbor's emergency.

11   Our goals may not even be achieved exactly as originally planned, and that is fine, too, because time has also brought us a sense of flexibility and an appreciation for the serendipitous properties of practically any action. The end product could turn out to be infinitely more complex, and in its way more perfect, more multifaceted and rich, than what we had first envisioned. The process is in itself an achievement.

12   They call us "late bloomers," they call us "returnees." We are sought by schools, thanks to the sheer numbers we represent, not to mention the life experience and the common sense that even the least bright among us brings to the classroom. We feel flattered and surprised, and our ego is bolstered by the realization that we are indeed quite capable.

13   There are fears, too ("Will it all make sense at some point?" "What if I'll never be able to get a decent job?"), but they are kept for only a few pairs of ears, where we know we will find support and understanding.

14   Graduation comes: the last papers have been handed in with trepidation, the test booklets carrying in their pages the very essence of our knowledge closed for the last time. Goodbyes, with promises and some tears, even a pho-tograph to keep as souvenir. We've made it: watch out world, here come the mothers and the grandmothers, ready to push, cajole, smile, and negotiate to achieve those goals we did not have a chance to effect the first time around.

15   We may just be beginning to feel a few arthritic pangs in our toes and fin-gers, but with our hair neatly streaked and some expensive dental work, we

know we still look good. We know we are still strong, smart, vital, and, most especially, ready to work. This time around we will make a big difference. We know, because, for sure, we already are different.

Definition Technique Questions

1. Why does Franco define her group as a "magic circle"?

_____

_____

_____

_____

2. What is the simile in paragraph 2? What is the fear the author shares with her friends?

_____

_____

_____

_____

Critical Reading and Thinking Questions

1. The author defines herself and her friends and others like them as "late bloomers" and "returnees." Why do schools seek them out as part of their student body?

_____

_____

_____

_____

_____

2. Why did Franco and her group of forty-year-olds not have a chance to reach their goals earlier in life? How will their education help them achieve their goals this time around?

_____

_____

Definition Writing Opportunities

1. Write a paragraph defining two groups that compete with each other, either in school or on the job.

2. Write an essay about your circle of friends. What were the circumstances under which you met? How have you supported each other during crises? Is your group still together, or has it broken up? Why?

CAUSE AND EFFECT

SPANGLISH SPOKEN HERE

Janice Castro

> In this essay, which originally appeared in *Time,* July 8, 1998, the author explores the causes and effects that the burgeoning Hispanic population has had on our language. Many citizens, having Standard American English as their first language, know some Spanish words and phrases, and some immigrants, having Spanish as their first language, know some Standard American English words and phrases. When people speak a language that is a mixture of both, a new language, Spanglish, develops.

Vocabulary Before you begin reading, look up the definitions of the following words that appear in the essay. The number in parentheses after each word refers to the paragraph number of the essay.

bemused (1)	context (5)	gaffes (10)	inadvertently (10)
linguistics (2)	mode (2)	patter (3)	syntax (3)

Spanglish Spoken Here

1 In Manhattan a first-grader greets her visiting grandparents, happily exclaiming, "Come here, *siéntate!*" Her bemused grandfather, who does not speak Spanish, nevertheless knows she is asking him to sit down. A Miami personnel officer understands what a job applicant means when he says "*Quiero un* part time." Nor do drivers miss a beat reading a billboard alongside a Los Angeles street advertising CERVEZA—SIX-PACK!

2 This free-form blend of Spanish and English, known as Spanglish, is common linguistic currency wherever concentrations of Hispanic Americans are found in the U.S. In Los Angeles, where 55% of the city's 3 million inhabitants speak Spanish, Spanglish is as much a part of daily life as sunglasses. Unlike the broken-English efforts of earlier immigrants from Europe, Asia, and other regions, Spanglish has become a widely accepted conversational mode used casually—even playfully—by Spanish-speaking immigrants and native-born Californians alike.

3   Consisting of one part Hispanicized English, one part Americanized Spanish and more than a little fractured syntax, Spanglish is a bit like a Robin Williams comedy routine: a crackling line of cross-cultural patter straight from the melting pot. Often it enters Anglo homes and families through the children, who pick it up at school or at play with their young Hispanic contemporaries. In other cases, it comes from watching TV; many an Anglo child watching *Sesame Street* has learned *uno dos tres* almost as quickly as one two three.

4   Spanglish takes a variety of forms, from the Southern California Anglos who bid farewell with the utterly silly "*hasta la* bye-bye" to the Cuban-American drivers in Miami who *parquean* their *carros*. Some Spanglish sentences are mostly Spanish, with a quick detour for an English word or two. A Latino friend may cut short a conversation by glancing at his watch and excusing himself with the explanation that he must "*ir al* supermarket."

5   Many of the English words transplanted in this way are simply handier than their Spanish counterparts. No matter how distasteful the subject, for example, it is still easier to say "income tax" than *impuesto sobre la renta*. At the same time, many Spanish-speaking immigrants have adopted such terms as VCR, microwave and dishwasher for what they view as largely American phenomena. Still other English words convey a cultural context that is not implicit in the Spanish. A friend who invites you to *lonche* most likely has in mind the brisk American custom of "doing lunch" rather than the languorous afternoon break traditionally implied by *almuerzo*.

6   Mainstream Americans exposed to similar hybrids of German, Chinese or Hindi might be mystified. But even Anglos who speak little or no Spanish are somewhat familiar with Spanglish. Living among them, for one thing, are 19 million Hispanics. In addition, more American high school and university students sign up for a Spanish than for any other foreign language.

7   Only in the past ten years, though, has Spanglish begun to turn into a national slang. Its popularity has grown with the explosive increases in U.S. immigration from Latin American countries. English has increasingly collided with Spanish in retail stores, offices and classrooms, in pop music and on street corners. Anglos whose ancestors picked up such Spanish words as *rancho*, *bronco*, *tornado* and *incommunicado*, for instance, now freely use such Spanish words as *gracias*, *bueno*, *amigo* and *por favor*.

8   Among Latinos, Spanglish conversations often flow easily from Spanish into several sentences of English and back again. "It is done unconsciously," explains Carmen Silva-Corvalan, a Chilean-born associate professor of linguistics at the University of California who speaks Spanglish with relatives and neighbors. "I couldn't even tell you minutes later if I said something in Spanish or English."

9   Spanglish is a sort of code for Latinos: the speakers know Spanish, but their hybrid language reflects the American culture in which they live. Many lean to shorter, clipped phrases in place of the longer, more graceful expressions their parents used. Says Leonel de la Cuesta, an assistant professor of modern languages at Florida International University in Miami: "In the U.S., time is money, and that is showing up in Spanglish as an economy of language." Conversational examples: *taipiar* (type) and *winshi-wiper* (windshield wiper) replace *escribir a máquina* and *limpiaparabrisas*.

10   Major advertisers, eager to tap the estimated $134 billion in spending power wielded by Spanish-speaking Americans, have ventured into Spanglish to promote their products. In some cases, attempts to sprinkle Spanish through commercials have produced embarrassing gaffes. A Braniff airlines ad that sought to tell Spanish-speaking audiences that they could settle back *en* (in) luxuriant *cuero* (leather) seats, for example, inadvertently said they could fly without clothes (*encuero*). A fractured translation of the Miller Lite

slogan told readers the beer was "Filling, and less delicious." Similar blunders are often made by Anglos trying to impress Spanish-speaking pals. But if Latinos are amused by mangled Spanglish, they also recognize these goofs as a sort of friendly acceptance. As they might put it, *no problema*.

Cause and Effect Technique Questions

A N A L Y Z I N G

1. The author's last name is Castro, and she uses many Spanish words and phrases. For whom do you think she is writing?

_____

_____

_____

2. The author ends the essay with a Spanglish expression: *no problema*. How does her doing this help develop the point she is making about Spanglish?

_____

_____

_____

Critical Reading and Thinking Questions

A N A L Y Z I N G

1. What are the positive effects of learning to speak a second language?

_____

_____

_____

2. What is the main economic effect of the expanding number of Hispanics in America?

_____

_____

Cause and Effect Writing Opportunities

W R I T I N G

1. Write a paragraph about the effects of learning another language.

2. Write an essay about the cultural benefits that America has gotten from the influx of a particular culture. Food, music, art, language, business, and religion are just some of the elements you might want to include in your essay.

WHY WE CRAVE HORROR MOVIES

Stephen King

> For the most part, people's lives are filled with fears about their jobs, paying the bills, their children, and a variety of crimes against people and property. Yet society doesn't respond well to those making their fears public. They are often seen as unbalanced, or troublemakers, or social misfits. Where do people go to release their pent-up fears? In this essay, the master of the macabre reveals his thoughts about why people are drawn to accounts of horror.

Vocabulary Before you begin reading, look up the definitions of the following words that appear in the essay. The number in parentheses after each word refers to the paragraph number of the essay.

anarchistic (11)	asylum (1)	depleted (3)
exalted (9)	innately (4)	menaced (6)
morbidity (12)	mythic (7)	normality (4)
penchant (7)	province (3)	remonstrance (10)
sanctions (10)	squinch (1)	status quo (9)
voyeur (6)		

Why We Crave Horror Movies

1   I think that we're all mentally ill; those of us outside the asylums only hide it a little better—and maybe not all that much better, after all. We've all known people who talk to themselves, people who sometimes squinch their faces into horrible grimaces when they believe no one is watching, people who have some hysterical fear—of snakes, the dark, the tight place, the long drop . . . and, of course, those final worms and grubs that are waiting so patiently underground.

2   When we pay our four or five bucks and seat ourselves at tenth-row center in a theater showing a horror movie, we are daring the nightmare.

3   Why? Some of the reasons are simple and obvious. To show that we can, that we are not afraid, that we can ride this roller coaster. Which is not to say that a really good horror movie may not surprise a scream out of us at some point, the way we may scream when the roller coaster twists through a complete 360 or plows through a lake at the bottom of the drop. And horror movies, like roller coasters, have always been the special province of the young; by the time one turns 40 or 50, one's appetite for double twists or 360-degree loops may be considerably depleted.

4   We also go to reestablish our feelings of essential normality; the horror movie is innately conservative, even reactionary. Freda Jackson as the horrible melting woman in *Die, Monster, Die!* confirms for us that no matter how far we may be removed from the beauty of a Robert Redford or a Diana Ross, we are still light-years from true ugliness.

5   And we go to have fun.

6   Ah, but this is where the ground starts to slope away, isn't it? Because this is a very peculiar sort of fun, indeed. The fun comes from seeing others menaced—sometimes killed. One critic has suggested that if pro football has become the voyeur's version of combat, then the horror film has become the modern version of the public lynching.

7   It is true that the mythic, "fairy-tale" horror film intends to take away the shades of gray. . . . It urges us to put away our more civilized and adult penchant for analysis and to become children again, seeing things in pure blacks and whites. It may be that horror movies provide psychic relief on this level because this invitation to lapse into simplicity, irrationality, and even outright madness is extended so rarely. We are told we may allow our emotions a free rein . . . or no rein at all.

8   If we are all insane, then sanity becomes a matter of degree. If your insanity leads you to carve up women, like Jack the Ripper or the Cleveland Torso Murderer, we clap you away in the funny farm (but neither of those two amateur-night surgeons was ever caught, heh-heh-heh); if, on the other hand, your insanity leads you only to talk to yourself when you're under stress or to pick your nose on your morning bus, then you are left alone to go about your business . . . though it is doubtful that you will ever be invited to the best parties.

9   The potential lyncher is in almost all of us (excluding saints, past and present; but then, most saints have been crazy in their own ways), and every now and then, he has to be let loose to scream and roll around in the grass. Our emotions and our fears form their own body, and we recognize that it demands its own exercise to maintain proper muscle tone. Certain of these emotional muscles are accepted—even exalted—in civilized society; they are, of course, the emotions that tend to maintain the status quo of civilization itself. Love, friendship, loyalty, kindness—these are all the emotions that we applaud, emotions that have been immortalized in the couplets of Hallmark cards and in the verses (I don't dare call it poetry) of Leonard Nimoy.

10   When we exhibit these emotions, society showers us with positive reinforcement; we learn this even before we get out of diapers. When, as children, we hug our rotten little puke of a sister and give her a kiss, all the aunts and uncles smile and twit and cry, "Isn't he the sweetest little thing?" Such coveted treats as chocolate-covered graham crackers often follow. But if we deliberately slam the rotten little puke of a sister's fingers in the door, sanctions follow—angry remonstrance from parents, aunts and uncles; instead of a chocolate-covered graham cracker, a spanking.

11   But anticivilization emotions don't go away, and they demand periodic exercise. We have such "sick" jokes as, "What's the difference between a truckload of bowling balls and a truckload of dead babies?" (You can't unload a truckload of bowling balls with a pitchfork . . . a joke, by the way, that I heard originally from a ten-year-old.) Such a joke may surprise a laugh or a grin out of us even as we recoil, a possibility that confirms the thesis: If we share a brotherhood of man, then we also share an insanity of man. None of which is intended as a defense of either the sick joke or insanity, but merely as an explanation of why the best horror films, like the best fairy tales, manage to be reactionary, anarchistic, and revolutionary all at the same time.

12   The mythic horror movie, like the sick joke, has a dirty job to do. It deliberately appeals to all that is worst in us. It is morbidity unchained, our most base instincts let free, our nastiest fantasies realized . . ., and it all happens, fittingly enough, in the dark. For those reasons, good liberals often shy away from horror films. For myself, I like to see the most aggressive of them—*Dawn of the Dead*, for instance—as lifting a trap door in the civilized forebrain and throwing a basket of raw meat to the hungry alligators swimming around in that subterranean river beneath.

13   Why bother? Because it keeps them from getting out, man. It keeps them down there and me up here. It was Lennon and McCartney who said that all you need is love, and I would agree with that.

14   As long as you keep the gators fed.

Cause and Effect Technique Questions

ANALYZING

1. Is there an identifiable thesis statement that clarifies the cause and effect nature of our craving for horror movies?

_____

_____

_____

_____

2. Point out one metaphor and one simile wherein King compares horror movies to something else.

_____

_____

_____

_____

Critical Reading and Thinking Questions

ANALYZING

1. In King's opinion, why do people enjoy being scared (the effect) by watching horror movies (the cause)?

_____

_____

_____

_____

2. In the last line of the essay, King says, "As long as you keep the gators fed." What does he mean by this?

_____

_____

_____

_____

_____

W R I T I N G

Cause and Effect Writing Opportunities

1. Horror movies are not the only type of film in which murder and mayhem take place. Choose another type of film and write a paragraph showing the cause and effect relationship that exists between it and the viewing public.

2. King states that there is a certain amount of insanity in the American population. Write an essay pointing out the causes and effects of an insane society.

PERSUASION

JUST SAY NO TO RANDOM DRUG TESTING

David Rocah

> This essay, written by American Civil Liberties Union attorney David Rocah, recounts a case he was to defend involving a Ridgefield Park High School student who was forbidden to play football because he refused to be randomly drug tested. The case never went to trial because the school district revoked their earlier policy on the advice of a judge who said there was not sufficient evidence of a widespread drug problem to warrant the enforcement of such a policy.
>
> In the next essay that follows, by former news writer and editor Claude Lewis, a contrary position is represented. Lewis believes that all students, not just athletes, should be randomly drug tested.

Vocabulary Before you begin reading, look up the definitions of the following words that appear in the essay. The number in parentheses after each word refers to the paragraph number of the essay.

affidavits (7)	bedrock (14)	coercing (8)	embodies (4)
illicit (1)	platitudes (14)	presumption (2)	toll (5)

Just Say No to Random Drug Testing

In our system, state-operated schools may not be enclaves of totalitarianism. School officials do not possess absolute authority over their students. Students in school as well as out of school are "persons" under our Constitution.

—*Justice Abe Fortas, Tinker v. Des Moines (1969)*

1 Ridgefield Park, like at least nine other school districts in New Jersey, recently decided that it would not permit its junior and senior high school students to participate in interscholastic sports unless they agreed to have their urine tested for traces of certain illicit drugs at random intervals during the athletic season. Because we believe that this intrusive and demeaning search of students' bodily fluids violates fundamental constitutional principles, the American Civil Liberties Union of New Jersey is representing a student and his parents in a legal challenge to the Ridgefield Park program.

2   One of the fundamental features of our legal system is that we are presumed innocent of any wrongdoing unless and until the government proves otherwise. Random drug testing of student athletes turns this presumption on its head, telling students that we assume they are using drugs until they prove to the contrary with a urine sample. The overwhelming majority of student athletes in Ridgefield Park, and throughout New Jersey, are law abiding citizens, and there is no basis in law or logic to presume otherwise or to treat them worse than accused criminals.

3   An equally cherished constitutional command is the rule that government officials may not search us without an adequate reason. Thus, for example, even though we know there is a drug problem in our society, we do not allow the police to randomly stop us on the street to see if we are carrying drugs.

4   The constitutional prohibition against "unreasonable" searches also embodies the principle that merely belonging to a certain group is not a sufficient reason for a search, even if many members of that group are suspected of illegal activity. Thus, for example, even if it were true that most men with long hair were drug users, the police would not be free to stop all long haired men and search them for drugs.

5   Unfortunately, many school officials concerned about drug use by students seem willing to ignore these principles. There is no doubt that the concern is well placed, and it is one that we share. Drug use is a scourge on our society, exacting a terrible toll in lost lives. And no one is arguing that we should tolerate students' use of illegal drugs. But zero tolerance for drugs should not lead us to have zero tolerance for constitutional limits. Sadly, that is exactly what is happening.

6   Parents and school officials currently have a wide variety of tools at their disposal to address drug use by students. Educating students about the dangers of drug use can be highly effective. A recent study by the Parent's Resource Institute for Drug Education shows that students who are warned about drugs by their parents use them 30 percent less often than those who are not, and students who said their parents set "clear rules" regarding drugs used them 57 percent less than those whose parents did not.

7   In addition, school officials currently have the power to require any student whom they reasonably suspect of using drugs to submit to a drug test. Indeed, if the affidavits submitted in court by the Ridgefield Park School Board are to be believed, school officials there have been grossly irresponsible in failing to act when they had reason to suspect particular students were using drugs. Not only did they not conduct drug tests, there is no indication that they even informed the parents of their suspicions.

8   Acting on the basis of individual suspicion ensures both that hundreds of innocent children are not subjected to a degrading search, and demonstrates that school officials care about all students who use drugs, not just student athletes. The Board also could have implemented a truly voluntary drug testing program, rather than coercing parents to consent by denying their children the opportunity to participate in interscholastic athletics. Had the Board done so, it is likely that no one would have objected, and the ACLU could not and would not have challenged it.

9   Given these tools, which, when employed vigorously can be an effective and constitutional means of dealing with drug use by the entire student body, why are school districts resorting to random drug testing of athletes? Because they improperly read a 1995 U.S. Supreme Court decision as giving them carte blanche. In a case involving a school district in Vernonia, Oregon, the Court decided that the district could constitutionally require student athletes to submit to random drug testing where officials testified that they were no longer able to maintain discipline in the school system because of a culture of

pervasive drug use and disrespect for authority, and where student athletes were the leaders of the drug culture.

10   Are the parents and administrators in Ridgefield Park prepared to admit that they cannot maintain order and discipline in their schools? There is no evidence of this, and we would be surprised if it were so. Ridgefield Park has a fine school system, which sent 73 percent of its graduates to college last year.

11   Are student athletes leaders of the drug culture? Although the Ridgefield Park School Board's court papers scandalously attempted to portray its student athletes as a pack of drug addled alcoholics, these same athletes won state championships in football for the past two years. Nationally, student athletes have been found to have higher academic achievement and fewer disciplinary problems than non-athletes, due in large part to the tremendous discipline required to balance a full academic program and the time demanded by practice and competition schedules. Singling out athletes in New Jersey because of a problem in Vernonia, Oregon, is both ridiculous and unfair.

12   School officials argue that random drug testing will deter drug use. But students should not use drugs because they are harmful and illegal, not because they might get caught. Moreover, random drug testing simply encourages students to defer drug use until after the athletic season is completed, rather than completely refraining from drug use.

13   School officials also argue that participating in interscholastic athletics is a privilege, not a right, and that they may therefore impose any conditions on the exercise of that privilege that they see fit. This ignores the well established constitutional doctrine that the government may not condition the receipt of a governmental benefit on the waiver of constitutional rights. Just as a school could not condition participation in interscholastic athletics on students giving up their right to free speech, they also may not condition participation on students giving up their right to be free from unreasonable searches.

14   Some also argue that students who aren't doing anything wrong have nothing to fear. This ignores the fact that what they fear is not getting caught, but the loss of dignity and trust that the drug test represents. And we should all be afraid of government officials who believe that a righteous cause warrants setting aside bedrock constitutional protections. The lesson that our schools should be teaching is respect for the Constitution and for students' dignity and privacy, not a willingness to treat cherished constitutional principles as mere platitudes.

NAÏVE COURT DIDN'T GO FAR ENOUGH WITH DRUG TESTING

Claude Lewis

Vocabulary Before you begin reading, look up the definitions of the following words that appear in the essay. The number in parentheses after each word refers to the paragraph number of the essay.

antithesis (3)	botched (1)	demise (5)	depraved (5)
draconian (2)	errant (7)	rony (9)	valid (10)

Naïve Court Didn't Go Far Enough with Drug Testing

1   This nation has so badly botched the war on drugs that I find myself in painful agreement with a Supreme Court ruling that public schools can require students to take drug tests as a condition of playing sports.

2   Indeed, my concern for an end to the devastation of drug abuse and addiction is so great that I find myself wondering why such tests should be restricted to athletes. Why not apply the pain all at once and permit random testing of all students? If such draconian solutions are necessary, why single out those who play sports? What about the millions of other students who don't? Should they not be required to undergo random drug tests?

3   Random drug testing is the antithesis of a free society. Yet, I am persuaded that since the drug problem is so pervasive, destructive and corrupt, and since the government has failed so miserably for so long in ending its corrosive effects, we have few alternatives other than poking our noses in places where they don't belong.

4   When it comes to drugs, we have reached a point where the only cure may have to be worse than the disease. We "must" take the strongest possible action to protect the young and the unsuspecting.

5   Most Americans have never seen firsthand the powerful and depraved activity in the world of illicit drugs. I have talked with addicts for years and have witnessed the demise and deaths of countless young men and women who were unable to end their enslavement.

6   I have seen young people with old faces, the result of persistent experimenting with drugs. Because government has failed at containing addiction and our nation has no sure method of treating the army of addicts living among us, extreme measures must be adopted.

7   No longer is it possible, if it ever was, to accept the pathetic lie that drug addicts exist mainly in the inner city. The problem has grown so great that in almost any community, children and errant adults can locate drugs within a half-hour of their homes.

8   If the court's decision is, as some say, a victory, it is one of the saddest victories I can imagine. It is distressing that we must resort to limiting Fourth Amendment privacy rights to student athletes in order to protect them from the danger of drugs. Students spend more time in school than in any other institution outside their homes. And it is the school where initial exposure to illegal drugs often takes place.

9   The irony in all this is that it is not the students who have failed, but the adults who are responsible for them. In Washington, the court's ruling was met with wide acceptance among young athletes.

10   Others argue if there's no reason to suspect illegal drug use, students should not be subjected to random testing. Such notions were valid in another era. No more.

11   How else do we begin to get at the problem? Drug education is good but won't provide a total solution. Education must be a part of the solution along with other firm approaches. Few of us come new to this problem. America is one of the world's most drug-dependent nations and the problem threatens to grow worse.

12   An enormous number of crimes committed every year—from petty thefts to bank robberies to murders—are connected to addiction.

13   Supreme Court Justice Sandra Day O'Connor holds a naïve notion on the matter, calling the collection of urine samples "particularly destructive of privacy and offensive to personal dignity."

14   What could be more offensive to personal dignity than addiction itself? The court's ruling may contain some frightening implications, but not nearly as frightening as the growing new armies of addicts who will poison the future of many young people for generations.

Persuasion Technique Questions

1. Both Rocah and Lewis use evidence to support their points of view. Which essay's evidence seems the most convincing? Why?

_____

_____

_____

2. Is there a thesis statement in each essay? If so, identify them.

_____

_____

_____

_____

Critical Reading and Thinking Questions

1. David Rocah suggests that most students and student athletes do not take drugs; therefore, he argues that a random drug testing policy is not necessary. Do you agree or disagree?

_____

_____

_____

2. Claude Lewis, on the other hand, says that the court's decision that public schools can randomly drug test athletes is a sad victory. How can a victory be sad?

_____

_____

_____

3. Even though these two essays are on different sides of the issue, can you suggest a way that a compromise can be reached?

_____

_____

_____

Persuasion Writing Opportunities

1. Write a persuasive paragraph defending or attacking random drug testing for high school athletes.

2. Write a persuasive essay supporting or rejecting the idea that random drug testing of all high school students will decrease drug use among them.

FATHERLESS AMERICA

David Blankenhorn

This essay is taken from Blankenhorn's book *Fatherless America: Confronting Our Most Urgent Social Problem*. The author is not writing this essay with a passing interest. He is the founder of the Institute for American Values. He also has been involved with an organization called the National Fatherhood Initiative.

Vocabulary Before you begin reading, look up the definitions of the following words that appear in the essay. The number in parentheses after each word refers to the paragraph number in the essay.

anthropologically (15)   coherent (13)   conscripted (16)   discourse (3)
disparate (8)   divergent (4)   narcissism (18)   parity (1)
patrimony (5)   puerile (22)   superfluous (9)

Fatherless America

1 The United States is becoming an increasingly fatherless society. A generation ago, an American child could reasonably expect to grow up with his or her father. Today, an American child can reasonably expect not to. Fatherlessness is now approaching a rough parity with fatherhood as a defining feature of American childhood.

2 This astonishing fact is reflected in many statistics, but here are the two most important. Tonight, about 40 percent of American children will go to sleep in homes in which their fathers do not live. Before they reach the age of eighteen, more than half of our nation's children are likely to spend at least a significant portion of their childhoods living apart from their fathers. Never before in this country have so many children been voluntarily abandoned by their fathers. Never before have so many children grown up without knowing what it means to have a father.

3 Fatherlessness is the most harmful demographic trend of this generation. It is the leading cause of declining child well-being in our society. It is also the engine driving our most urgent social problems, from crime to adolescent pregnancy to child sexual abuse to domestic violence against women. Yet, despite its scale and social consequences, fatherlessness is a problem that is frequently ignored or denied. Especially within our elite discourse, it remains largely a problem with no name.

4 If this trend continues, fatherlessness is likely to change the shape of our society. Consider this prediction. After the year 2000, as people born after

1970 emerge as a large proportion of our working-age adult population, the United States will be a nation divided into two groups, separate and unequal. The two groups will work in the same economy, speak a common language, and remember the same national history. But they will live fundamentally divergent lives. One group will receive basic benefits—psychological, social, economic, educational, and moral—that are denied to the other group.

5   The primary fault line dividing the two groups will not be race, religion, class, education, or gender. It will be patrimony. One group will consist of those adults who grew up with the daily presence and provision of fathers. The other group will consist of those who did not. By the early years of the next [twenty-first] century, these two groups will be roughly the same size.

6   Surely a crisis of this scale merits a response. At a minimum, it requires a serious debate. Why is fatherhood declining? What can be done about it? Can our society find ways to invigorate effective fatherhood as a norm of male behavior? Yet, to date, the public discussion on this topic has been remarkably weak and defeatist. There is a prevailing belief that not much can—or even should—be done to reverse the trend.

7   When the crime rate jumps, politicians promise to do something about it. When the unemployment rate rises, task forces assemble to address the problem. As random shootings increase, public health officials worry about the preponderance of guns. But when it comes to the mass defection of men from family life, not much happens.

8   There is debate, even alarm, about specific social problems. Divorce. Out-of-wedlock childbearing. Children growing up in poverty. Youth violence. Unsafe neighborhoods. Domestic violence. The weakening of parental authority. But in these discussions, we seldom acknowledge the underlying phenomenon that binds together these otherwise disparate issues: the flight of males from their children's lives. In fact, we seem to go out of our way to avoid the connection between our most pressing social problems and the trend of fatherlessness.

9   We avoid this connection because, as a society, we are changing our minds about the role of men in family life. As a cultural idea, our inherited understanding of fatherhood is under siege. Men in general, and fathers in particular, are increasingly viewed as superfluous to family life: either expendable or as part of the problem. Masculinity itself, understood as anything other than a rejection of what it has traditionally meant to be male, is typically treated with suspicion and even hostility in our cultural discourse. Consequently, our society is now manifestly unable to sustain, or even find reason to believe in, fatherhood as a distinctive domain of male activity.

10   The core question is simple: Does every child need a father? Increasingly, our society's answer is "no," or at least "not necessarily." Few idea shifts in this century are as consequential as this one. At stake is nothing less than what it means to be a man, who our children will be, and what kind of society we will become.

11   This [essay] is a criticism not simply of fatherlessness but of a culture of fatherlessness. For, in addition to losing fathers, we are losing something larger: our idea of fatherhood. Unlike earlier periods of father absence in our history, we now face more than a physical loss affecting some homes. We face a cultural loss affecting every home. For this reason, the most important absence our society must confront is not the absence of fathers but the absence of our belief in fathers.

12   In a larger sense, this is a *cultural* criticism because fatherhood, much more than motherhood, is a cultural invention. Its meaning for the individual man is shaped less by biology than by a cultural script or story—a societal code that guides, and at times pressures, him into certain ways of acting and of understanding himself as a man.

13   Like motherhood, fatherhood is made up of both a biological and a social dimension. Yet in societies across the world, mothers are far more successful than fathers at fusing these two dimensions into a coherent parental identity. Is the nursing mother playing a biological or a social role? Is she feeding or bonding? We can hardly separate the two, so seamlessly are they woven together.

14   But fatherhood is a different matter. A father makes his sole biological contribution at the moment of conception—nine months before the infant enters the world. Because social paternity is only indirectly linked to biological paternity, the connection between the two cannot be assumed. The phrase "to father a child" usually refers only to the act of insemination, not to the responsibility for raising a child. What fathers contribute to their offspring after conception is largely a matter of cultural devising.

15   Moreover, despite their other virtues, men are not ideally suited to responsible fatherhood. Although they certainly have the capacity for fathering, men are inclined to sexual promiscuity and paternal waywardness. Anthropologically, human fatherhood constitutes what might be termed a necessary problem. It is necessary because, in all societies, child well-being and societal success hinge largely upon a high level of paternal investment: the willingness of adult males to devote energy and resources to the care of their offspring. It is a problem because adult males are frequently—indeed, increasingly—unwilling or unable to make that vital investment.

16   Because fatherhood is universally problematic in human societies, cultures must mobilize to devise and enforce the father role for men, coaxing and guiding them into fatherhood through a set of legal and extralegal pressures that require them to maintain a close alliance with their children's mother and to invest in their children. Because men do not volunteer for fatherhood as much as they are conscripted into it by the surrounding culture, only an authoritative cultural story of fatherhood can fuse biological and social paternity into a coherent male identity.

17   For exactly this reason, Margaret Mead and others have observed that the supreme test of any civilization is whether it can socialize men by teaching them to be fathers—creating a culture in which men acknowledge their paternity and willingly nurture their offspring. Indeed, if we can equate the essence of the antisocial male with violence, we can equate the essence of the socialized male with being a good father. Thus, at the center of our most important cultural imperative, we find the fatherhood script: the story that describes what it ought to mean for a man to have a child.

18   Just as the fatherhood script advances the social goal of harnessing male behavior to collective needs, it also reflects an individual purpose. That purpose, in a word, is happiness. Anthropologists have long understood that the genius of an effective culture is its capacity to reconcile individual happiness with collective well-being. By situating individual lives within a social narrative, culture endows private behavior with larger meaning. By linking the self to moral purposes larger than the self, an effective culture tells us a story in which individual fulfillment transcends selfishness, and personal satisfaction transcends narcissism.

19   In this respect, our cultural script is not simply a set of imported moralisms, exterior to the individual and designed only to compel self-sacrifice. It is also a pathway—indeed, our only pathway—to what the founders of the American experiment called the pursuit of happiness.

20   The stakes on this issue could hardly be higher. Our society's conspicuous failure to sustain or create compelling norms of fatherhood amounts to a social and personal disaster. Today's story of fatherhood features one-dimensional characters, an unbelievable plot, and an unhappy ending. It reveals in our society both a failure of collective memory and a collapse of

moral imagination. It undermines families, neglects children, causes or aggravates our worst social problems, and makes individual adult happiness—both male and female—harder to achieve.

21   Ultimately, this failure reflects nothing less than a culture gone awry: a culture increasingly unable to establish the boundaries, erect the sign-posts, and fashion the stories that can harmonize individual happiness with collective well-being. In short, it reflects a culture that increasingly fails to "enculture" individual men and women, mothers and fathers.

22   In personal terms, the end result of this process, the final residue from what David Gutmann calls the "deculturation" of paternity, is narcissism: a me-first egotism that is hostile not only to any societal goal or larger moral purpose but also to any save the most puerile understanding of personal happiness. In social terms, the primary results of decultured paternity are a decline in children's well-being and a rise in male violence, especially against women. In a larger sense, the most significant result is our society's steady fragmentation into atomized individuals, isolated from one another and estranged from the aspirations and realities of common membership in a family, a community, a nation, bound by mutual commitment and shared memory.

23   [A good father] is a cultural model, or what Max Weber calls an ideal social type—an anthropomorphized composite of cultural ideas about the meaning of paternity. I call him the Good Family Man. As described by one of the fathers [I] interviewed . . ., a good family man "puts his family first."

24   . . . A good society celebrates the ideal of the man who puts his family first. Because our society is now lurching in the opposite direction, I see the Good Family Man as the principal casualty of today's weakening fatherhood script. And because I cannot imagine a good society without him, I offer him as the protagonist in the stronger script that I believe is both necessary and possible.

Persuasion Technique Questions

1. What types of evidence does the author use to try to sway the reader? Identify at least two.

_____

_____

_____

_____

_____

_____

_____

2. Persuasion, like definition, uses many mode techniques to present evidence to support conclusions and to convince readers. Identify several mode techniques used by the author in this essay.

_____

_____

_____

_____

3. In his attempt to persuade the reader, the author makes several assumptions that are not necessarily true or factual. Identify them, and comment on how you felt when you first read them, as opposed to how you feel about them now that you have thought about them again. Do they help convince you, or do they make you think they weaken Blankenhorn's argument?

_____

_____

_____

_____

_____

_____

_____

Critical Reading and Thinking Questions

1. Is there a thesis statement in the essay? If so, point it out. If not, what do you think is the author's thesis?

_____

_____

_____

2. What concluding paragraph techniques does the author use? Do you think they are effective in giving the essay an appearance of completeness? Do they influence your feeling about his conclusions about a fatherless America?

_____

_____

_____

3. What does Blankenhorn see as an additional danger to a culture of fatherlessness? Why is this danger even more threatening to our culture?

_____

_____

_____

_____

_____

_____

Persuasion Writing Opportunities

1. Write a persuasive paragraph opposing or defending Blankenhorn's idea that fatherhood is more of a cultural invention than is motherhood.

2. Now, write an essay expanding on the topic in Exercise 1. As you write, consider the following: your definition of what being a "man" entails; your definition of what "fatherhood" means; the effects on children if the father is not present for a significant amount of time. And finally, psychologists say that the greatest influence in a child's development is the same-sex parent. If true, how might fatherlessness generate a cycle of fatherlessness?

CHOOSING VIRGINITY

Lorraine Ali and Julie Scelfo

> This essay is a bit different from most persuasive essays in that it does not rely on the authors' preferences or researched facts; rather, it offers interviews with young people opposed to premarital sex. As you read the essay, consider not only what is being said but who is saying it.

Vocabulary Before you begin reading, look up the definitions of the following words that appear in the essay. The number in parentheses after each word refers to the paragraph number in the essay.

abstract (11)	beleaguered (2)	cacophony (4)	dire (22)
ethos (1)	inherent (3)	proponent (25)	semblance (4)

Choosing Virginity

1 There's a sexual revolution going on in America, and believe it or not, it has nothing to do with Christina Aguilera's bare-it-all video "Dirrty." The uprising is taking place in the real world, not on "The Real World." Visit any American high school and you'll likely find a growing number of students who . . . have decided to remain chaste until marriage. Rejecting the get-down-make-love ethos of their parents' generation, this wave of young adults represents a new counterculture, one clearly at odds with the mainstream media and their routine use of sex to boost ratings and peddle product.

2 According to a recent study from the Centers for Disease Control, the number of high-school students who say they've never had sexual intercourse

rose by almost 10 percent between 1991 and 2001. Parents, public-health officials and sexually beleaguered teens themselves may not be relieved by this "let's not" trend. But the new abstinence movement, largely fostered by cultural conservatives and evangelical Christians, has also become hotly controversial.

3   As the Bush administration plans to increase federal funding for abstinence programs by nearly a third, to $135 million, the Advocates for Youth and other proponents of a more comprehensive approach to sex ed argue that teaching abstinence isn't enough. Teens also need to know how to protect themselves if they do have sex, these groups say, and they need to understand the emotional intensity inherent in sexual relationships.

4   The debate concerns public policy, but the real issue is personal choice. At the center of it all are the young people themselves, whose voices are often drowned out by the political cacophony. Some of them opened up and talked candidly . . . about their reasons for abstaining from sex until marriage. It's clear that religion plays a critical role in this extraordinarily private decision. But there are other factors as well: caring parents, a sense of their own unreadiness, the desire to gain some semblance of control over their own destinies. Here are their stories.

The Wellesley Girl

5   Alice Kunce says she's a feminist, but not the "army-boot-I-hate-all-men kind." The curly-haired 18-year-old Wellesley College sophomore—she skipped a grade in elementary school—looks and talks like what she is: one of the many bright, outspoken students at the liberal Massachusetts women's college. She's also a virgin. "One of the empowering things about the feminist movement," she says, "is that we're able to assert ourselves, to say no to sex and not feel pressured about it. And I think guys are kind of getting it. Like, 'Oh, *not* everyone's doing it.'"

6   But judging by MTV's "Undressed," UPN's "Buffy the Vampire Slayer" and just about every other TV program or movie targeted at teens, everyone is doing it. Alice grew up with these images, but as a small-town girl in Jefferson City, Mo., most teen shows felt alien and alienating. "You're either a prudish person who can't handle talking about sex or you're out every Saturday night getting some," she says. "But if you're not sexually active and you're willing to discuss the subject, you can't be called a prude. . . ."

7   Alice, a regular churchgoer who also teaches Sunday school, says religion is not the reason she's chosen abstinence. She fears STDs and pregnancy, of course, but above all, she says, she's not mature enough emotionally to handle the deep intimacy sex can bring. . . .

The Dream Team

8   Karl Nicoletti wasted no time when it came to having "the talk" with his son, Chris. It happened five years ago, when Chris was in sixth grade. Nicoletti was driving him home from school and the subject of girls came up. "I know many parents who are wishy-washy when talking to their kids about sex. I just said, "No, you're not going to have sex. . . ."

9   Today, the 16-year-old from Longmont, Colo., vows he'll remain abstinent until marriage. So does his girlfriend, 17-year-old Amanda Wing, whose parents set similarly strict rules for her and her two older brothers. "It's amazing, but they did listen," says her mother, Lynn Wing. . . .

10   "Society is so run by sex," says Chris, who looks like Madison Avenue's conception of an All-American boy in his Abercrombie sweat shirt and faded baggy jeans. "Just look at everything—TV, movies. The culture today makes it seem OK to have sex whenever, however or with whoever you want.

© 2014 Wadsworth, Cengage Learning

I just disagree with that." Amanda, who looks tomboy comfy in baggy brown cords, a white T shirt and chunky-soled shoes, feels the same way. "Sex should be a special thing that doesn't need to be public," she says. "But if you're abstinent, it's like *you're* the one set aside from society because you're not doing it.". . .

11   To most abstaining teens, marriage is the golden light at the end of the perilous tunnel of dating—despite what their parents' experience may have been. Though Amanda's mother and father have had a long and stable union, Karl Nicoletti separated from Chris's mother when Chris was in fifth grade. His fiancée moved in with Chris and Karl two years ago. . . . Chris and Amanda talk about marriage in the abstract, but they want to go to college first, and they're looking at schools on opposite sides of the country. "I think we could stay together," Chris says. Amanda agrees. "Like we have complete trust in each other," she says. "It's just not hard for us.". . .

The Survivor

12   Remaining a virgin until marriage is neither an easy nor a common choice in Latoya Huggins's part of Paterson, N.J. At least three of her friends became single mothers while they were still in high school, one by an older man who now wants nothing to do with the child. "It's hard for her to finish school," Latoya says, "because she has to take the baby to get shots and stuff."

13   Latoya lives in a chaotic world: so far this year, more than a dozen people have been murdered in her neighborhood. It's a life that makes her sexuality seem like one of the few things she can actually control. "I don't even want a boyfriend until after college," says Latoya, who's studying to be a beautician at a technical high school. "Basically I want a lot out of life. My career choices are going to need a lot of time and effort."

14   Latoya, 18, could pass for a street-smart 28. She started thinking seriously about abstinence five years ago, when a national outreach program called Free Teens began teaching classes at her church. The classes reinforced what she already knew from growing up in Paterson—that discipline is the key to getting through your teen years alive. Earlier this year she dated a 21-year-old appliance salesman from her neighborhood, until Latoya heard that he was hoping she'd have sex with him. "We decided that we should just be friends," she explains, "before he cheated on me or we split up in a worse way.". . .

15   Her goal is to graduate and get a job; she wants to stay focused and independent. "Boys make you feel like you're special and you're the only one they care about," she says. "A lot of girls feel like they need that. But my mother loves me and my father loves me, so there's no gap to fill."

The Beauty Queen

16   Even though she lives 700 miles from the nearest ocean, Daniela Aranda was recently voted Miss Hawaiian Tropic El Paso, Texas, and her parents couldn't be prouder. They've displayed a picture of their bikini-clad daughter smack-dab in the middle of the living room. "People always say to me 'You don't look like a virgin,'" says Daniela, 20, who wears supersparkly eye shadow, heavy lip liner and a low-cut black shirt. "But what does a virgin look like? Someone who wears white and likes to look at flowers?"

17   Daniela models at Harley-Davidson fashion shows, is a cheerleader for a local soccer team called the Patriots and hangs out with friends who work at Hooters. She's also an evangelical Christian who made a vow at 13 to remain a virgin, and she's kept that promise. "It can be done," she says. "I'm living

proof." Daniela has never joined an abstinence program; her decision came from strong family values and deep spiritual convictions.

18   Daniela's arid East El Paso neighborhood, just a mile or so from the Mexican border, was built atop desert dunes, and the sand seems to be reclaiming its own by swallowing up back patios and sidewalks. The city, predominantly Hispanic, is home to the Fort Bliss Army base, breathtaking mesa views—and some of the highest teen-pregnancy rates in the nation. "There's a lot of girls that just want to get pregnant so they can get married and get out of here," Daniela says.

19   But she seems content to stay in El Paso. She studies business at El Paso Community College, dates a UTEP football player named Mike and works as a sales associate at the A'gaci Too clothing store in the Cielo Vista Mall. . . .

20   Daniela has been dating Mike for more than a year. He's had sex before, but has agreed to remain abstinent with her. "He's what you call a born-again virgin," she says. "Or a secondary abstinent, or something like that. We just don't put ourselves in compromising situations. If we're together late at night, it's with my whole family.". . .

The Ring Bearer

21   Leneé Young is trying to write a paper for her Spanish class at Atlanta's Spelman College, but as usual she and her roommates can't help getting onto the subject of guys. "I love Ludacris," Leneé gushes. "I love everything about him. Morris Chestnut, too. He has a really pretty smile. Just gorgeous." But Leneé, 19, has never had a boyfriend, and has never even been kissed. "A lot of the guys in high school had already had sex," she says. "I knew that would come up, so I'd end all my relationships at the very beginning." Leneé decided back then to remain a virgin until marriage, and even now she feels little temptation to do what many of her peers are doing behind closed dormitory doors. "I feel that part of me hasn't been triggered yet," she says. "Sex is one of those things you can't miss until you have it."

22   Last summer she went with a friend from her hometown of Pittsburgh to a Silver Ring Thing. These popular free events meld music videos, pyrotechnics and live teen comedy sketches with dire warnings about STDs. Attendees can buy a silver ring—and a Bible—for $12. Then, at the conclusion of the program, as techno music blares, they recite a pledge of abstinence and don their rings. "My friend, who's also a virgin, said I needed to go so I could get a ring," Leneé says. "It was fun, like the music and everything. And afterwards they had a dance and a bonfire.". . .

The Renewed Virgin

23   Lucian Schulte had always planned to wait until he was married to have sex, but that was before a warm night a couple of years ago when the green-eyed, lanky six-footer found himself with an unexpected opportunity. "She was all for it," says Lucian, now 18. "It was like, 'Hey, let's give this a try.'" The big event was over in a hurry and lacked any sense of intimacy. "In movies, if people have sex, it's always romantic," he says. "Physically, it did feel good, but emotionally, it felt really awkward. It was not what I expected it to be."

24   While the fictional teens of "American Pie" would have been clumsily overjoyed, Lucian, raised Roman Catholic, was plagued by guilt. "I was worried that I'd given myself to someone and our relationship was now a lot more serious than it was before," he says. "It was like, 'Now, what is she going to expect from me?'" Lucian worried, too, about disease and pregnancy. He promised himself never again.

25   Lucian, now an engineering major at the University of Alberta in Canada, is a "renewed virgin." His parents are strong proponents of chastity, and he attended school-sponsored abstinence classes. But the messages didn't hit home until he'd actually had sex. "It's a pretty special thing, and it's also pretty serious," he says. "Abstinence has to do with, 'Hey, are you going to respect this person?'" He has dated since his high-school affair, and is now hoping a particular cute coed from Edmonton will go out with him. "But I'll try to restrict myself to kissing," he says. "Not because I think everything else is bad. But the more you participate with someone, the harder it's going to be to stop."

26   It's not easy to practice such restraint, especially when those around him do not. Lucian lives in a single room, decorated with ski-lift tickets and a "Scooby-Doo" poster, in an all-male dorm, but he says most students "get hitched up, sleep around and never see each other again." . . . Lucian figures he can hold out until he's married, which he hopes will be by the time he's 30. "I'm looking forward to an intimate experience with my wife, who I'll truly love and want to spend the rest of my life with," says Lucian. "It's kind of corny, but it's for real."

Persuasion Technique Questions

ANALYZING

1. Is there a thesis statement in the essay? If so, identify it. If not, what do you think is the authors' thesis?

_____

_____

_____

_____

2. Stereotypes are often used in persuasive essays to convince readers to a particular way of thinking. They usually rely on the reader's unfamiliarity with a certain group's lifestyle. Stereotyping relies on an immediate and simplistic image of someone or something, foregoing a more deeply and richly defined picture. How do the lifestyles or backgrounds of some of the interviewees defy the usual weakness of stereotypical images and, quite dramatically, make the authors' argument more convincing?

_____

_____

_____

_____

_____

_____

_____

_____

_____

_____

_____

_____

_____

_____

Critical Reading and Thinking Questions

ANALYZING

1. Is there a thesis statement in the essay? If so, identify it. If not, state what you think is the thesis in your own words.

_____

_____

_____

2. Discuss which of the interviewees you agree with the most and the least. Give specific reasons.

_____

_____

_____

3. From what the interviewees say, how much influence do parents have on their children's decision to have sex or not?

_____

_____

_____

_____

_____

_____

_____

Persuasion Writing Opportunities

WRITING

1. Write a persuasive paragraph on how your friends feel about premarital sex.

2. Write a persuasive essay opposing or defending the idea of premarital sex. Did the ideas of your friends that were expressed in Exercise 1 influence your decision? What about your parents, religion, or what you have read or seen in the media?

LIMITED ANSWER KEY

Chapter 2

PRACTICE 1

1. Paragraph 2, sentence 3, and sentence 12: gene therapy might evolve to allow scientists to alter a fertilized egg in ways that differ from how it would have developed naturally.
3. Paragraph 2: Dr. Anderson of USC stated that within just a few years he would ask the National Institutes of Health for permission to alter the genes of a fetus with an inherited disease. Paragraph 3: Many scientists agree that gene therapy is an ethical procedure. Paragraph 5: Researchers are already experimenting with introducing gene self-destruct cells in cells that become eggs and sperm.

Chapter 3

Answers will vary in all of the practices.

Chapter 4

PRACTICE 1

1. Reading a newspaper each day <u>is important</u> <u>because it keeps you informed about current events.</u>
3. Working while going to school <u>should teach</u> <u>young people responsibility.</u>
5. The Beatles <u>remain popular,</u> <u>even after their breakup decades ago, because of their versatile musical style.</u>

PRACTICE 2

2. <u>The aging process, talented newcomers, and constant travel</u> make maintaining a sports career a difficult lifestyle.
4. A successful career often hinges on <u>hard work, dedication, and intelligence.</u>

PRACTICE 3

Answers will vary.

PRACTICE 4

1. <u>Fruits</u> <u>are a good source for vitamin C.</u> (The essay map is missing.)
3. Many <u>students</u> <u>make college a worthwhile experience by joining fraternities and sororities, playing intramural sports, and participating in student government.</u> (All elements are present.)
5. <u>Styling, construction, and value make</u> the Breitling a popular wristwatch for collectors. (All elements are present.)
7. <u>Skydiving and bungee jumping</u> <u>are dangerous activities.</u> (The essay map is missing.)
9. *Star Trek* <u>has been a long-running television series</u> because of <u>special effects, interesting characters, and fascinating stories.</u> (All the elements are present.)

PRACTICE 5

Answers will vary.

PRACTICE 6

Answers will vary.

Chapter 5

Answers will vary in all the Practices.

Chapter 6

Answers will vary in all the Practices.

Chapter 7

Answers will vary in all the Practices.

Chapter 8

Answers will vary in all the Practices.

Chapter 9

PRACTICE 1

Answers will vary.

PRACTICE 2

1. Cybersex <u>is becoming a popular activity.</u>
3. <u>Binge drinking at parties</u> <u>is increasing.</u>
5. <u>A positive attitude</u> <u>can help fight illness.</u>

Chapter 10

Answers will vary in all the Practices.

Chapter 11

Answers will vary in all the Practices.

Chapter 12

Answers will vary in all the Practices.

Chapter 13

Answers will vary in all the Practices.

Chapter 14

PRACTICE 1

Answers will vary.

PRACTICE 2

2. The problem is one of *coincidence.* The problem may have nothing to do with overeating or being exposed to cold weather on a walk. It would be unusual for the person never to have overeaten on other holidays. Did

the person become sick then? Most likely the person is exposed to cold weather during the winter months on other occasions, such as playing in the snow with family or friends, waiting for a bus, or walking the dog. Did illness occur after these events? If the answer is no, then the cause lies elsewhere. A good candidate would be an allergy to a specific food such as turkey, cranberries, or pumpkin pie, foods that are commonly eaten on holidays.

Chapter 15

PRACTICE 1

Answers will vary, but sample responses are provided.

1. Pro: Selling cigarettes to teens under eighteen years of age should be legalized. Con: Teens under eighteen years of age should not be permitted to buy cigarettes.

3. Pro: Organized prayer should be permitted in public schools to promote morality. Con: To ensure the separation of church and state, organized prayer should not be allowed in public schools.

5. Pro: All eighteen-year-olds should be drafted into the armed services. Con: Eighteen-year-olds should not be drafted into military service.

7. Pro: The government should require periodic safety inspections for automobiles. Con: The government should not require periodic safety inspections for automobiles.

9. Pro: The income tax must be increased. Con: The income tax must not be increased.

PRACTICE 4

2. Either-or
5. Red herring

Chapter 17

PRACTICE 1

Essay responses will vary. Key terms:

2. evaluate
4. contrast

GLOSSARY

Absolute phrase: a group of words consisting of a noun or pronoun and a **participle** (not the regular verb form) plus any other completing words. Absolute phrases modify the entire sentence and cannot be punctuated as a complete sentence.

Abstract language: general words that refer to ideas or concepts that cannot be perceived through the senses.

Action verb: a verb that states what a subject does (in the past, present, or future tense).

Active voice: a verb form in which the subject of the sentence does the acting (using an action verb or a transitive verb).

Adjective: a word that modifies (or describes) a noun or pronoun. Adjectives usually come before the nouns they describe, but they can also follow the noun (in the predicate of the sentence).

Adverb: a word that modifies (describes) a verb, an adjective, or another adverb. Often adverbs end in *-ly*. Many adverbs answer the question *where, how,* or *when*.

Adverbial conjunction: a word that often follows a semicolon to explain how or in what way the two clauses joined by the semicolon are logically related.

Antecedent: the **noun** to which a **pronoun** refers in a sentence.

Apostrophe: a punctuation mark used to indicate contractions (isn't) or possession/ownership (Anna's papers).

Appositive: a word or phrase that renames the preceding word or phrase. Appositive phrases are often called noun phrases.

Argument: developing a topic by persuading the audience to agree with, or be convinced by, a particular point of view.

Article: a type of word that introduces a noun and indicates whether it is specific or countable. Frequently used articles are *a, an,* and *the.*

Attitude: a word or phrase in the thesis sentence/statement that expresses the writer's conclusion about a topic as an opinion, not a fact. Most often, it is expressed in the verb, such as *are/are not, is/is not, should/should not,* and *can/cannot.*

Audience: the person or group you are writing for. This could be a professor, a classmate, a boss, a coworker, or even a member of a club to which you belong.

Block citation: a quotation of five or more typed lines separated from the text by being indented ten spaces from the left margin and followed with parenthetical citation of the source.

Body paragraphs: the central section of an essay that explains the thesis statement of the essay.

Brackets: punctuation marks used in quoted material to set apart editorial explanations. (The dean wrote, "All faculty must teach sumer [sic] school.")

Brainstorming: a form of freewriting in which the writer lists thoughts freely, at random.

Causal chain: a series of events that can develop; the relationships that exist between events.

Causal relationship: the connection between cause and effect.

Cause-effect: an organization system that examines why something happens or the consequences stemming from causes.

Chronological order: an organization system for events according to how they occur in order of time. This order is used most often in narratives, process analysis, and cause-effect essays.

Class definition: the indication of a word's meaning by its placement in a broad class of similar things that readers will readily understand. A class definition usually includes a specific detail that distinguishes the original term or word from the others in the class.

Classification: an organization system that divides the subject matter into categories determined by one criterion or basis for grouping.

Clause: a group of related words containing both a subject and a verb. Clauses are either **independent** or **dependent**. They also can be **restrictive** or **nonrestrictive**.

Clustering: a type of prewriting in which the writer explores and organizes thoughts in a chart that begins with putting the main topic in a circle in the center of the page, then connecting related ideas (in smaller circles) with lines (branches).

Coherence: a quality in which the relationship between ideas is clear throughout a paragraph or essay.

Coincidence: two or more events that occur around the same time but with no direct cause-effect relationship.

Colon: a punctuation mark most often used to show that a list or explanation will follow. (Eat plenty of green vegetables: broccoli, spinach, and cabbage, for example.)

Comma: a punctuation mark used for separating ideas, independent clauses, and items in a list, and for enclosing descriptive phrases.

Comma splice: a sentence containing two independent clauses incorrectly joined by a comma.

Comparison-contrast: an organization system showing similarities (comparisons) and differences (contrasts) between two or more subjects or topics. The organization can be blocked by topic or point by point by criteria.

Complex sentence: a sentence that contains an independent clause and a dependent clause.

Compound sentence: a sentence consisting of two or more independent clauses.

Compound subject: two or more simple subjects joined by a coordinating conjunction.

Compound verb (predicate): a predicate (the part of the sentence containing the verb) containing two or more verbs.

Concluding paragraph: the paragraph that ends an essay and gives a sense of completeness.

Conclusion: the last sentence of a paragraph or the last paragraph of an essay that ties together the preceding ideas.

Concrete language: particular, specific words used to portray the unique complex nature of the real world.

Conjunction: a joining word or phrase (see **coordinating conjunction**, **adverbial conjunction**, and **subordinating conjunction**).

Connotative language: use of words that have (or develop) associations and implications apart from their explicit sense.

Controlling idea or attitude: the focus concerning the topic or how the author feels about the topic.

Coordinating conjunction: a word that joins grammatically equal structures. The most frequently used are *and, but, or, yet, for, nor,* and *so.*

Coordination: joining two or more grammatically equal structures, most often with a coordinating conjunction or a semicolon.

Countable nouns: nouns that can be either singular or plural.

Criterion: the standard used to classify things (basis for grouping, evaluating, comparing, and contrasting).

Cross-examination: a prewriting technique used to discover ideas about a topic. You can interview yourself or a partner by using sets of questions regarding definition, relationship, compare and contrast, testimony, and circumstances.

Dangling modifier: a descriptive phrase or clause that does not modify (describe) any word or phrase in a sentence.

Dash: a punctuation mark used to set apart parenthetical information that needs more emphasis than would be indicated by parentheses. (Irina's professor—a dynamic sociology teacher—helped her understand American society.)

Definition: an organization system that explains the meaning of a term or concept using a variety of strategies (examples, contrast, description, etc.).

Definition by negation: saying what a given word or term *is not* before saying what the word or term *actually is.*

Demonstrative pronoun: a pronoun used to point out or specify certain people, places, or things (*this, that, these, those*).

Denotative language: use of words in their accepted, dictionary-defined sense.

Dependent clause: a group of words with a subject and verb that cannot stand alone and must be joined to an independent clause to complete its meaning. Most dependent clauses begin with subordinating conjunctions or relative pronouns.

Description: the mode of writing that develops a topic through the use of vivid sensory detail.

Direct object: the word or words (usually nouns or pronouns) following and receiving the action of an action verb.

Directional process: the explanation of how to do something. The intent of directional process writing is to enable the readers to do something (to duplicate some process) after they have followed the directions.

Dominant impression: the overall feeling or emotional response the writer wants the reader to take away from descriptive writing.

Draft: a draft is another word for *version.* Several versions of a paper should be written until the topic is explored, organized, and expressed for optimum clarity.

Editing: one of the final steps in the writing process during which the writer checks the draft of the essay for misspelled words, grammatical errors, missing words, and other errors.

Essay: an organized written work on a topic in a series of paragraphs, including an introduction that attracts the reader's attention and states the thesis of the essay; body paragraphs that present the supporting points of the thesis and develop them with facts, details, and examples; and a conclusion that summarizes the ideas and coherently ends the work.

Essay map: in the thesis statement of an essay, the indication of the subtopics that the essay will cover.

Example: an instance or case used to illustrate or explain a point.

Expository writing (exposition): informative writing, the primary purpose of which is to explain a concept.

Extended definition: a definition explained in several sentences or a paragraph by means of any one mode of development or any combination of the modes of development: description, narration, example, classification, process, comparison and contrast, and cause and effect.

Fact: a statement that can be proven to be true.

Figurative language: the device of describing a person or thing in terms usually associated with something very different.

Forecasting thesis sentence: see **thesis sentence/statement.**

Fragment: an incomplete sentence because it is missing a subject or verb or the verb is incomplete; a dependent clause not attached to an independent clause.

Frame or signal phrase: an introduction to or explanation for a quotation. The frame or signal phrase states the name of the person quoted, the person's title or expertise, or a brief comment on the quotation's content. This information can be placed before the quotation, after the quotation, or in the middle of the quotation.

Freewriting: writing that is used to explore ideas without concern for grammar, spelling, or organization.

Future tense: a tense used to indicate action or being that has not yet occurred.

Gerund: the *-ing* form of a verb that functions as a noun in a sentence.

Gerund phrase: a **gerund** and its completing words.

Helping verb: a part of the verb before the main verb, conveying information about tense. Helping verbs usually are forms of *have, be, do,* and *will.*

Hyphen: a punctuation mark used to join descriptive adjectives before a noun, to join compound words, to attach some prefixes, or to separate syllables at the end of a line.

Image/imagery: a word, phrase, or figure of speech (such as a simile or metaphor) addressing the senses, suggesting sounds, smells, sights, feelings, tastes, or actions.

Indefinite pronoun: a pronoun used to refer to general or indeterminate people, places, or things (*everyone, everybody, someone, somebody, everything, something, nothing, anyone*).

Independent clause: a clause that can stand alone as a sentence, containing a complete subject and verb.

Indirect object: a noun or pronoun following a verb that receives a direct object. (Jane gave *her* the book.)

Infinitive phrase: a group of words consisting of *to* plus a verb and its completing words. An infinitive phrase can function as a noun, adjective, or adverb.

Informational process: the explanation of how something was made, how an event occurred, or how something works.

Interrupter: a clause or phrase that clarifies or provides additional meaning.

In-text citation: quoted or paraphrased material of no more than three or four typed lines incorporated into the text of the paper rather than set apart in block form. This material should be followed by parentheses containing the author's name and the page number of the source.

Introductory paragraph: the paragraph that introduces the reader to the topic of an essay.

Introductory sentence: the sentence that often precedes the thesis statement. The purpose of introductory sentences is to catch the reader's attention and clarify your **tone**.

Irregular verb: a verb that does not form the past tense by adding *-ed* or *-d*. Some verbs do not change forms at all, or they form the past tense by changing the spelling of the entire word (stem-changing verbs).

Linking verb: a verb that does not express action but links the subject to the word or words that describe the subject. The most common linking verbs are forms of *be*.

Listing: a prewriting technique used to discover ideas about a topic. The topic is written at the top of a blank piece of paper, and the writer writes down a list of ideas associated with the topic. This technique also is called *free association*.

Main idea: the writer's basic approach to the subject. It is the problem to be solved or the issue being raised for consideration.

Main verb: the most important word in a verb phrase, usually conveying the action of the sentence.

Metaphor: a way to describe a topic in terms of another concept (love is *a rose*).

Modes of development: the different viewpoints from which to write about a topic: description, narration, example, classification, process, comparison and contrast, definition, cause and effect, and persuasion.

Modifier: a word or group of words that functions as an adjective or adverb (providing description).

Narration: a story, usually told in chronological order, usually building to a climax and then resolving.

Nonrestrictive clause: a clause that is not essential to complete the meaning of a sentence. If you remove a nonrestrictive clause from a sentence, the basic meaning of the sentence will remain clear.

Noun: a word that stands for a person, place, or thing. It can be singular or plural.

Noun clause: a clause functioning as a noun, usually beginning with *a, the, what, where, why*, or *when*.

Object: a word or words (usually nouns or pronouns) following prepositions, action verbs, and words formed from verbs (participles, infinitives).

Objective description: factual description, using sensory details of what is seen, heard, tasted, smelled, or touched without any emotional response or interpretation.

Paragraph: a group of sentences that discuss or develop a topic.

Parallel construction (parallelism): the repetition of the same grammatical structure for coherence or emphasis.

Paraphrase: restating someone's ideas in your own words and sentence structure (not directly quoting the other person's words).

Parentheses: a mark of punctuation used to set off specific details giving additional information, explanations, or qualifications of the main idea in a sentence. *Many students name famous athletes as heroes (Barry Bonds and Mia Hamm, for example)*.

Participial phrase: a group of words consisting of a participle and its completing words.

Participle: a verb form ending in *-ed* or *-ing* that is used as an adjective or used with helping verbs to form present perfect or past perfect forms. See **past participle** and **present participle**.

Passive voice: a verb form chosen when the actor of the sentence is not important or when the writer wishes to avoid naming the subject. In the passive voice, the object of an active verb becomes the subject of a passive verb (*be* + past participle).

Past participle: a verb form used to help form the present perfect and past perfect tenses and the passive voice. Past participles usually end with *-d, -ed*, or *-en*.

Past perfect tense: a tense used to describe past action or events occurring prior to a later time in the past. The past perfect is formed from *had* and the verb's past participle form.

Past tense: a tense used to discuss completed past actions. All **regular verbs** in the past tense end in *-ed*.

Period: a punctuation mark that is used to end a complete statement or is included in an abbreviation.

Personal pronoun: a pronoun that refers to a specific person or thing (*I, me, you, he, him, she, her, it, we, us, they, them*). There are three forms, depending on how the personal pronoun is used in a sentence: subjective (used as a subject), objective (used as an object), or possessive (used to indicate possession or ownership).

Personification: a form of metaphor in which nonhuman things are given human characteristics.

Persuasion: argument that seeks to convince others of the rightness of a belief, point of view, or course of action.

Phrasal verb: a two-word or three-word expression that combines a verb with another word, changing the meaning (such as *pick it up*).

Phrase: a group of related words missing a subject or verb, or both. Phrases are used in sentences to complete thoughts or add descriptive detail; they may be restrictive or nonrestrictive. See **prepositional phrase, participial phrase, gerund phrase, infinitive phrase**, and **absolute phrase**.

Plagiarism: presenting someone else's ideas or words as if they are your own.

Point of the story: in narrative writing, what is interesting about the subject.

Predicate: the part of the sentence containing the verb, making a statement or asking a question about the subject.

Preposition: a word that connects a noun or pronoun to the rest of the sentence, often showing location or time. Frequently used prepositions are *in, on, over, before*, and *after*.

Prepositional phrase: a phrase that contains a preposition and its object (e.g., *in the car* or *on the table*).

Present participle: a verb form ending in *-ing* that is used to help form the **progressive tenses** and that may be used as an adjective.

Present perfect tense: a tense used to describe an action or condition that started in the past and continues up to the present. The tense is formed by combining *has* or *have* and the past participle.

Present tense: a tense used to discuss habitual actions, facts, or conditions that are true of the present.

Prewriting: the step in the writing process in which the writer thinks about the topic, purpose, and audience and explores ideas for development through **brainstorming**, **clustering**, or **freewriting**.

Process: a series of actions leading to a concluding point.

Process analysis: an organizational structure that explains how to do something or how something works.

Progressive tense: a tense that discusses actions that are or were happening or are planned for the future. This tense is formed by adding a form of the verb *be* (*is, am, are*) to a verb ending in *-ing*.

Pronoun: a word that takes the place of, or refers to, a noun. The word or phrase that the pronoun refers to is the **antecedent** of the pronoun. See **personal pronoun**, **relative pronoun**, **demonstrative pronoun**, **indefinite pronoun**, and **reflexive pronoun**.

Proofreading: checking the final draft for spelling, punctuation, sentence fragments, and grammar.

Question mark: the punctuation mark that ends a direct question.

Reflexive pronoun: a pronoun ending in *-self* or *-selves* that is used to indicate action performed to or on the antecedent.

Regular verb: a verb ending in *-ed* in the past tense or past participle, or forming its third-person singular form by adding *-s* or *-es*.

Relative clause: a clause that functions as an adjective and begins with a **relative pronoun** (*who, whom, which, that*).

Relative pronoun: a pronoun used to introduce a qualifying or explanatory clause (*who, whom, which, that, whoever, whichever*).

Restrictive clause: a clause that is essential to identify nouns or to complete the meaning. These clauses follow the nouns or ideas they modify. No commas are used to offset restrictive clauses.

Revising: rewriting drafts for both content and organization.

Run-on sentence: a sentence containing two or more independent clauses with nothing that joins them together (a serious grammatical error).

Semicolon: a mark of punctuation that usually joins two independent clauses; it occasionally is used to separate items in a series containing internal commas.

Sensory image: descriptive writing evoking the five senses: sight, touch, smell, sound, and taste.

Sentence: a complete statement or question containing a subject and a verb and expressing a complete thought.

Simile: a comparison using *like* or *as* (My love is *like a rose*).

Simple definition: a brief explanation such as found in a dictionary. There are three types of simple definition: definition by synonym, class, and negation.

Subject: the topic (who or what) about which a clause makes a statement or asks a question. Usually the subject is a noun or pronoun, and usually the subject precedes the verb.

Subjective description: description that creates an easily identifiable emotion or impression. This type of description communicates the writer's emotional response to what he or she encounters.

Subject-verb agreement: Subjects and verbs should agree in number. Thus, singular subjects require verbs with singular endings, and plural subjects require verbs with plural endings.

Subordinating conjunction: a word that joins two clauses by making one clause dependent on the other (independent) clause (for example, *although, after, because, while*).

Subordination: joining a dependent clause to an independent clause.

Subtopic: the topic or subject of a paragraph. Subtopics are more specific topics used to help explain or clarify the more general overall topic of the entire essay. For instance, the overall topic of an essay might be *surgery* while the subtopics might include *plastic surgery, Lasik surgery,* and *cardiovascular surgery.*

Summary Paragraph: a presentation of the substance of a body of material in a condensed form or by reducing it to its main points.

Support sentence: a sentence that explains, clarifies, or defines the subject stated in the topic sentence.

Symbol: an object, person, image, word, or event that represents more than the literal significance of the term, often evoking complex ideas or themes in literary works.

Synonym: a word with the same, or close to the same, meaning as another word.

Synonym definition: defines a word by supplying another (often simpler) word that means the same thing.

Tense: the form of the verb that shows when in time an action occurred (present, past, future).

Thesis sentence/statement: one or more sentences, usually included in the introduction, that state the main idea of an essay and often outline the subtopics of the essay (**essay map**).

Three-item essay map: three items listed in a thesis statement that will support the thesis.

Tone: the author's implied attitude toward the reader or the places, people, and events in a literary work, revealed by the style and word choice.

Topic: the subject or focus of a paragraph or essay.

Topic sentence: a sentence stating the main idea of a paragraph.

Transitional expression: a word or phrase explaining how or in what way two ideas are related. These are often **adverbial conjunctions**.

Uncountable nouns: nouns that represent an idea or concept that cannot be counted (water, air) and cannot be made plural.

Unity: a clearness, coherence, and consistency in the purpose, theme, or organization of a literary work.

Verb: a word indicating action, feeling, or being. The form of the verb can indicate the time of the action: present, past, or future (tense).

Works Cited list: a list of the reference works referred to in a research paper. In both MLA and APA, the quotes are cited parenthetically in the text of the paper.

INDEX

© 2014 Wadsworth, Cengage Learning